Borges the Poet

BORGES *the Poet*

Edited by Carlos Cortínez

The University of Arkansas Press
Fayetteville   1986

Design: Patricia Douglas Crowder
Typeface: Linotron 202 Palatino
Composition: G & S Typesetters, Inc.
Printing: Thomson-Shore, Inc.
Binding: John H. Dekker & Sons, Inc.

The paper used in this publication meets the minimum requirements of the American
National Standard for Permanence of Paper for Printed Library Materials Z39.48—1984. ∞

LIBRARY OF CONGRESS CATALOGUING-IN-PUBLICATION DATA
Main entry under title:

Borges, the poet.

   1. Borges, Jorge Luis, 1899–   —Criticism and interpretation—Congresses.
I. Cortinez, Carlos, 1934—   .
PQ7797.B635Z63483   1986   861   85-8690
ISBN 0-938626-37-X
ISBN 0-938626-48-5 (pbk.)

Contents

Borges the Poet

Introduction

"Stars and men move in cycles," says a line by Borges, recalling the teachings of Pythagoras. To the examples of Eternal Return given to us by the poet, one might add the periodic gathering of the readers of Borges. These congregations of scholars reappear in the United States like the seasons. Borges attributes the growing American fascination with his work to three of his distinctive characteristics. He is old, he is blind, he is South American. His readers don't have to reach for such reasons.

Much has been said at various gatherings about the enthusiasm created by the presence of Borges himself. While the abiding interest of those in attendance rests of course on the originality and depth of his work, it is the enchanting personality of the poet that converts into memorable occasions congresses that might otherwise fall into tedium.

When I convened a symposium on Borges (and with Borges) at the University of Maine in 1976 (collecting commentary for *Simply a Man of Letters*) I had no inkling that in a few years I would again be involved in that pleasant task, inviting a group of the closest readers of Borges to go on with the same conversation. With one difference: this time the focus was to be—to my satisfaction—on the poetry of Borges, upstaged so long by his stories.

Gathering at Dickinson College in April, 1983, we could not help remembering that this was sixty years after the timid appearance, in the far south of the hemisphere, of a slender volume of poems entitled *Fervor de Buenos Aires*. Since then, at uncertain intervals, there have come from that same remote corner poems equally vigorous and passionate, testifying to an exemplary devotion, a fierce loyalty, to the art and to the unsure destiny of the poet. Even though a newcomer to the lines of Borges must finally be directed to the work itself, to the wise and serene poems, I believe that publication of some of the commentary which came out of the symposium on the poems might make them even more accessible. The transcription of the dialogue (sometimes rambling in delightful ways), enlivened and informed by Borges, may give an idea not only of the peculiar genius and wisdom of the writer, but also of the marvelous freshness and expansiveness of his spirit.

Carlos Cortínez
Carlisle, Pennsylvania
1985

THE MORGAN LECTURES
DISCUSSIONS WITH BORGES

I. Jorge Luis Borges Discusses Emily Dickinson with James Michos Hughes and others.

(Some preliminary remarks while Borges is being seated. BANKS: There is a chair right here if you would like to be seated. BORGES: I'm clumsy. BANKS: You are never clumsy. BORGES: I'm clumsy all the time. BANKS: You are far more agile than we, sir. BORGES: Yes, of course—at the ripe age of eighty-three. BANKS: Marvelous age. BORGES: Yes, I'll be eighty-four at any moment.)

SAMUEL ALSTON BANKS (President of Dickinson College): Perhaps the most foolhardy of missions is attempting to say something meaningful on the same program with Jorge Luis Borges.

BORGES: Thank you, sir.

PRES. BANKS: I am delighted to be here with him. I shall try to limit my remarks. I have a letter from the governor of the state of Pennsylvania that he has asked me to read.

"As governor, I am pleased to send greetings on the occasion of your visit to Dickinson College and our commonwealth, Señor Borges. In your own country you have been called Argentina's best-known and most significant native cultural figure. In this country, one of our national magazines recently described you as the 'greatest living poet, essayist, and story writer in the Spanish language, and a universal figure in modern literature.'"

BORGES: What can I do about it?

PRES. BANKS: "Your work is known and admired throughout the world. Indeed on behalf of all Pennsylvanians, it is an honor for me to welcome you to our state and wish you well during your visits to the campuses of some of our finest colleges and universities.

—Dick Thornburgh, Governor"

If one were to say something meaningful, albeit succinct, I think it would be that there is a special appropriateness in Señor Borges' presence here.

BORGES: Really?

PRES. BANKS: Of the two pillars of the liberal arts, Borges has been a contributor to both: the lively imagination and the clear and fresh perspective that are so essential, both of these—both perspective and imagination—to the nature of life itself. In order to have such depth of perspective, one must have both the humor and the humility to see oneself clearly. Many of you will know these words, for they are his: "It's to the other man, to Borges, that things happen. I walk along the streets of Buenos Aires, stopping now and then, and perhaps out of habit, to look at the arch of an old entranceway or a grillwork gate. Of Borges, I get news through the mail, and glimpse his name among a committee of professors or in a dictionary of biography. I have a taste for hourglasses, maps, eighteenth-century typography, the roots of words, the smell of coffee, and Stevenson's prose. The other man shares these likes, but in a showy way that turns them into stagy mannerisms. It would be an exaggeration to say that we're on bad terms. I live, I let myself live, so that Borges can weave his tales and poems. And those tales and poems are my justification."

Such clarity of perspective lacks only one thing, that which all of us as human beings need, and that is the testimony of gathered people who at times say to the single artist, poet, writer: "You do matter so deeply to us." And in a poem, which you may not know quite as well, another written by him, I offer him as our gift his words, for these are the words of appreciation which he gave to James Joyce in "Invocación a Joyce":

BORGES: (whispers) That's right.

PRES. BANKS:

> What does our cowardice matter if on this earth
> there is one brave man?
> What does sadness matter if in time past
> somebody thought himself happy?
> What does my lost generation matter,
> that dim mirror,
> if your books justify us?
> I am the others. I am all those
> who have been rescued by your pains and care.
> I am those unknown to you and saved by you.

Señor Borges, you do not know us all, but you have touched us all.

BORGES: Thank you, sir.

PRES. BANKS: I ask that you bear with us for one more minute, because in this moment you represent not only Dickinson College, but a history here, and you are part of a lectureship which Dean Allan will describe. Then we will hear you.

GEORGE ALLAN (Dean of Dickinson College): The Morgan Lectures are named in honor of James Henry Morgan, Dickinson College's first dean of the college and its eighteenth president. Jim Henry was appointed to the dean's position in 1903 as part of an effort by President George Reed to improve significantly the quality and reputation of this sleepy, small town college. A decade later Reed was dead, and his successor had spent the college's endowment and plunged it into debt. Jim Henry was appointed president in 1914, returned Dickinson to financial health and doubled the size of the student body, from two hundred and fifty students to slightly over five hundred. Morgan is an unlikely figure to provide the aegis for tonight's lecturer; President Morgan was a tight-fisted, authoritarian administrator. One might say he was a little tyrant. There was no budget in those days, just Jim Henry's personal decisions regarding how to spend money. I don't think salaries were ever raised during the whole of the twenty years in which he was in charge. He opposed all curricular reforms, and was a hopeless curmudgeon on social matters. He was, in short, a narrow-minded, parochial little Caesar who was not beneath instigating a vicious rumor campaign that succeeded in destroying the reputation of his reform-minded successor. But he had his virtues, few as they were. He believed deeply in the classics and the classical education, and was instrumental in sustaining Dickinson's Latin graduation requirement until its demise with the Second World War. He prevented the trustees from expelling all female students and returning Dickinson to an all-men's college, and he hauled the editors of the yearbook before the campus judiciary when they put the picture of the senior class's only black student at the end of the book rather than in the proper alphabetical location. He set high standards for admission, and was not afraid to dismiss poor students, even at a time when enrollments were dangerously low. He strengthened literature and the arts. Above all, he stood for something he thought worthwhile and pursued that ideal with unfailing energy and optimism until his health failed him in 1934, and he resigned his duties for good. This slender thread of perseverance for the sake of worthwhile human matters is what links Jim Henry Morgan to Jorge Luis Borges. The one parochial, the other cosmopolitan; the one parsimonious in thought and feeling, the other generous and overflowing, yet both are sensitive to the fragile value of human accomplishment, the importance of our cultural heritage in shaping who we are and to what we aspire, and both are optimistic concerning the human prospect despite its unlikely, absurd, befuddling character. The slender thread connecting Emily Dickinson with our own John Dickinson is even a thinner one. John was one of the Virginia Dickinsons, a member of an old and aristocratic family, proud to contribute its sons to national leadership, and not surprised that one of them should author the Articles of Confederation and become the first governor of Pennsylvania and of Delaware. Emily came from a strain of New England Dickinsons, hovering around Amherst and other chilly villages where winter nights and Puritanism made for brooding self-reflection and led great minds to poetry instead of politics. The two families, New Englanders and Virginians, linked together only in Southern England, where William the Conqueror gave land and pelf to Walter DeCaen and to the DeCaen sons. The Duke at Caen in Normandy was a Norseman, of course, and thus all Dickinsons trace back eventually to the language and poetry of those Northern adventurers whom Borges studies so avidly. So tonight we celebrate the slender threads of history and interpretation; they have brought us Borges as our Morgan lecturer, speaking on the poetry of Emily Dickinson. Our strategy tonight is as follows: Professor James Hughes of Wright State University will be the interlocutor to Socrates; he will ask questions of Borges, inviting his reflections on Emily Dickinson and maybe on other matters. Eventually all of you will be invited to join in the exchange, the slender thread of our conversation.

PROFESSOR HUGHES: I want to thank you all for the opportunity of being here at this conference. It is an historic event, when a great writer in one century from one part of the world comes to speak about a writer from another time and another part of the world. And I think that these two writers have a great deal in common, despite their many differences in experience and style. I know that many of you are jealous of the fact that I'm up here and you would like the opportunity to ask questions, and I assure you that you will have it. I would like to begin with a question about your acquaintance with Emily Dickinson: how did you become acquainted with her poetry, when did you begin to be interested in her, and what is it about Emily Dickinson that you think is important?

BORGES: Emily Dickinson was revealed to me, I think, through *The History of American Literature* by Lewisohn.

HUGHES: All right.

BORGES: I recall a few examples, and then I went on and read all her poetry.

HUGHES: And did you read it in English or Spanish?

BORGES: Well no, in English. Why in Spanish? God forbid! Emily Dickinson should be read in English!

HUGHES: All right.

BORGES: Besides, I've done most of my reading in English.

HUGHES: Do you know of anyone who has attempted to translate Emily Dickinson into Spanish?

BORGES: Yes, Silvina Ocampo. She's translating it at this very moment, I think, in Buenos Aires.

HUGHES: Have you seen any of those translations?

BORGES: Yes, they're very fine. Of course they're not close translations, but somehow Emily Dickinson is there, in her own magic way.

HUGHES: Well, some of us believe that Emily Dickinson is probably here in a magic way—

BORGES: Why not?

HUGHES: What *is* the magic of Emily Dickinson?

BORGES: I was captured by a few verses quoted by Lewisohn in *The History of American Literature* and I can recall them at this moment. One is, "This quiet Dust was Gentlemen and Ladies." Now, the idea is trite, of course: "Dust thou art, to dust returneth," but the expression is wonderful. How to say it? "Men are dust"; "Men fall to dust" are really nothing. But "This quiet Dust was"—and then you get a prosaic statement, "This quiet Dust was Gentlemen and Ladies." Then another two verses that come back to me at this moment—you know them by heart, I suppose: "Parting is all we know of heaven, And all we need of hell." I should like to stress the word "need," because it means that the human soul needs misfortune, that misfortune is really a blessing in disguise—especially if you are a poet. Then you have to be unhappy, since otherwise you cannot write. You have to begin with unhappiness. That should be a tool for the poet. In the case of Emily Dickinson, I suppose words such as "lonely," "lonesome"—she must have been sad, as many of us are, because sadness is needed. Even in the case of Whitman, he did all he could to be happy, since he thought happiness was an American duty, but I wonder—I suppose he failed, as all men do, as most of us do. But perhaps, thinking over those things, I should say that at the end of a day, we have been sometimes in heaven, most of the time in hell perhaps, and that is the idea behind James Joyce's *Ulysses*—the idea that, in a single day, within the compass of twelve hours, all things happen to every man. After, let's say, nine o'clock or so, during the daytime, we have been in all places, we have suffered all things, and that is one of the revelations of Joyce. So that Emily Dickinson must have been very unhappy, since her poetry is so good. I don't think poetry can be analyzed, or explained. If it is explained, it is explained away. I believe what Whistler said once; he was discussing art, influences, political problems, genealogy and all that, and then he said these fine words: "Art happens." That is to say, art is a miracle, but happily for us, a very common miracle. Art happens. Things beautiful are happening all the time. That would be the same thing as what Angelus Silesius said, "Die Rose ist ohne warum." That might be translated "The rose has no why." It doesn't come off in English; the verse is German. In Spanish it can be done: "La rosa es sin por qué": The idea that art should not be analyzed and cannot be analyzed. But of course, analyzing is a pleasure, also. Why deny ourselves that pleasure? I mean, the search for explanation is a pleasure, even if we don't find it. Now, in the case of Emily Dickinson, what really matters are the cadences—I mean her voice. When we read five or six poems by Emily Dickinson, we know her—as well as we could know anybody. I mean, Emily Dickinson today is clear-voiced; Emily Dickinson today is—she's not quiet dust, no—she's that living voice going on and on, and it's speaking to us. I think of her as if I had known her personally. I saw her house when I was in New England. By the way, it is a very strange thing (maybe astrology can explain it) why most of the dreaming, most of the writing in America (when I talk of America I think both of my South America and your North America, and what's in between), most of the dreaming, and thinking, and writing has been done in New England. There should be some astrological explanation. From a small land, relatively small, you get such figures as Emily Dickinson, Herman Melville, Emerson—my favorite poet, a cool poet, Emerson, so full of emotion—you have Emerson, you have Melville, you have Thoreau, you have William James, you have Henry James, and you've got Edgar Allan Poe, of course, and they all came from New England. There must be some reason for that. I suppose that reason's known only to astrologers.

HUGHES: I'm wondering about what you said about the feeling that you know Emily Dickinson personally—are you at all acquainted with her letters?

BORGES: No, I'm sorry to say I haven't read them. That would be a pleasure to come—

HUGHES: Well, I recommend them to you, because her letters—

BORGES: My bounden duty, of course, to read those letters! My pleasure also, since I enjoy her poetry so much, but at this moment I can only recall a few verses.

HUGHES: You know, I have a feeling that her poems are letters, and, in fact—

BORGES: That her letters are poems.

HUGHES: —that the only poems that she published were, with a few exceptions, poems that were sent as letters to people, to special people, and I'm wondering if you feel that poetry is that kind of communication, that kind of letter.

BORGES: Yes, I think I have received those letters that Emily Dickinson sent me. I got them, duly. Here they are with me. I can only quote a few lines, but they are there, they're all there, in my memory, my unhappy memory.

HUGHES: And you send letters in turn, of your own.

BORGES: Yes.

HUGHES: Your own poems are letters.

BORGES: Yes, they truly are, sir, of course. We keep on a secret correspondence, that ghost and myself, Emily Dickinson and myself, a mere South American practitioner.

HUGHES: But in a sense your letters are not as secret as hers—

BORGES: No, unhappily they are not—they should be kept secret.

HUGHES: With all these people?

BORGES: "Mum's the word," concerning me, eh?

HUGHES: It may be, then, that one of the differences between you and Emily Dickinson—

BORGES: There are so many differences.

HUGHES: Well, but one of them—

BORGES: She was a real poet, and I'm not!

HUGHES: But she had to reveal herself secretly to individuals, and if you have, unlike Emily Dickinson, a large readership, a large correspondence—

BORGES: Yes, but what can I do about it? Those things happen.

HUGHES: And yet you say, "Mum's the word." Is it possible then that your poems are—

BORGES: I think that two or three of them are good, maybe, I should say. No, the rest is silence, as Hamlet had it. I may have written, in the course of eighty-odd years, I may have written a few pages, a few tales, and perhaps some stanzas, some lines at least—

HUGHES: And that's all?

BORGES: That's all, but that should prove sufficient. I've written far too much. What one writes, one writes at the end. Every book is a rough draft of the next book. They are all rough drafts, and nothing definitive. They are all rough drafts, and then, in the end, if the gods allow you, then you may find the real cadences, the words you're looking for, the metaphor that somehow eluded you. Both may be found at the end. But you begin by trying, at least I do, and you go on to other and I hope better things. I never look for subjects. I want the subject to find me. I do not hunt for them. I do not think I can invent metaphors. I think we have already, let's say, the few essential metaphors. And those are, of course, life and a dream, death and sleep, stars and eyes, time and the river, women and flowers. Those metaphors are sufficient. But every generation has to say them in a certain dialect, with a certain cadence, not known before. All poetry is telling the same tale over and over again, with some slight but precious variations.

HUGHES: Do you, when you communicate this poem to other people, and other people think that it's very good, and you yourself feel—

BORGES: Well, I disagree with them, of course.

HUGHES: You disagree.

BORGES: Yes, we have to go on to other things then. I don't have to remember what I have done. I have to forget. I want to forget and go on dreaming and writing.

HUGHES: And when the response to the poem that you really feel good about is good, isn't that a special—

BORGES: It is. I'm duly thankful. So I think, yes, I think I'm greatly overrated, but still, what can I do about it? People overrate me because they're fond of me. I suppose in this case, I have several assets. For example, I'm a South American—very picturesque, no? I'm an old man. I am blind. In a sense, I'm almost Homer or Milton.

HUGHES: Are you familiar with Emily Dickinson's poem, "Before I Got My Eye Put Out"?

BORGES: No. Could you recite it to me? I'd be duly thankful.

HUGHES: I can't—

BORGES: Or you can read it.

HUGHES: I can't recite the whole thing, and I don't have a copy with me, but the point of the poem is that it was safer to see, and that when she lost her eye, she saw too much. Does that make any sense at all?

BORGES: I think that being blind may be a blessing in disguise. I went blind for reading purposes in 1955, and then, of course, I have time for rereading and for thinking, and for dreaming, also. I spend most of my time by myself. I have young friends; we have a good time. But I spend most of my time alone, and then I'm always scheming, and planning, and dreaming, going over rough mental drafts, versifying also. Yesterday—yes, last night—I dictated a poem to María Kodama called "The Last Wolf in England." I saw a picture of a wolf and that set me to thinking of wolves. The poem I think is quite good, though I have to wonder.

HUGHES: Can you recite it?

BORGES: No, don't worry—I can't. It has to be licked into shape. That wolf is still a cub. We have to lick it into shape. Yes.

HUGHES: Possibly a werewolf.

BORGES: Well, why not? I'm very fond of werewolves. We call them *lobizones* in my country; that's the word for werewolf. In French it's

Loup-garou I think, no? And then *capiangos*—those are men who turn into tigers, not into wolves.

HUGHES: I think you already can tell that the pattern we have established is a very open one, and—

BORGES: "Give-and-take" would be the right word.

HUGHES: Give-and-take—

BORGES: Give-and-take, yes. A colloquial expression, but why not? Let's be colloquial, no? We're among friends.

HUGHES: We have agreed that in order to make this a real symposium, you all should feel free to ask questions about any of the subjects that have come up or anything else that occurs to you.

BORGES: Yes, any subject. The universe is before us.

DEAN ALLAN: I'd like Señor Borges to say some more about Emily Dickinson's voice. Do you mean that in a way that pays attention to subject matter? Her nature poetry? Love poetry?

BORGES: When you think of a poet you think of his voice. You don't think of printed pages. You think of particular cadences, a way of speaking, a way of thinking. I think I know her voice. I think I know her personally in that sense, though I have never met her in the flesh, of course, since history forbids it, since chronology forbids it. But I wonder if I could do without her. I wonder if I could do without American literature. I can't, of course. Nobody can, eh? I think that such men as Edgar Allan Poe, Emily Dickinson, Walt Whitman, changed things—everything's different now, since they happened. They happened to us, to everyone of us personally. And so poetry is different.

HUGHES: How is it different? What did it do to you personally?

BORGES: In the case of Poe, you can't think him away. Because if *he's* not, we have no Baudelaire, no symbolism, no Mallarmé perhaps, no pre-Raphaelites also, begotten by him. In the case of Walt Whitman, he stands for all public literature, or poetry—it was invented by Whitman. You can think away other poets, perhaps Longfellow. But not Edgar Allan Poe. I'm not saying this against Longfellow. But there are poets that can be thought away. But at least we've named four or five American poets that cannot be thought away. For example, Herman Melville, that splendid nightmare *Moby Dick*, then Poe, especially *The Narrative of Arthur Gordon Pym*. Arthur

Gordon Pym—a Saxon name, a Scots name, and then Pym, for Poe, Arthur Gordon Pym for Edgar Allan Poe. And Whitman, of course, invented so many things we would want to talk about him forever and a day, and Henry James, William James also, particularly the tales of Henry James, so rich, so inexhaustible, so deliberately ambiguous, they can be read in so many different fashions. Every time you read them the text is different. I think America has done much for the whole world. Everything has been changed. And why not remember Mark Twain, also? He wrote *Huckleberry Finn* and I think that from *Huckleberry Finn* came *Kim*, because *Kim* is the same: you have a young man, you have a boy, and then you have a country seen through their eyes, and that was Mark Twain's invention when he wrote *Huckleberry Finn*. And then suppose Kipling was growing out of that when he wrote *Kim*. That was way back in 1900, I think; he published the book in 1901, two years after I was born.

PRES. BANKS: Señor Borges, as you mention symbolic activity, especially as a poet and the son of a psychologist, could you say something of the nature and significance of dream? Anything you wish to deal with on that?

BORGES: I have thought much about dreams. Dreams are the first art. Since animals dream, and men dream, there's a kind of theatrical performance, and all that happens within our heads, so that every night in a sense, we are dramatists. We make small pieces and sometimes we get the tiger of the species—the nightmare, and that also is a dream—that also is a horrible dream. Dreams give us many things. They gave Coleridge "Kubla Khan." And I was once given a quite bad poem by a dream. But it was not my fault—it was the dream. Maybe I remembered it wrong when I woke up. And then I am about to publish a short story called "Shakespeare's Memory." We were in East Lansing, María Kodama and I, and I had a very tangled dream. When I awoke, the only thing that I remembered was the sentence, "I sell you Shakespeare's memory"—that was all. Then I thought that this would prove sufficient. I thought the idea of selling was too commercial for me. So, instead, I amended the dream and I said I give you, or, I bestow on you, no—that's too pompous—I give you Shakespeare's memory. And then a story came, not too bad a story, about a German scholar who is given Shakespeare's personal memory, and of course he does nothing with it.

HUGHES: I've just suddenly had an Emily Dickinson line flash through my mind: "Dying in drama is never dead."

BORGES: There should be more of the idea, more variation I think, no? Dying, drama.

HUGHES: It's that whole idea that dreams are safer.

BORGES: I suppose they are, because of the dying and drama.

HUGHES: It's when you wake up.

BORGES: Yes.

HUGHES: And then she says, "Shriek." The real expression of danger, the fear, is on waking, not within the sleep, not within the dreams.

BORGES: Every morning, when I wake up, I say to myself, "Here I am: Jorge Luis Borges. I hate him, I'm tired and bored with what I do. Every morning I have that feeling. Not here, because I think, "Well, I'm in Pennsylvania, in America," well, that's different, no? Buenos Aires is very dreary, at least in our time.

HUGHES: Do we have any questions?

BORGES: Oh, we should have any amount of questions. The night is young (to use a trite metaphor, but a very good one). Any amount of questions. As Borges, I'm very shy, far more shy than any of you, or a whole lot of you put together.

QUESTION FROM THE AUDIENCE: How were you influenced by Emanuel Swedenborg?

BORGES: Greatly. I'm writing a book on him. I've read four books of his done into English in Everyman's Library, and several lives of him. I think that William Blake was begotten by Swedenborg. I think that he was the real one; Blake was his dream. Blake was a fine poet, and Swedenborg wasn't. But I think that his idea of ethics is a new idea. The idea, for example, that we're not punished, we're not rewarded, that in a sense we create our own heaven and our own hell—that came from Swedenborg and was taken up by Blake, and lastly, of course, as you all know, by Bernard Shaw in his *Man and Superman*, the same idea, of heaven and hell being states of mind, not punishments or gifts.

QUESTION (Donald Shaw, University of Edinburgh): You once said, in one of your works, that you thought Schopenhauer was perhaps the only person who really understood how the world was. I wonder why you said that.

BORGES: I said that he has really read the riddle of the world, no? Well, I think it's true. At least if I think of philosophy, I think of Schopenhauer as *the* philosopher. Though of course I owe much to Berkeley, to Bradley, to Hume, to Mauthner and so on and so forth, but still I think of Schopenhauer as being *the* philosopher. I taught myself German in order to read Schopenhauer. And I read him in English, *The World as Will and Idea*, but "Idea" isn't too good, no? *Die Welt as Will und Forstellung*, no? In Spanish it comes off better, eh? *El mundo como voluntad y representación.* "Representación" is surely "Forstellung," but not "Idea"—I don't know why it's translated as "Idea." But I still keep on reading Schopenhauer, and thinking. Of course I don't know whether the world can be explained or expressed in words. Perhaps not. But in any case I think he did the trick and not the others. I owe so much to Schopenhauer. I'm so happy to be reminded of him. So I stick to that statement. I stick to the statement that Schopenhauer made, perhaps, the best map of the universe that has ever been designed.

QUESTION FROM THE AUDIENCE: You've been writing poetry for over fifty years now. How would you describe your poetic evolution? How would you compare your most recent poetry with the stuff you wrote when you were younger?

BORGES: When I was a young man I was baroque. I did my best to be Sir Thomas Browne, or Quevedo, or Lugones, or somebody else. But now, now I think I can fall back on myself, if I exist. So that I began by being very complex, I wallowed in newfangled words or archaic words, and I wrote in a very complicated way. Now I do my best to be simple, since I know that things are complex. So that even if my sentences are simple, the meaning is never simple, since the world is not a simple thing, but a very complex thing. I think I began by being baroque, by being a seventeenth century writer, by attempting to be Shakespeare. We all do that, I suppose. But now, I fall back on being myself. I try to record with dictionary words; I try to be as simple as I can, since I know that things cannot be really simple; they are not. So that even if they are really simple, they are deceptive; they deceive us. But I think in terms of the reader also. I think that reading should be pleasant, should be an experience of happiness. Then I try to make the reader as happy as I can, well, by not being too vainglorious, by avoiding pomp and circumstance, by telling my stories as simply as I can, by not meddling with them. I do my best not to meddle with what I write. I let the dream have its way with me. And I think that my best books are my last ones. That may be an illusion, but a necessary illusion. I think that perhaps we might choose, let's say *Doctor Brodie's Report*—or *The Book of Sand*, that's better; you must have *The Book of Sand* for prose. And for poetry, a book called *La Cifra—The Cipher*, or *The Many Things*; I don't know what title you have. But let us stick to those two books. Perhaps two too many, for all I know. So *The Book of Sand* the *The Cipher*. One stands for my prose, the other for my verse.

QUESTION (Tom Reed, Dickinson College): When you were speaking about writing poetry, you mentioned your desire to please the reader. But William Blake, someone you've just mentioned, wrote a letter later to a friend about "Jerusalem" saying he doubted he'd ever find a buyer for that particular engraved manuscript.

BORGES: But he was a fine poet, I am sure.

REED: But can you imagine writing without an audience?

BORGES: Of course I can. I'm like Robinson Crusoe and I keep on writing, for example. Crusoe is a good example, no? In my island, I keep on writing. What else can I do? You see, I am blind, I am old, I can't read—what else can I do but dream and write? Or dictate, rather, since I can't write by myself. My letters overlap.

QUESTION FROM THE AUDIENCE: You mentioned Whistler, in passing, when you were discussing "art happens." I wonder if there are other painters and visual artists you were particularly moved by, or that you've been particularly affected by, in addition to the literary artists that you've mentioned.

BORGES: Yes, I think I would mention Turner, I would mention Rembrandt, Velázquez, and perhaps some expressionist painters also. I mean Franz Marc, perhaps, Kubin, Kandinsky, and that's that. You see, I am old and more or less blind, but I still think certain paintings are more or less essential, no? And Blake, of course. I remember some wonderful lines by Blake. They come back to me quite often. I will give them to you in a moment:

> But silken nets and traps of adamant
> will Oothoon spread,
> And catch for thee girls of mild silver,
> or of furious gold; . . .

That kind of thing is forgotten, I think, no? "Girls of mild silver, and of furious gold." "Mild silver" of course inspired "furious gold," but "furious gold" is wonderful, I should say. You can do so many things with the English language, all things *are* being done with the English language, I should say.

QUESTION (Jaime Alazraki, Harvard University): In *La Cifra* you wrote, "I should live to forget about myself"—"Viviré para olvidarme." Can you reflect on that?

BORGES: I didn't quite understand my quotation. Can you go over it once more?

ALAZRAKI: "Viviré para olvidarme."

BORGES: Did I write that? Well, why not? Thank you sir. Yes, of course. To go on living, one has to forget of living as a duty, a very pleasant one, also. If you had a perfect memory, you'd die. I wrote a story about that, a man who was burdened down by an endless memory. "Funes, el memorioso," I think, was the name of that story. Yes, to go on living one has to forget. Because if not one would be overwhelmed by the too-minute past, by too many days, by too many circumstances. So oblivion is a part of memory, a very precious part of memory.

QUESTION FROM THE AUDIENCE: Señor Borges, to return to where we started the evening, with the consideration of Emily Dickinson, it's hard to think of her without thinking of the other great female poet of the Americas, Sor Juana Inés, and is perhaps—

BORGES: Two who have nothing in common whatever, eh?

QUESTION: I don't know.

BORGES: I don't think they have anything in common.

QUESTION: Except that, as women, and as poets, they both had a life of denial. Do you think it paradoxically was part of their poetry and part of their inspiration that they had to face this?

BORGES: Yes, but I can do without Sor Juana Inés; I can't do without Emily Dickinson. That is a personal heresy, perhaps, but I can do without Sor Juana Inés.

QUESTION: You see no connection, then?

BORGES: No. Well, of course, all things are linked, but no special connection, nothing standing out, a thin thread perhaps . . . a really thin thread, the thinnest of threads.

QUESTION FROM THE AUDIENCE: You mentioned earlier the possibility of thinking away certain American authors. Can you contrast the role of literature and the role of personal experience in your own writing?

BORGES: I suppose literature is a personal experience, only different, really a book is a . . . it's falling in love, let's say, no, . . . reading is a personal experience and a very vivid and intense personal experience.

HUGHES: Do you feel that the universities and schools have hurt literature? If we teach literature as a subject and analyze it, are we inhibiting it from being a personal experience?

BORGES: No, we should teach our students to think of it as a personal experience. That is the real duty, no? To teach, not the content of books, but the love of books, the love of literature. That's what I did. I taught my students—not to memorize names endlessly—but the love of English and American literature.

HUGHES: To rephrase the question, would you make any distinction between the experience of literature and the other personal experiences in one's life? Is there anything particularly distinctive about . . .

BORGES: In my case I think literature has been the keenest experience of all. Literature is a very keen experience, especially poetry.

HUGHES: Intensified; keen, very sharp?

BORGES: Yes. Nothing dull about it. Nothing blurred, nothing misty— on the contrary, it stands out. When I think of my boyhood, I fall back on my first reading of Stevenson, Kipling, Mark Twain, and so on—those are personal experiences. Much as the fact that I loved my father, I fell in love with Miss So-and-so, and so on. Yes, it was all personal experiences. Reading is a very personal experience, a very enjoyable one. Not a duty, certainly, but a pleasure—an easy form of habit, as I should say.

HUGHES: There was another question here.

BORGES: There should be any number of questions, yes?

QUESTION FROM THE AUDIENCE: Señor Borges, can you tell us what poetry means to you, or what is your own definition of poetry?

BORGES: I should say it means everything to me. Poetry and philosophy, and friendship, naturally—meeting people or meeting books. I don't think they're essentially different. Discovering Mark Twain, or discovering Miss So-and-so—more or less the same thing, no?

QUESTION: Can you explain to me why you titled your last book *La Cifra*, *The Cipher*?

BORGES: Yes; I was thinking that all experiences were given us, say, a certain number of times. We should see the moon, I don't know—nine thousand times, but not one time more. So there is a cypher to everything, for doing things for the last time. For example, maybe this is the last time I will be speaking concerning poetry, for all I know. Maybe I will die tonight. Many things at my age are a farewell, a goodbye to things. I called the book *The Cipher* because I was thinking of that poem where a man is told that he is allowed to see the moon a certain number of times, not a single time more. That's a kind of tragic poem. I have written many poems about that. One called "Límites," that we do things only a certain number of times, that we are doing many things for the last time, unaware of it. Yes, that would be the explanation, I think. But I wonder if that will be the title, because when the book comes out it may be called, for all I know, *The Many Things* and not *The Cipher*. We were discussing that with the translator. *The Cipher* is not good in English; in Spanish it is all right, but in English . . .

QUESTION: Yes sir, I understand that you are fascinated with the English language—

BORGES: Of course I am.

QUESTION: —at that stage of the Anglo-Saxon and Middle English language. Is there anything about the quality of the English language at that point that you especially like?

BORGES: Well, I think that it's very simple. It's that English is not only a Germanic, but a Romance language. For example, if I go over those famous verses which are found in *Macbeth*, "The multitudinous seas incarnadine," that's splendid and Latin, and then you have the short section, "Making the green one red"—the same thing said twice over, but each time it's different. First we have splendor: "the multitudinous seas incarnadine," and then the short Saxon words, "making the green one red." English has that peculiar quality. For example, in Norwegian or in German, all the words are Germanic, or most of them. In Spanish, most of the words are Latin, except for a few other words that are not felt as being different. While in English you feel the difference between, let's say, "kingly" and "regal"; "fraternal" and "brotherly." Those words have a slight difference, but it makes all the difference. For example, if you are writing a poem it would make all the difference in the world if you spoke of the "Holy Spirit" or of the "Holy Ghost." The "Holy Spirit" is the light, Latin word. The "Holy Ghost" is the dark Saxon word. It makes all the difference to the poem. The sense is the same, but the connotation is different; the feeling behind those words is different. You can do so much with English. I've done most of my readings in English, by the way. I think in terms of Edward William Lane and Captain Burton. The Bible is to me what it was to my Methodist forefathers, the English Bible, the King James Bible, and so on.

QUESTION (David Kranz, Dickinson College): Your quotation from *Macbeth* and also your anecdote about the memory of Shakespeare make me ask whether you sense that you've heard the voice of Shakespeare as well as the voice of Emily Dickinson.

BORGES: Yes, I think I have.

KRANZ: If so, what is it?

BORGES: It's as mysterious as the rest of the universe. It can't be explained. Why should I explain it? We all know that voice, I think, as with all writers. Walt Whitman's voice, for example, is with us all the time. And so is Frost's voice—another great poet—and Browning's voice. Though Browning has so many voices it's hard to tell, no? Browning has so many voices.

QUESTION (Beverley Eddy, Dickinson College): I'm fascinated by what you said about English, that English has the ability, because it is partly Germanic and partly Romantic—

BORGES: Well, it does have that—

EDDY: —to pinpoint certain meanings, and I wonder if this isn't a limitation on the poet, that in—

BORGES: No, to have several meanings, to be able to choose between two slightly different words, no, on the contrary.

EDDY: But in the translations that you've been mentioning, you've been saying that English does not capture the entire richness of the word, the way "Vorstellung," for instance, does.

BORGES: Yes, but don't blame English for that one mistake! In that case yes—I think "idea" is hardly "Vorstellung." "Idee" in German, or "Gedanke," and those are not the same as "Vorstellung," evidently, you know?

EDDY: Right.

BORGES: In that case, yes, I think English made a slight mistake, which we will forgive.

EDDY: I would follow that up, though, by asking what languages you personally find the most poetic, or the best for writing poetry.

BORGES: I think when poetry happens, it may happen in any language, as far as I know. It's happening all the time. Poetry: it's something everlasting—it goes on; it flows on. Personally, I'm very fond of German, since I like compound words. I'm very fond of English, of course, and Spanish still has the dignity of the Latin. Yet the French hasn't, you know. French is quite different. I mean, Spanish and Italian are the voweled languages, while French is not. English isn't either. The vowels died out somehow, though you do find open vowels in Old English, in Middle English, but not in Modern English, because it is made of consonant sounds, not open vowel sounds; while in Spanish you get the open vowels of Latin, and perhaps, for all I know, of the Greek.

QUESTION: My question is more about the universe than about poetry.

BORGES: Well, why not? The universe is with us all the time, no?

QUESTION: Of course. Do you remember your essay–story about the library of knowledge, the library that is a honeycomb with all the hexagons—

BORGES: Of course I do. It is a kind of methodical nightmare, I should say, no? Yes. It's not a real nightmare. I view the universe as an endless library, with endless meaningless books. It's horrible, that story. I wrote that story some forty years ago, I think.

QUESTION FROM THE AUDIENCE: Yes, sir. My question is—

BORGES: I was trying to be Kafka, of course, when I wrote that story, and failing, utterly failing. I did my best to be Kafka; my worst. I wrote "The Lottery in . . ."

AUDIENCE: Babylon.

BORGES: Yes, ". . . in Babylon," yes, and then the book called "The Endless Library," yes. Both attempts at Kafka, of course. Unsuccessful attempts I should say, no? Quite unsuccessful.

QUESTION: There are six sides to the hexagon. That seems to suggest more than four dimensions; that is, six dimensions. If there is a God, sir, is the God within the honeycomb, which is endless in all directions, or is the God without the honeycomb?

BORGES: Well, but I wonder if there is a God—outside or inside the honeycomb? I'm not too sure about him, or about it, since we don't even know whether to call him "him." Yes, "Our Father *which* art in heaven"—that suggests a thing, rather than a person. "Our Father *which* art in Heaven." No, I would think of the God as being the honeycomb, what Bernard Shaw was saying when he wrote, "God is in the making," and we are in the making, of course. We are the making of God, at this very moment. We are somehow at the Godhead. I can't believe in a personal God, but why not in a God who may be evolving through stones, through plants, through beasts, through men, through ourselves, through the days to come, through many days to come?

QUESTION FROM THE AUDIENCE: Señor Borges, you've given a lot of lectures and you've answered a lot of questions. Is there a question that no one's ever asked you that you've always wanted to have a chance to answer?

BORGES: I'm afraid not. I can't provide you with a new question. The questions seem to be more or less endless.

PRES. BANKS: Like the honeycomb.

BORGES: Like the honeycomb, yes. But it is a good word, honeycomb, yes?

PRES. BANKS: Yes.

BORGES: "Honey" is a beautiful word.

PRES. BANKS: That's right. It is a beautiful word.

BORGES: "Honey." "Miel"—no, it's not too good, no? "Miel" in Spanish isn't as good as "honey."

HUGHES: That's correct.

BORGES: "Honey" is sweeter. I prefer "honey" to "miel" any day.

QUESTION FROM THE AUDIENCE: Do you have a muse of poetry—a poetic muse who helps you write?

BORGES: Yes, maybe the Holy Ghost, for all I know. Why not? A muse. Why not? Yes, a muse, or the Holy Ghost, the Rûwach, the Spirit of Elohim, yes, a Semitic people.

QUESTION FROM THE AUDIENCE: What do you think is the main difference between poetry in free verse and poetry in rhyme? Do you think there should be a different word for poetry in free verse?

BORGES: Well, in German we have "Das Stück"—that stands for prose and verse—why not? And poetry may stand for prose also. Think of Carlyle or Herman Melville—that's poetry, surely. So there's no essential difference, except perhaps in the mind of the reader. If you read something as a poem, you should react to it in a different way, no? In prose, you expect information, or arguments; in poetry, you don't. In poetry, all the time you're receiving very mysterious gifts, and you're thankful for them. Perhaps the difference is not in the text, but in the reader—the reader's mood. You may read the Bible as prose, or as poetry. So there is no essential difference between them.

QUESTION (Winifred Woodhull, Dickinson College): I was wondering about your remark earlier about women as one of the few metaphors in your poetry. And I'm wondering whether it's a particularly propitious metaphor for forgetting or remembering yourself through poetry.

HUGHES: Would you mind repeating that for us?

WOODHULL: I'm coming back to Borges' remark about woman as one of the few metaphors in his poetry, along with mirrors and flowers, et cetera—

BORGES: No, I didn't say that—

WOODHULL: Whether this is a particularly propitious metaphor for forgetting or remembering yourself.

BORGES: I don't see what woman has to do with it. Do *you* understand?

PRES. BANKS: I can give it a shot. She wants to know whether the metaphor of woman has something to do with the forgetting or remembering of yourself in poetry.

BORGES: I don't think it has, but you may be right, for all I know. I know very little concerning myself. I know little or nothing about myself, as Whitman had it. Of course, I'm thinking of women all the time, even at my age. But what can I do about it?

QUESTION FROM THE AUDIENCE: You've spoken a bit about voices this evening, and due to your experience with literature and your greatness—

BORGES: "Greatness"—that's an overstatement.

QUESTION: Perhaps.

BORGES: I'm very tiny, really. Quite inoffensive. No greatness about me. I mean no harm to anybody.

QUESTION: I'm going back to your experience, though. Out of your great experience and in deference to your age, perhaps we feel that—the way you speak of a voice, it sounds as if it's very much a presence for you, as if these people are alive, they are—

BORGES: Well, they *are* present, of course.

QUESTION: The question I want to ask is, this may be presumptuous, but perhaps in the audience they feel that this is some special ability you have either had given to you or you have earned, whereas—

BORGES: No.

QUESTION: Whereas I would like to speak to how you listen to a poem, how you invite these voices, how they come to you, how they work.

BORGES: Well, they're given to me. I accept them. That's that. I just accept them. I take them in.

QUESTION: Might they come to us also?

BORGES: Why not? They're coming to you all the time, I suppose.

QUESTION: Yes, I would think so—

BORGES: But maybe you're deaf, perhaps. I do my best not to be deaf. Being blind I'm in no need of deafness.

QUESTION FROM THE AUDIENCE: James Joyce came up twice tonight.

BORGES: Joyce is coming up all the time.

QUESTION: And one of the things Borges mentioned was the possibility in *Ulysses* for a man to have multiple experiences in one day.

BORGES: Yes.

QUESTION: I wonder what you make of Joyce's *Finnegans Wake* and all that simultaneity.

BORGES: *Finnegans Wake*. I think Virginia Woolf said that *Ulysses* was a defeat, a glorious defeat. I say the same thing of *Finnegans Wake*. It is a defeat. But there are such wonderful lines. For example, these come back to me at this very moment: "The rivering waters of." Period. "The hither and thithering waters of." Period. "Night." Full stop. Wonderful, eh? They don't make for a novel but for a poem.

They're a poem in themselves, I think, no? But I wonder if the whole book is a novel. I don't think so. Far too many puns, and then reading it is hardly direct. It makes for labor. I think of Joyce as being essentially a poet, not a novelist, though he wrote that one fine novel, *A Portrait of the Artist as a Young Man*, and then those fine tales of *Dubliners*. I think he was essentially a poet.

QUESTION FROM THE AUDIENCE: Borges, you have frequently made an equivalence between the Holy Ghost and the Muse. And you have made this equivalent to what you call the—

BORGES: Well, the spirit, I should say.

QUESTION: —"poor mythology of our time," the subconscious. Why do you use "poor mythology" when you refer to the subconscious?

BORGES: The subconscious is a very ugly myth, while the Holy Ghost is a very pleasant one. And the Spirit is far better, of course, the Rûwach. The subconscious has something tawdry and ugly and unattractive about it, no? I dislike the subconscious, no? I suppose we all do.

PRES. BANKS: The word "Rûwach" that you're using, the Hebrew word for the wind coming through the canyons that the Hebrew commonwealth used—why is that more beautiful to you?

BORGES: Perhaps it's a mere superstition, eh? But I prefer it.

PRES. BANKS: Yes. But what does it call forth from you?

BORGES: Well, I think of the Bible, that very strange idea, inviting beauty, the one very plural book, to a single mind—

PRES. BANKS: Many voices.

BORGES: Very strange, the Hebrews did that, no? It's as though *Pilgrim's Progress*, *Huckleberry Finn*, and *The Tragedy of Hamlet, Prince of Denmark* were all written by the same man—very strange idea. It makes you think of all those books being written by the one Holy Spirit, dictated in different periods to different men in different countries—very strange idea.

PRES. BANKS: Yes, yes, that's clear. I think you have another question.

BORGES: Only one?

PRES. BANKS: No, many.

QUESTION FROM THE AUDIENCE: Señor, you have said that you try to write simple—

BORGES: Well, I do my best. I fail, of course.

QUESTION: Yet we know that there are many poets out there who are writing very obscurely and difficultly for the general public to understand. We know that there are journals devoted just to explication of poetry. It's become a very difficult thing for the average person to read. What do you think about this trend?

BORGES: Well, I don't feel guilty. It's their funeral, not mine.

QUESTION FROM THE AUDIENCE: Have you ever written any poems that you thought were very, very good and that you have deliberately never shown to anyone else?

BORGES: Well, I wish that were true, but it isn't. I'm very sorry. I apologize.

QUESTIONS FROM THE AUDIENCE: I find it hard to understand some words that you wrote once, that I have read recently. And I hope I am not misrepresenting them. But I thought you said that when you write your words you are no longer Borges. They belong to the Spanish language or to the tradition.

BORGES: Yes, if I succeed—

QUESTION: Did you say that, and what did you mean?

BORGES: I mean they're not personal to me. They just happen and then they go on, living their own lives. A book has a life of its own, a fate of its own. Maybe a heaven or a hell of its own, for all I know. That's what I meant.

QUESTION FROM THE AUDIENCE: In a literary biography of Federico García Lorca, it was said that you once walked out on a dramatic play put on by him, and I would like to know if you have reassessed the theatre of Lorca and if you still feel the same.

BORGES: It is very boring.

HUGHES: And do you feel the same way that you used to feel about it?

BORGES: Yes, I do. Yes, I stick to that heresy. I am wedded to that heresy. A very minor poet, I should say. Though a pleasant one. Quite a minor poet.

QUESTION FROM THE AUDIENCE: I'd like to go back to when you were talking about personal experiences, and books being personal experiences.

BORGES: Yes, of course they are. What else can they be but personal experiences?

QUESTION: But don't you have to have some other personal experiences that you bring to the book, in order for the book to have any meaning for you?

BORGES: Yes, of course you do. You bring your whole life, your whole lifetime; you bring all your past, all the present. You bring yourself.

QUESTION: Does a book have any meaning other than the one you bring to it?

BORGES: I suppose a book has a different meaning to each reader. It's changing all the time. It's growing, like a plant, like a wilderness. It keeps on growing, and evolving, throughout time.

QUESTION: When you talk about your books with other people, then, do you get any sense of what they're talking about? Do you understand their meaning when they talk about your books?

BORGES: Well, off and on, I should say. I wonder what they make of my books. I do my best to forget them, to keep on dreaming and keep on writing.

QUESTION FROM THE AUDIENCE: I've read of your experience with Ultraism, a movement in your youth. I was wondering what you felt about movements like Cubism and Futurism, especially in contrast to a singular figure like Emily Dickinson, who was associated with no movements during her whole life.

BORGES: Literary movements are a mistake! An oversimplification. Besides, I'm an individualist, and don't believe in movements. They're necessary to very young writers, perhaps, then they're wearying to the flesh.

QUESTION FROM THE AUDIENCE: Borges, you said that you can hear Emily Dickinson's voice.

BORGES: Yes. I'm hearing it at this very moment.

QUESTION: In which of your books, in which of your poems, do you hope that the reader can hear your voice best?

BORGES: Perhaps—there's a poem of mine called "Otro poema de los dones." Maybe that poem. Or perhaps a poem called "The Other Tiger." Quite a good one, I should say. You have those two. Pick and choose.

QUESTION: What qualities about those poems allow for your voice to come through?

BORGES: I can hardly explain that, but I feel it. Yes, I feel it, very keenly. But I can't explain it. The whole thing can't be explained. Tradition is all substitution; tradition changes things. Either poetry comes through you or it doesn't—it can't be explained. If you explain it, you explain it away.

QUESTION (Sue Norman, Dickinson College): Señor Borges, you have been associated with libraries at various times in your life, and the image of a library appears from time to time in your short stories and poems. Could you comment on what "library" might mean to you?

BORGES: I think libraries are a wealth of possible experiences, and you can choose among them. At the library, you can choose, you can find personal experiences, but you should do the choosing yourself, rather than have choices dictated to you. The library offers thousands of opportunities, wonderful experiences, several forms of happiness; or unhappiness, perhaps. There are a million possibilities.

QUESTION: Earlier you mentioned that some of the best American literature came out of the New England area. I was wondering to what you attribute that connection. Also, one of my favorite personal voices from that area is the voice of Henry David Thoreau.

BORGES: But of course. I forgot him. I feel very guilty about it. Of course, Thoreau. He is duly remembered.

QUESTION: To what do you attribute the connection between New England life and the great love of literature that comes out of it?

BORGES: I suppose New England was Old England trying to be something else, no? That made all the difference. It was really Old England trying to be America. You see it in Emerson; Whitman, of course, but he came from Long Island, beyond that privileged area, New England.

HUGHES: We have time for three more questions.

QUESTION FROM THE AUDIENCE: Señor Borges, in the old Spanish proverb, the man with one eye is characterized as king in the land of the blind.

BORGES: There's a story by Wells about that: "The Country of the Blind."

QUESTION: How would you characterize the man who is blind in the land of the seeing?

BORGES: I suppose a blind man has more time for thought, and for dreaming, than a seeing man. At least I have to believe that, since I am blind. I have to think of it as being a boon, a blessing in disguise. "En el país de los ciegos el tuerto es Rey." That is a very fine story by H. G. Wells, "The Country of the Blind."

HUGHES: Yes, over on the right.

BORGES: That's the second.

QUESTION FROM THE AUDIENCE: You've written about the detective stories of Edgar Allan Poe and Chesterton. Some of your own stories have been—

BORGES: Detective stories.

QUESTION: Could you say something about your feeling about the genre of detective stories? You have an affinity for it?

BORGES: I think the genre was invented by Poe, and taken up by Dickens and Stevenson. It is a very interesting game. I think Poe wrote the essential books, the essential stories: "The Murders in the Rue Morgue," "The Mystery of Marie Rogêt", and then, "Thou Art the Man," and of course "The Purloined Letter," one of the best stories ever written. And that was taken up, "The Purloined Letter," by Chesterton, in his story about "The Invisible Man." The same story was told over again, with great fantasy and wonderful style. Yes, I think that the detective story is a very fine intellectual game, and a very amusing one. And of course, I should remember Wilkie Collins, *The Moonstone*, *The Woman in White*; they are very fine detective stories, novels also. And why not our old friend, Ellery Queen? I've read most of his stuff.

HUGHES: All right. Could we have a third question?

BORGES: And Phillpotts. I keep on remembering men who wrote mystery stories.

QUESTION (Donald Shaw): Señor Borges, after a lecture you gave at Harvard a long time ago, someone asked you a question about life after death. And you said something I've never forgotten. You said, "I am out for oblivion." Are you still out for oblivion?

BORGES: Yes, I am.

SHAW: Why?

BORGES: Very hopeful of it.

SHAW: Why do you not want to live after death?

BORGES: Eighty-three years is a long time. I do not want to outstay my welcome, no? At eighty-three . . . one is thoroughly tired. That's it. And yet, I go on living. When I was a young man I thought of suicide; now I go on living. Time will take care of that; any moment, I suppose.

DEAN ALLAN: We have been attempting to understand and grab hold of the real Borges tonight. Each time we've cast a net of words around him, he has managed to elude it, reminding us once more that the real Borges can't be captured by any of our words.

BORGES: I can't capture myself.

DEAN ALLAN: And though he continues to elude us, he does remind us that the quest, though hopeless, is well worth it. I would invite you to continue it amongst yourselves and with him in Drayer Lounge, where a reception will convene as soon as you can manage to find your way there. Thank you very much for coming tonight.

II. *Jorge Luis Borges Discusses Hispanic Literature, with Gonzalo Sobejano, Carlos Cortinez, and others.*

This section has been translated from the original Spanish conversation by Mauricio Roberto Rosales.

CORTÍNEZ: Well! What a relief to speak Spanish!

BORGES: Yes, indeed!

CORTÍNEZ: It's going to be a very easy job to moderate this session, because I believe all of you know at least one of the participants. We all knew the Borges of the encyclopedias, but now we have come to know the other Borges, right? Since yesterday we know the "charming" Borges.

BORGES: Thank you very much.

CORTÍNEZ: And as the Bible says, "By their fruits ye shall know them." Recently, in the reading of his poems, we have seen a sample of the poetic fruits which Señor Borges has given and this morning we have also witnessed the fruits of Professor Sobejano, because we have listened to two magnificent works by Christopher Maurer and Jaime Alazraki, who themselves are the fruits of Professor Sobejano to some degree—they are former students of his—so it's not necessary to introduce them. And we can begin to bombard Señor Borges immediately.

BORGES: Sure, why not? Here I am.

CORTÍNEZ: Well, keeping in mind that today is April 7th, which is the day Gabriela Mistral was born, who is not an Argentine . . .

BORGES: Well, but what can you do?

CORTÍNEZ: Borges had the opportunity of knowing Gabriela Mistral, so that we may, perhaps, begin with her. Yesterday we spoke of another woman. He calls her the greatest woman poet, or poet—

BORGES: Emily Dickinson.

CORTÍNEZ: Emily Dickinson. But in South America we also have Gabriela, right?

BORGES: Yes, of course.

CORTÍNEZ: Did you know her?

BORGES: I met her in the home of Victoria Ocampo, in Mar Del Plata. She insisted on being Indian and I insisted *we* weren't Indian. There were conversations like that, kidding around a little bit. She insisted on her Indian blood. I have some, but I didn't insist. But everything was very pleasant. A kind of child's play, which we have every morning about Indian America,—if we have or don't have anything to do with the Indians. It was a kind of game we both had—so many years ago.

CORTÍNEZ: I believe you share an affinity for the Bible, right?

BORGES: Ah, certainly. Well, that's because the Bible, I don't know if we can speak of it, is really a library, seeing that its name is plural, no? What a unique idea—the idea of joining texts by different authors, from different epochs, and attributing them to one sole author, the Spirit! That's marvelous, no? That is to say, works as disparate as the Book of Job, the Song of Songs, Ecclesiastes, the Book of Kings, Genesis, the Gospels too. To attribute all this to one invisible author. The Jews had a unique idea. It's as if one set about uniting in only one tome, and signing with only one author's name, the work of Emerson, the work of Carlyle, the work of Melville, the work of Henry James, the work of Chaucer, the work of Shakespeare, and say that it's all by one author. The Jews had a splendid idea—to reduce their books, their entire library, to that book which is called "The Books"—the Bible. It's really a very curious idea; now if we could only do it again! There are too many books; and it would be better to have all of them united. Each country could do it—gather its greatest books and attribute them to one sole anonymous author—the Spirit.

SOBEJANO: Well, if it's my turn to speak now . . .

BORGES: I believe so.

SOBEJANO: Not speak, but rather ask. I didn't know whether to call this a conversation, a questionnaire, an interrogation . . .

BORGES: Catechism, also—a catechism. What do you think?

SOBEJANO: Well, then, I'll begin with one question. Let's see how you like it. You've made it clear that you're a poet who doesn't like to be a poet who sings but tells.

BORGES: Yes, that's true. We Argentineans are not interjectory. Our poetry is mostly oral, rather exclamatory, no?

SOBEJANO: But, at the same time, you also express admiration or a special respect for a few poets from Spain.

BORGES: But of course, certainly!

SOBEJANO: For example Jorge Guillén, Jorge Manrique—

BORGES: Jorge Guillén seems to me the greatest poet in the Spanish language, no? Without offending anyone, I hope.

SOBEJANO: Of these two poets, do you think that one of them is grandiloquent?

BORGES: No, happily, not.

SOBEJANO: Guillén?

BORGES: No, no, happily, not.

SOBEJANO: What Spanish poet would you consider grandiloquent and musical? That is, who "sings" and doesn't "tell."

BORGES: I think there are so many the list would be infinite, no?

SOBEJANO: Would you save Manrique?

BORGES: Yes, and many others, of course.

SOBEJANO: And Guillén. How do you feel about Quevedo?

BORGES: Above all, the best poem in the Spanish language to me is the "Epistola Moral" by sevillano anónimo. I don't think there is any doubt, no? "Oh muerte, ven callada, como sueles venir en la saeta. . . ."

SOBEJANO: Don't you think it's too didactic, too moralistic and didactic, a bit . . . ?

BORGES: But we need didactic people, sensible people. We are all easily genial and easily irresponsible. It's better for a person who is not genial, who is responsible and clear-sighted to write admirable verses, for example: "Augur of the faces of the deprived," is a verse that had been written forever, no? Or "before time dies in our arms . . ." And so many other verses like that.

SOBEJANO: I remember, you spoke of those verses, "Oh muerte, ven callada como sueles venir en la saeta. . . ."

BORGES: Yes. The last time I saw Henríquez Ureña, we decided these lines had to be from some Latin, since in the seventeenth century it was fashionable to imitate classical themes. And he said, "I'll find out who it was." I never saw him again after that. Possibly Guillén has found the source of these verses that seem so Latin to me.

SOBEJANO: A short time ago I read the observation you shared with Henríquez Ureña, and I consulted a book, the first book that exists on the "Epístola moral," by Dámaso Alonso, someone you also know.

BORGES: Yes, certainly.

SOBEJANO: Okay, then. The origins of that verse are inexplicable, no?

"Todo lo pasas de claro con tu flecha," Manrique says.

BORGES: Yes, I know, but "todo lo pasas de claro con tu flecha" is not "Oh muerte, ven callada como sueles venir en la saeta."

SOBEJANO: Exactly, and first of all you put attention on "callada," no?

BORGES: Yes, of course.

SOBEJANO: . . . which is the one that doesn't appear to be explained in this book. That is why I say I'm trying to confirm that poetry—

BORGES: . . . that poetry cannot be explained. By the same token, art happens.

SOBEJANO: Yes.

BORGES: I repeat what Whistler said: "art happens." Art occurs and cannot be explained. But we enjoy explaining it so much. An innocent pastime: the analysis of literature, why not?

CORTÍNEZ: Well, now it's Latin America's turn, I believe, right?

BORGES: Yes, of course.

CORTÍNEZ: Beginning with the same country that produced Gabriela Mistral . . .

BORGES: It's that I know so little of that continent! Or in the case of the Argentine Republic, I know it too well, eh? Which is dangerous, yes.

CORTÍNEZ: But you knew Vicente Huidobro, right?

BORGES: Yes. Vicente Huidobro, yes. We spoke with him one night. Ulises Petit de Murat and he were there. And something funny happened. We were riding the subway to Ramos Mejía, a town west of Buenos Aires. Huidobro talked about his poetry, spoke with a certain vanity, and then Ulises and I said, "Now, this is too much, really!" And then he realized that he had gotten a little carried away, and he said, "of course, my poetry isn't worth anything." Soon we were all laughing and we changed the topic. It was a funny situation. We shared opinions with each other and I never saw Huidobro again in my life. It was the last time I saw him. We didn't talk about Huidobro's poetry that night, but other things. Well, the universe is always infinite, always leaves us a few subjects. But perhaps tonight we will exhaust them.

SOBEJANO: I was asking about the condition of the poet who does not sing but tells, and this coincides with what Jorge Guillén practices: a poetry of minor eloquence that does not scream, does not clamor, does not pretend to sing, but—

BORGES: If I could sing, I would sing, but I lack a voice; I don't really have a voice. Everything is tied to that poetry, well, which is almost prose, and many times is; ultimately, that is the only sincere thing in me—to live in this fashion. And I have no desire for interjections.

SOBEJANO: A student asked me once, "does the poetry of Jorge Guillén somewhat resemble the poetry of Jorge Luis Borges?"

BORGES: If only my poetry resembled Guillén's, but I'm not that ambitious!

SOBEJANO: But he referred mainly to the attitude, and I answered what occurred to me at that moment, which was that the poetry of Guillén is much more complacent in the affirmation of nature, the earth, pleasure, where as yours is, in effect, more desperate.

BORGES: No, not desperate; resigned. Quietly resigned.

SOBEJANO: So you consider yourself a peaceable man?

BORGES: Yes, certainly. I try to be. I've never gotten angry in my life. But I don't know, it may be better to get angry and vent one's feelings. I'm incapable of anger, incapable of wrath, but I am capable of patience, and capable of forgetfulness above all.

SOBEJANO: Certain adjectives abound in your poetry. For example, "arduous," "precise," "numerous," so much so that I think I can trace in their imprints the influence you've had on writers, or critics, and Latin American poets, who also use words like these a lot.

BORGES: But do these words seem strange?

SOBEJANO: Excuse me, no, no, no. They are not strange. But—

BORGES: Because a tree is precise, stars are precise, sand is precise, so many things are precise, that they would be too numerous, yes?

SOBEJANO: My question was whether you believe that these words, which are not strange, but often repeated, characterize your writings.

BORGES: In my case, very often repeated. Jean Cocteau said that style is a series of "tics." And he is right, I believe. All styles are a series of habits, repetitions; that is style. But one should try to write in an anonymous fashion, say, without "tics," without preferences; also without disdain.

CORTÍNEZ: Well, to finish up with the poets of my country . . . You know there was another who won the Nobel Prize.

BORGES: But why do you want to finish up with them?

CORTÍNEZ: So as not to have competition!

BORGES: But, really, they are not that bad. Why do you want to be done with them?

CORTÍNEZ: Well. We know that of Neruda's work, you don't like the love poems but the political poems. Could this suggest an ideological affinity?

BORGES: No, on the contrary. Let us say, that communism served to make him an excellent poet, the way democracy served Whitman, imperialism did Kipling, etcetera. Each poet requires his inspiration. And this inspiration is different in each case. For example, I admire, I love Whitman, but I do not believe in democracy. Ultimately, opinions are simple inspirations for each poet, and anything could be an inspiration. For many, well, I don't know, the Christian religion, for example. For Dante, it was inspiration; for me it wouldn't be because I don't believe in it. But that doesn't mean I don't believe in Dante. I don't believe his religion, his opinions, which is not to disbelieve him. Because he is something essential, something which goes beyond his opinions. Besides, opinions change so much; one changes so much with time, and you should not judge anyone for an opinion. It is the least of things, the most superficial, the most ephemeral.

SOBEJANO: And now for a completely peninsular question. You admire a Portuguese novelist, Eça de Queiroz, very much, to the point of affirming that his novel *El Primo Basilio* seems superior to you than *Madame Bovary*.

BORGES: This seems obvious to me. This is an axiom. I sound like Euclid now, speaking of axioms.

SOBEJANO: My question is peninsular because it incorporates a Portuguese and a Spaniard. You have barely spoken, that I know of (but it could come from my ignorance), about a novelist often compared with him, Clarín (Leopoldo Alas), who wrote short stories as well as novels.

BORGES: But I don't know if they are that similar. I recognize more the differences than the similarities. No doubt both things exist; it's impossible that they would not exist.

SOBEJANO: Well, this is precisely why I meant to ask you, if you thought that the modern short story which you have cultivated, and brought to such a masterful level, has in Leopoldo Alas any important inspirational value, as almost an embodiment of the short story in Spanish letters. I'm referring, of course, to Spain.

BORGES: I don't know. I don't remember his short stories. I remember his novel—

SOBEJANO: Stories, some of them fantastical and parabolic—

BORGES: I don't remember them. I think the short story is an essential genre and the novel isn't. In the novel there is always an excess. There are always too many pages, even in the case of Joseph Conrad, who is for me the supreme novelist. Even in his case there is always excess. A short story, on the other hand, a good story by Kipling, say, or a good story by Conrad, can be essential, have no leftover, not lack one sole word. The novel is successive, and the novelist can't contain it. But a short story can be contained. A story might contain itself, the way a sonnet can. But a novel can't. A novel is successive, for the readers and the author. A novel, after it's been read may form a whole, and maybe books are not written for what they give us page by page, but for their lasting image. Perhaps a man's life is this. The important thing is the image he leaves behind. And this image could be spread out in his entire work and not be in one particular book. For example, to me the supreme prose writer in the Spanish language is Alfonso Reyes. Alfonso Reyes is not in any one book. He is in all the books, like the God of the pantheists, and maybe this is true for many writers. For example, Poe is not in any one of his books, not even in *Arthur Gordon Pym*. But he is in all his work, in the image he has left us. It's the same with Byron. We can easily imagine Byron and not even think of *Don Juan* and of his other poems. Perhaps that is the fate of a writer. And perhaps the *Quijote* is more in our memory as a whole than in each page. I don't know if it's in each page, perhaps not. Unless, perhaps, it's in the admirable last chapter, in which Cervantes bides farewell to his friend and ours, Alonso Quijano. Perhaps that is where the *Quijote* is. Maybe that last chapter requires the weight of the previous ones; maybe it wouldn't mean anything, published by itself.

CORTÍNEZ: Last night, you were telling us that you don't believe in literary movements, weren't you?

BORGES: Ah, of course! I think they're a mistake. Perhaps because I am an individualist, no? And in English literature, which for me is *the* literature, there are hardly any movements. And those which do exist are less important than the ones who participated in them. For example, I think that Coleridge or Wordsworth is more important than the Romantic movement. And, generally, you can say that. Besides, the notion of schools strikes me as being rather dismal. Of course, it's convenient for those who chronicle literature historically, but it's a rather new discipline. I don't believe there are historical studies of any literature in the eighteenth century that began in the nineteenth century. And now we see everything historically; we see everything as a function of dates, which strikes me as being more or less dismal. One would have to think about each book as the book of the present moment. For me, the greatness of Kafka lies in this—in the fact that his novels, and above all his short stories, came out splendidly and were very ancient. They didn't need to be contemporary. And that's a virtue. Right now I recall (I'm going to digress; why not?) I recall a statement which Kipling attributes to a Hindu poet, but which he possibly invented himself. The phrase is so beautiful that it doesn't matter if it's the work of Kipling, or the work of an anonymous Hindu poet, or a commonplace thing in the literature of India. It goes like this: "If no one had told me it was love, I would have thought it was a naked sword." I think this would be an admirable phrase if it were written this morning or two thousand years ago. Literature should seek this out. It should strive to be eternal, and not to correspond exactly to an era, seeing as how we are unfortunately condemned to an era. I think we should search for eternities even if we do not find them.

CORTÍNEZ: That is why I won't mention Modernism to you. But may I ask you about Lugones?

BORGES: No. But Modernism, to me, was like a good breath of air in the Spanish language. So many things began because of Modernism. Naturally, among those things, I too began, which is something to lament. I believe we are all children of Modernism, that is to say, the offspring of, well, Jaimes Freire, Lugones, and Rubén Darío above all. I may have spoken with Lugones five or six times in my life, and each time he changed the conversation to speak affectionately and nostalgically about "my friend and master Rubén Darío." He liked that brotherly relationship with Darío. He was a lone, disagreeable man; and Darío was very *querible* ("loveable," as they say in English), very charming, and Lugones was no doubt awed by Rubén Darío, who had showed him so many things. I think that everything that has been done afterwards comes from Modernism. We could, ultimately, grow tired of swans and lakes; the Modernists themselves did grow tired of them as subjects. I believe it was like a great freedom, a great breath of air for the language. So many ideas entered, so many others, all the themes. Soon after, Lugones, in *Lunario*, changed the meter and other games like that, metric, rare. And then a music, a music definitely taken from Verlaine and Hugo, but to switch the music of one language to another is very difficult. If I could take the music of English into Spanish I would be a great poet, but this I am not. For example, a music like "Ligero sueño de los crepúsculos suaves, como la negra madurez del higo, sueño de un lugar que se goza consigo mismo, con sus propias alas." This morose music is new in the Spanish language. And it is absurd to say that Lugones took it from Verlaine or Darío, seeing as how those books are at everyone's disposal, and not all write these verses. Or the other one goes: "El jardín con sus íntimos retiros, hará a tu lado el sueño, fácil jaula," where metaphor is downplayed and cadence is all. No, I think we owe a debt of gratitude to Modernism. In the end, everything has changed because of Modernism, although the word is a bit ridiculous. But that doesn't matter, does it?

SOBEJANO: May I ask you a question? In a recent anthology of your poetry, there's a poem to Baltasar Gracián, or about Baltasar Gracián—

BORGES: Well, I think I can explain that. That's not a poem that makes fun of Baltasar Gracián. It's a poem that makes fun of me. I am the Gracián of that poem. That's why I consider myself unworthy of heaven, seeing as how I tend to think in literary forms, riddles, puns, rhymes, alliterations, and that poem is really an autocaricature, say. I never thought of the historical Gracián; I thought of myself. Maybe I'm being unfair, but Gracián is a pretext in the poem, a kind of metaphor.

SOBEJANO: In the same anthology there's a note of yours saying precisely this, that the poem is a parody, that it avails itself of parody. . . .

BORGES: Dear me, I tried to say something new and I seem condemned to repetition, no?

SOBEJANO: No, but my question was if you thought it was a statement made too late. Because for years the reader has perceived it to be a poem against Baltasar Gracián.

BORGES: Fine. It could be against the both of us, then. It could be against the two together, eh? Against Baltasar Gracián, S.J., and against me.

SOBEJANO: Do you consider yourself an ingenuous poet or a sentimental poet? Taking off from that famous distinction by Schiller of the poet who is nature and the poet who seeks nature but who knows too much and feels too much and who isn't nature.

BORGES: Unfortunately, I am sentimental in that sense, yes, but what can you do? We spend our lives reading. Emerson said, "poetry comes from poetry"; in my case from the books I have read of course, and from emotions. Without emotion there is no poetry possible.

SOBEJANO: It seems it would be impossible for there to exist ingenuous poets nowadays, don't you think?

BORGES: But, why? Our era is so ingenuous . . . Nobody knows anything! We should not fear knowledge; we should fear ignorance, seeing as how we are so ignorant.

SOBEJANO: Yes. Nonetheless, one could perhaps know too much. No?

BORGES: No. The universe is infinite. What *can* we know? The number of books is infinite. What amount have we read of all those pages? How many languages are there? Thousands. And we know one or two. Our life is very brief—in my case, too long—but ultimately, it is brief, naturally. What *can* we know? Very little. The universe always remains. The universe is infinite; no matter what we take from it, the infinity remains. That is, of course, the infinite minus something, and what remains is infinity, always. No, I don't think we should resist knowledge, since we know so little. How can we resist knowledge? We are semi-barbarians!

CORTÍNEZ: I think you also say this in a poem to Peru, in *La moneda de hierro*. You speak of—

BORGES: I don't recall this poem.

CORTÍNEZ: Well, I can help you remember.

BORGES: Yes, thank you.

CORTÍNEZ: You say that all you have from Peru is the silver that your grandfather brought or your great-grandfather.

BORGES: Yes. And the *History of the Conquest of Peru* by Prescott. And I think that is all, no? No, and a few pleasant memories, personal memories.

CORTÍNEZ: Well, the point is that you also mention a Peruvian poet, Eguren. Do you recall?

BORGES: Eguren, of course. Alberto Hidalgo, a minor poet, introduced me to Eguren, a major poet, I would say. What is the book called? "La niña . . ."

CORTÍNEZ: Well, just one poem, "La niña de la lámpara azul."

BORGES: Yes, "La niña de la lámpara azul," yes.

CORTÍNEZ: Do you think the title too pretty?

BORGES: Well yes, too decorative, no? But it was made to be decorative. The girl of the lamp, and blue at that, is already too much for me. I'm very sober, a Puritan, and for me these excesses, these orgies are really damnable. No? "Niña de la lámpara azul?" No. I am not orgiastic.

CORTÍNEZ: Well, and concerning "blue," whom can we talk about?

BORGES: It seems clear to me that we talk about Mallarmé: "L'azure, l'azure, l'azure," and afterwards Rubén Darío adopted them, no? I think one can talk about basic colors, for example, one can talk about blue, or red, or yellow, or white, perhaps green, but not hues. For example, Chesterton, whom I unconditionally admire, has a poem in which he says, "the violet and silver leopard of the night." I think that is a mistake—I think he should say "black and silver." "Violet," it seems to me, is a shade that doesn't fit. I don't know what you may think. "The black and silver leopard of the night" would be better because "violet and silver," and I don't know why, seem like a drawing; like an engraving. And "black and silver" go well together, I think. But who am I to correct Chesterton?

SOBEJANO: One question. In your first poems (and I think this still continues), the late afternoons, the street, the last streets of the city, and above all, the patio—all have a significance for you, pleasant places, violent places in which you find—

BORGES: That's because I was born in a house with patios. All of Buenos Aires was like that. I was born in the middle of Buenos Aires. And the whole block was a many-storied house. Everything had been made of low houses, with flat roofs, cisterns, each with a turtle at the bottom to keep the water pure, back doors, patios, that was

Buenos Aires. Of course, now it's something else. Since I'm blind, I continue to live in that Buenos Aires that no longer exists. I have written a poem that begins like this—a very sad poem. I will not inflict it on all of you. It begins like this: "I was born in another city that also was called Buenos Aires," since everything has changed so much. No, but, actually, I no longer care for late afternoons, nor suburbs. I like the center of town, I like the city, and I like the morning. I like the morning, mid-town, the hope one has, that illusion that each day could be the beginning of something, which wears away as the day passes. That illusion at the beginning of each morning is what I like, and I encourage it. That is to say, now I like the morning and the late morning.

CORTÍNEZ: If we stay now on this side of the Andes, and think about Argentinean poetry—you have always liked Gaucho poetry, right?

BORGES: Yes. I have always liked Ascassubi, and Hernández. But in Ascassubi there is a happiness that isn't in Hernández. A happiness that is a kind of flowering courage. In Hernández there's courage, but it's sad. Not in Ascassubi. For example, "Vaya un cielito rabioso, cosa linda en ciertos casos, en que anda un buen hombre ganoso de divertirse a balazos." Well, that is Ascassubi, very different from the tone of Hernández, which is a sad tone, more or less, no?

SOBEJANO: A Spanish critic, perhaps resentful of some of your opinions, attacks you for being a universal man, cosmopolitan, educated in Switzerland and England, and so forth, and says that you have an enormous culture, universal, but that this very thing makes you devalue less developed cultures. Naturally, we're talking about a socialist critic. What do you think about that?

BORGES: The culture of underdevelopment?

SOBEJANO: I suppose you think—

BORGES: Argentinean culture, isn't it?

SOBEJANO: And the Spanish, of course. And all Hispanic countries. But I suppose he was thinking about your Buenos Aires of the suburbs, of the milongas, of "The Man on the Pink Corner"—

BORGES: But this isn't damnable. I don't think it is damnable. Besides, we've gone to the moon, or further, I hope.

SOBEJANO: Do you find this opinion tendentious, unfair?

BORGES: No. No. I try to be universal. Of course, I don't achieve it. But I spent five splendid weeks in Japan, and I felt like a barbarian among civilized people. Later, well, I was in Egypt. I felt the weight of time, so many yesterdays accumulated there. In Europe you feel the same. And here, too, in certain places. In New England, for example, you feel a time that isn't felt in Texas, certainly, although I love Texas. There are so many countries! I would like to know all languages, know all literatures, but my God! I'm eighty-three years old and I know very little. But I'm studying Icelandic at this moment—I think it's good to do that—and with María Kodama, we study Anglo-Saxon, Old English. That was something magical, too. Then I taught myself German in order to read Schopenhauer, and I did it in a way I want to recommend to you: begin the German not with grammar, which is dismal, but with *Buch der Lieder* by Heine and with the *Intermezzo* . . . that's how I came to enjoy German literature, though I couldn't converse well in it. Now I'm studying Icelandic. I would like to learn other languages, and like you, like all of you, perhaps, I feel the nostalgia for Latin, which at one time I thought I had but which I've lost. But the nostalgia for Latin is good, since without it we wouldn't have el anónimo sevillano, the works of Quevedo, the works of Góngora, the works of Saavedra Fajardo, all which are based on a nostalgia for Latin. Perhaps you could say the same about Milton, who also felt a longing for Latin and Greek. It's a beautiful longing.

SOBEJANO: That reminds me that somewhere you say you tried to learn in the beginning from Latinized writers, like Saavedra Fajardo, like Quevedo.

BORGES: That's true.

SOBEJANO: Then you left that for—

BORGES: I don't know why Saavedra Fajardo has been forgotten. He was a very lucid man, besides being an admirable writer.

SOBEJANO: And finally, you believed you had arrived at a simpler style.

BORGES: When I sit down to write now, I do it with a minimal vocabulary. I try to avoid synonyms. That is to say, if I write "reddish" I keep saying "reddish" and not "red" later on. It seems better to write this way, to write in a way that isn't noticed, no? I return to el anónimo sevillano: "a style so plain and moderate that no one who sees it notices." That's what I look for. It may be the most difficult thing to achieve, doubtless, no?

SOBEJANO: Yes, precisely, in that last trajectory of yours, that last line contrasts strongly, I think with—

BORGES: With the baroque.

SOBEJANO: With the baroque which is practiced so often now, used so often.

BORGES: Well, I feel youth is baroque out of fear. A young person thinks, "if I say what I feel, they will know it's a stupid remark. Let's disguise it." Then he disguises himself as a contemporary, or a man of the future, a writer from the seventeenth century; or a young writer easily disguises himself as Shakespeare, for example. But that's a mistake, isn't it? At my age, on the other hand, you're resigned to being who you are; above all, you know your limits, you know full well if there's anything at the center, but you know that there are things you shouldn't try. In my case, the novel, for instance. Nor a story that runs a little long. I know I shouldn't try it. A story that's a little long too. On the other hand, I feel less insecure in a sonnet or in a one page poem, in free verse, or in blank verse, which is so easy and pleasant on the ear.

SOBEJANO: These brief forms—the poem, the story, the short essay— do you feel that they favor intensity and density? I suppose so, naturally.

BORGES: Yes, and in every case it's almost impossible for them to be tedious. A haiku lasts three lines. It doesn't have time to bore you, no? Five, seven, and five syllables. The tanka: five, seven, five, then seven and seven. This doesn't give you time to be bored either.

CORTÍNEZ: Borges, are you anticipating the work that María Kodama is going to read tomorrow?

BORGES: Right. Actually, I'm usurping her theme. No, but I say that because she said it to me this afternoon. I'm very clever.

CORTÍNEZ: Well, talking about the novel and poetry, there are two writers in your country that nearly all of our students know as prose writers; these are Güiraldes, the novelist, and the essayist Martínez Estrada. But they were also poets, right?

BORGES: Yes, but Martínez Estrada was an *admirable* poet. How strange that is! Martínez Estrada is inconceivable without Lugones, and he's superior to Lugones. I would say the same about the great Mexican poet who wrote "La Suave Patria."

CORTÍNEZ: López Velarde, no?

BORGES: Yes, López Velarde. I think he's inconceivable without Lugones, but better than Lugones. But that's fine—in general the child is superior to the parent, no? In the case of Martínez Estrada, his best poems are, well, better than the best ones of Lugones. But he's one child of Lugones. And he's very proud too. And Lugones was also a child of Laforgue, ultimately, and a child of Darío too.

CORTÍNEZ: And Güiraldes, does he convince you as a poet?

BORGES: I don't think he was too convinced, himself, no? He wrote the book *El Cencerro de Cristal*, a kind of imitation of the *Lunario*. For example, let's see, well, don't be offended: "Luna, frígido ovillo, pulcro botón de calzoncillo." I don't know if it's worth remembering it. Well, I apologize for mentioning that intimate button.

SOBEJANO: Since you've quoted López Velarde, do you think that in Velarde there is the beginning of prosaicness done to the hilt but badly?

BORGES: Prosaicness is one of the poetic mediums, I think, if it's used carefully, no? If you don't abuse it, it can be very helpful.

SOBEJANO: Prosaicness I think is continued a bit by César Vallejo, and then there is the neo-realist movement, with novelists like Arguedas, or Ciro Alegría, who in the 40s and 50s, cultivated a kind of novel and literature very responsive to daily life, work, suffering and did it not trying to give a merely informative testimony, of course, but rather a work of art. I see a continuation there from the prosaicness of López Velarde, through the poetry of Vallejo, to Arguedas.

BORGES: I don't know these poets. I know López Velarde, yes, but not the others. I can't speak with any authority. Besides, well, I've been blind, as a reader, since fifty-five; truly, I do not know my contemporaries.

SOBEJANO: But I asked it because it's a movement that doesn't look for complexity, or refinement, but a lyrical beat, drawn from daily things, the most humble things, the life of the poor.

BORGES: Those two things can be united, I think—refinement and that intimate rhythm you speak of. I don't think they are mutually exclusive.

SOBEJANO: No, of course. You have a collection of Quevedo, and other anthologies. What criteria do you use to gather a collection of a poet's work? An aesthetic preference, or that it be complete, or what?

BORGES: No, no. A hedonistic criterion, say, aesthetic, of pleasure. There are famous works by Quevedo that I didn't include because I thought they were awful. Well, but I don't know. It's better not to recall them at this moment; I have not included them. I also made an anthology of Góngora, and did not include, say, "ande yo caliente y ríase la gente"; I find this quite miserable, no? And also, "era del año la estación florida, en que el mentido robador de Europa," I find all this horrible. But Góngora has splendid verses. How curious that one of the best sonnets by Quevedo should have been written by Góngora. That typically Quevadian sonnet that says: "Las horas que limando están los días, los días que royendo estan los años." Góngora wrote Quevedo's best verses. And before him too. A real scoundrel, really! He anticipated Quevedo.

CORTÍNEZ: Well, it was known in Spain, although the vote was secret, that when they voted the Cervantes Prize for Onetti there was a dissident vote for Octavio Paz. And the rumorous tongues say that that vote was cast by you.

BORGES: Not the rumorous tongues. The good and true tongues.

CORTÍNEZ: Which means I can ask you about Octavio Paz?

BORGES: How strange. I admire Octavio Paz very much. I like what he writes. I find nothing interesting to say about him right now. I am simply a grateful reader of Octavio Paz. And I voted for him. I feel the prize to Onetti was a mistake, but ultimately life is made of errors, above all my life, which is a kind of anthology of errors.

CORTÍNEZ: But they made up for that mistake, because they did give the Cervantes prize to Octavio Paz the following year.

BORGES: True.

CORTÍNEZ: And we, there are many here who think that the last Nobel Prize was a mistake, not with regards to the person but the order in which it was given. I don't know if you agree with us.

BORGES: No. The prize has been well given. I frankly do not deserve the Nobel Prize. The Swedes are very sensitive. They are totally right.

Who am I to compare myself with Neruda, with Kipling, with Bernard Shaw, with Bertrand Russell, with André Gide, with William Faulkner? I am nobody, evidently. I think the Swedes do very well. Besides, it's a kind of ritual that's well established. I've lost count of the years—they promise me the prize every year, they give it to another, and I know that's the way it is. It's like a drawing that repeats itself. Now it's a habit of time.

CORTÍNEZ: Well, García Márquez said he was very surprised because he got it before you.

BORGES: Well, I must be grateful to him for that error. He deserves it and I don't.

SOBEJANO: You say that they've given you too much attention, you say this modestly.

BORGES: It's true. Libraries have been written about me. I haven't read them, as of now, but I'm grateful for them just the same. I'm a very timid man; I don't usually read what's written about me. I'm very timid.

SOBEJANO: Bearing in mind that you had a body of work that was much developed and important by the forties and fifties, and that you didn't have then such an extensive and universal popularity, don't you think . . .

BORGES: No, the people were right then and they made a mistake afterwards.

SOBEJANO: No, no, there is a compensation there and a justice. We Spaniards read almost with an amused curiosity the many disqualifications you make of our writers. For example, Gracián, Calderón, the entire eighteenth century, the entire nineteenth century, Azorín, Juan Ramón Jiménez, García Lorca, Camilo José Cela—

BORGES: No, no. Juan Ramón Jiménez, no, eh? A great poet, of course.

SOBEJANO: Do you think the nineteenth century is an embarrassment in Spain?

BORGES: Not even an embarrassment, I think. I think that's too strong a word, no?

SOBEJANO: A century with writers like, say, Larra, Bécquer, Galdós, Leopoldo Alas, four or five writers of—

BORGES: Well, my sense pains me!

SOBEJANO: Well, then nothing. Agreed.

CORTÍNEZ: How about the *Poema del Cid*? I think you've also disqualified the *Poema del Cid*.

SOBEJANO: Well, the *Cid*, no, I don't think so. But, yes, yes, a little.

BORGES: They told me they were going to make a version of that poem for adults, but I don't know if it's true or not, no? I had the other one. Not the one for adults.

SOBEJANO: Continuing with Spain, do you feel that Spain is rough, rude—I think—a bit cruel, or very cruel, radical?

BORGES: Well, but they boast about being rough! I say that to praise them, to praise them I say they are rough.

SOBEJANO: No, no, my question was if you weren't referring solely to Castilla, because, for example, say Galicia, Andalucía . . . much sweeter, no?

BORGES: Yes, in that case I am from Andalusian and Portuguese stock. Sweeter, eh? On the other hand, Castilla, so many military types, so many friars, nothing good.

CORTÍNEZ: Well, I think the public has the right to stick their two cents in here, right?

BORGES: Very well, it's been a long time since I've heard that expression. Fine, let's see—

QUESTION FROM THE AUDIENCE (the exchange was in English): Yes sir, I've come a long way to hear you talk and to see and extract—

QUESTION: —your words of wisdom. One day I read something in one of your stories that said, "there isn't a man alive who isn't credulous outside his own specialty." I have to admit, I laughed with the rest, I understood some things you said. My specialty isn't Spanish—I don't speak a word—but I'd like to ask you a question. I'm not a man of faith, but there's a story that's troubled me for years since I've read it: "Three Versions Of Judas."

BORGES: Oh, really? I apologize, in that case, for troubling you.

QUESTION: And what I wanted to know is—since I'm naive in this way—the person who introduced your character in the story, Nils Lindberg, is this person real? Or is he just a character of your imagination?

BORGES: Will you tell me again the name of the story?

QUESTION: "Three Versions Of Judas."

BORGES: Yes, that whole thing, I'm sorry to say, is invented. There is no such man.

QUESTION: Oh, so there was no such man.

BORGES: I'm sorry to say it.

QUESTION: Oh, no, that's okay. Maybe there was, I don't know.

BORGES: No one has ever read that story except you, eh? You are the one reader in the world.

QUESTION: Maybe.

BORGES: Quite sure, yes. I wrote it, you read it, and that's that, eh?

QUESTION: That's that. Thank you. Thank you, sir.

CORTÍNEZ: Well, we don't have anything against the verbal music of England, but we prefer questions in Spanish, right? If it's possible, because today is the Spanish day here.

BORGES: Of course.

CORTÍNEZ: If someone would like to come to the other side and ask a question.

BORGES: Why not.

CORTÍNEZ: Because if not, we'll continue up here.

BORGES: Fine, continue yourselves, and the others as well. I talk too much, maybe.

QUESTION (Donald Shaw, University of Edinburgh): Borges, we all know, or at least we can conjecture, what Macedonio Fernández was for you. Do you think Macedonio signifies something special in Argentinean literature?

BORGES: No, I think Macedonio was above all an oral man. What he wrote is not easily understood, but in the spoken word he was a man of genius. Well, there is Pythagoras, Buddha, Jesus, Socrates, who never wrote. I think he was an oral man above all, very taciturn. All night long he would say four or five things; he referred constantly to the questioner. That is to say, "che, you notice that . . ." and then something surprising would follow. This he said in a low voice. Well, there were people who waited the whole night to hear Macedonio say three or four things, said in a very low voice and which had to be repeated later. I'm sure he was a man of genius though the work written by him does not confirm it. I felt the same about Rafael Cansinos Assens, a Jewish-Andalusian writer. I felt he was a genius. But later, re-reading his books, I've realized that you cannot look for it in his books, but only in my personal memory, and the same for Macedonio.

SHAW: You will excuse me if I don't express myself well—I too suffer somewhat from timidity, especially before such a gathering. My question is the following: a large portion of literature is created in the memory, and our memory is very short, as you . . .

BORGES: But precisely because of that the mind can imagine. If we remembered everything we wouldn't be able to imagine anything. It's beneficial that our memory is short. Forgetfulness is the most valuable thing about memory.

SHAW: Nonetheless, forgetfulness is much larger, right? Is it possible to create out of forgetfulness rather than memory?

BORGES: I'm incapable of creating in any way. But perhaps both tools are helpful.

SHAW: What I refer to—for example, you, in your story "The Immortal," refer to the theme of forgetfulness.

BORGES: Well yes, I wrote that story, and at the end it occurred to me that it would be better if the protagonist were Homer, the forgotten one, at the end of all these centuries. It's a good story but the style is too fancy, I think. If I were to write it now, I would do it in a simpler style. But perhaps that story required that style, since each theme dictates its own language. For example, something occurs to me, and that something tells me to employ the sonnet, to employ free verse, to employ the story, or to employ the essay. In short, I don't think there is an absolute rhetoric. There are themes that should be treated in rhymed verse; others allow or demand blank verse or free verse. That depends on each theme. I don't think there can be a general aesthetic. But ultimately, you could teach me much about this undoubtedly.

SOBEJANO: I had another question concerning circularity and repetition. Did you read much Nietzsche?

BORGES: No, very little. But the notion of circular time comes much before Nietzsche. The Stoics, The Pythagoreans . . . There is an entire book in *The City Of God* dedicated to refuting the idea of circular time. There is a very beautiful poem by Rossetti, "I Have Been Here Before," with this theme. The idea of circular time dates from very much before Nietzsche, of course. You find it rationalized in a book by Hume, *Dialogues on Natural Religion*. And he says: if we suppose that the number of elements in the universe is limited (and there is no reason to believe it is infinite) then, since time is infinite, these combinations must repeat themselves and we have a cyclical history. That is to say that we find here what we have found thousands of times. But Hume rationalizes the idea of eternal return. He shows in one page, more or less, that if we accept an infinite number, say of atoms, and a time without beginning or end, history must be circular. Or that each moment comes from, is created by a preceding moment, and engenders the next.

SOBEJANO: And do you think this repetitious eternity or eternal return, because of this limitation of atoms or of elements, should be of any consequence to us?

BORGES: No, I don't believe so, because if we don't remember then it doesn't exist. Unless there is an angel keeping count somewhere, I don't know; I don't believe in angels most of all. Mostly those angels who keep track of the centuries.

SOBEJANO: Don't you think that it's just as easy to believe in linear time as in repetition and return, in the consequence of days, that is to say that yesterday precedes today and today precedes tomorrow and there comes a time when we disappear?

BORGES: But everything is mysterious. Everything is equally enigmatic, circular time and infinite linear time. Everything is equally enigmatic, fortunately. It's good that we have enigmas.

SOBEJANO: It seems to me that life, co-existence and collective life, would make one believe in linear progression more, no?

BORGES: I think so.

SOBEJANO: On the other hand, solitude tends to bring one to dreams and isolation.

BORGES: Well, possibly, when one has reached eighty-three years of age, one has said everything one had to say, one has done all the possible acts, and one is condemned to repetition. But, ultimately, it is a sad topic. You are young and have many years ahead of you, you may not repeat yourselves, but with me, I don't know, I don't know if I can avoid repeating myself. Perhaps my lot is to be condemned to repetition, to say the same things, to feel the same emotions.

Nonetheless, this afternoon, when you gave me away, when you made me listen to my own poems, when my entire past came back to me, when I heard people here in Pennsylvania speaking about the hoodlum Paredes, speaking about so many habits of my thought, of Swedenborg, speaking of Spinoza too—all that and habits of mine, chess, the suburbs of Buenos Aires, the city of Montevideo—so many things returned to me; I was very moved. I had the impression that all that was new.

CORTÍNEZ: We have a question from the audience.

QUESTION (José Hernández, Gettysburg College): Yes, thank you. Señor Borges, there is a theme in your work that fascinates, enchants and confuses me and I don't know if the answer is simple or complicated. Please tell me something of how you use mirrors.

BORGES: Ever since I was a child I've felt the terror of mirrors. In my room there was a dresser from Hamburg with three mirrors. I saw myself repeated in them and I felt the horror of the mirror. The thought that I could be lying down and see myself in the mirror and three times at that—terrible! And since then I've continued to feel the terror of mirrors and a fascination as well. But now I'm protected from them by blindness. There's a beautiful poem by Johannes R. Becher called "Spiegelmensch," ("The Man of the Mirror"). He imagines a man in a rectangular cell; in that cell, the walls, the floor, and the ceiling are made of mirrors, and that man is there and sees himself repeated infinitely. The poem was written by someone who no doubt also felt the horror of mirrors. I think Poe felt that horror; we have an article by him on interior design where he says that if there is a mirror, it should be placed in such a fashion, perhaps very high up, that a seated person could not see himself repeated in it. And you can see this in the short story "William Wilson," of the double, which is a variant of the mirror.

QUESTION FROM THE AUDIENCE: You wrote three works whose subject was the "caudillo," Juan Facundo Quiroga: two poems: "Los llanos" and "El General Quiroga va en coche al Muere," and also "Díalogo de muertos" in *El hacedor*.

BORGES: I think the "Díalogo de muertos" is the best. We can forget the rest, eh? Besides, it's better to forget them. Since Sarmiento has already told that story so well, it's a presumption, an audacity to tell it.

QUESTION: Then my question is: to what degree did Sarmiento influence your works or is it more likely something historical?

BORGES: No, I don't believe so. I believe that if we Argentineans had adopted *Facundo* as a work typical of us, our destiny would be different. Unfortunately, we chose *Martín Fierro*, which, well, it's too late now, we can't help it, even though it's an inferior work. It would have been better to canonize the *Facundo*, and not *Martín Fierro*.

QUESTION FROM THE AUDIENCE: There has been, it seems, a lot of talk over García Lorca's *The Poet In New York*. Some say that it's a strictly surrealist book; others say it's a book of misunderstood metaphors, that it is not surrealist. I like to play with these concepts. Do you?

BORGES: I can't speak with any authority about García Lorca, since I've read him so little. He struck me as a professional Andalusian, but aside from that I don't know. But I remember a few verses of his with much pleasure—only pleasure, nothing more, no enthusiasm. On the other hand, if I think, I don't know, about Antonio Machado, about Manuel Machado, about Juan Ramón Jiménez, I feel a kind of reverence and a kinship too. On the other hand, in the case of Lorca, I feel that he's a small curiosity in literature, nothing else, no? A type of bric-a-brac, for example, yes. Now I don't think anyone appreciated Manuel Machado, and I think it's a mistake. Cansinos Assens said that Manuel was better than Antonio. I don't believe one should prefer one over the other; one can prefer the two of them, which is what I do.

QUESTION FROM THE AUDIENCE: Señor Borges, it seems that some authors end up hating their characters a bit, like Unamuno maybe with Augusto Pérez. Is there a Borgesian character that you don't like that much now, or one for which you lack any affection at all?

BORGES: But I've never created a character. It's always me, subtly disguised. No, I can't invent anyone—I'm not Dickens, I'm not Balzac—I can't invent people. I'm always myself, the same self in different times or places, but always, irreparably, incurably, myself.

QUESTION FROM THE AUDIENCE: Borges, I would like to know if it's true that you've advised people to read the resumes of novels rather than the novels themselves.

BORGES: But no! Why? I don't believe that! With that criterion why not read indexes, or catalogues? No, of course not! A novel should be read. A novel is each word of that novel, not a summary. That's false.

Why not go directly to the author? Biography also seems like a mistake to me. I taught English Literature and said, "do not read any biographies. Deal directly with Dickens, directly with Emerson, directly with Shaw or with Chesterton"—or with Stevenson, of course, whom I refer to so often, and whom I must have mentioned many times today.

QUESTION (Sandra Wheaton): Maestro, you speak much about infinite time and infinite space. Allow me to ask you, of all your stories, which one do you feel treats the theme of infinity best?

BORGES: One story of mine?

SOBEJANO: Yes, yours.

BORGES: I think there is one story, "El Aleph," which isn't bad. But it's been a long time since I read it. I think I remember it well. Yes, and its theme is the infinite, precisely, infinite space in any case, since there is no infinite time. You would have to create another "Aleph" for infinite time.

WHEATON: And what do you think of the story, "The Book of Sand"?

BORGES: I think it's one of my best stories, but it's a variant of "El Aleph," the notion of an impossible object. I say a book of sand; a point in which are all the points of space. Well, "Funes el Memorioso," as well—a man overwhelmed by an infinite memory. They are the same story actually. And I have another story, "Blue Tigers"; it's the same notion of impossible objects. But, finally, I won't offer it to you because I haven't published it yet.

QUESTION FROM THE AUDIENCE: Señor Borges, it's said that Cortázar is your spiritual heir. What do you think of this? Do you like his works?

BORGES: I was the first to publish a text of Cortázar in Buenos Aires. I was managing an almost secret—or secret—magazine—*Los Anales de Buenos Aires*. And a tall young man came to see me and brought me a story. He said to me: "What do you think of this story?" I said to him: "Come back in ten days." But he was back in one week and I told him, "I've got two bits of news for you. One: your story is being published. Two: my sister is doing the illustrations for it." That story was called "Casa Tomada," by Cortázar. It is the only thing by him I have read, and it's excellent, of course. I forgot all about it and when we met in Paris he thanked me for it. He had never published anything before. He was a totally unknown writer in Buenos Aires. And he thanked me for my sister's illustrations, which were very good, and the story is very good. "Casa Tomada"— the gradual takeover of a house by ghosts or evil spirits—I'm not sure. A "haunted house."

QUESTION (Celia Escrig, Wilson College): Borges, you say that the young are baroque because of their timidness.

BORGES: I believe that's right. In my case it was. I was baroque because of my timidity.

ESCRIG: What do you think young people are afraid of?

BORGES: I think a person lives in fear of everything. Besides, a young person still doesn't know who he is, if he's Alexander the Great, or Admiral Nelson, or Kant, or Swedenborg. He doesn't know yet. On the other hand, later, with time, yes, one knows one isn't Nelson, or Swedenborg. One knows who one is, and resigns oneself.

CORTÍNEZ: At what age, Borges, does one find out who one is?

BORGES: I haven't hit one hundred yet—I can't answer, eh? I don't know.

CORTÍNEZ: Well, if there aren't any other questions. . .

BORGES: No, no, are there maybe three questions?

CORTÍNEZ: Could there be three questions? Let's see . . .

BORGES: Three is the magic number.

CORTÍNEZ: Let's see if we can get three final questions.

BORGES: Let's extract three questions. A difficult trinity.

QUESTION FROM THE AUDIENCE: Señor Borges, before I ask my question I would like to greet you with a very Mexican kiss and hug.

BORGES: Thank you very much. *Caramba!* A Mexican speaks to me. Very good. A Mexican with an x, of course, not with a j, eh?

QUESTION: Of course—

BORGES: Mexico Street in Buenos Aires, also with an x, where I've lived.

QUESTION: In an interview with Dick Cavett, you stated that you like certain sounds in the English language. Do you do any writing in English, and if so what are those writings?

BORGES: No, I respect the English language too much. There are words which I like very much, for example, "dim," and "eerie," and "uncanny," for example, and "wistful"—so many others, perhaps all the others, eh?

QUESTION: I also know that you like to dream very much. Do you dream in various languages?

BORGES: No, in two languages. On the other hand, Captain Burton boasted, (but he was a cheat) of being able to dream in fourteen languages. But these are Burton's lies—we shouldn't pay attention to them.

QUESTION: Thank you.

BORGES: That's one, no?

CORTÍNEZ: That was one, yes.

BORGES: That was one. Let's see.

CORTÍNEZ: Is there another question there?

BORGES: If the hourglass allows us two more questions. If the water-clock is generous . . .

QUESTION FROM THE AUDIENCE: Señor Borges, why do you say that it's unfortunate that *Martín Fierro* was taken as a national book in Argentina?

BORGES: *Martín Fierro* is an admirable book, but the hero is an horrendous character. Well, he's a deserter, a drunkard, a fugitive, an assassin, very sentimental, who pities himself and not others. It's a shame to have this character as an example. Simply for this reason. Now, aesthetically, it's an admirable poem. I know it by heart, especially the first part, "La muerte de cruz." Also the second part I know by heart.

CORTÍNEZ: The third question is for you to recite the whole of *Martín Fierro* by memory.

BORGES: "Aqui me pongo a cantar . . ."—no, I'd better not start singing, we'd be here till the candles burn out. Now for the third question—the defeated one.

CORTÍNEZ: Here it comes.

QUESTION FROM THE AUDIENCE: You occupy yourself often with contemptible characters like, for example, Juan Muraña el Cuchillero. Why an interest in definitely real characters, but ones not worthy of admiration?

BORGES: When I was little I loved pirates—Stevenson's pirates, now the cuchilleros, why not? But I don't know, maybe it's the love of personal courage, not courage for a cause. I think it's an admirable idea, no? The idea of a man who doesn't fight for a cause, who simply just fights, well, because he's brave, because fighting is a habit of his. I think there can be something admirable in people like that. Maybe it's a dangerous cult, the cult of courage. Personally, I'm a coward; maybe that's why I admire courage.

CORTÍNEZ: Do you think that Juan Muraña is a protective shadow?

BORGES: No, not a protective one; I expect to have better protectors. Stevenson, for example, and Mark Twain, seem to be better than Muraña.

SOBEJANO: A question about—

BORGES: No, no, no, no, there have to be five, because four is bad luck. They told me that in Japan. No, there must be two more then. Four, no. That won't do at all, no? Dangerous number, four.

CORTÍNEZ: Well, there is an Argentinean woman there who likes milongas, who wants to ask you something.

BORGES: But of course! I too like milongas.

QUESTION (Ana Cara-Walker): The question is about Muraña again, and you say that probably you, well, liked pirates and now why not the "cuchillero"?

BORGES: Sure, they are land pirates.

CARA-WALKER: In *Evaristo Carriego*, in your book, you mention Juan Muraña as the character who tells Carriego who he is.

BORGES: It's only a guess on my part, maybe true, eh? Could be.

CARA-WALKER: Yes, but why did you choose Juan Muraña?

BORGES: Because Carriego spoke a great deal about him, and knew him. He talked with him in his house a lot. I don't remember ever seeing him, but—

CARA-WALKER: Was he his hero?

BORGES: Yes, he was a friend, sure, Carriego was older than I. And Carriego—it's hard to get this right—died in 1912 at the age of 29. How old was I? Impossible to say.

CARA-WALKER: But I refer to Juan Muraña—was he admired by Carriego?

BORGES: He was the most famous knife slinger in north Buenos Aires, in barrio Tierra del Fuego, the Penitentiary, the Recoleta, the Maldonado, that neighborhood, yes. He knew it. He was a truck driver and he was responsible for many deaths, or so I was told. But a friend of mine told me: "who wasn't responsible for at least one death in our time? Even the most wretched!" Everyone was responsible for one death; it was part of being human.

SOBEJANO: One question: nowadays there is much talk about the reader, about the importance of the reader; the reader is indispensable to the creation of a work. This has always been clear, but these days the fact is taken more seriously in criticism. You are very generous with the reader, and you say on one occasion that—

BORGES: No, the author is an invention of the reader's, a superstition of the reader's, and I thank everyone a great deal for having read me, and having enriched me so much by reading.

SOBEJANO: You've gone so far as to say that it's pure chance that one is the reader, the other is the writer, haven't you?

BORGES: I said that in my first book, in 1923, I just now remembered. Well, that's the only thing I can remember.

SOBEJANO: There's always one reader that's more determined, more penetrating than the others, and that's the critic.

BORGES: I wouldn't know about that, since I haven't read anything written about me, out of timidity, of course. I feel uncomfortable reading about myself.

SOBEJANO: But would you prefer that your works be studied from an analytical point of view, informative, descriptive? Or do you prefer the kind of criticism that uses a work of the imagination to make another work of the imagination?

BORGES: Yes, the latter, undoubtedly. Reading has got to be a pleasure. It's a joy you have to tell people about. Required reading is absurd, no? Why impose joy? A book is a great happiness.

SOBEJANO: I mean, would you prefer that your story, for example, be doubled by another story?

BORGES: I would like it very much, and there's no doubt that has happened, no? It's good that reading functions in this way.

SOBEJANO: Do you think a critic should recreate the work?

BORGES: But, certainly, Shakespeare, for example, is richer now than when he wrote . . . Cervantes, too. Cervantes was enriched by Unamuno; Shakespeare, by Coleridge, by Bradley. A writer grows this way. After his death, he continues to evolve in the minds of readers. And the Bible, for example, is richer now than when its books were written. Time is responsible for this. It's all part of the work, too. Incomprehension can help an author. Everything can help him. The reader's distractions. A work can be read and be badly remembered later, that is to say, amended by memory. This happens to me often. *Caramba!* I don't know if I dare say it. Every time I quote Shakespeare I realize that I've made him better.

CORTÍNEZ: It would be bad luck to continue. We've gone past the fateful four questions. I think this is a good time to thank you for your presence this evening . . .

BORGES: Thank you very much, thank you very much.

CORTÍNEZ: . . . and to thank our writer.

BORGES: Thank you.

III. *Jorge Luis Borges Discusses English and North American Literature with Miller Williams, Kenneth Rosen, and others.*

ROSEN: Good evening, ladies and gentlemen. Welcome to the final event of Dickinson College's symposium on "Borges the Poet." In a recent interview, one of the questions was, "did you dream last night, Señor Borges?" His response was—

BORGES: I dream every night.

ROSEN: Sí, Señor.

BORGES: I have a nightmare every other night.

ROSEN: "I dream every night. I dream before I go to sleep, and I dream after waking up. When I begin to say meaningless words, I'm seeing impossible things. I remember that a dream gave me a story. I had a very confused, a very tangled dream. And the only thing I remembered was this: 'I sell you Shakespeare's memory.'"

BORGES: But *I* said that!

ROSEN: You did.

BORGES: I thought you were cribbing.

ROSEN: I am cribbing. "And I wrote a story about that—"

BORGES: Your bounden duty.

ROSEN: Right.

BORGES: My duty also, to crib. That's a traditional classicist's duty, cribbing.

ROSEN: And that's what I'm doing.

BORGES: Let's go ahead.

ROSEN: "I wrote a story about that—the memory of Shakespeare. What a fine name Shakespeare is, yes? But he was quite bad, don't you think so? A man who wrote, 'England, that demi-paradise'? Sounds like a bad joke, no?"

BORGES: It is. I mean, "demi" is funny, sounds like O. Henry, no?

ROSEN: "I mean, Shakespeare's letting you down all the time. A very uneven writer. He's not dependable. You have a very fine line and then you have, well, rhetoric." To talk about this and about English and North American literature in general with Borges tonight, we have with us Miller Williams, Professor of English and Foreign Languages at the University of Arkansas, a translator, and a prize-winning poet in his own right. In keeping with the informal format of these presentations for the last few nights, we will entertain questions from the audience as the discussion up here progresses. I'd like to ask you, however, if you are going to ask a question, if you possibly can, to come to the mike at either side here of the platform, please.

BORGES: A thousand and one questions, I hope.

WILLIAMS: We are all set to talk about Borges' thoughts on English and North American literature . . .

BORGES: If any.

WILLIAMS: I have a very strong feeling, however, that we're going to talk about whatever Borges wants to talk about. We have a couple of small problems to overcome first. It's difficult to interview a writer before an audience who knows his life and work as well as this audience knows the life and work of Borges.

BORGES: A lot more than I do.

WILLIAMS: Dick Cavett had it a lot easier. Also, Borges has said that he doesn't like to think in terms of the literature of a nation, or even the literature of a language, in isolation, and that's what I've been asked to get him to do.

BORGES: The whole thing's a game!

WILLIAMS: Another thing is that I have laryngitis. But since my job is to get *Borges* to talk, that shouldn't bother us too much.

BORGES: I'm a tired old man; I'm eighty-three; my country's falling to pieces; I'm very sad.

WILLIAMS: Whenever you're asked about writers in the English language, you consistently mention such people as Chesterton, Wells, Stevenson, Kipling, Lewis Carroll, Whitman, Thomas Browne, DeQuincey, Emerson. These are—

BORGES: Bernard Shaw . . .

WILLIAMS: These are Victorians—

BORGES: Well, I'm a Victorian also. I was born in 1899. I *am* a Victorian.

WILLIAMS: I was going to ask you if that's the only reason that this is your favorite circle of writers. Is it perhaps because when you were in school they were moderns?

BORGES: No, I think of them as personal benefactors, as friends of mine, all of them, and DeQuincey of course, Coleridge, Wordsworth, Sir Thomas Browne. I knew so many of his cadences by heart, but now they've left me, and I still keep on thinking of him.

WILLIAMS: What about some others that are Victorian or generally taken to be, like Hardy?

BORGES: No, I'm afraid I'm unworthy of Hardy. My mother wasn't; she loved him. I didn't.

WILLIAMS: That's a marvelously generous way to say that you don't care to read him.

BORGES: Well, no, I'm unworthy of him. I attempted him, and I failed. He didn't; I did.

WILLIAMS: What about—turning to poetry, mainly—Gerard Manley Hopkins? Another Victorian, of sorts.

BORGES: I think of him as a very great poet, and I think that what he did with the English language was something quite new. I remember, of course, the lines we're all remembering at this moment, "Mastering me God! giver of breath and bread." Hear those thick sounds, akin to Anglo-Saxon, perhaps, and then the Saxon half-rhyme, the alliteration: "Mastering me God! giver of breath and bread"—so unlike anything else in the language, except for perhaps the very early poems, the Old English poems.

WILLIAMS: If you don't mind, I'd like to mention a few other writers and just let you respond to them off the top of your head.

BORGES: Of course, you can go ahead. There are a thousand and one writers before us, from an endless literature.

WILLIAMS: Matthew Arnold.

BORGES: I think of his prose, rather than his verse. But I've read and re-read that book on Celtic literature. And I think he was perhaps too sensible a man to be a poet. A poet should not be too intelligent. In most cases they are not, of course. But I think he was too self-conscious to be a good poet, or a real poet. But his prose is, of course, wonderful. I keep on reading and rereading him.

WILLIAMS: Conrad.

BORGES: Conrad to me is *the* novelist. Were we to choose a single novelist—and why should I choose one?—I would choose Joseph Conrad. The others can be safely forgotten. Even the greatest. Let us forget Tolstoy, Dostoievski, Flaubert, of course, but not, not Conrad. And I would like to add, since I'm talking in terms of the novel, why not Cervantes; you may have heard of him. I think he was quite good, often dumb, of course, a very fine novelist. But Conrad has something epic about him, something you don't find in Proust, for example. There's something petty about Proust, while in the case of Conrad, you think of him as being all over the world, you think of him as you think of the ocean, perhaps, and then you look back on such brief masterpieces as "The End of the Tether," "The Duel," *Youth*, and the others. I think I will read and reread Conrad, for all my life. We all know, according to professors, that the novel was begotten by the epic. But the novel has forgotten that past and gone, well, to mere chattering. But in the case of Conrad, you feel that the epic is still there; at least in the case of such a masterpiece as *Lord Jim*, I know that the novel goes on being the epic. It has not become the novel; it still is the epic. And that, I should say, is one of the chief aims of literature, to save the epic. I am more or less untouched by sentimentality, by the pathetic—those things hardly touch me. But anything epic makes me glow. For example, *The Ballad of Chevy Chase*. Or, why not?, Bunyan's *Pilgrim's Progress*. And then the epic poetry, the iron poetry of the Saxons—I studied Old English because I wanted to read them in the texts, and María Kodama can do it far better than I. She's here; she'll give us some stanzas out of "The Battle of Maldon." But to go back to Conrad—what a strange benefactor! He had to choose, since his language was a secret language, between French and English, and happily for us, his choice was English, and now I suppose he will go on and on retelling those same wonderful stories, those stories not only of the sea, but of that other, more complex sea, the mind of man. I'm very glad that Conrad has been mentioned. I'm always thinking about him. I think of him, I repeat, as being *the* novelist. The others can be safely forgotten, and should be forgotten. But in the case of Conrad, Conrad goes on, very happily for us and for mankind.

WILLIAMS: Thank you. Mark Twain.

BORGES: Mark Twain was, of course, a man of genius. Mark Twain wrote perhaps the first novel I ever read through in my life, *Huckleberry*

Finn. That was the first novel I ever read through, and the first book of history I ever read through was Prescott's *Conquest of Perú*. What a pity that Tom Sawyer is allowed to step in at the end and to spoil the novel. But still you can forget the last chapters and remember the first. And I have a personal opinion or heresy about *Huckleberry Finn*. I think that *Huckleberry Finn*, read and reread by Kipling of course, begat *Kim*, since *Kim* was published in 1901. I forget the date of Mark Twain's *Huckleberry Finn*, but it was some twenty or so years before. And from *Kim*—the framework is the same—in both books, in *Kim* and in *Huckleberry Finn*, you have a country, a civilization, seen through the eyes of a child and of an old man: in one case, of course, Nigger Jim and Huck; in the other, Kim and the lama. And an Argentine writer read *Kim*, Ricardo Güiraldes. From Güiraldes there came another book with the same framework, *Don Segundo Sombra*. The same thing, except that what he sees is simpler; he's seeing the problems of Buenos Aires and the "troperos," or "drovers," who are driving the cattle. And then another fine book came from *Don Segundo Sombra*. I forget the author's name, but the book, I read it (it was read to me) is called *Shane*, and the frame of it is the same also. So that when Mark Twain wrote *Huckleberry Finn*, he was really, in a sense, engendering *Kim*, *Don Segundo Sombra*, and *Shane*. Besides, I think of Mark Twain as a personal friend. I share all his jokes, his bitterness also. He was—yes, I'm sure that he was a man of genius. But he wrote off and on; he didn't know when to stop, but that is a mark of genius—the fact that he's irregular, that he's not watching his own work too closely. I don't think a writer should look too closely on what he is writing. He should let the dream have its way with him. Well, thank you, Mark Twain.

WILLIAMS: Let me ask you a mischievous question, to go back a minute. Can you speculate on what Conrad might have written if he had written in French?

BORGES: I'm glad to say he didn't write in French. Well, no, I think if the subject is the sea—well, the subject is not the sea, of course; the subject is man's soul. But had he written in French I don't think he would have done as well. And I'm thankful that he wrote in English; I love France, but I feel closer to English. Why not? My paternal grandmother was English. I've done most of my reading in English. When I talk of the *Arabian Nights* I think in terms of Edward William Lane and of Captain Burton. When I speak of the Bible, I think of the Bible my English grandmother read. She knew it; she knew it chapter and verse, and I was brought up—the first books I read were the *Arabian Nights*, and then the Bible was pouring into me, because my grandmother was easily biblical, as all Protestants are. So, those two things, they made for good.

WILLIAMS: You asked me as we were having wine before we came in here what was the difference between beer and ale. And I stopped—

BORGES: I wonder if you could tell me. I don't know.

WILLIAMS: —I stopped and asked a Britisher, Donald Shaw, and he said that ale is brewed from the top and beer is brewed from the bottom. I thought I'd tell you that before I forgot.

BORGES: Yes, but I wonder what that means as far as ale is concerned.

WILLIAMS: I have no idea what it means.

BORGES: I don't either. Perhaps he doesn't, either. Perhaps nobody does. The whole thing's a dark mystery.

WILLIAMS: Mr. Shaw, would you like to answer the question?

SHAW: All I can say is that what I've always heard is that it's a question of where the fermentation process takes place. That is to say, if you have the vat with the malt in it and it's fermenting, if it's beer, the fermentation is artificially made to take place at the bottom of the vat, and if it's ale it's at the top. I mean, you can tell by the taste— that's the real point, isn't it?

WILLIAMS: I hope you're getting all this down.

BORGES: I am not. I wonder what fermentation is?

SHAW: Come back to Edinburgh, and I'll teach you.

BORGES: That's it, yes. I think of Stevenson, of Wordsworth, and then of course, Carlyle was a Scotsman, David Hume, and so on. Yes, let's go back to it.

WILLIAMS: Let's get a little more modern. What about Wallace Stevens? Have you read Stevens?

BORGES: I haven't. I'm really sorry.

WILLIAMS: It seemed to me that you translated a Stevens poem a long time ago.

BORGES: It must have been before my birth. Some reincarnation. Sorry.

WILLIAMS: And that's all you want to say about Stevens?

BORGES: Yes, since I don't know him, why should I slander him?

WILLIAMS: All right. Robert Frost?

BORGES: Robert Frost is to me, perhaps, one of the finest poets. I remember a poem of his called "Acquainted with the Night," a poem in tercets. And then, of course, that other poem about woods at midnight. But I think of Frost as being, let us say, to repeat that easy metaphor, as being begotten by Browning. I think of Frost as coming from Browning, as an heir of Browning. But Frost is a great poet. When I was a young man, I preferred, I'm sorry to say, Sandburg. Well, now he's too loud for me. Sandburg is too loud; Frost isn't. Frost has the force of William Empson; Frost has discovered the many uses of ambiguity. He's writing at the same time several poems, even as Henry James, when he pretended he was writing a single story, was writing several stories, many stories. And that's all to the good, since poetry should, I think, be ambiguous.

WILLIAMS: What about Robert Graves? Do you know him?

BORGES: Yes, Robert Graves, we saw him, María Kodama and I, we saw him twice in Majorca. The first time we thought he was quite unaware of us. He was in some kind of splendid ecstacy. He seemed to be aloof, far away, and when I came to say good-bye, he shook my hand and he kissed María's hand. That was the first time. The last time he was unaware of us and I, being blind, was unaware of him. At this moment he's quietly dying, in Majorca. No news has come. I have so much to thank Robert Graves for. Besides that splendid book, work of fiction I should say, *The White Goddess*. There, he supposes that all poetry comes from the myth of the white goddess, a myth of his own invention, of course. But the book is there, and a very fine book. Another book called *The Common Asphodel*, very ungenerous, but not only bitter, a very eloquent book. And then I remember a poem of his, not to be found in his collected works, about Alexander. In that poem, he supposes that Alexander does not die in Babylon. Alexander is lost, and he goes through a forest, thinks he is about to die, and he then sees a fire, the fire of a Tartar army. And he goes there, he's dying, and he's saved by the Tartars, and since his trade, his office, is to be a soldier, he's a soldier in that unknown army of yellow men with slanting eyes. Then years go on, he finds he's merely an obscure soldier. Nobody takes him into account, but he does his duty: he fights, he does not know the names of his generals, he goes on fighting, and the day comes when the troop receives their pay. He looks at the coins, and there is one coin that strikes him, and he says, "Yes, that was the metal I coined when I was Alexander and I defeated the King of Persia." And that's that. That's so good that it should be very ancient. That, I think, is a quality of things good: they may have existed forever. That I should say is the measure of Kafka. I don't think of him with the nations of the twentieth century. You think of him as having been there forever. I also think of that myth of Robert Graves as having existed forever, or at least since the time of Alexander.

WILLIAMS: Since we're talking about North American poetry, it occurs to me that I was going to ask you about some younger poets; in a book called—

BORGES: I'm an ignorant old man. Don't ask me about—

WILLIAMS: That's why I'm not going to ask—you're not an ignorant man, but—

BORGES: Think of me as posthumous. I died twenty some years ago. I'm a mere ghost. I am Hamlet's father, in a sense.

WILLIAMS: I'm not going to name names, but there's a volume called *Directory of American Poets* in which there are about five thousand names listed—

BORGES: Perhaps five thousand too many.

WILLIAMS: And I'm wondering—the poet Karl Shapiro says there haven't been five thousand poets in the history of the human race, and—

BORGES: I don't think so.

WILLIAMS: And I'm wondering—

BORGES: Let's hope so.

WILLIAMS: That's an inordinately high number, isn't it?

BORGES: Overwhelming. That's overwhelming.

WILLIAMS: What about Hemingway?

BORGES: I dislike him thoroughly.

WILLIAMS: William Faulkner?

BORGES: A great writer. A great writer, William Faulkner, undoubtedly. He got the Nobel prize, and he deserved it. I was so glad when I heard the news. Faulkner stands for the South, a region I greatly love, and I love it more because I was in New Orleans, and blues and spirituals were overwhelming me, pouring all over me, from every side of Bourbon Street. I've always loved the South. And I think the phrase, the common phrase, "the Deep South" is a good one. Had it been "the Profound South" it would have been no good. But "the Deep South" is all right. In Spanish it goes well also. If I say "el hondo sur" that sounds as it should. Yes, of course I love Faulkner. His first book I most liked, *Sanctuary*, because in the others he went in for, well, for games with time, hardly exhilarating.

WILLIAMS: Let's move back a little bit to Chaucer.

BORGES: Well, you mention Chaucer and a line of Chaucer comes back to me, because I think what's important in a poet is not his biography, or his opinions, or the time he lived in, but the verses he has left us. And, pronouncing them in my own South American, twentieth-century way, the lines are found at the beginning of *Troilus and Cressida*, and they run thus: "But ye loveres, that bathen in glad-nesse." I suppose Chaucer would have said, "But ye loveres, that bathen in gladnes-se." But I think, what a fine metaphor. When Mallarmé spoke of "la blanc couple nageur," that's too precise to be poetry, but the idea of bathing in gladness evokes what not too subtly Shakespeare called "the act of darkness" or "the deed of darkness," I'm not sure. "But ye loveres, that bathen in gladnesse." And then also comes back to me the final lines of that very fine poem (I hope I pronounce it right, but I think it should be pronounced in this way): "That regnest ay"—he's thinking of the Godhead in the Trinity, of course, "that regnest ay in thre, and two, and oon." What a good thing that he wrote "oon" and not "one." Because "in three and two and one" would be nowhere, while "thre, and two, and oon"—they boom.

ROSEN: We'll be glad to entertain questions from the audience.

BORGES: Any questions you like, concerning any subjects. Except ale and beer, of which I still remain ignorant.

QUESTION FROM THE AUDIENCE: Jack Kerouac, and William Seward Burroughs—what do you think of them as writers?

BORGES: No, I can only plead my ignorance.

QUESTION FROM THE AUDIENCE: What about Lewis Carroll?

BORGES: Well, I remember I saw Silvina Ocampo, a great Argentine poet,

and she said to me, "After all, Lewis Carroll invented everything."
When he wrote *Alice in Wonderland*, *Through the Looking Glass*, and
Silvie and Bruno, he was attempting very daring experiments, but
they came off so well, you think of them as having been there all the
time. I think that Lewis Carroll is perhaps the most imaginative of
all nineteenth century writers, except that he succeeded so well
that people take him for granted. And since he's read in childhood,
people think of him as writing for children. What Silvina Ocampo
said to me, I fully think that she was saying the truth, was that
Lewis Carroll invented almost everything, at least if things can be
invented, since we're supposed to keep on repeating the same
things. But those books are so daring, and so felicitous, that we
think they were easy. That I think is the mark of success—that
something should appear to be inevitable even though it cost a lot
of work. You don't think of a rough draft of Carroll; you think of
those things as flowing from somewhere—perhaps the muse, perhaps the Holy Ghost, who knows? But you think of them as being
necessary. I don't think I could do without Lewis Carroll. And I've
also read his books on mathematics, and so on, and I have a first
edition of *Sylvie and Bruno*, a book compounded, according to him,
out of personal dreams. I can give you a stanza I remember out of
that book, "He thought he saw an elephant, but it proved—"no,
I've forgotten, "that proved he was the pope," no, no—(whispers)
Well, what a pity, it won't come back to me. (Whispers). No,
I'm very sorry. Oh—"He thought he saw an elephant / Revolving
round the lamp / He looked again / And saw it was / A penny
postal stamp." That's right. An impossible mistake, of course.

QUESTION FROM THE AUDIENCE: What are some of your favorite English
words? What are some of the words that just don't work in English?

BORGES: I only know the ones that work. Those words are, firstly, "dim,"
a beautiful word, a dim word, and of course akin to German the
"Dämmerung," the twilight. But "dim" is better. I think Shakespeare has, in *Romeo and Juliet*, speaking of the vault, he says, "That
palace of dim night." "Dim" is perfect. Had he said "dark night" or
"black night" that would have been awkward. Then you have those
two fine Scottish words, "uncanny" and "eerie." "Uncanny," you've
heard it in German, where you can say, "unheimlich." But "eerie" I

think has a witchcraft of its own. So that we have "dim," "eerie," and "uncanny." But perhaps, far more than the words, is the fact that you can do many things with verbs and prepositions that cannot be done beyond the English language or at least beyond Germanic languages. For example, we've not spoken of Kipling as yet. But I can remember, I'm sure, two lines out of *The Ballad of East and West*. The two British officers are chasing an Afghan horse thief, and that lasts a long time, then Kipling says, "They have ridden the low moon out of the sky / their hoofs drum up the dawn . . . ." Now you can't ride the moon out of the sky in Spanish; the language doesn't allow it. And you can't drum up the dawn either. So really those two verses have the richness of English, I think. And there are other verses, where you have the English sounds and also the sounds of Asia, both the sounds of the Afghans and the Arabs. What other words can I remember at this moment? Well, of course, why not fall back on the moon? One thinks that all names for the moon are mistaken. Because in Greek we have "Selene." Far too complicated for the moon. The moon is a simple white thing. And in Spanish, and in Latin, and in Italian, and in Portuguese, you have "luna." That I think is quite a good word. But in German you have "der Mond." That's a he-moon. I don't think that will do at all. I don't want a he-moon. And in Old English the word was rather ugly: "Mona," also he-moon. And "mona" means an "ape" in Spanish, of course. Quite a bad word. In English you have that fine, lingering word, "moon." You have to say it slowly. It's as slow as the moon itself. "Moon" is a word you can go on pronouncing forever and forever. I may die, and go on saying "the moon." "Moon"—what a beautiful word. That sound is very beautiful, the double-o sound: "moon." And "loom" always—well, you can't "loom over" in Spanish, either, no. "Loom over," "moon": those are beautiful sounds. In French, the name is a good one, also, because "lune" is a fine word, far better than "la luna," as you say, "la lune." A slight word, a slender word, even as the English "moon."

WILLIAMS: The title of this symposium is "Borges, the Poet." It was not carelessly named, as you can see.

QUESTION FROM THE AUDIENCE: How do you think literature ought to be taught?

BORGES: Well, I've done my best, or my worst, to teach English, and not least American, literature. I always tell my students to disavow biography, and go to the writers themselves, and enjoy it. If you don't enjoy a book you're not really reading it. If you read out of a sense of duty, that reading does you really no good. You're bored stiff. While if you read, looking for happiness or for emotion, then you're right. So I told my students—I had to teach English, and not least American literature, during four months—I told them, "I can't teach you those two literatures, they're endless. I have hardly read a page or so out of the millions of books, but I can teach you the love of literature. And at the end of four months, one of my students was in love with DeQuincey, another with Chaucer, another with Dr. Johnson, another with Bernard Shaw, another with George Moore, and so on—another with Mark Twain, and with Browning, many of them. Many of them love the work of Browning. So I think that literature should be thought of as an easy form of happiness, as an easy way for attaining happiness.

QUESTION FROM THE AUDIENCE: Señor, are you familiar with the works of J. R. R. Tolkien, and, if so, what do you think of them?

BORGES: I was certainly defeated by them. I attempted them, several times over, and in the end he was the victor. I was defeated, and I left off reading him. I never understood them. To me, they were pointless. But perhaps not to more astute readers.

QUESTION FROM THE AUDIENCE: Borges, have you ever studied Hebrew, or Arabic?

BORGES: No, I'm sorry to say I haven't. It was my bounden duty to do so, since I come of Jewish stock, and of course Arabic, my being Spanish. No, I haven't. I know a few words, and those common Arabic words that are part of the Spanish language, but are not felt as being different.

QUESTION FROM THE AUDIENCE: We enjoy the humor in your work; you've already given us a couple of indications of it tonight. But what books make *you* laugh?

BORGES: Well, I think Charles Dickens makes me laugh. I think Mark Twain makes me laugh. Bernard Shaw makes me laugh. Oscar Wilde makes me laugh. That's that. I've mentioned four writers; in the case of other writers, I laugh at them, but that's different, no?

QUESTION FROM THE AUDIENCE: Why do you admire William Morris?

BORGES: Why shouldn't I admire William Morris? William Morris is a great benefactor. My father gave me a copy of the *Volsunga Saga* as done into English by Morris. I fell in love with that book and a handbook of Norse mythology. And when I've read one of those fine books of his, I have remembered so many things by heart, especially *The Earthly Paradise*. I remember the king, he's talking to a Breton and to a Norseman, and then he gives one of them a ring and the other a horn, and he tells the Breton—no, the Norseman—"Remember me, who am of Odin's blood." I have mentioned Odin. María Kodama can vouch for the truth of what I'm saying. We were, a few months ago, in Iceland. We talked to the vicar of some village or other and he said to us, "You should see, you should meet, the heathen priest." And I said, "What do you mean by heathen priest?" "Well," he said, "the priest of the three hundred people in Iceland who still worship Odin, or Wotan of the Old English, Odin and Thor." When we met him I saw he was a tall man, a giant, like most Icelanders, I'm told, with a fresh face and a white beard. He had no books in his house. He was a shepherd and a very poor man, and he was the priest of Odin and Thor. He intoned to us some verses in Icelandic. I'm learning the language now, and I could make out those two names, not out of the past, but out of the very living present. I could make out the names, pronounced in reverence, of Frea, Othan, Othid, and Thor, with a hard Scottish "r." And I said to myself, "How lucky I am!" I met a priest of the Germanic gods, whose gods were worshipped all over Germany, all over Holland, all over England, all over Sweden, Norway and Denmark, and there are three hundred men worshipping them now in Ultima Thule, Iceland. This was one of the great boons of my life. I felt very happy about it.

In the case of Morris, I remember so many poems by him, but I think he was wrong when he attempted English as a merely Germanic language, because you see, I read the two versions of the *Odyssey*: Pope, of course, and William Morris. And Pope has it. Yes, "The Man, for Wisdom's various arts renown'd / Long exercis'd in woes, O Muse! resound." That's very fine I think; I mean, in a Latin way. While Morris, I'm sorry to say, has only, "Tell me, Muse, of the

Shifty, the man who wandered afar / After the Holy Burg of Troy he had wasted with war." "Holy Burg" sounds like slang, no? "The Holy Burg," instead of, let's say, "the Citadel." I'm sorry to say that he wrote that. But there are also many good things. A bad painter and a great poet.

QUESTION: What about D. H. Lawrence and Henry Miller?

BORGES: Well, I was defeated by Miller, but—who did he say?

ROSEN: D. H. Lawrence.

BORGES: No, I prefer the other Lawrence. I prefer Lawrence of Arabia. I've no use for David Herbert Lawrence—writing smutty stories, smutty novels, I've no use for him. He's beyond my ken; I'm unworthy of him. But the other, Lawrence of Arabia, is of course a great writer, another epic writer, even as Conrad was.

QUESTION (Professor Dunn, Dickinson College): You spoke of epics. I'd be interested in your opinion of *Moby Dick* and Herman Melville.

BORGES: I think *Moby Dick* is a splendid nightmare. I have read and reread it several times over. Of course he wrote under the influence of Shakespeare and of Carlyle, two very good influences, I should say. But I think of *Moby Dick* as being a wonderful book. Still, there is a point, and the point is this: that in ancient literature, a quest was successful . . . I mean, the Argonauts found the Golden Fleece, and Ulysses came back to his island. But in the case of contemporary literature, since Cervantes, perhaps, you know that the quest always ends in defeat. We know that man shall never be the victor. We get that in *Don Quijote*, we get that—not in *Treasure Island*, in *Treasure Island* they find the treasure, good for Stevenson!—But in *Moby Dick* we know the whole scheme is doomed to failure. We know that Ahab will not find the whale or when he finds it, will, of course, be defeated by the whale. And I think that's a sign of our times. We're too cowardly to think in terms of victory. We think in terms of failure and we duly fail, of course.

QUESTION FROM THE AUDIENCE: What do you think of e. e. cummings?

BORGES: Well, at this moment, if you mention a poet, a stanza comes:

> god's terrible face, brighter than a spoon,
> collects the image of one fatal word;
> so that my life (which liked the sun and the moon)
> resembles something that has not occurred: . . .

Those four lines come back to me; for the rest—I know I enjoy them but I can't bring them back to me. I think of poets in terms of quotations. I mean, if the verse sticks to me, then it is good. If it doesn't, then the poet's forgotten.

QUESTION: What is it about the literature and the language of the Anglo-Saxons that appeals to you?

BORGES: I lost my eyesight for reading purposes way back in 1955. And then I said to myself, quoting somebody else, cribbing as I am all the time, "When something ends, something else is beginning." And then I got to work to create the beginning. Then, I thought, "Why not Old English? Since after all, Middle English and Modern English are so good, why not attempt the real thing, why not attempt Old English?" And then my students and I looked over a book I had at home on a top shelf, the *Anglo-Saxon Chronicle*; we came on two words and fell in love with Old English. Those two words, I'm making you a gift of them today, you'll thank me, are the names for London and for Rome. London is the "Lundenburg"; isn't that fine, ponderous? And Rome is the "Romaburg." We fell in love with those two words, and afterwards we came across a sentence, saying, "Julius Caesar was the first of all Romans to seek out Britain." That's more or less irrelevant in English. But when we read it in Old English, "Iulius Casere aerest Romana Brytene land sohte," we fell in love with Old English, and we, well, we ran through Peru Street of Buenos Aires shouting, "Iulius Casere aerest Romana Brytene land sohte!" People stared at us. We were discovering Old English, and then we went on, went on to many things.

QUESTION (Ralph Slotten, Dickinson College): Which of Emerson's poems is your favorite, and why?

BORGES: Well, there are so many favorite poems of Emerson. But I think of the poem called "The Brahma," I think that is one of the finest poems. It's four or five stanzas. And then another poem, a long one, where you find, you come across, a very uncanny sentence, a sentence that Edgar Allan Poe could never have achieved. The sentence is: "Things are of the snake." He means things are evil. But "things are evil" is no good; "things are of the snake" has something mythic and ancient about it. I love Emerson's cold poetry. He was a passionate man and a cold poet. And perhaps the first of all intellectual poets. The only one who ever thought, while the others were merely, well, versifying different subjects. But Emerson was thinking all the time, even when he wrote poetry. He was a thinking man. He was thinking all day long, perhaps all night long, perhaps in his dreams he was thinking also. But I should say "Brahma," and so many more of them. I love him so much that only to quote one, I would feel I was leaving out the others. So let us stick to "Brahma": It begins "If the red killer thinks he slays . . ." "Red killer" is perfect, of course, "the red killer thinks he slays."

QUESTION FROM THE AUDIENCE: Henry James—which do you prefer, the very late works, *Wings of the Dove* or *The Golden Bowl*, or the earlier ones?

BORGES: No, I have no taste for the novels. I think the novels were a mistake. But the tales are very fine. I've read and reread them many times over. While the novels are far too—perhaps too delicate, or too long-winded, why not? or shouldn't I say that word?—But what he wrote, his stories, are unequalled by anything. In his tales he foreshadows Kafka, of course. But that's not his chief importance. I mean, he's a writer in his own right, and a teller of tales in his own right. Strangely enough, he was a friend of Kipling, and they both admired each other, yes, as writers of course—they were friends.

QUESTION FROM THE AUDIENCE: Sir, we've had transitions in the education about literature in America in recent times. And evidently you went to school in the time when memorization was favored.

BORGES: No, I think that when one likes something, there's no need to memorize it. It sticks to you. Why do it on purpose? If a thing is good it stays with you, and gives you company for the rest of your life. You shouldn't memorize poetry. That's a duty, and duty, I think, well, should be avoided, no?

QUESTION FROM THE AUDIENCE: When you write a poem similar to "The Rose," where you take one little, one short subject, do you find yourself sitting down and it all comes out at once and that's it, and maybe you might toy with it, or are your poems scholarly works that you spend a great deal of time on? How do they come to you?

BORGES: No, suddenly a revelation, but the word is too ambitious a one, is given me. And then I know something is about to happen, and then that something may be a sonnet, may be a short story, may be a poem in free verse, may be a poem in blank verse. And then—

well, I sit back, I let the dream have its way with me, and then in due time I dictate it to somebody—I can't see, the letters overlap when I attempt writing, and in due time it's whipped into shape. But the whole thing is very slow. In the beginning the whole thing is passive. I merely receive something. And then I have, well, in my own way I have to find out for that particular subject whether it needs free verse, or needs the regular forms, or needs to be told in the past, or needs to be told in the first person, or the third—these things I need to find out. In the case of a story I always know the beginning and the end. And I have to invent, or discover, the words being the same, what happens in between. But I always know the beginning, not the first sentence, but the beginning itself. Not the actual words, of course. And I always know the end. And then the rest of the story has to be worked out in my own South American way.

QUESTION FROM THE AUDIENCE: Do you think that there is a kind of kinship between poets and mathematicians?

BORGES: My mathematics is very slight. But I have read and reread Bertrand Russell. And I think there *should* be a kinship. And I suppose there is. There is a kinship between all things, especially between poets and mathematicians, and poets and philosophers, who are a measure of poets, I should say.

QUESTION FROM THE AUDIENCE: What do you think of the poetry of Edna St. Vincent Millay?

BORGES: Well, I plead my ignorance once more.

QUESTION FROM THE AUDIENCE: What are your thoughts, sir, on John Gardner's verse?

BORGES: I plead my ignorance over and over again, eh? This is a really thorough examination. With very bad marks, low marks. If this kind of thing goes on—

QUESTION FROM THE AUDIENCE: Over the years, have we either been blessed or cursed with various schools of criticism—

BORGES: Cursed, I should say.

ROSEN: I could have answered this one for you. He would like to know in fact what your views are on "deconstructionism."

BORGES: My views are, well, nowhere. The whole thing's a mistake. A really pedantic mistake. That's no good, I should say.

QUESTION FROM THE AUDIENCE: What do you think about Jonathan Swift?

BORGES: Well, one of the many gifts Ireland has given us, eh?—especially the last chapters of *Gulliver's Travels.* And in a sense I think Voltaire, or Voltaire's themes, came from Swift, since *Gulliver's Travels* came before the novella of Voltaire. Except that Voltaire was a happy man, and a pessimist; Jonathan Swift was a pessimist and a very embittered man—perhaps a madman, for all we know. In one of the biographies I read that, in the end, he was mad. Then he lived in a big house in Dublin, and he walked all over the house, and he said to himself those Biblical words, "I am that I am." And I remembered Shakespeare, one of his comedies—there is a coward who is detected, he's a soldier, he's shamed in the presence of the others, and then he says to himself, "Simply the thing I am shall make me live." I suppose that Swift meant the same. "I am that I am." That is to say, "I can't remember my own name, but I am something living." And we can all say, "I am that I am," and that "I am" may be, for all I know, revealing the will of Schopenhauer, or the Holy Ghost, or perhaps God. Since Bernard Shaw wrote, "God is in the making." And we are in the making. In the case of Swift, when I was a child, I read him for the sake of—for amusement. I read *Gulliver's Travels*, I read just the beginning. And then I went on, later on in life, I went on to the Yahoos and I wrote a story more or less imitated from Swift. The story is called "Doctor Brodie's Report." The whole thing is taken from Swift, and I used the word "Yahoos" purposely.

QUESTION FROM THE AUDIENCE: What do you think of Nikos Kazantzakis?

BORGES: Well, I am sorry again. You see, my eyesight left me in 1955, and I have done some rereading, but no new reading. And I am very ignorant concerning contemporary literature, if he's a contemporary writer.

QUESTION (Cecilia Heydl): Which would be one of your favorite Whitman poems?

BORGES: I think we make a mistake when we speak of Whitman's poems, because he thought of the whole book as being one poem, a single American epic. But whenever I translate him into Spanish, "The Song of Myself," (not "to myself" but "of myself"). And also, well, that other poem, yes, "Starting from—" I don't remember, sorry.

What are the first words? "Starting from fish-shape Paumanok where I was born, / Well-begotten and rais'd by a perfect mother, / After roaming many lands, lover of populous pavements." "Starting from Paumanok," no? And then of course, those very fine, fleshy poems, "Children of Adam." Most of the things he wrote are very fine. But I think that we should think of them, and we'll talk about that tomorrow and after tomorrow, of the whole book as being a single epic, not as being an anthology or a series of short poems. I think he intended the whole book to be a single book. That is why he kept on republishing, and adding to, *Leaves of Grass*. The first book published was way back in 1855, the year that Longfellow's *Hiawatha* came out. He kept on republishing the book. And then he added to it, "Drum Taps" and so on.

QUESTION (Beverly Eddy, Dickinson College): How would you describe the art of the translator, and what would you say are the qualities that a person needs to be successful at it?

BORGES: I think a translator should be a poet in his own right. The classic example, of course, is Edward Fitzgerald; he took several pieces from a Persian astronomer and turned them into a single poem. But I think a poem should be recreated. If not, the whole thing is merely pedantic. The poet has to recreate—things. And that happens many times, I suppose. Perhaps the King James Bible is a recreation, for all I know. I don't know Hebrew. Perhaps the King James Bible is a more subtle book than the original Hebrew version.

QUESTION FROM THE AUDIENCE: Would you say something about the relation of idea to style?

BORGES: I think that every subject dictates its own style. I mean, a subject wants to be written in a certain fashion. I have no theories whatever. For example, the case of rhyme. I suppose that Whitman was quite right when he discarded it, since rhyme would have done him no good. And Swinburne was right when he used it, since it did him good. So it depends.

QUESTION FROM THE AUDIENCE: What about the relation of a poet's ideas to the worth of the poetry?

BORGES: Well, in the case of Whitman, the ideal of democracy made him into a great poet. In the case of Neruda, communism made him into a great poet. In the case of Kipling, the idea of the empire, the

British empire as a duty, made him into a great poet. Now, those three ideas are, of course, quite different, and hostile to each other. But, still, Whitman stood in need of democracy, Neruda stood in need of communism, Rudyard Kipling stood in need of the British empire; that's that.

QUESTION FROM THE AUDIENCE: I would like to hear you talk just a little bit about Dante. Does he mean as much to you as your favorite English poets and American poets?

BORGES: Yes, I think that he means—well, were I to save a whole book, but why should I save one book, there are so many of them that are so good—I think I would save the *Divine Comedy*. And yet, I cannot believe in its mythology, either the heathen or the Christian one. I don't believe in Hell, in Purgatory, or in Heaven. I don't believe in rewards and punishments. But I believe in them, or at least there is a willing suspension of disbelief, as Coleridge had it, when I read the *Divine Comedy*. I have no Italian, but I have read the *Divine Comedy* some ten or twelve times over, in different editions. Italian editions are so good, that they have, many of them—for example, Momigliano, Grabher, Torraca, and so on—perhaps a note to every line. No such thing has been attempted in other literatures, as far as I know. I've gone over editions of Shakespeare, but you don't find an explanation to every line. But in Dante, particularly those editions I mentioned, especially in the one by Atilio Momigliano, the Jewish scholar, you do. In the case of Grabher also. And in my case, since my language is Spanish, I stand in no need of learning Italian, since the two languages are two illustrious dialects of Latin. And if you have one, you understand the other. I mean, I don't understand Italian if it's spoken to me, I may not be a witness—I may not see an Italian play, or Italian film—but if I have an Italian book before me, let's say the *Divine Comedy*, why not the *Furioso* also, another very fine poem, in that case I can read on slowly, I don't think I can understand everything, but I can enjoy everything, and be sensitive to everything, and that's far more important. The fact that I am not a Christian, the fact that I disbelieve utterly in punishment, Hell, in purification, in Purgatory, or in rewards, Heaven, that makes my judgment of Dante to be simply an aesthetic one. I think of Dante as being *the* writer, as being *the* poet. Though I might add Vergil, perhaps. But, we think of Vergil in terms of Dante, so they go together. But had I to choose one poet and one book, in spite of all my love for all things Germanic, for all things English, for all things Scandinavian, I think that I would choose Dante and the *Divine Comedy*.

ROSEN: We have time for one or two questions.

QUESTION FROM THE AUDIENCE: Since you seem to dislike punishment, what do you think of children's literature that deals with that, like fairy tales?

BORGES: Well, in the case of *Alice in Wonderland*, it doesn't. In the case of *Through the Looking Glass*, it doesn't. I don't think punishment is the right idea. As Bernard Shaw said, or a character in Bernard Shaw said, "I have left behind me the bribe of heaven." So you think of heaven as being the bribe and hell as being the threat, and those things are wrong, of course. Why punish, why threaten? Those things are beyond me.

QUESTION FROM THE AUDIENCE: What is the visionary quality of your dreams?

BORGES: Well, in my dreams I haven't lost my eyesight. I keep on dreaming in colors. I suppose the colors are not too subtle. Still I know that every night when I am asleep, I have my eyesight, and then I see things. Sometimes when the nightmare visits me, then I see very awful things, and I do my best to forget them. In daytime I am blind. At nighttime, when I am asleep, I see.

ROSEN: Señor Borges said to keep going, so we'll keep going for a few more minutes.

QUESTION FROM THE AUDIENCE: What do you think of Freud?

BORGES: I think he was a nasty old man, eh?

QUESTION FROM THE AUDIENCE: For two days we've been asking you questions about your literary benefactors. Do you have any benefactors who are not literary?

BORGES: All of *you*, I should say. Every single one of you, you're all so kind to me. America is so kind, and so forgiving, in my case. Why not? I think, well, my father was a great friend, my mother also. I have had so many fine friends; I still have them. Of course I suppose all people are benefactors, even the ones you don't know. They may be doing good to you. Since language, Emerson said, language is fossil poetry. And in that case, if you use a language, you are indebted to those unknown poets who made the language. But when I am speaking in English, I am receiving the gifts of many dead men, the gifts of many ghosts, and in the case of Spanish the same thing, of course. In the case of all languages. All those dead men are still giving me their gifts. And I'm duly thankful for them, though I don't know their names.

QUESTION FROM THE AUDIENCE: Which writer, for you, best captures the way common Americans speak?

BORGES: Yes, one moment . . . The man who wrote, "Some Like Them Cold" and "Haircut"—what was his name?

ROSEN: Ring Lardner.

BORGES: Yes, I should say Ring Lardner. But of course I'm not an authority. Yes, Ring Lardner, why not? And Mark Twain—perhaps he started the whole thing. And Carl Sandburg could always handle the vernacular. Whitman couldn't.

QUESTION FROM THE AUDIENCE: What do you think about James Joyce?

BORGES: I think that Joyce made a mistake in attempting the novel. He really was a poet. And, since I am a man of quotations, I'll give you this one that you know by heart, perhaps. The last sentence of the first chapter of *Finnegans Wake*, and it runs thus (it cannot be done into other languages): "The rivering waters of." Period. "The hitherandthithering waters of." Period. "Night." Full stop. I think that—that is a wonderful verse. Not the idea, the idea of comparing time with a river is a very old one. But the way it's stated. And then you have "rivering waters of." And then, "hitherandthithering" and that can't be done, let's say, outside the English language, or beyond the English language. "Hitherandthithering"—that would be awful in Spanish: "aquí y acullá." And then you have "Night." So the punctuation is also a fine invention of his. Because had it been written, "The rivering waters of" comma "the hitherandthithering waters of" comma "night." And there would be no point—you need that, the period, and the full stop at the end. And of course I remember well his *Chamber Music* and the very fine stories and *Portrait of the Artist as a Young Man*. The book itself I think is a mistake, I mean, *Ulysses* is unreadable. So is, of course,

Finnegans Wake. They were defeats. But they were, as Virginia Woolf said, "Glorious defeats." And they are glorious, of course.

QUESTION FROM THE AUDIENCE: What do you think of Ralph Ellison's *Invisible Man*?

ROSEN (to Borges): Are you familiar with Ralph Ellison's novel, *Invisible Man*?

BORGES: H. G. Wells' novel?

ROSEN: No, no—an American writer.

BORGES: No, I think in terms of Wells, rather. I enjoy that novel greatly. But this is another invisible man.

ROSEN: Right. A different one.

BORGES: A different invisible man. I do my best to be an invisible man, but I don't succeed.

QUESTION (Betty Billings): Did you have any influence from either Schiller or Goethe? Do you have any preference between the two or from any other particularly well-known German poet?

BORGES: I think I owe much to the first German novelist I ever read through, Gustav Meyrink, who wrote *Der Golem.* And then, my memory is full of the German verses, because I think the language is so beautiful:

> Noch spür ich ihren Atem
> auf den Wangen.
> Wie kann das sein
> dass sie in einem Tage fortziehn
> für immer fort
> und ganz vergangen.

And then, of course, Heine:

> Das küsste mich auf deutsch und sprach auf deutsch
> (Man glaubt es kaum
> Wie gut es klang) das Wort: "Ich liebe dich!"
> Es war ein Traum.

And Hölderlin, of course. We have Hofmannsthal, Heine and Hölderlin, and so many others, novelists; German literature is so rich, especially in poetry. And of Goethe, I think I recall the *Roman Elegies.* I also think that *Faust* should be forgotten. And forgiven, I should say.

QUESTION FROM THE AUDIENCE: How do you feel that the heart, the soul, and the mind of man interrelate in poetry, and how should they interrelate in life?

BORGES: Whew! That's too tangled a question for me. Would you say it all again, because somehow I was lost in that maze, eh?

QUESTION: The three separate parts—or at least considered as separate—the intellect, the emotions, and the spirit—seem to come together in some poets' poetry, Whitman for example. And I wondered how you thought that they interrelated, and if they were separate in reality.

BORGES: I don't think poetry should be attempted without emotion. It is in that case a mere game of words. That is hardly important. I think that emotion, well, there is a need for it. We cannot do without it. Why should we? So I think of styles of writing as growing out of emotion. If not, the whole thing is meaningless. When I write, I always begin by emotion. And then I go on to words. I don't begin by the words. Those words are given me after the emotion, after that exhilaration that we are speaking about.

QUESTION FROM THE AUDIENCE: How do you evaluate the poetry of John Keats?

BORGES: Well, he's so uneven. In the case of Keats, well, you find wonderful verses, the one about Ruth, for example,

> ". . . when sick for home
> She stood in tears amidst the alien corn."

And then you get very early lines, for example, "The pleasant flow / Of world's unopening a portfolio." That is Keats, I am sorry to say. Or "I stood tip-toe upon a little hill." Keats again. But he wrote some fine verse. And a poet should be remembered by his successes, not by his failures. Well, he was failing all the time, I should say. For example, "With beaded bubbles winking at the brim." That's obviously ugly. And yet people forgive him.

QUESTION FROM THE AUDIENCE: Would you comment on G. K. Chesterton, and your interest in his work?

BORGES: I think of Chesterton first as a poet. But he was a poet all the time. Especially when he wrote detective stories. He was a great poet. But also when he was actually a poet. For example,

But I shall not be too old to see
Enormous night arise
A cloud that is larger than the world
And a monster made of eyes.

And then Chesterton wrote a very fine epic poem on King Alfred and the Danes, the book called, well, it's horse, I think, no? *The White Horse.* I'm not sure about the title.

ROSEN: *The Ballad of the White Horse?*

BORGES: Yes, *The White Horse.* And then all the Father Brown, the saga of Father Brown, those are wonderful. They are many things at the same time. I mean, they are detective stories, they are parables, and they are poems, also. But perhaps when the detective novel has died out, and it will die out in due time, those books will be read for what is fantastic in them. As I say, not for the solving of the puzzle, for the puzzle itself. Chesterton was a great writer, of course. But I think that, in a sense, he came from Stevenson, since the idea of London as a fairy city was given him, not only by London itself, which is, I suppose, a fairy city, but also by Stevenson's *The New Arabian Nights*, *The Suicide Club*, "The Rajah's Diamond," and so on. Therein we find London thought of as a fairy city. And maybe it *was* a fairy city for Stevenson, who came from the north, who came from Scotland, and then when he found himself in London, he thought of it as being a fairy city. He got that sense down, especially in *The Suicide Club*. There are also those books of Chesterton on Browning, on Dickens, on Blake, very good books. I think Chesterton was a man of genius, but people think of him in terms of his opinions, and that is wrong. I am not a Catholic, but I enjoy Chesterton. Chesterton had no love for Germany; I love Germany, but I love Chesterton also. So I think of Chesterton as being far beyond his mere opinions. And he was a whimsical man.

QUESTION FROM THE AUDIENCE: Are there any women writers that you enjoy?

BORGES: Of course. Emily Dickinson, Lady Murasaki, Silvina Ocampo. Three. Jane Austen, no. My mother enjoyed her; I never could. And yet Kipling admired Jane Austen very much.

DEAN ALLAN: It's my job to do the obvious, and announce that what began a couple of days ago in fact now comes to an end, which is the characteristic of all things, it seems.

BORGES: "All good things may not last," as George Moore says.

DEAN ALLAN: Yes, indeed. It seems to me appropriate to turn the end
   back upon the beginning, or the beginning on the end, by closing—

BORGES: —the circle.

ALLAN: With circling back on Emily. I found in her poetry a poem that I
   think Borges wrote. And what a better way to send us on our
   flights and walks home?

> Many a phrase has the English language—
> I have heard but one—
> Low as the laughter of the Cricket,
> Loud, as the Thunder's Tongue—
>
> Murmuring, like old Caspian Choirs,
> When the Tide's a'lull—
> Saying itself in new inflection—
> Like a Whippoorwill—
>
> Breaking in bright Orthography
> On my simple sleep—
> Thundering its Prospective—
> Till I stir, and weep—
>
> Not for the Sorrow, done me—
> But for the push of Joy—
> Say it again, Saxon!
> Hush—Only to me!

BORGES: Who wrote that?

DEAN ALLAN: Emily Dickinson.

BORGES: Congratulate her.

DEAN ALLAN: I think you did.

BORGES: We all do.

THE POETRY ITSELF

I. *On Borges' Poetry*

THORPE RUNNING

The "Secret Complexity" of Borges' Poetry

Ever since the final years of the ultraist decade of the 20s in Argentina, Borges has tried to undo or to discredit almost everything that he believed or wrote during those years. This purposeful rejection of what was, after all, a synthetic approach to art, a catch-all of avant-garde theory and practice, has led him into new areas of poetic investigation which paradoxically place him once again in the forefront of current theoretical development.

Although Borges rejects the militant tone of his early ultraist pronouncements, as well as a belief in the supreme powers of the metaphor which they expressed, he retains, in spite of his apparent reticence and self-effacement, an insistent resolve to discover—to rescue—the basis for a true poetic image. In contrast to the intended difficulties imposed by the Ultraists' contrived metaphors which had correlated ever more "distant realities," he now "modestly" advises us that his later poetry has a "secret complexity" underlying its apparently ordinary language. Borges' careful consideration of the characteristics of the words he uses in his poetry parallels the concerns of other Latin American poets, especially the more adventurous ones who deal with what Octavio Paz labels the "zone of language." This focus on words and their limitations also carries Borges' poetry into the realm of theory currently dominated largely by French literary critics and philosophers such as Maurice Blanchot, Jacques Derrida, Michael Riffaterre and Gérard Genette.

Both of those groups share an awareness of the limits of language and a lack of confidence in its ability to express anything in concrete or unequivocal terms. Specifically, they mistrust the meanings engendered by words; thus, they tend to concentrate on the word as signifier only, and to disregard the ambiguous "signifieds" that they have been saddled with. This focus on the word stripped of its various meanings has necessarily also led more recent poets to reject a poetry built on analogy, since analogy is based on mental associations made between the implications of words. Their rejection of analogy places them perfectly in line with Borges' own rejection of ultraism and its glorification of the metaphor. The ultraists were supremely confident that they had found in the metaphor the ultimate creative source; however, new critics and poets who reject both the word with a fixed meaning and the metaphor it makes possible, now find greater creative possibilities in the view of a word seen primarily as signifier. Jacques Derrida, for example, makes this succinct comment regarding the linguistic sign: "L'absence de signifié transcendental étend à l'infini le champ et le jeu de la signification."[1] As a result of this absence of transcendental signification the word can now be seen as a *significant flottant*—a "floating signifier."

Such open-ended possibilities within a word can be responsible for a shattering effect upon language, as Octavio Paz shows in these lines from *Pasado en claro*.

> Una sonaja de semillas secas
> las letras rotas de los nombres:
> hemos dispersado a los nombres,
> hemos deshonrado a los nombres.
> Ando en busca del nombre desde entonces.

But, in the same poem, he shows that in spite of the disorienting effect of this dispersal of meaning, a continual creative process (*espiral, rotación*) is set in motion because of the inherent possibilities within words which have an "infinite field of meaning."

> Alcé con las palabras y sus sombras
> una casa ambulante de reflejos,
> torre que anda, construcción de viento.
> El tiempo y sus combinaciones:
> los años y los muertos y las sílabas,
> cuentos distintos de la misma cuenta.

Espiral de los ecos, el poema
es aire que se esculpe y se disipa,
fugaz alegoría de los nombres
verdaderos. A veces la página respira:
los enjambres de sonidos y sentidos,
en rotación magnética se enlazan y dispersan
sobre el papel.[2]

In this same vein, Roberto Juárroz, an Argentine who bases his entire poetics on the "floating" sign, clearly summarizes a view of language with no meaning attached to its signs.

Porque aquí y ahora la palabra no existe.
Tan sólo queda su identificación
en los archivos policiales
de la historia del hombre.
Su sonido es un coágulo en el tiempo.
Su escritura es un pálido diafragma
para las tácticas funestas
del corredor de la memoria.[3]

Borges is as aware of the fallibility and the futility of language and its signs as are those other poets and thinkers; in fact, his prose writing owes its original and easily identifiable technique to his belief that language does not have the ability to "name" things, as Sylvia Molloy has shown in her article on "simulacro y causalidad textual" in his fiction.[4] This concern becomes an even greater dilemma for the poet, as Borges explains in his postscript to *Historia de la noche* (1977).

La materia de que dispone el lenguaje es, como afirma Stevenson, absurdamente inadecuada. ¿Qué hacer con las gastadas palabras—con los Idola Fori de Francis Bacon—y con algunos artificios retóricos que están en los manuales?

He then elaborates on the "inadequacy" of what he elsewhere calls "ambiguous language."

Whitehead ha denunciado la falacia del diccionario perfecto: suponer que para cada cosa hay una palabra. Trabajamos a tientas. El universo es fluido y cambiante; el lenguaje, rígido.[5]

That last reference to a fluid and changing universe recalls the "floating signifier," and also parallels Derrida's explanation for that phenomenon, namely the lack of a fixed "center" for each word. Derrida's term for that ungraspable sign is the "trace,"[6] which Borges again almost echoes

with the words *vástago* (descendent) and *reflejo* (reflection) in these two
selections from the poems "A Johannes Brahms" and "Juan 1,14."

> Mi servidumbre es la palabra impura,
> Vástago de un concepto y de un sonido;
> Ni símbolo, ni espejo, ni gemido,
> Tuyo es el río que huye y que perdura.[7]
>
> He encomendado esta escritura a un hombre cualquiera;
> no será nunca lo que quiero decir,
> no dejará de ser su reflejo.[8]

In Borges' later poetry this inability to "name," and the frustration
with a "worn out" and "ambiguous" language is an ever present concern; his famous poem "El otro tigre" from *El otro, el mismo* (1967),
clearly illustrates this preoccupation which carries into all of the subsequent volumes. In the last line of the first quotation above, we see part of
the reason ("tuyo es el río") why this holds such fascination for a writer
whose favorite topic is time. For Borges, language's failings are linked
with human weaknesses, since both share a temporal nature; language is
both worn out (*gastado*) and undermined (*universo fluido y cambiante*) by
time, as are its practitioners. But he is not content to just play on this
awareness; he does not simply turn the "game of signification" into a
"spiral of echoes." Borges points out in the prologue to *La moneda de
hierro*, in which he discusses the limitations of art, that in spite of its
shifting meanings, language—the word—literally has a future.

Cada sujeto, por ocasional o tenue que sea, nos impone una estética peculiar.
Cada palabra, aunque esté cargada de siglos, inicia una página en blanco y com-
promete el porvenir.

In the face of an impure language and his own mortality, he insists on
establishing a poetry with a durable meaning, and this insistence is personal and solidly affirmative, in spite of the "secret" aspects which it will
entail.

The first way in which Borges' texts face up to an ambiguous language is to demonstrate how a word "loaded down by centuries" can
have an almost unlimited richness in its multiplicity of meanings. The
poem "El otro tigre" does just that, showing that, as Roman Jakobson
says, "the context is variable and each new context gives the word a new
signification. In that fact resides the creative force of the literary sign."[9]

"Blake," a poem in *La cifra*, contains the same kind of assertion about its subject, the rose.[10] It is important to note that Borges is not casual about selecting these subjects: both the rose and the tiger already have poetic (or as Borges would say, "archetypal") associations. Another poem on the same topic, "The Unending Rose," carries this idea of a multiplicity of meanings within a single word to an almost unlimited degree, a concept reinforced by the related title of the book it is contained in, *La rosa profunda*. That adjective, "profundo," is one that Roberto Juárroz also uses in his *Poesía vertical* in order to indicate the unlimited verticality— the open-ended depth of signification—of the poetic word. At the end of "The Unending Rose" it is evident that "the rose" has taken on a wealth of associations; addressing the rose, the poet says:

> Cada cosa
> Es infinitas cosas. Eres música,
> Firmamentos, palacios, ríos, ángeles,
> Rosa profunda, ilimitada, íntima,
> Que el Señor mostrará a mis ojos muertos.[11]

This awareness that the word in poetry has the potential to evoke a vast range of meanings within the reader underlies, then, all of Borges' mature poetry, and is an important part of his poetry's "secret complexity." Although in "The Unending Rose" Borges shows how a word's endless implications can provide poetic depths, he does not exclusively exploit the idea which some poets also see as the way to unlimited expression; Juárroz, for example, sees it as the key to a *poesía explosiva*. Rather, Borges seems to turn his back on this penetrating vision of what an ambiguous but unlimited language can do, incongruously insisting on consciously disregarding that knowledge. He explains the contradiction in his poem "El ingenuo" from *La moneda de hierro*.

> Cada aurora (nos dicen) maquina maravillas
> Capaces de torcer la más terca fortuna;
> Hay pisadas humanas que han medido la luna
> Y el insomnio devasta los años y las millas.
> En el azul acechan públicas pesadillas
> Que entenebran el día. No hay en el orbe una
> Cosa que no sea otra, o contraria, o ninguna.
> A mí sólo me inquietan las sorpresas sencillas.
> Me asombra que una llave pueda abrir una puerta,
> Me asombra que mi mano sea una cosa cierta,

> Me asombra que del griego la eleática saeta
> Instantánea no alcance la inalcanzable meta,
> Me asombra que la espada cruel pueda ser hermosa,
> Y que la rosa tenga el olor de la rosa.

The poem is, in spite of its title, anything but a reflection of naïveté. Perhaps, "El otro, el mismo" would have been a more fitting title for a poem which devotes the first half to a demonstration of poetic self-consciousness and the second half to a declaration of self-limitation. The opening seven lines are made up of the kind of exotic images which have characterized all modernist poetry, and also relate extraordinary events connected with modern society. Its imagery becomes almost a parody of avant-garde verse. As in the ultraists' poetry there is dehumanization; human elements are referred to through metonymy (*pisadas humanas, insomnio, públicas pesadillas*), but the images in these lines are all formed by the ultraists' favorite means, personification (*cada aurora maquina maravillas*, etc.). The verbs used are all in the creationist mold—dynamic and assertive (*maquinar, torcer, medir, devastar, acechar*). At the end of these seven verses ("no hay . . . una cosa que no sea otra . . .") Borges restates his frequently expressed belief that there is an excess of analogies and nihilistic pessimism in the world and in language.

In contrast to that conscious "modernity" of both expression and content, the second half of the poem deals with unremarkable things which nevertheless "astonish" him, and it is written in an apparently flat and prose-like style which still adheres to the strict form of the poem, with its fourteen-syllable lines and consonantal rhyme. This poem, which could well be seen as the poetics for all of Borges' later work, is a fleshing out of a key statement from the prologue to *El otro, el mismo*.

Es curiosa la suerte del escritor. Al principio es barroco, vanidosamente barroco, y al cabo de los años puede lograr, si son favorables los astros, no la sencillez, que no es nada, sino la modesta y secreta complejidad.[12]

This "secret complexity" is his understated rebellion against the more obvious "baroque" difficulties of modernist or imagist poetry. In "Browning resuelve ser poeta" Borges explains his plan of attack against overworked poetry:

> Como los alquimistas
> que buscaron la piedra filosofal

en el azogue fugitivo,
haré que las comunes palabras
—naipes marcados del tahur, moneda de la plebe—
rindan la magia que fue suya
cuando Thor era el numen y el estrépito,
el trueno y la plegaria.

Besides becoming the basis for this alchemistic transformation of simple words into sources of magic, common, everyday words give Borges' later work a pronounced "intimacy" as Jaime Alazraki has shown.[13] Because of the obvious personal connection which Borges feels for the things he writes about, his later poetry becomes what Maurice Blanchot calls the author's "journal," filled as it is with the writer's own "insignificant details."[14]

Even a casual reading of the poet's later collections quickly reveals the frequent repetition of what Borges often calls "habitual" details. This is done consciously, with Borges even forewarning the reader in the prologue to *El otro, el mismo* about "las previsibles monotonías, la repetición de palabras y tal vez de líneas enteras." The repetition, which is really a self-conscious exercise of "intertextuality," counteracts the ambiguousness of language by concentrating the reader's attention on the word within the text. As both Blanchot and Michael Riffaterre emphasize, repetition thus fulfills a poetic purpose, with the restated words themselves becoming images or symbols.[15] Borges confirms that even when dealing with familiar words he is using a form of image. In a recent interview he said, referring to Emerson, that "all words are metaphors—or fossil poetry, a fine metaphor itself."[16] Borges' remarks on the word "fossil" are significant, since the word leads us to think of rock-hard remnants of an original life form and suggests further that Borges' approach to poetic language might have an archeological cast. Indeed, much of his later work reflects a desire to go back to original linguistic models, very much the same desire that Derrida sees in Lévi-Strauss, "[une] nostalgie de l'origine, de l'innocence archaïque et naturelle." "Archaic and natural innocence" is precisely what Borges is looking for in his new approach to the image, as in the poem "Un sajón." Its third strophe virtually describes "fossil poetry."

Era tenaz. Obraron su fortuna
Remos, redes, arado, espada, escudo;

> La dura mano que guerreaba pudo
> Grabar con hierro una porfiada runa.

Fossils are often seen as hard outlines of original life forms preserved in stone, and that is exactly what runes are, namely sculpted outlines of the first writers' symbols. Even the act of carving them is seen as a firm and laborious process done by a "hard" hand, which engraves with an iron tool. And just as the carver must be "tenacious," so too must the symbol he carves persist with "stubbornness." As if to illustrate the durable word-as-image ideal derived from this process, the second line here is comprised only of five words—five things—which are personified into images by the introductory phrase, "they worked out his fate." This poem's final four strophes describe the original process of language formation which had the magical quality Borges is working toward in his own verse.

> Para cantar memorias o alabanzas
> Amonedaba laboriosos nombres;
> La guerra era el encuentro de los hombres
> Y también el encuentro de las lanzas.
>
> Su mundo era de magias en los mares,
> De reyes y de lobos y del hado
> Que no perdona y del horror sagrado
> Que hay en el corazón de los pinares.
>
> Traía las palabras esenciales
> De una lengua que el tiempo exaltaría
> A música de Shakespeare: noche y día,
> Agua, fuego, colores y metales.
>
> Hambre, sed, amargura, sueño, guerra,
> Muerte y los otros hábitos humanos;
> En arduos montes y en abiertos llanos,
> Sus hijos engendraron a Inglaterra. (*El otro*, 46)

Even for the purpose of singing, the archaic linguistic development is described here as a hard, solid "coining" operation; the coined word could well be seen, then, as a "moneda de hierro," the title of Borges' 1976 book. These laboriously fabricated words were used to symbolize the magical relationship which the Saxon had with his world. And, just as importantly, these are "essential words" describing "human habits," the words and the functions to which Borges wants to return through the "alchemy" he mentioned in the "Browning" poem. This recapturing of a magical experience explains the astonishment seen in the four-times-repeated "me asombra" that Borges expresses in connection with essential things in the poem "El ingenuo"; and those lines in turn recall this one from "El mar": "the astonishment that elemental things leave."

Borges makes explicit his desire to return to linguistic origins, to a *lenguaje del alba*, as he calls it, in "Al iniciar el estudio de la gramática anglosajona," from the same book.

> Símbolos de otros símbolos, variaciones
> Del futuro inglés o alemán me parecen estas palabras
> Que alguna vez fueron imágenes
> Y que un hombre usó para celebrar el mar o una espada;
> Mañana volverán a vivir,
> Mañana *fyr* no será *fire* sino esa suerte
> De dios domesticado y cambiante
> Que a nadie le está dado mirar sin un antiguo asombro. (*El otro*, 105)

Again it is the original word as metaphor (*símbolos de otros símbolos*) an image that Borges describes here, and that he wants to use in the same way in order to "compromise the future" (*mañana volverán a vivir*). The future effect will be, once again, a sense of astonishment which goes back to the original magical relationship—an *antiguo asombro*.

We see now that Borges' "secret complexity" lies in the words he uses—and in the people who read them. This "secret" even allows him to write a poem to the moon, a subject scorned during the ultraist period as being nothing but an outworn poetic cliché. He explains why he can now write about this essentially poetic topic.

> El secreto, a mi ver, está en usarla
> con humildad. Es la palabra *luna*.

In the next strophe he states that he does not dare spoil the moon "with a vain image"—an indictment of both Modernismo and Ultraism—explaining in the following verses that the word *luna* already provides sufficient "complexity."

> Sé que la luna o la palabra *luna*
> Es una letra que fue creada para
> La compleja escritura de esa rara
> Cosa que somos, numerosa y una. (*El otro*, 74)

The "secret complexity" already exists in the "complex script" of human experience. It lies in the multiple associations a word has gathered

over the centuries. Or, at an even deeper level of difficulty which requires ingenuousness, it involves stripping away the word's timeworn
complications in order to experience the original astonishment that fab-
ricators of language felt when they made their first metaphorical connections between words and objects.

Translations by T. Running

1. A rattling of dry seeds
   the broken letters of the names;
   we have scattered the names,
   we have dishonored the names.
   Ever since then I have been walking in search of the name.

   I raised with words and their shadows
   a walking house of reflections,
   a tower which walks, a construction of wind.
   Time and its combinations:
   years, the dead, syllables,
   different stories from the same account.
   A spiral of echoes, the poem
   is air which is sculpted and dissipates, a
   fleeting allegory of true names.
   At times the page breathes;
   the clusters of sounds and senses,
   in a magnetic rotation, connect and disperse
   on the page. (O. Paz, *Pasado en claro*, 1975)

2. Because here and now the word does not exist.
   Its identification only remains
   in the police files
   of man's history.
   Its sound is a clot in time.
   Its script is a palid diaphragm
   for the ill-fated tactics
   in the hall of memory. (Juarroz, *Poesía vertical*)

3. My obligation is the impure word,
   descendent of a concept and a sound;
   neither symbol, nor mirror, nor moan
   yours is the river which flees and which remains.

4. I have entrusted this writing to any man at all;
   it will never be what I want to say,
   it will be nothing but its reflection.

5.   Each thing
   Is infinite things. You are music,
   Firmaments, palaces, rivers, angels,
   Profound rose, unlimited, intimate,
   That the Lord will show to my dead eyes.

6. *The Naive Person*   (J. L. Borges)
   Each dawn (they tell us) fabricates marvels
   Capable of twisting the most stubborn fortune;
   There are human steps that have measured the moon
   And insomnia devastates years and miles.
   Public nightmares lie in wait in the blue
   And make the day gloomy. In the sphere there is
   Nothing that is not another or contrary thing, or nothing.
   Only the simple surprises disturb me.
   It amazes me that a key can open a door.
   It amazes me that my hand may be a certain thing.
   It amazes me that the Greek's
   Instantaneous Eleatic arrow does not reach the unreachable goal,
   It amazes me that the cruel sword can be beautiful,
   And that the rose can have the smell of a rose.

7. Like the alchemists
   who looked for the philosophers' stone
   in the fleeting mercury,
   I will make the common words
   —cards marked by the gambler, common coins—
   produce the magic that was theirs
   when Thor was divine and noisy,
   thunder and prayer.

8. He was tenacious. These things worked out his fate:
   Oars, nets, plow, sword, shield;
   The hard hand that fought was able
   To carve with iron a stubborn rune.

9. To sing of memories or praises
   He coined laborious names;
   War was the collision of people
   And also the clash of spears.

His world was one of magic on the seas,
Of kings and wolves and fate
That does not pardon and of the sacred horror
That lies in the heart of the pine groves.

He brought the essential words
Of a language that time would raise
Into Shakespeare's music: night and day,
Water, fire, colors and metals.

Hunger, thirst, bitterness, sleep, war,
Death and other human habits;
In arduous forests and in open plains,
His/Their children will produce England.

10. Symbols of other symbols, variations
Of the future English or German are these words
Which at one time were images
And which a man used to celebrate the sea or a sword;
Tomorrow they will live again,
Tomorrow *fyr* will not be *fire* but rather that kind
Of domesticated and changing God
Which nobody is allowed to see without an ancient astonishment.

11. The secret, in my view, is in using it
with humility. It is the word *moon*.

I know that the moon or the word *moon*
is an inscription that was created for
The complex script of that rare
Thing that we are, numerous and one.

NOTES

1. Jacques Derrida, *L'ecriture et la différence* (Paris: Editions du Seuil, 1967): 411.
2. Octavio Paz, *Pasado en claro* (Mexico: FCE, 1975): 230.
3. Robert Juárroz, *Poesía vertical* (Caracas: Monte Avila, 1976): 230.
4. Sylvia Molloy, "'Dios acecha en los intervalos': simulacro y causalidad textual en la ficción de Borges," *Revista Iberoamericana*, 100–101 (Julio-Diciembre, 1977): 381–398.
5. Jorge Luis Borges, *Historia de la noche* (Buenos Aires; Emecé, 1977): 139.
6. Jacques Derrida, *Positions* (Paris: Les editions de minuit, 1972): 40.
7. Jorge Luis Borges, *La moneda de oro* (Buenos Aires: Emecé, 1976): 73.
8. Jorge Luis Borges, *Elogio de la sombra* (Buenos Aires: Emecé, 1969): 16.
9. Roman Jakobson, *Ligüística, poética, tiempo* (Barcelona: Editorial Crítica, 1981): 97. My translation.
10. Jorge Luis Borges, *La cifra* (Madrid: Alianza tres, 1981): 47. The reference to archetypes here is not a casual one. In *La cifra* Borges repeatedly brings up the notion of a Pla-

tonic ideal; it seems obvious that he would like to extend the return to original linguistic symbols all the way back to an archetype.

11. Jorge Luis Borges, *La rosa profunda* (Buenos Aires: Emecé, 1975): 156.

12. Jorge Luis Borges, *El otro, el mismo* (Buenos Aires: Emecé, 1967): 10.

13. Jaime Alazraki, "Borges o el difícil oficio de la intimidad; reflexiones sobre su poesía más reciente," *Revista Iberoamericana* 100–101, 449–463.

14. Maurice Blanchot, *L'espace littéraire* (Paris: Gallimard, 1955): 20.

15. Blanchot, *L'espace littéraire*, 14. Michael Riffaterre. *Semiotics of Poetry* (Bloomington: Indiana University Press, 1978): 49.

16. Willis Barnstone, *Borges at Eighty* (Bloomington: Indiana University Press, 1981): 165.

BIBLIOGRAPHY

Alazraki, Jaime. "Borges o el difícil oficio de la intimidad: reflexiones sobre su poesía más reciente." *Revista Iberoamericana*. 100/101 (n.d.) 449–463.
Barnstone, Willis, ed. *Borges at Eighty: Conversations*. Bloomington: Indiana University Press, 1982.
Blanchot, Maurice. *L'espace littéraire*. Paris: Gallimard, 1955.
Borges, Jorge Luis. *Elogio de la sombra*. Buenos Aires: Emecé, 1969.
Borges, *El otro, el mismo*. Buenos Aires: Emecé, 1967.
Borges, *Historia de la noche*. Buenos Aires: Emecé, 1977.
Borges, *La cifra*. Madrid: Alianza tres, 1981.
Borges, *La moneda de oro*. Buenos Aires: Emecé, 1976.
Borges. *La rosa profunda*. Buenos Aires: Emecé, 1967.
Derrida, Jacques. *L'écriture et la différence*. Paris: Editions du Seuil, 1972.
Derrida. *Positions*. Paris: Les editions de minuit, 1972.
Jakobson, Roman. *Lingüística, poética, tiempo*. Barcelona: Editorial Crítica, 1981.
Juárroz, Roberto. *Poesía vertical*. Caracas: Monte Avila, 1976.
Molloy, Sylvia. "'Dios acecha en los intervalos': simulacro y causalidad textual en la ficción de Borges." *Revista Iberoamericana*. 100/101 (1977) 381–398.
Paz, Octavio. *Pasado en claro*. Mexico: FCE, 1975.

ARTURO ECHAVARRÍA FERRARI

From Expression to Allusion: Towards a Theory of Poetic Language in Borges[*]

In several youthful essays, Borges repeatedly pointed to the fact that poetry was forced to use a language consisting of words which, being in
everyday use and constituting common currency, was alien to its very
nature: the poet's intent to convey something personal and unique. Noting that there was no such thing as a "poetic language," he called for its
invention through the use of new combinations of words which would
transmit "unheard-of visions" of reality. This possibility was at the time
clearly grounded on two suppositions: that language is capable of reflecting the world in all its complexity, therefore being *expressive*; and
that the *expressive* capability of language is for all purposes limitless,
judging by all the possible word combinations that can be carried out.

The mature Borges thinks differently. Language is not *expressive* at all;
words are not images of reality and in fact can only be used to *mention* or
allude to, but not to *express* ("Alguna vez yo también busqué la expresión; ahora sé que mis dioses no me conceden más que la alusión o mención,"[1]), and therefore what can be said is limited. Taking these premises
as a point of departure, Borges goes on to structure a personal poetic
language using such everyday words as *río, noche, sombra,* or *sueño.* He
manages to do this through an extremely complex intertextual system

[*]This is a translated, abridged and revised version of the second chapter of my book
Lengua y Literatura de Borges (Barcelona: Ariel, 1983).

based on allusion, which, for the sake of clarity, may be spoken of as "external allusion" (allusion to the texts of other writers), and "internal allusion" (allusion to his own texts). This framework results in the enrichment and transmuting of the habitual meaning of "common" words in such a way that some of them (primarily *noche*, and *sombra*) become metaphors of a total conception of literature as a virtual world of *sombras* (shadows/images), which contains imbedded in it the *sombra* of the writer, which in turn can only be realized through the reader.

Such words as *noche*, *sombra*, and to a lesser extent *oro*, thus become the cornerstone of a personal poetic vocabulary which in turn projects a particular view of literature.

In the poem "Un lector" (*Elogio de la sombra*), Borges writes: "Mis noches están llenas de Virgilio." The verse is interwoven with others that allude to his growing blindness: "Cuando en mis ojos se borraron / las vanas apariencias queridas . . ."[2] Interpreted on a primary level, *mis noches* (my nights), alludes to the darkness which is insidiously invading the world of the poet-reader and transforming his "days" into "nights." But it might be asked if indeed these words refer only to the poet's blindness.

In "Invocación a Joyce" he writes:

> pero la memoria tiene sus talismanes,
> sus ecos de Virgilio,
> y así en las calles de la noche perduran
> tus infiernos espléndidos,
> tantas cadencias y metáforas tuyas,
> los oros de tu sombra. (p. 342)

The reader could very well ask if the metaphors of Joyce, *los oros de tu sombra* ("the golds of your shadow") can endure in *las calles de la noche* ("the streets of night"). What does *en las calles de la noche* really mean? In a poem written many years before, "La noche cíclica" (1940), after stating that the battle between Lapiths and Centaurs will again take place in the future, that the monster in the Labyrinth of Crete will once again wail "en la infinita Noche," the poet concludes with the following words:

> Vuelve la noche cóncava que descrifró Anaxágoras;
> Vuelve a mi carne humana la eternidad constante
> Y el recuerdo ¿el proyecto? de un poema incesante:
> "Lo supieron los arduos alumnos de Pitágoras . . ." (p. 177)

The last line, as has been noted frequently, is a quote of the first line of the poem. *La noche (night)*, it is insinuated, or *infinita noche* ("infinite night"), symbolizes memory as it registers myths which are received through literature, since to read—and to remember what has been read— is equivalent to the registering of images, and equivalent to dreaming. But at the same time in that *noche* Borges is trying to compose a poem, and *la noche* transforms itself metaphorically into a space peopled by his own dreams, a space in which a new myth arises. And yet, if the reader wishes to search so to speak, for the roots of *la noche* in the context of Borges' work, he must reach back to an essay written in the poet's youth, in the book *El tamaño de mi esperanza* (1925):

> . . . for any human being in the process of poeticizing, night is another thing. It is a simultaneous vision of earth and heaven, it is the celestial vault of the Romantics, it is a long-lasting and perfumed freshness, it is a spatial image not a concept, it is a showcase of images [*un mostradero de imágenes*].

Further on, he adds that writers have also contributed to the construction of *la noche*:

> Without my willing it, in my vision of night there is also the Virgilian *ibant obscuri sola sub nocte per umbram*.[3]

La noche then becomes a *mostradero de imágenes* ("a showcase of images"), and also a space in which Borges remembers the verses of other poets, or other people's words which in turn project upon the reader's fantasy, other images. But as has been noted, Borges' poetic thought deepens and becomes further refined with age. Years later, in the "Prologue" to *El hacedor* (1960), just before invoking *la sombra de Lugones* (his "ghost"/"shade") to whom he will "deliver" the book, he observes in the great hall of the library, people reading, *soñando* ("dreaming"), and suddenly recalls that same line by Virgil, "*ibant obscuri sola sub nocte per umbras*," like that, *umbras* (*sombras*). Borges seems to be alluding to the *Aeneid* (VI), where the verse is found, where it serves as the preamble to Aeneas' descent into Hades, who himself as a "*sombra*" ("shade"), will come face to face with other "*sombras*" (Charon and the centuars, for example), which are in effect the projections of words belonging to men of the past. This reading seems to be confirmed by a poem written even later, "El desterrado" ("The Exile," 1975), in which Ulysses substitutes for his literary precursor, Aeneas:

En el confín del orbe yo, Ulises,
Descendí a la Casa de Hades
Y vi la sombra del tebano Tiresías
Que desligó el amor de las serpientes,
Y la sombra de Heracles
Que mata sombras de leones en la pradera . . . (p. 449)

Sombras (shadows/images) face and interact with other *sombras* (images), which in turn are projections of the words of other poets, who today are nothing but mere words themselves, mere names. Thus, in another poem published in 1975, *noche* and *sombra* are unequivocally connected with each other, and these *sombras* are made to encompass, in very explicit terms, their "creators." When, in the poem "A un ruiseñor" ("To a Nightingale") Borges invokes *"el ruiseñor de la sombra"* ("the nightingale of shadows" or of night), he invokes simultaneously those who *named* him in different poetic contexts. *"El ruiseñor de la sombra,"* refers to the dreamt nightingale, the image by which sheer and marvelous chance becomes also a "bird of darkness [shadows]," and is meant to include Shakespeare, Keats, Heine, Virgil, and especially the Persian poets who constructed a highly complex mystical literature around this symbol:

¿En qué noche secreta de Inglaterra
O del constante Rhin incalculable,
Perdida entre las noches de mis noches,
A mi ignorante oído habrá llegado
Tu voz cargada de mitologías,
Ruiseñor de Virgilio y de los persas? (p. 426)

In *la noche,* the night of Borges, the poet where the song of that nocturnal bird materializes, other *noches* and other songs are included such as the songs of Shakespeare, of Keats, of Heine, of Virgil and the Persians. Songs which reciprocally include other songs, that of the nightingale itself and those of the poets, all materialize under the benevolent protection of a truly vast and multiple and *unánime* (unanimous) *noche*.

It would be very hard indeed to trace and explain with a semblance of precision all the simultaneous referents of the word *noche*. Certain words, in the context of Borges' mature poetry, acquire, as has been noted, through his own poems—and sometimes through his essays and stories—a multiplicity of meanings which endow them with a power to hallucinate. The words *mis noches* in the context of "mis noches están llenas de Virgilio . . ." may have then, as simultaneous referents: Borges' blindness, that space in which his poetic images arise (and thus the presence of Virgil in his poetry); the images (*sombras*) of Virgil's words that keep echoing in his memory; and finally, the name of *Virgil*, which is nothing more than a composition of letters, a word that projects a *sombra*, a "shade" of Virgil himself. *Joyce* is also a word, a *sombra* whose existence is due to the multiple power he managed to instill in words, metaphors with the power to hallucinate, *los oros de su sombra* (golds of his shadow or shade).

In *Sub nocte*, Virgil and Joyce are both *sombras*. *Sombras* that project other *sombras*, through words, and poetic images. Thus, upon rereading the title of the book which is perhaps Borges' greatest collection of poems, we begin to acknowledge the astounding truth. *Elogio de la sombra* can be read as praise of his growing blindness, but simultaneously it is praise for poets who endure in their work through the "magical" virtue of words, praise for the night in which poems come forth, praise for the power of words to project images in the minds of the readers, praise, in sum, of the power of language, and of poetry and of immortality.[4] Throughout the book, it may be noticed that in many of the poems Borges either expressly mentions the word *sombra* (shadow) or creates the *sombras* through the power of his own words.

But of all those poems which evoke *sombras* (shades or ghosts) of writers such as Joyce, López Merino, or Ricardo Güiraldes, just to mention a few, none is more eloquent than the one which bears the title "A cierta sombra, 1940" ("To a certain shade [ghost], 1940"). In this poem, Borges addresses De Quincey, the *sombra* alluded to:

> Que nos salven ahora las indescifrables arquitecturas
> que dieron horror a tu sueño.
> Hermano de la noche, bebedor de opio,
> padre de sinuosos períodos que ya son laberintos y torres,
> padre de las palabras que no se olvidan . . . (p. 328)

It is important to note that in the last two lines, one proceeds from De Quincey (*sombra*/shade) to the *indescifrables arquitecturas* ("indecipherable structures") of his dream, that is, the images conceived in creative trance (*sombras*/shadows), and from there, through language, to the images (*sombras*) which these words project in the mind of the reader: "padre de sinuosos períodos que ya son laberintos y torres / padre de las palabras que no se olvidan . . ."

Other poems in the *Elogio* reveal, through a skillful and lucid use of language, that Borges "creates" with the actual cooperation of the reader the *sombra* (shadow/image) through words. In the poem "The Unending Gift," the *I* that writes manages, as the poem is being read, to bring forth the existence of a painting that a painter friend named Jorge Larco promised him but was never able to deliver:

> Ahora, en New England, sé que ha muerto . . .
>   Pensé en el hombre y en el cuadro
>   perdidos . . .
> Pensé después: si estuviera ahí, sería con
>   el tiempo una cosa más, una de las va-
>   nidades o hábitos de la casa; ahora es
>   ilimitada, incesante, capaz de cualquier
>   forma y cualquier color y no atada a
>   ninguno.
> Existe de algún modo. Vivirá y crecerá como una
>   música y estará conmigo hasta el fin . . . (p. 321)

The painting exists through Borges' imaginative power, through the "magic" of his own words. Moreover, the deliberate ambiguity used to describe the picture itself ("capaz de cualquier forma y cualquier color") reflects, in the reader's imagination, an object which conforms to his preferences and wishes, and that, in truth, will vary each time the poem is read. The painting not only exists but, as a function of a multitude of readers, is and will be, in form and color, infinite.

The fact that Borges is able to create *sombras* (shadow/images) through words—Jorge Larco's "picture," for example—*sombras* which, in a first instance, belong only to his imaginative powers, implies that the poet impresses in these *sombras* a portion of time as he experiences it, a portion of his own identity as a writer. In the poem "Heráclito," where the poet states that he is *"hecho . . . de tiempo"* ("made up of time"), he concludes: *"Acaso el manantial está en mí. / Acaso de mi sombra / surgen, fatales e ilusorios, los días"* ("Maybe the source is in me. / Maybe out of my shade/the days arise, relentless and unreal").

Thus, if time constitutes Borges, Borges the poet reconstitutes time in his works through language. And yet, in such diverse poems as "El reloj de arena" ("The Hourglass") and "El alquimista" ("The Alche-mist")—whose analysis cannot be deliberated here—the poet speaks of the impossibility of finding *"el oro aquel que matará la Muerte"* ("that gold that will kill Death"). But this is not entirely so. The contest with time—the subject of these as so many other of his poems—is in itself a way of capturing it. The will of the poet displayed as he tries to modify language, to transmute and enrich the meanings of words, transfigures him, in the end, into a triumphant alchemist. This process is clearly alluded to in a recent poem, "Browning decide ser poeta" (1975):

> Como los alquimistas
> que buscaron la piedra filosofal
> en el azogue fugitivo,
> haré que las comunes palabras
> —naipes marcados del tahur, moneda de la plebe—
> rindan la magia que fue suya
> cuando Thor era el numen y el estrépito,
> el trueno y la plegaria. . . (p. 418)

In what is perhaps one of his most extraordinary poems, "Una rosa y Milton," Borges willingly becomes the alchemist. Mingling what has been read (past literature) with what he literally imagines, the poet tries to inscribe his own poetic time in a word which stands for an image of the rose, an image that he wills unique and personal since the rose, and the word "rose," in the context of the poem, initially exists only in his own mind:

> De las generaciones de las rosas
> Que en el fondo del tiempo se han perdido
> Quiero que una se salve del olvido,
> Una sin marca o signo entre las cosas
> Que fueron. El destino me depara
> Este don de nombrar por vez primera
> Esa flor silenciosa, la postrera
> Rosa que Milton acercó a su cara,
> Sin verla. Oh tú, bermeja o amarilla
> O blanca rosa de un jardín borrado,
> Deja mágicamente tu pasado
> Inmemorial y en este verso brilla,
> Oro, sangre o marfil o tenebrosa,
> Como en sus manos, invisible rosa. (p. 207)

The flower is a *sombra* (shadow) before the dead eyes of Milton, a *sombra* (shadow/image) in Borges' fantasy, and through the word *rosa*, a *sombra* in our imagination, a *sombra* (shadow/image) inextricably tied to *la noche* (the night), to the imaginative spaces in which the poet traced it. Moreover, the mere fact that he invokes it in a poetic context such as this, constitutes Borges' rose in such a way that we are bound to find imbedded in it the roses of Dante, of Ronsard, of Marino, of the Persian poets. *La tenebrosa flor* (the shadowy flower), moreover,—like Jorge Larco's picture—shall be archetypal and infinite, since it is neither tied to a specific color or form. Borges' time, and that of his precursors, flows and changes with the time of the reader through *sombras*, through words.

But in order for this to happen, as we have just pointed out, writing must be transformed into reading, his dreams must be re-dreamt, our *sombras* (shadows) must somehow reflect his *sombra* and his *sombras*. In a poem, "La moneda de hierro," it is so stated:

> En la sombra del otro buscamos nuestra sombra;
> En el cristal del otro, nuestro cristal recíproco. (p. 501)

Reading, thus, becomes the process through which we see literally "through a glass darkly." Without this mutual reflection, without the interaction of writing and reading, everything will vanish, as everything vanishes in that unstable world conceived by Berkeley once the perceiver disappears. In the poem "Historia de la noche" (1977), Borges once again alludes, in a deliberately ambiguous way, to the power of recreation inherent in the reader, whose perception is the only guarantor of the existence of that evanescent world of letters. The poem sets out to write a history of "night," from the very beginning when it is a univocal name which denotes a period of darkness to the point when, through a complex process of literary elaboration (that of Virgil, Pascal, Fray Luis de León, among others), it becomes a symbol which has multiple and simultaneous designations:

> A lo largo de sus generaciones
> los hombre erigieron la noche.
> En el principio era la ceguera y el sueño
> y espinas que laceran el pie desnudo
> y temor de los lobos.
> Nunca sabremos quien forjó la palabra

para el intervalo de sombra
que divide los crepúsculos;
nunca sabremos en qué siglo fue cifra
del espacio de estrellas.
Otros engendraron el mito.
La hicieron madre de las Parcas tranquilas
. . . .
Doce casas le dieron los Caldeos;
infinitos mundos, el Pórtico.
Hexámetros latinos la modelaron
y el terror de Pascal.
Luis de León vio en ella la patria
de su alma estremecida.
Ahora la sentimos inagotable
como un antiguo vino
y nadie puede contemplarla sin vértigo
y el tiempo la ha cargado de eternidad.

But, the poet hastens to add, neither a night that one can observe directly, nor, even less so, that which time has *cargado de eternidad* ("burdened with eternity") and whose nature is indeed virtual, would possess any reality at all if it was not perceived. Thinking of the *inagotable noche* (unfathomable night), he concludes:

Y pensar que no existiría
sin esos tenues instrumentos, los ojos.[5]

Without the reader, then, everything will vanish and dissolve in forgetfulness. In the poem "Ariosto y los árabes," Borges regrets that the *Orlando Furioso* is a dream that nobody dreams any longer:

Por islámicas artes reducido
A simple erudición, a mera historia,
Está solo soñándose. (La gloria
Es una de las formas del olvido).
Por el cristal ya pálido la incierta
Luz de una tarde más toca el volumen
Y otra vez arden y otra vez se consumen
Los oros que envanecen la cubierta . . . (p. 148)

In the melancholy dusk in the poem, the word *oro* acquires a new designation. Los oros (the golds) here represent the engraved title and the name of the author on the cover. It is not through these visible "golds" that Borges the poet would like to remain in the world, but rather through *los oros invisibles* (the invisible golds), his metaphors, intimate time transcribed in words.

Borges has apparently accomplished what he originally set out to do many years before. He has managed to say something unique and personal, not by expressing, but by *naming* and above all, *alluding to* (*mención y alusión*). *Padre de las palabras que no se olvidan* (creator of unforgettable words), Borges calls his *hermano de la noche* (brother of the night), the *sombra* of De Quincey. And like De Quincey, he would like to continue existing as a *sombra* (shadow/shade/ghost) who projects other *sombras* (images) in the halls of memory; he would wish to endure by *"el oro de los tigres,"* *los que no están en el verso* ("the gold of the tigers," those which are absent from the verse), like Virgil and Joyce, by "los oros de *su* sombra," by the richness and diversity with which he endowed words that, belonging to everyone or to no one, he has definitely made his.

NOTES

1. Jorge Luis Borges, *Antología personal* (Buenos Aires: Sur, 1966): 8.
2. Jorge Luis Borges, *Obra poética* (Buenos Aires: Emecé, 1977): 353. Further quotes will pertain to this edition and the page number will be included in parentheses in the text.
3. Jorge Luis Borges, *El tamaño de mi esperanza* (Buenos Aires: Proa, 1926): 111–12.
4. Guillermo Sucre, in an article which deals mainly with the *Elogio de la sombra*, also sees in the title of the book a "variado símbolo" (multiple symbol) Sucre, "Borges: el elogio de la sombra" in *Revista Iberoamericana*, vol. XXXVI, No. 72, julio-agosto, 1970, reprinted in Jaime Alazraki (editor), *Jorge Luis Borges. El escritor y la crítica* (Madrid: Taurus, 1976): 106. If, on the one hand, I find myself in agreement with Professor Sucre when he notes that Borges' *persona* is "creada e inventada por su obra" ("created and invented by his own literary work"), I differ as to the implications of this concept. My reading varies from Sucre's, for example, with respect to what I consider the "central" meaning of the word *sombra* (shadow)—which Sucre reads as referring primarily to death and dispossession—, and also with respect to the ways the writer uses language to create and project that literary *persona* in the mind of the reader. *Sombra* (shadow), as will be noted above, has indeed multiple meanings, but these meanings point to some central aspects of a theory of literature.
It is interesting to note, in passing, that Borges' concept of *sombras* as images registered in the mind of the reader is very similar to that of Coleridge when he defines "poetic faith." In the writing of poetry, he strives for ". . . a semblance of truth sufficient to procure for these *shadows of the imagination* that willing suspension of disbelief for the moment which constitutes poetic faith." S. T. Coleridge, *Biographia Literaria* ed. George Watson (London: J. M. Dent and Sons, 1965): 168–9. (Emphasis mine.)
5. Jorge Luis Borges, *Historia de la noche* (Buenos Aires: Emecé, 1977): 135–6.

BIBLIOGRAPHY

Alazraki, Jaime, ed. *Jorge Luis Borges. El escritor y la crítica*. Madrid: Taurus, 1976.

Borges, Jorge Luis. *Antología personal*. Buenos Aires: Sur, 1966.

Borges, *El tamaño de mi esperanza*. Buenos Aires: Proa, 1926.

Borges, *Historia de la noche*. Buenos Aires: Emecé, 1977.

Borges, *Obra poética*. Buenos Aires: Emecé, 1977.

Coleridge, Samuel T. *Biographia Literaria*. Edited by George Watson. London: J. M. Dent and Sons, 1965.

Sucre, Guillermo. "Borges: el elogio de la sombra." *Revista Iberoamericana*, 72 (1970).

JOSÉ MIGUEL OVIEDO

Borges: The Poet According to His Prologues

Borges' readers will have noticed that nearly every book he has written has been accompanied, at some moment in its published history, by a prologue which fulfills more important functions than those usually attributed to these preliminary texts. In the case of his poetic works, these functions are much more precise and revealing than those in other collections, thus meriting particular attention.

His *Obras Completas*[1] of 1974 brings together sixteen books of poems, essays and fiction, thirteen of which are preceded by prologues. The other three (*El aleph, Otras inquisiciones, El hacedor*) don't have, strictly speaking, prologues (although *El hacedor* presents us with a dedication "A Leopoldo Lugones" which almost constitutes a prologue); however, all three do have epilogues and one (*El aleph*) includes a postscript to the epilogue. There is, it seems, in Borges, a very personal tendency to present his works with preliminary or concluding texts, as if establishing between them and the body of the book a textual dialogue—a verbal sequence which attempts to close the circle of text, author's voice and reader's response. The *Obras Completas* also closes with a general epilogue, a brief autobiography disguised as a note in the apocryphal *Enciclopedia Sudamericana*, "to be published in Santiago de Chile in the year 2074" (*OC*, 1143). In that ideal autobiography the author writes: "The renown that Borges enjoyed during his lifetime, documented by an accumulation of studies and polemics, continues to amaze us today. Yet he was the first to be surprised at his fame, always fearful that he would be declared an impostor or a bungler, or a mixture of both" (*OC*, 1144).

This is how Borges wishes to be remembered: as a humble practitioner of literature, diligent but not completely satisfied with his merits, or rather, disdainful of them.

Of course, a number of these prologues were written later than the works they accompany, the majority in 1969. This was a key year in the life of the author: he turned seventy years old; for the first time he reissued his three earliest books of poetry in independent volumes;[2] and also published a new book of poems, *Elogio de la sombra*, of which he said: "This . . . is my fifth book of verse. It is reasonable to assume that it won't be better or worse than the others. To the mirrors, labyrinths, and swords, which my patient reader already expects, two new themes have been added: old age and ethics" (*OC*, 975). It is this confrontation between his earlier and his present poetry which seems to have awakened in him the need to write new introductory texts. In them one sees Borges in the process of rereading the poet that he was, who in turn announces the poet that he is. In this way, his older collections can be read as parts of a fluid process unified in the memory of the man who wrote the poems and these new texts. In a poem from *Elogio*, evidently written a year before, titled "Junio, 1968," Borges gives us a clue to his personal and intellectual views which preside over his production from that time forward. The poem speaks of an afternoon during which a man reviews the books in his library:

> On a golden evening,
> or in a quietness whose symbol
> might be a golden evening,
> a man sets up his books
> on the waiting shelves,
> feeling the parchment and leather and cloth
> and the satisfaction given by
> the anticipation of a habit
> and the establishment of order.

And later, remembering his models (Stevenson, Andrew Lang, Alfonso Reyes, and Virgil) he concludes:

> (To arrange a library is to practice,
> in a quiet and modest way,
> the art of criticism.)

The man, who is blind,
knows that he can no longer read
the handsome volumes he handles
and that they will not help him write
the book which in the end might justify him,
but on the evening that perhaps is golden
he smiles at his strange fate
and feels that special happiness
which comes from things we know and love. (*OC*, 998)

Those "handsome volumes," those "things we know and love," are his own early books which the now older apprentice poet would like to have written differently, although these books, mysteriously, explain his recent poetry.[3] The justification of which the poem speaks should not be understood as only referring to the critical reaction that his poetic work produces, but also to his own reaction, as author and reader of his own books, books which dictate "the establishment of order." This order is indicated by the prologues.

It is interesting to observe that, in at least two instances, Borges has rejected the prologues which appeared in the original editions and has written new ones. Such is the case with "A quien leyere" from *Fervor de Buenos Aires* (1923) and "Al tal vez lector" from *Luna de enfrente* (1925). Today we would barely recognize Borges in them: they are arrogant defenses of a literary program, which at that time combined Expressionist traces, Ultraist novelties and a certain "criollista" belligerence.[4] They are written in that style—sharp, emphatic, bellicose, and extremely conceptual—which he refers to as his "baroque period," perhaps to indicate his literary pretension and his worship of new form.

Not only does Borges consign these original prologues forever to oblivion and replace them with others more in line with his mature thoughts, but he subjects the books themselves to substantial changes, suppressions and substitutions—while assuring us that he has made only indispensable corrections, not wanting to make new books of them.[5] Besides the fact that a writer is entirely free to suppress or revise his *juvenilia* as he sees fit, we have here a model case with which to examine the masterful exercise of a fundamental aspect of Borges' art: the rereading of himself, the first step towards self-criticism and rewriting. In the new prologue (1969) to *Fervor de Buenos Aires* he indicates that the very process of correction has taught him something: in spite of the book's "baroque excesses," the "harsh notes," the "sentimentalities and vagaries," "I feel that the youth who wrote it in 1923 was already, essentially, the man who now resigns himself and corrects" (*OC*, 13).

In other prologues, that notion of an identity which blankets the differences yields to a certain sense of distance with respect to the accompanying works: the author doesn't recognize himself in them. In *Luna de enfrente*, for example, the final line of the prologue summarizes: "I have changed this book very little. It is no longer mine" (*OC* 55). Yet it is surprising to find this same distance in the epilogue of a much more recent book like *El hacedor* (1960) where he excuses himself for "the essential monotony of this miscellany" due to the fact that it contains "previous pieces which I haven't dared to alter, because I wrote them with a different concept of literature" (*OC*, 854). The task of rereading is infinite if it searches for the unity of the process; it is useless if it seeks unattainable perfection: between these two poles moves Borges, the prologue writer. Publishing one's past works usually puts an end to a process which otherwise would be endless; it is not strange therefore that Borges uses a quotation from his beloved Alfonso Reyes as an epigraph to *Discusión*: "This is the trouble with not publishing one's works: a lifetime is spent in reworking them" (*OC*, 175).

Actually, the reader discovers in the prologues to his lyrical work, that Borges, always so unwilling to give aesthetic definitions or to formulate literary creeds, has been sketching, subtly, a poetic theory and ethics of the creative act. This theory begins with the criticism of the poet he once was. That young poet of the 1920s—remembers the mature Borges in his later prologues—wanted, above all, to be two things: *modern* and *Argentine*. The novelty of the form, that sensational manner of capturing the instantaneous, dominant in the spirit of the era, coupled with the proud affirmation of his own culture (the Argentina that Borges knew and which was reduced to a particular Buenos Aires, to certain neighborhoods which generated a domestic mythology), are dominant stimuli in the poetic inspiration of those first three books. With them, Borges wanted to create a new poetic tradition, specifically Argentine, which although it may have echoed notes of European origin (avant-garde, idealist philosophy, German metaphysical speculations, etc.), was a challenge to tradition and the Hispanic legacy, a gesture of radical independence. The argentinisms and neologisms of his early poetry (which have been erased or revised in later editions) were a defiant sign of his literary stance of that decade: a verbal schism that gave him the feeling of beginning anew, of being original. Borges has repeatedly abjured this pretension. In the new prologue to *Luna de enfrente*, he suggests that his modernity doesn't affect him, or rather, that it exists in spite of him, in the same way that he is Argentine:

> To be modern is to be contemporary, current; we are all fatally modern. . . . There is no art that is not of its age. . . . We know nothing of the literature of Carthage, which was presumably rich, except that it could not include a book like Flaubert's. Forgetting that I already was one, I also wanted to be an Argentine. (*OC*, 55)

For similar reasons, he distrusts all aesthetics, including his own, because "they are no more than useless abstractions" (*OC*, 975). But in the prologue to *El otro, el mismo* he points out an appropriate kinship for his mature poetry, and converts his first avant-garde affinities into echoes of another aesthetic direction: "On rereading these pages, I have felt closer to *Modernismo* than the subsequent sects engendered by its corruption, sects which now deny it" (*OC*, 858). What is surprising is that in the original prologue to *Fervor* . . . he had attacked Rubén Darío's rhetoric and had praised Carriego's *criollista* simplicity;[6] now he abjures those early excesses, accepting the linguistic ideals of *Modernismo*:

> I am doubtful of literary schools, which I judge didactic stratagems to simplify that which they teach, but if I were obliged to declare the origin of my verses I would say it is *Modernismo*, that great freedom, which renewed the many literatures whose common language is Spanish and which reached, certainly, to Spain. (*OC*, 1081)

His identification with Lugones is both the vehicle and the result of that process of encounter with his true poetic self, which is, for Borges, one of the higher rewards of writing poetry. In fact, in a recent introduction to an anthology of Lugones' work, Borges writes a very revealing passage on his relationship with the great Argentine poet, and clarifies the context in which his own work belongs:

> Lugones was a simple man, a man of elemental passions and convictions, who forged and manipulated a complex style. Two great Spanish American poets, Ramón López Velarde and Ezequiel Martínez Estrada, inherited and elaborated his style which is now more their own than his.[7]

It is an almost irresistible temptation to add Borges' name to that list of heirs, precisely because the conclusion of the paragraph reiterates one of his most deeply rooted ideas: an author can recognize himself better in the books of others. Styles and literary modes are transitive and creation is nothing more than the patient exercise of possibilities which another author discovered and did not exhaust. To find one's own identity and know what it is one writes, is a slow process which offers more surprises than certainties. For Borges, this exercise has taken the form of a progressive refinement—stylistic as well as conceptual—which in his latest poetic works might seem extreme. His poetry has narrowed its limits, his motifs have been reduced to a minimal group which restructures itself in predictable forms; his diction has become increasingly oral—an utterance rather than a written text. Upon rereading Borges' poetic work in chronological order, one has the impression of retracing one's steps on a road, of passing places already explored but now devoid of detail, more austere in the images they evoke. It might seem a loss, yet is actually a secret gain, which charges each word, no matter how simple they may be, with a more intense and deeper significance. The author confesses:

> A writer's fate is strange. At first he is baroque, vainly baroque, as the years pass, he can achieve, if the stars favor him, not simplicity, which is nothing, but modest and secret complexity. (*OC*, 858)

In his prologues, Borges discreetly indicates the direction in which his idea of poetry has been evolving. Not only readers and critics have associated his work with "intellectual poetry." He himself has maintained that of the two basic poetic attitudes (the lyrical and the intellectual), unfortunately only the latter is visible in the poems of *Cuaderno de San Martín*: "I now believe that in all poets which deserve to be reread, both elements co-exist . . . In reference to the exercises of this volume, it is evident that they aspire to the second category" (*OC*, 79).

The reason is clear: "the baroque is intellectual" (*OC*, 39) because it is an aesthetic of distortion and exaggeration that is close to the grotesque. Rejecting Poe's theory that "writing a poem is an operation of the intelligence" (*OC*, 1021), and refuting Walter Pater who sees poetry as "an abstract system of symbols" subjected to the musical necessities of language (*OC*, 858), Borges subscribes to a theory of the essentially magic character of the poetic word. He sees the poem as an instrument which can restore to us that mysterious vibration of the original word, a word which can stay the tide of time and defeat death:

> The root of language is irrational and of a magical character. Poetry wants to return to that ancient magic. . . . Poetry is a mysterious chess, whose board and pieces change as if in a dream and over which I will yet lean after I have died. (*OC*, 1022)

Following this line of thought, Borges will say something which may seem quite strange to the readers of his poetry: "As for the rest, literature is nothing more than a directed dream" (*OC*, 1022). It's not that he is subscribing, of course, to the Surrealist theory of automatic writing, but underscoring the idea that the writer is only the partial author of a work, and that he is manipulating and adapting forces largely beyond his control; just as the reader responds to these stimuli with his own intuitions and affective preferences, dictated by the dominant ideas of the age. Poetic communication is a spark ignited by the friction and coincidence of many elements only implied in the text. The importance lies in the protagonists' participation in that communication, not in the identity of the actors. At the beginning of *Fervor . . .* there is a note "A quien leyere":

> If the pages of this book include a felicitous line, may the reader forgive me the discourtesy of having usurped the line first . . . the circumstances which make you the reader of these exercises, and me the writer, are trivial and fortuitious. (*OC*, 15)

The prologue to *Elogio de la sombra* (1969), contains statements that we now find in critics who stress the intersubjective nature of the text: "A volume in itself is not an aesthetic act . . . the aesthetic act can only occur when it is written or read" (*OC*, 975). As a result, Borges declares that he is without an aesthetic theory. He presents himself in the prologues as an author who has, with time, learned a repertory of "artifices," "skills" and "habits" which attempt to diminish in the reader the monotonous effect of "my writing routine" (*OC*, 1081) and to give him an illusion of novelty. For Borges, poetry *pretends* to say for the first time (sometimes successfully) that which the author himself or others have said before; the poetic act consists of borrowing voices until one finds the voice which fits, and then, of projecting that unique voice into the ear of the reader. Borges refers to this process in the prologue to *El otro, el mismo*. He tells a significant anecdote from his avant-garde years, during which he was associated with the Peruvian poet Alberto Hidalgo, then an exile in Buenos Aires:

> In his Victoria street dining room, the writer—if we can call him that—Alberto Hidalgo commented on my habit of writing the same page twice, with minimal variation. I regret having answered him that he was no less binary, except that in his particular case the first version belonged to someone else. Such were the deplorable manners of that period, which many view with nostalgia. We all wanted to be heroes of trivial anecdotes . . . What is strange and what I can't understand, is that my second versions, like distant and involuntary echoes, are usually inferior to the originals. (*OC*, 857)

This explains the ethical justification which always accompanies Borges' comments on his own poetry. One can understand that he is "resigned to being Borges," his timid hope that some of the lines of his books do not "dishonor" him, his belief that "beauty is common to all" and that anyone can attain it, as simple manifestations of his intellectual modesty. But if one perceives the very delicate irony of these formulas, one could interpret them another way: as a device to diminish the reader's expectations, inducing him to read the work as Borges himself has read it; seeing, in its totality, not the differences, but the similarities which blend the younger poet, the mature poet and the older artist beneath the mask of one literary *persona*. That is, he has come to conceive the poetry as a destiny, through which he discovered himself and realized his identity, found his true models, and learned his possibilities and limitations. Poetry is an intimate revelation, which the poet tries to share with the reader, attempting to create for him the sensation of a precise act that can "touch us physically, like the proximity of the sea."[8] That essential unity of his search, in which even the detours are a way of confirming the main path, has never been synthesized with greater beauty and precision than in the impeccable final phrase of his new prologue to *Fervor de Buenos Aires*: "At that time, I sought out the afternoons, the suburbs and misfortune; now I seek the mornings, downtown and serenity" (*OC*, 13).

More may be said about Borges' prologues. Their abundance and their specific function within his work require further explanation. I believe that they are a key part of his literary art. Few authors have appended more than he, not only prologues, but as we have seen, epilogues, postscripts, inscriptions, notes, and peripheral texts (sometimes apocryphal) to his poems, stories and essays. Some of his main texts can, and even should, be read as variations of others, a relationship which pertains to "Hombre de la esquina rosada" and "Historia de Rosendo Juárez" on the one hand, and to "Tlön, Uqbar, Orbis Tertius" and "Utopía de un hombre cansado" on the other, and yet again to the two "Poemas de los dones." His is the art of a scholiast, of systematic commentary on his own texts, whose web of quotations, images and symbols tends to be represented as a homogenous whole, continuous in time. It is also an art of fragments, palimpsests and textual superimposing, complicated by texts which include falsely attributed quotations and references to real people in fantastic contexts. They are versatile and porous texts, sometimes interchangeable and ambiguous through their lack of generic definition: stories which are false bibliographical notes, essays with the characteristics of poems, poems (like "El Golem") which refer us to specific stories, new versions, parodies, etc. This singular quality of Borgesian texts is certainly associated with their brevity and the cumulative effect that they have on the memory of the reader. Wolfgang Iser has pointed out that while we can perceive certain aesthetic objects in their totality, a literary text is an exception; it can only be grasped "by way of different consecutive phases of reading." That is, in the act of reading "there is a moving viewpoint which travels along *inside* that which it has to apprehend."[9] To read is a game of expectations and memory which do not lie exactly within the text, nor in the imagination of the reader, but in the point of encounter between the two: it is an ideal projection which momentarily fuses their respective realities. Literature is an open experience, not a given product. Borges' texts intensely stimulate that fusion, proposing to the reader to see in them moments of a recognizable and coherent process, while at the same time perceiving the variation which each fragment introduces into the fabric of the work as a whole. On being activated by the reader's performance, these texts are organized into a larger unity which lends them greater significance and heightens the pleasurable effect: they are pieces of a rigorous design whose arrangement we believe to be our own.

Borges has often defended the virtues of literary brevity. These lines from the prologue to *Ficciones* are famous:

> To compose vast texts is a laborious and diminishing extravagance; that of expounding in five hundred pages an idea whose perfect oral exposition takes a

few minutes. A better device is to pretend that those books already exist and to offer a summary, a commentary. (*OC*, 429)

His disdain for the novel as a genre is also well known, an opinion which allows a few exceptions: Cervantes, Stevenson, Conrad. This disdain may be influenced by the ideas of Ortega y Gasset, who called the novel a "sluggish genre."[10] But not only the story teller loves concise expression; the essayist and the poet also cultivate brevity, so that the exposition and images are concentrated in precise focal points. The ridiculous and pedant figure of Carlos Argentino Daneri of "El Aleph," who intends to write a poem which coincides with the universe, transforming each object into words, is an exact opposite of the author. Borges proceeds through concretion and violent syntheses which fuse the remote and the immediate, the immense and the infinitesimal. In the epilogue to his *Obras Completas*, the author explains his own literary taste while speaking in the third person:

> He enjoyed stories, a trait which reminds us of Poe's dictum *There is no such a thing as a long poem*, which confirms the poetic customs of certain oriental nations. (*OC*, 1143)

Borges' books tend to be rhapsodic; the unity of his work is not in them, but rather in the texts they contain and in the dialogue between those texts, overflowing the lax and conventional limits of each collection. Asking the reader's indulgence for that lack of formal unity, Borges has repeatedly said that his books are the fruit of "my resignation, my carelessness, and sometimes, my passion" (*OC*, 857). Among his own books those which please him most are the miscellanies, his *Antologías Personales*, books composed of other books, or *El hacedor*, which he calls "*silva de varia lección*" (*OC*, 854). As befits books of brief poems, the prologues are also brief, written in a tone which attempts to be a faithful *mimesis* of the poetic voice. The prologues are not added to the book: they are part of it, an important part because they contain, as we have seen, Borges' poetics, as well as a guide for the reader and an intellectual and moral self-portrait. In that sense, they tend to represent one of the most creative moments of the book: they invent, for the texts which they precede, a synchronic coherence, and connect them diachronically with the previous texts, claiming the reader's attention for the *system* that they compose. Borges surely recalls that once, in antiquity, one of the main purposes of the prologue was the *captatio benevolentiae* of the reader through simplicity and brevity.[11] We have here an art and a strategy that Borges, the poet, developed after the publication of his first three books of poems. The difficult style of the original prologues which Borges has eliminated from his *Obras Completas* is impossible to translate into English because it is a pretentious language of his own invention, to prove that Spanish could also be written in another fashion:

> Suelen ser las prefaciones de antes una componenda mal pergeñada, entre la primordial jactancia de quien ampara obra que es propiamente facción suya y la humildad que aconsejan la mundología y el uso. (*Fervor*, 5)

Borges has used the prologue with another intention also: to remind us that prologues are a genre of great literary dignity, whose virtues we have today forgotten or misused due to intellectual laziness. Fortunately, we also know precisely what Borges thinks of the prologue as a literary genre. That opinion appears, quite logically really, in a special prologue which Borges wrote to introduce one of his most curious and least read books: simply titled *Prólogos*, it collects various prologues written between 1923 and 1974.[12] The prologue to this volume is titled, predictably, "Prólogo de Prólogos," "a type of prologue," says Borges, "raised to the second power" (*Prólogos*, 7). He complains that "no one has formulated a theory of the prologue" and that it is usually confused with mere hyperbole and eulogy. Borges recalls that in some great works (Wordsworth's *Lyrical Ballads*, Montaigne's *Essays*, and the *Thousand and One Nights*) the prologue constitutes "an inseparable part of the text" (*Prólogos*, 8). He also remembers that "in Elizabethan theatre, the prologue was the actor who declared the theme of the play" (*ibid.*). This is particularly significant when applied to his own poetic prologues: because of their theatrical origin, the prologue is, above all, a *voice* which advises us what we will find in the text, and how we should judge it. Thus, Borges concludes, "the prologue, when the stars are propitious, is not a spurious form of toast, but a lateral type of criticism" (*ibid.*). Not only texts require and produce prologues; the process can also be inverted—prologues themselves can constitute a literary work. At the end of this "Prólogo de Prólogos," Borges imagines a utopian work, a book whose hypothetical nature tempts him: "The book which I foresee, would consist of a series of prologues to nonexistant books. It would abound in exem-

plary quotations from those possible books" (*Prólogos*, 9). It is not difficult to discern, in this project, a disciple of Macedonio Fernández, author of the fifty-six prologues which compose the unfinished text of *La
novela de la eterna*.[13]

The prologues serve Borges as a field for games played by his imagination, and the exercises of his intellect, always ready to review his texts,
leaving on them the signs of his reading: retrospections, self-defenses,
definitions, recognition of his debts to other authors belonging to unexpected poetic traditions, quotations and glosses of his own quotations.
But even more, the prologues present a moral portrait and rectify and
compensate for the inevitable deformation of celebrity. The image offered by those prologues and poems is that of a man reconciled to being
himself, perfectly lucid about his capabilities and limitations, intimate
but never maudlin, confessional and yet discreet, not only an artist, but a
man who has learned from his art. In his prologue to Lugones' work,
Borges writes: "A poet is not only an artificer, a maker, but also a man
who feels with intensity and complexity" (*Lugones*, 10). His poetry is
written in such a way that one sees first, not the artifice, but the man.

Translated by Candelyn Candelaria

NOTES

1. Jorge Luis Borges, *Obras completas 1923–1972* (Buenos Aires: Emecé, 1974). (Further
references are indicated *OC*, with a page number.)
2. Jorge Luis Borges, *Fervor de Buenos Aires, Luna de enfrente y Cuaderno San Martín* had
already been collected in *Poemas* (Buenos Aires: Losada, 1943).
3. Norman Thomas Di Giovanni, *Borges on Writing* (New York: E. P. Dutton, 1973):
78–83.
4. Alfred J. Mac Adam, "Borges the *Criollo*: 1923–1932." *Review*, No. 28 (January-April
1981): 65.
5. Emir Rodríguez Monegal, *Jorge Luis Borges. A Literary Biography* (New York: E. P.
Dutton, 1978): 177–178.
6. There we read: "Cómo no malquerer a ese escritor que reza atropelladamente palabras sin paladear el escondido sombro que albergan, y a ese otro que, brillantador de en-
debleces, abarrota su escritura de oro y de joyas, abatiendo con tanta luminaria nuestros
pobres versos opacos, sólo alumbrados por el resplandor indigente de los ocasos de suburbio." *Fervor de Buenos Aires* (Buenos Aires: Imprenta Cervantes, 1923): 6.
7. Leopoldo Lugones, *Antología poetica*. Selección e introducción de Jorge Luis Borges.
(Madrid: Alianza Editorial, 1982): 12.
8. Jorge Luis Borges, *La rosa profunda* (Buenos Aires: Emecé, 1975): 10.

9. Wolfgang Iser, *The Act of Reading* (Baltimore: The Johns Hopkins University Press, 1980): 109.

10. José Ortega y Gasset, *Ideas sobre el teatro y la novela* (Madrid: Alianza Editorial, 1982): 23. It is well known, however, that Borges differed seriously with Ortega's literary and philosophical opinions. Regarding this, see Rodríguez Monegal (note 5): 182–3, and "Nota de un mal lector" (on Ortega and Unamuno) reproduced in *La Gaceta del Fondo de Cultura Ecónomica*, no. 143 (November 1982): 10.

11. A. Porqueras Mayo, *El prólogo como género literario* (Madrid: Consejo Superior de Investigaciones Cientificas, 1957): 133.

12. Jorge Luis Borges, *Prólogos* (Buenos Aires: Torres Agüero Editor, 1975).

13. Macedonio Fernández, *Museo de la novela de la eterna* (Buenos Aires: Centro Editor de América Latina, 1967).

BIBLIOGRAPHY

Borges, Jorge Luis. *Fervor de Buenos Aires*. Buenos Aires: Imprenta Cervantes, 1923.

Borges, *La rosa profunda*. Buenos Aires: Emecé, 1975.

Borges, *Obras completas 1923–1972*. Buenos Aires: Emecé, 1974.

Borges, *Poemas*. Buenos Aires: Losada, 1943.

Borges. *Prólogos*. Buenos Aires: Torres Agüero Editor, 1975.

Di Giovanni, Norman Thomas. *Borges on Writing*. New York: E. P. Dutton, 1973.

Fernández, Macedonio. *Museo de la novela de la eterna*. Buenos Aires: Centro Editor de América Latina, 1967.

Iser, Wolfgang. *The Act of Reading*. Baltimore: Johns Hopkins University Press, 1980.

Lugones, Leopoldo. *Antología poética*. Madrid: Alianza Editorial, 1982.

Mac Adam, Alfred J. "Borges the Criollo." *Review*, 28 (Jan.–April 1981), 65.

Mayo, A Porqueras. *El prólogo como género literario*. Madrid: Consejo Superior de Investigaciones Científicas, 1957.

Ortega y Gasset, José. *Ideas sobre el teatro y la novela*. Madrid: Alianza Editorial, 1982.

Rodríguez-Monegal, Emir. *Jorge Luis Borges. A Literary Biography*. New York: E. P. Dutton, 1978.

WILLIS BARNSTONE

Borges, Poet of Ecstasy

The author of a very famous Spanish novel, *Don Quijote de la Mancha*, was born in Buenos Aires in the year 1899. His name appears to be Jorge Luis Borges, although this is questionable since he has largely dropped his Christian names and is, in his own words, merely and "unfortunately . . . Borges." But here too the Argentine author of the *Quijote* eludes us and even puts in doubt the American authorship of the Spanish masterpiece by signing the work with the name of an intermediary, an invented Borges, who calls himself Pierre Menard.

Now there are some Spanish nationalists who would claim that the work was actually invented much earlier by a man from Alcalá de Henares named Cervantes. But this is immediately countered by Islamic nationalists who further predate the work, assigning it to the pen of an obscure Arab historian, Cide Hamete Benengeli. But Borges does not mind this receding mirror of Plotinian illusions, nor does it even matter when an outrageous upstart, Avellaneda, attempts to steal the show and to rewrite the Borges masterpiece as his own.

In these multiple creations of creations, we find the essential dilemma in Borges: Borges is a character created by Borges who will always escape into a new creation; but no sooner will he become the other, *el otro*, the *yo* of Borges y *yo*, no sooner does that shy man Borges wielding a mighty club of modesty shift into the writer Borges and into a text and into a reader's vague memory and (according to Borges' own hope) into a few anonymous phrases that have entered the Spanish language, than we outsiders, like the old counters of Catullus's infinite kisses, lose track so that Borges can return once more to that original Borges, whoever he is, and start again.

From all this I wish to propose that Borges is a very unstable compound, a mysterious compound, who searches relentlessly to find a stable single condition, a label or formula or key to his essence, but is one fated to eternal metamorphosis. Like space abhorring a vacuum, Borges abhors a condition of *stasis*. For this reason he moves from *enstasis* (being in himself) to *ekstasis*, (being elsewhere). As a poet of ecstasy, he is fated to follow the voyage of the seeker, not the finder, to wander, following the original Greek usage of the word *ekstasis*, "outside himself." If we need any further proof of Borgesian mutability, we can find it by looking again at Borges' favorite creation, the *Quijote*, where we see that the main character himself, Alonso Quijano, cannot be quiet and moves, as one moves in dream and oblivion, into the figure of a lanky, helmeted knight, who some very uninformed amateurs of art claim originated in an etching by a more recent Spaniard, living in France, under the name of Picasso.

The Greek word *ekstasis* signifies "being or standing elsewhere," that is, a displacement from a condition of stasis. The early classical meaning is bewilderment, insanity, seizure, anger, terror, reflecting a movement from the ordinary to the extraordinary, from a normal to an "altered state," from being self-contained and standing in oneself (*enstasis*) to standing elsewhere (*ekstasis*). To be "beside oneself" or "out of mind" follows the etymological meaning. But in late Greek the word received another application. The Oxford English Dictionary refers to "withdrawal of the soul from the body" and "mystic trance." So for Neoplatonic and Christian mystics ecstasy occurs when the mind is emptied of all sensory-intellectual phenomena and then is filled with ineffable rapture in anticipation of divine union. Plotinus uses the word to mean a returning movement outward and upward to the emanation from the One. For Longinus ecstasy is transport and elevation, related to his principal idea of the *hypsos*, the sublime, which he finds eminently in Sappho's "concourse of passions" (*pathon te synodos*). In Borges this Neoplatonic ecstasy of ineffable rapture is most pertinent. Later, I will refer to two specific mystical experiences which Borges speaks of in an interview. This is the Borges of ecstatic contemplation, of mystical ecstasy.

But the more common ecstasy in Borges is not mystical, secular or religious. His is the ecstasy of otherness, a movement from Borges to the *yo* in "Borges y *yo*," from public man to private dreamer. He shifts slyly from streetcorner knifer to Persian mystic to Chuang-tzu's Chinese butterfly, dreaming it is Chuang-tzu. The protean Borges cannot be formulated and pinned against a wall of reality or illusion. While his quest is self-knowledge, that anagnorisis and elation comes tantalizingly only at the instant of extinction (as at the end of the "Poema conjetural") where none can report the ultimate gnosis. In reading Borges, we are at least prepared to witness the transformation of the spirit or, more modestly, to be alerted to the possibility of ultimate transcendence. But Borges will tell us no ultimate truths. He will not fall into the easy prevaricating trap of prophetic truth and revelation.

Borges' central obsession is Borges: how to get away from that "coward and pedant" he knows too well, whom he must wake to each morning, whose books he won't let in the house. To be free of the old man, he turns his identity into a dream or a simulacrum, and sees the image reflected endlessly in a mirror until "el otro que lo observa / es apenas un sueño del espejo?" ("Beppo").[1] When the other, *el otro*, finally escapes his master Borges, he may become, as in the poem "Beppo" a Plotinian archetype, a shadow. And what we think is our true identity is merely an image in a broken mirror, going back to an Adam before Paradise or to an indecipherable divinity. To become a god, to know the secrets and have the power of that divinity, would be ideal. But Borges knows that that divinity will always be indecipherable and, moreover, unattainable. *El otro* will always be *el otro*, immeasurably remote, as Borges will always be Borges. Yet this is all to the good, for the other, whom Borges would become, offers the foreign port, the Ithaca to use Homer's goal. Or to use Constantine Cavafy's redeeming notion of Ithaca, it promises even more: it offers the voyage. En route Borges will search for algebras, wisdom, answers to riddles; his search would end, however, if he ever became *el otro*. Indeed, Borges is smart enough to know that if he became any of those ideal others he aspires to (including the dead man with the key to the universe), it would be a boring disappointment. (Remember that Ithaca, which gave us the voyage, is itself poor.) So without exception,

Borges' movement toward the other, into ekstasis, is a process, never a completed action. Ithaca is a vision. But to arrive and anchor in the port is inert stasis and death.

Borges has a second obsession, equally nightmarish. While he seeks his way out of labyrinths, back through mirrors and sunsets and clocks, to be *free* of Borges, to experience the ecstasy of otherness, at the same time he *returns* relentlessly to the maker of his travels, to that dubious character, Borges, who may offer a secret or two. Yet he will never wholly find Borges any more than he will wholly be free of himself to find the other.

To move from one identity to another, one must begin some place. At least most of us would like to fix our point of departure. Not Borges. In his enigmatic poem "Descartes" Borges makes clear only that all is in doubt, including the existence of the Descartes he evokes. More than simply asking *what* am I and *who* am I, he has Descartes of the poem go further and ask *do* I, Descartes, even exist? Of course the historical Descartes also doubted his own existence—I doubt that I am but I cannot doubt that I doubt, therefore I think, followed by *je pense, donc je suis*. But the real Descartes is playing circular syllogistic games. Descartes invented by Borges is more serious. He has Descartes jeopardize his very being by casting it into dream:

> Quizá no tuve ayer, quizá no he nacido.
> Acaso sueño haber soñado.
> Siento un poco de frío, un poco de miedo.
> Sobre el Danubio está la noche.
> Siguiré soñado a Descartes. . . .

But there is a further trick in all this. (Borges is never reluctant to create wondrous mischief.) For while Descartes is questioning his own existence, suggesting that it may have been a dream or that he may not even have been born, there is obviously a Borges-invented Descartes who is raising questions. Therein lies the mischief. For we need not conclude simplistically as does the historical Descartes, yes, for all these reasons I must exist. We may affirm, rather, that the so-called real Descartes of the poem, that ordinary everyday Descartes, is an illusion, a dream. In that case, then, since we have already posited that some speaker called Descartes raised these questions, then only that Descartes, the doubter, the dreamer, the one outside the everyday Descartes of the poem, exists. In this instance, there is a movement of identity from that everyday Descartes of the poem, who turns out to be a false dream, to the real dreamer whose voice we hear. That real dreamer is, in regard to the everyday Descartes, in *ekstasis*, outside his normal self (which may never have existed). The doubting dreaming Descartes whom Borges has invented is, in regard to ordinary mortals, someone else. And that someone else, whom Borges would have us return to, that dreamer of philosophers and gods and timeless beasts, is of course another Borges—the elusive figure whom neither he nor we will ever spot clearly in the mirror, who will never be caught in an act of epiphany, spilling the truth. The artist as well as the philosopher Borges would never allow such an inept, anticlimatic ending.

While Borges never appears to leave himself completely—that is for mystics and saints—he does confess that this experience of total otherness occurred twice in his life. "In my life I only had two mystical experiences and I can't tell them because what happened is not to be put into words, since words, after all, stand for a shared experience. . . . Twice in my life I had a feeling. . . . It was astonishing, astounding. I was overwhelmed, taken aback. I had the feeling of living not in time but outside time. I don't know how long that feeling lasted, since I was outside time."[2] In these two instances when Borges reaches into "the other time," communication between that other condition and the normal one is poor. Hence the notion of oblivion and ineffability associated with mystical transport.

Borges says that such a moment of ecstasy, when one is really elsewhere, in another time, another place, in another being, is not a shared experience. But the ineffable nature of mystical contemplation is not due simply to the lack of a common system of words; the mystic plainly lacks a clear memory of his or her experience. Dreams as well as trances as well as any foray into the unconscious or up to and beyond the heavens are rather hard to put on tape recorders. About this, Borges says simply "in the case of ecstasies, that can only be told through metaphors." But he expresses this discomfort with eternity much better in verse. After going through all the dreams of ancient places and art works which the New York Cloisters has brought to mind—the maze at Knossos, tapestries of the white unicorn which do not obey time, the sands of America which Leif Ericsson devised—he is weary and a bit skeptical of such ventures. He writes in "The Cloisters":

> Siento un poco de vértigo.
> No estoy acostumbrado a la eternidad.

Perhaps the last Borges we must address is the first: the Borges who is Borges the writer, the maker. Although Borges is sick and tired of being himself, of looking at the public which is looking at him, it is his duty, given him by his father, as a compensation for his military unfitness, to be a maker. He has been a maker now for six decades and more, and he has found neither the right words nor himself. But he knows very well the habits of that minor maker from the southern hemisphere. As always he is the best conspirator to spy on and denounce himself. Here is what he has to say about the other, "*Aquél,*" who is Borges:

> Aquél
> Oh días consagrados al inútil
> empeño de olvidar la biografía
> de un poeta menor del hemisferio
> austral, a quien los hados o los astros
> dieron un cuerpo que no deja un hijo
> y la ceguera, que es penumbra y cárcel,
> y la vejez, aurora de la muerte,
> y la fama, que no merece nadie,
> y el hábito de urdir endecasílabos
> y el viejo amor de las enciclopedias
> y de los finos mapas caligráficos
> y del tenue marfil y una incurable
> nostalgia del latín y fragmentarias
> memorias de Edimburgo y de Ginebra
> y el olvido de fechas y de nombres
> y el culto del Oriente, que los pueblos
> del misceláneo Oriente no comparten
> y vísperas de trémula esperanza
> y el abuso de la etimología
> y el hierro de las sílabas sajonas
> y la luna, que siempre nos sorprende,
> y esa mala costumbre, Buenos Aires,
> y el sabor de las uvas y del agua
> y del cacao, dulzura mexicana,
> y unas monedas y un reloj de arena

> y que una tarde, igual a tantas otras,
> se resigna a estos versos.

Borges the maker is the ultimate process. That is the one condition in which Borges is most clearly the other Borges. This activity of the maker is his "*Aquél*," his other, and is his experience of supreme ecstasy. All the images he makes, he tells us in "El hacedor," make up the cumulative self:

> Otra cosa no soy que esas imágenes
> Que baraja el azar y nombra el tedio.
> Con ellas, aunque ciego y quebrantado,
> He de labrar el verso incorruptible
> Y (es mi deber) salvarme.

Here, in this poem written in his eighth decade, Borges no longer derides this other self, the maker, as he did in "Borges y yo"; in fact, now after so many years of labor and intimacy with the public Borges, his true self has become the writer. When he ended his essay "Borges y yo" with "I do not know which one of us is writing this page," he was prophetic but in unexpected ways, for now not only has the public Borges commingled indistinguishably with the private intimate *yo* (indistinguishable to us as well as to himself) but the substantial *yo*, the anguishing, passionate and dreaming *yo*, has become the public Borges.

This Argentine born in 1899 in Buenos Aires has at last become his other, *el otro*, the author of the *Quijote* as well as of the austerely confessional poems of *La cifra*. This mere South American, as he would say of himself, has become Borges. Or to recall the lines from the above lyric "El hacedor," this lonely, broken, blind man, carrying out his scribal tasks, *is* the writer, which is his salvation. And his ecstasy is precisely in moving from the loneliness of the *yo* to the curious loneliness of the creator.

Borges finds his destiny in the ministry of words, and he performs his job, to the end, as an artist. In his mission of self-discovery, he must go beyond words into silence, project himself into a symbol, into some object outside himself. And what better symbol for a poet, unafraid of beauty as he is of intellect, than the moon? In *La cifra*, his last published book of poems, the title poem "La cifra" refers to the great lunar circle of the night, the zero to which we aspire. The day before Constantine Cavafy died he took a pencil and drew a large Plotinian circle on a hospital napkin. It was his full circle. Borges composes a circle in this last poem, and urges us strongly to contemplate it, for one day

> *No volverás a ver la clara luna.*
> *Has agotado ya la inalterable*
> *suma de veces que te da el destino.*
> *Inútil abrir todas las ventanas*
> *del mundo. Es tarde. No darás con ella.*

So he (or that maker called Borges) warns us that while we are alive we are to pursue its vision, to look at it carefully:

> vivimos descubriendo y olvidando
> esa dulce costumbre de la noche.
> Hay que mirarla bien. Puede ser última.

The night activity of a blind poet is to waken us. Although it will one day be too late to open all the windows of the world, Borges moves us for a while, and hopefully himself, into the morning of his created light. Clearly, the ecstatic labor of the blind man is to be the maker, the writer, is to open our eyes and make us see.

NOTES

1. All references to poems are from Jorge Luis Borges, *La cifra* (Buenos Aires: Emecé, 1981).
2. Other quoted material is from *Borges at Eighty: Conversations,* ed. and with photographs by Willis Barnstone (Bloomington: Indiana University Press, 1982).

BIBLIOGRAPHY

Barnstone, Willis, ed. *Borges at Eighty: Conversations.* Bloomington: Indiana University Press, 1982.
Borges, Jorge Luis. *La cifra.* Buenos Aires: Emecé, 1981.

RAMONA LAGOS

The Return of the Repressed: Objects in Borges' Literature

Contrary to the physical and spiritual plenitude of his poems written during the decade of the twenties, Borges' work after the thirties begins to exhibit a deep change that exalts the disjunction, restlessness, frustration, and breaking up of the harmony that impregnates his first three books. The pleasant strolls are no longer a current activity, and there is no joy either in contemplating the country landscape or in remembering his idyllic childhood. The serenity of the poems becomes internal agitation. The process becomes invisible torture, insomnia, and agony.

His lyric process starts reflecting the rupture with limitless confidence in the two forces that are the bases for poetic certainty and emotional serenity (the youthful quasi-boasting): first, an illuminating and absolute ability of his early experiences to achieve *The Poem* and secondly, an actual ability to be able to build the poems. It would seem that during the thirties, his faith in a capability to accede to poetic revelation, or at least its imminence, is gone. This change is simultaneous with the irruption of the narrative that hides a similar process under the structure of the spectacular stories of *Historia universal de la infamia*.[1]

The lyric texts written in these years do not signify, therefore, a mere thematic change in Borges' works. Neither do they represent a newborn vocation of intimacy. Rather, they reflect a profound transformation of his view of literature, the world, and of himself.

This decisive change in Borgesian literature can be attributed to the same years in which he wrote and published *Historia universal de la infamia*. From this period, his lyric and narrative texts start exhibiting, systematically, a serious questioning of the literary work and of its expressive possibilities.

This transformation can be seen in one of the many levels of the discourse, in the coded presence of objects and diverse materials that, expressing a metaphysical dimension, also show "las interjecciones del cuerpo," the instinctive, the sense of doubt and the sense of failure. In other words, the world has changed, from certainty to uncertainty, from Heaven to Hell.

Borges' early poetry associates Heaven with the library, with intellectual activity, with an idealized childhood, and with Adrogué. In "The Thing I Am" from *Historia de la noche*, the reference to ordinary coexistence between Heaven and Hell is clearly explicit for the first time in this highly coded poetry.

In the early texts the sense of happiness and plenitude is evident. Hell is also there but hidden, and potentially ready to develop. In the poems written during the twenties in recollection of Borges' childhood, Hell is perceived as waiting to appear at the first sign of self doubt or pain. The signs of the painful side of life are, from this point of view, expressed by realities or objects such as labyrinths, felines, coins, jails, bars, gratings, parks, stones, iron, precious metals, mirrors, sand, nails and mud. It is easy to see in each one of these materials the obvious metaphysical power which they contain. But we can also perceive, in the cyphered and paradoxical discourse, the presence of instinct and elementary fear repressed by a powerfully intellectual literary thought.

Without attempting to demonstrate in detail how all these objects function in relationship to each other, their similarities and differences, their nuances and shades of meaning, an attempt will be made to show how some of them function in these texts. The purpose is to illustrate how they express a more secret and carefully hidden aspect of life in the literature of Borges and also how they reflect a strong lyric dimension that develops through the years and through his texts.

Adrogué is one of the privileged spaces in the work of Jorge Luis Borges. The name appears in poems, serves as titles for some of them and also for an anthology in 1977. If the name is mentioned, it is also suggested by smells and sensations which the reader learns to identify with relative ease. Adrogué is the space of a Utopia which, around 1923, he wants to find again, gives up around 1960, and, toward 1977 remembers again. Adrogué is the paradise within his memory, although in maturity Adrogué often becomes the labyrinth implying loss and at times horror.

Toward 1930, Borges' conception of horror is still an aesthetic experience. It is still the "pleasant horror" of nights spent with his favorite books, with his youthful readings. In these readings, recollected around 1930 in the prologue to *Evaristo Carriego*, the labyrinth, the Minotaur, and even fear, are each perceived *as one of the forms of existence in Paradise*. This is a sort of pleasant horror, protected from the outside world, and controlled by imagination and intelligence as well as by the library. We notice that Adrogué (one Paradise) includes the library of the poet's father (the other Paradise), thus making up two heavens, one inside the other. Nevertheless, in all of these youthful poems the demoniac virtualities are potentially present from the beginning. Adrogué is also the labyrinth; at the same time, the library also represents Babel. At what point do the infernal virtualities latent in these spaces come to predominate over the idyllic atmosphere?

The poems written in the decade of the thirties, show that the exciting horror becomes real agony during this period. In the texts of *Fervor de Buenos Aires*, *Luna de Enfrente*, and *Cuaderno San Martín*, Adrogué, the library, the labyrinth and objects in general, represent a state of happiness, a state of delight. The labyrinth and the reading activities have an intellectual and playful function which is manifested in "perplexity": "I thought: If I had a magnifying glass and the luck to see well, I could discover the Minotaur."

The same thing occurs in *the South*, identified with Adrogué: it is also the definitive place of dreams and imagination.

In Borges' more mature works, the labyrinth becomes inhabited by the Minotaur, who is perceived as a prisoner who "waits" for his redeemer or his immolator. From that point on, the labyrinth acquires the connotation of a jail, horror, and a true inferno. Erik Lönnrot, one of the Borgean characters, is destroyed in a physical and intellectual labyrinth, and in spite of himself, it is in a labyrinth that Yu Tsun murders Albert. In *Elogio de la sombra* (1969), the poem entitled "Labyrinth" has the

Minotaur as its lyric subject, a pathetic prisoner of "the stone nets," of the "road of monotonous walls," still awaiting its liberator. The monstrous and desolate nature of the locked up beast is also quickly transferred, very early, to the tiger, to Oedipus, and to Janus, who appear in several poems in *El hacedor* (1960).

The atrocious glimpses of life, experienced as a prison, can later be seen in the poet's abundant use of gratings, bars, cages, swords, daggers, and other immurements. One also becomes aware of limitations, of frontiers which confine vibrant and bloody tigers anxious for freedom. The library which has been Paradise becomes a jail and a labyrinth made more painful by the blindness which impedes (prevents) its full enjoyment. The consciousness of anguished living is also expressed by the poet's mentioning ungraspable materials such as sand.

Nevertheless, and in spite of the insistence of the poems, and of the short stories, in expressing the horror of life, there is also a subtle development of a parallel line of feelings whose meaning is to expose the return of vital exaltation always carefully repressed in the Borgesian discourse. This is the presence of instinct, which also assumes an enigmatic coded form.

Referring to the afternoon of Socrates' death, Borges comments on the *Phaedon* and what the philosopher said when they set him free from his chains: "How strange! The chains were heavy. It was a form of pain. Now I feel relieved because they've taken them off. Pleasure and pain go together, they are twins!" Borges adds: "How remarkable it is that at that moment, on the last day of his life, he shouldn't say that he's about to die, but rather that pleasure and pain are inseparable."[2]

Immediately thereafter, Borges' explanation centers on an apology of the senses, of the material, concrete aspect of life in order to finally postulate the dialectic of the desire to live, against the desire to cease. The process may be seen within the structure of his texts from the moment in which living becomes intolerable. This phenomenon explains a kind of recovery of lyric serenity in the poet's later texts. A brief and curious example can be seen in *Tigres azules*, a story in which there is an allusion to the generative, engendering capacity imposed on some magic blue stone disks. This story relates the adventure of Alexander Craigie "professor of Western and Oriental logic," in the process of trying to catch a blue tiger that has lived in his dreams. He travels to the area of the Ganges River and arrives at a remote village. The atmosphere is primitive and dominated by the physical pullulation of the jungle "which almost penetrates the huts." One night he escapes this village and goes toward a forbidden plateau. There he finds the obsessive color: "Incredibly, it was the blue color of the tiger of my dreams. I wish I had never seen it. I looked closely. The crack was filled with little stones, every one of the same circular form: very smooth and only measuring a few centimeters in diameter."[3]

The stones represent the sacred tiger. Their function is to engender. In the midst of the tribe's terror, the character, (and narrator, at the same time) displays his discovery.

Finally, the village becomes the stones, the jungle becomes the swamp and the swamp, the jungle. All of the germinal, elemental traits, are here associated with physical, primordial reproduction. This association is not strange to the work of Borges. In "The Circular Ruins," the magician who is prepared to dream up and to engender his son, arises out of the mud, from substance: "No one saw him disembark in the unanimous night, no one saw the bamboo canoe sinking in the sacred mud." The old man kisses the mud. When the story ends with a fire, an observation is made concerning the sky which "was rose-colored like a leopard's gums." In the same manner, in *Tigres azules* the presence of the tiger appears (sublimated and hidden in the circular stones), of the mud, of the jungle, of procreation.

In "Simón Carvajal" a poem from *La rosa profunda*, the lyric conclusion identifies the tiger's fate with human destiny, which is simultaneously a destructive force and a destroyed victim: "He was always killing the same immortal tiger. Don't let his destiny surprise you too much. It's yours and mine, except that our tiger has shapes which change endlessly. It's called love, chance, each moment, hate."[4]

Everything seems to lead to the idea that Borges' tiger is a symbolic cypher of man in a manner different from that of the minotaur or Janus (whose connotation is basically tragic, trapped), because they are divided figures. On the contrary, the tiger, the panther and the leopard, become cyphers of a more elementary dimension of the living carnal being: the cypher of the body, of the instinct repressed and displaced by the sublimating discourse which attempts to manifest this only under the form of aesthetic experience. Expressions concerning felines such as "that fateful splendor" (*Del cielo y del infierno*, 1942) and "terrible elegance" (*Tigres azules*, 1977) also show this.

When an animal is incarcerated, as they appear in many poems, the agony manifest between a purely biological energy and the state of imprisonment clearly illustrates the homology between the beast, tragically cornered by iron bars, and human destiny. Indeed, an obvious meaning of the physical and metaphysical level of life. In "El otro tigre," the lyric text shows the savage and free animal animated by the imagination, next to "the vocative tiger" of the verse, the tiger that is a cypher of man, "shape" of his dreams, and verbal signifier. It is in this tiger that the double clue of the feline is centered: one dimension is the tellurian and the atavistic, which are repressed and carry the implication of torture and suffering; the other one is the principle of life and imagination (the "vocative tiger" of the poems or the free tiger in the poet's dreams) which breaks through the repression either to denounce the prison or to wander lively in the jungle imagined by the lyric subject. It is precisely the latter one that establishes the balance in the texts.

These animals and objects and their dialectic connotation convey the most complex lyricism in Borges' texts due to their symmetrical balance of intimate confession and, at the same time, their masterful art of hiding the true being who pretends (in the explicit dimension of the texts) only to be playing with thoughts, with "the labyrinths of the spirit."

NOTES

1. It has been studied in detail how the short stories of *Historia universal de la infamia* (Buenos Aires: Emecé, 1954) destroy the narrative verisimilitude, secretly throughout the irony of the discourse which distorts history, and throughout the manipulative power of human language as it is used by the narrators.
2. Translation mine.
3. Translation mine.
4. Translation mine.

BIBLIOGRAPHY

Borges, Jorge Luis. *Cuaderno San Martín*. N.p., n.d.
Borges, *El hacedor*. Buenos Aires: Emecé, 1971.
Borges, *Elogio de la sombra*. Buenos Aires: Emecé, 1969.
Borges, *Fervor de Buenos Aires*. Buenos Aires: Imprenta Cervantes, 1923.

Borges, *Historia de la noche*. Buenos Aires: Emecé, 1977.

Borges, *Historia universal de la infamia*. Buenos Aires: Emecé, 1954.

Borges, *La rosa profunda*. Buenos Aires: Emecé, 1975.

Borges, *Libro del cielo y del infierno*. Buenos Aires: Sur, 1960.

Borges, *Luna de Enfrente*, N.p., n.d.

Borges. *Tigres azules*. N.p., 1977.

JAIME ALAZRAKI

Enumerations as Evocations: On the Use of a Device in Borges' Latest Poetry

Enumerations in literature are as old as the Old Testament, but in modern times they have achieved the status of an established rhetorical device only since the writing of Walt Whitman. Such are the conclusions of Detlev W. Schumann and Leo Spitzer, two critics who have studied enumerations in contemporary poetry. Spitzer summarized his findings in a well known essay entitled "Chaotic Enumerations in Modern Poetry."[1] There he says: "All seems to indicate that we owe chaotic enumerations as a poetic device to Whitman."[2] In a different essay devoted to Whitman, Spitzer defines the device as "consisting of lumping together things spiritual and physical, as the raw material of our rich, but unordered modern civilization which is made to resemble an oriental bazaar. . . .[3] If enumerations have been, until Whitman, one of the most effective means of describing the perfection of the created world in praise of its Creator, it was Whitman's task to render that same perfection and unity into attributes of our chaotic modern world."[4] Whitman did not invent the device, but he used it with such intensity and skill that his poetry became a showcase of the rich possibilities offered by the device for poets who succeeded him. In Spanish America, Darío and Neruda were deeply influenced by Whitman and his enumerative style. So was Borges, who wrote about Whitman and on enumerations as early as 1929.

In a short note entitled "The Other Whitman," he argued that Europeans misread Whitman: "They turned him into the forerunner of many provincial inventors of free verse. The French aped the most vulnerable

part of his diction: the complaisant geographic, historic, and circumstantial enumerations strung by Whitman to fulfill Emerson's prophecy
about a poet worthy of America."[5] Borges viewed enumerations and free
verse—at that time—as foundations of European avant-garde poetry.
"Those imitations," he concluded caustically, "were and are the whole of
today's French poetry."[6] He then added, on the subject of enumerations,
"many of them didn't even realize that enumeration is one of the oldest
poetic devices—think of the Psalms in the Scriptures, and of the first
chorus of *The Persians*, and the Homeric catalogue of the ships—, and
that its intrinsic merit is not its length but its delicate verbal balance. Walt
Whitman didn't ignore that."[7]

Almost fifty years later, in a footnote to his latest collection of poems,
La cifra, Borges restated the same notion. Referring to the poem "Aquél,"
he wrote, "this composition, like almost all the others, abuses chaotic
enumerations. Of this figure, in which Walt Whitman abounded with so
much felicity, I can only say that it should impress us as chaos, as disorder, and be, at the same time, a cosmos, an order."[8] There are three
elements here that need to be emphasized. The first is that Borges adopts
in 1981 the term coined, or rather divulged, by Spitzer as it was used
earlier by Schumann. Raimundo Lida translated Spitzer's article into
Spanish and it was published in Buenos Aires in 1945. It is presumable
that Borges read it, but he didn't have to, since the term has become part
of our literary jargon and we use it familiarly, unaware of our debt to
either Schumann or Spitzer. What matters is that this is the first reference
Borges makes to the device under the name of "chaotic enumerations."

The second point is that Borges emphasizes the idea of order in the
guise of chaos underlying the effectiveness of chaotic enumerations in
Whitman. This is the very core of Spitzer's definition: "Whitman's catalogues," he says, "present a mass of heterogeneous things integrated,
however, in a majestic and grand vision of All-One."[9]

The third and last point is Borges' explicit recognition that his last
collection, *La cifra*, abuses chaotic enumerations. He is right. Although
enumerations appear already in his early collections, and reappear
throughout his entire poetic work, the device is considerably more frequent in his latest book. Following is an attempt to track the course of
enumerations in Borges' poetry, and an attempt to define the implications of the device in the development of his art.

For a writer who has been an early reader and admirer of Whitman, who has written a couple of essays on him, who has acknowledged his debt to Whitman in numerous texts, early and late, and who has (more recently) translated *Leaves of Grass* into Spanish, it is not at all surprising to find in Borges' own poetry the use and abuse of enumerations. They appear as early as 1925 in his collection *Luna de enfrente* in such poems as: "Los Llanos," "Dualidá en una despedida," "Al coronel Francisco Borges," "La promisión en alta mar," "Mi vida entera," and "Versos de catorce." With the exception of "Mi vida entera" ("My Whole Life"), the other poems use enumerations either partially or for the rhythmic element performed by a repeated word or anaphora. What sets "My Whole Life" aside from the others in his early poetry is the use of enumerations in a manner that will become characteristic of his later work. Note the poem in a translation by W. S. Merwin:

> Here once again the memorable lips, unique and like yours.
> I am this groping intensity that is a soul.
> I have got near to happiness and have stood in the shadow
>   of suffering.
> I have crossed the sea.
> I have known many lands; I have seen one woman and two
>   or three men.
> I have loved a girl who was fair and proud, and bore a
>   Spanish quietness.
> I have seen the city's edge, an endless sprawl where the
>   sun goes down tirelessly, over and over.
> I have relished many words.
> I believe deeply that this is all, and that I will neither see
>   nor accomplish new things.
> I believe that my days and my nights, in their poverty and
>   their riches, are the equal of God's and of all men's.[10]

With the years, the list will become longer, the lines shorter, the voice deeper, the tone calmer, but the effort to survey his whole life through enumerations will remain the same.

But what exactly do enumerations enumerate in poetry? In the case of Whitman, they list the diversity or even chaos of a country, time, or people, in order to cluster that diversity into a unity: the poem renders that oriental bazaar of our unordered civilization—in the words of Spitzer—into "the powerful Ego, the 'I' of the poet, who has extricated himself from the chaos."[11] This is not the use Borges makes of enumerations. In his second essay on Whitman, he comments on this use of enumerations reminiscent of the holy texts found in most religions: "pantheism," he writes, "has disseminated a variety of phrases which declare that God is several contradictory or (even better) miscellaneous things." He then brings up examples from the *Gita*, Heraclitus, Plotinus, the Sufi poet Attar, and concludes: "Whitman renovated that device. He did not use it, as others had, to define the divinity or to play with the 'sympathies and differences' of words; he wanted to identify himself, in a sort of ferocious tenderness, with all men."[12] Borges himself has employed this particular type of enumeration, proper to pantheism, in his fiction, in the description of divine visions or theophanies in stories like "The Aleph," "The Zahir," and "The God's Script," but not in his poetry.

There is another use of enumerations. It is best summarized by Whitman himself toward the end of his poem "A Backward Glance Over Traveled Roads" when he writes, "*Leaves of Grass* indeed has mainly been the outcropping of my own emotional and personal nature—an attempt from first to last, to put a *Person*, a human being (myself, in the latter half of the 19th Cent., in America) freely, fully and truly *on record*."[13] But for Whitman to put a human being on record was to write about Humanity and Nature, History and Politics, America and Sex, or, as he says elsewhere, "to sing the land, the people and the circumstances of the United States, to express their autochtonous song and to define their material and political success."[14]

Borges shares this task of poetry ("to articulate in poetic form my own physical, emotional, moral, intellectual and aesthetic Personality" in Whitman's words), but in a much more modest and restricted way. Compared to the cosmic world of Whitman, Borges' poetry is an intimate environment peopled by sunsets and cityscapes, streets and outskirts, authors and books, branches of his family tree, Argentine heroes and counter-heroes, obsessions and mythologies, metaphysical and literary reflections, Old English and Germanic sagas, time, blindness, memory, oblivion, old age, love, friendship and death. There is no need to reconcile these two different perceptions of poetry belonging to Whitman and Borges, but rather how to explain the latter's admiration for the former.

In the preface to *Elogio de la sombra* he wrote, "I once strove after the vast breath of the psalms and of Walt Whitman."[15] And in his poem

"Buenos Aires," from the same collection, he writes: "Buenos Aires is a tall house in the South of the city where my wife and I translated Whitman whose great echo, I hope, reverberates in this page."[16] And again in the preface to *El otro, el mismo* he insisted, "In some of these poems, Whitman's influence will be—I hope—noticed."[17] That Whitmanesque "vast breath" is present, paradoxically, in poems where enumerations convey intimate evocations of the poet's personal past, as in his early poem "My Whole Life," written in 1925. Another example, chronologically, of this type of intimate evocation is the second of the "Two English Poems" written in 1934. Like the previous one, this too is a sort of family album in which the most significant experiences and events of the poet's personal life are recorded: desperate sunsets, lean streets, ragged suburbs, a lonely moon, his grandfather killed on the frontier of Buenos Aires, his great-grandfather heading a charge of three hundred men in Perú, the memory of a yellow rose, books, explanations, theories, the poet's loneliness, darkness, and his heart. The poem can be read, indeed, as a microcosm of his entire poetic work; most of his major themes and motifs are spun in this early cocoon.

What needs to be pointed out, though, is that this poem typifies the kind of enumerations that will be predominant in later poetry. There is no chaos here, in the sense used by Spitzer, as an expression of modern world disorder. There is a random survey of experiences we call chaotic enumerations, but the chaos refers mainly to the nature of the presentation rather than to the disorder of the representation (be that a country, a civilization, or the world). Borges too strives "to put a person on record," but not, as in Whitman's case, in the crucial latter half of the nineteenth century, during the rise of America as a world power, but in a very familiar time and in a place that is perceived more in personal than in historical terms.

Enumerations in which the specified material belongs to a strictly intimate space and a highly personal time may be illustrated by this passage:

> Stars, bread, libraries of East and West,
> Playing cards, chessboards, galleries, skylights, cellars,
> A human body to walk with on the earth,
> Fingernails, growing at nighttime and in death,
> Shadows for forgetting, mirrors busily multiplying,
> Cascades in music, gentlest of all time's shapes,

> Borders of Brazil, Uruguay, horses and mornings,
> A bronze weight, a copy of the Grettir Saga,
> Algebra and fire, the charge at Junín in your blood,
> Days more crowded than Balzac, scent of the honeysuckle,
> Love and the imminence of love and intolerable remembering,
> Dreams like buried treasure, generous luck,
> And memory itself . . . All this was given to you . . .[18]

This scrutiny of things past and present comes from "Matthew XXV: 30" written in 1953. It is a recasting, slightly modified, of the enumeration put forth in the second "English Poem" of 1934 which in turn rewrites the earlier inventory recorded in "My Whole Life" of 1925. They are not the same poem: each one has a different intent and a different tone suitable to that intent. In the first, the emphasis is on the admission that, as the poem declares, "this is all, and I will neither see nor accomplish new things," a lucid anticipation, in 1925, of Borges' basic approach to writing as rewriting. The second is a love poem, and in it the poet's life is inscribed through its most memorable assets to be offered, as a trophy, to the beloved one: "I am trying to bribe you with uncertainty, with danger, with defeat."[19] The third poem recounts those same items, concluding: "You have used up the years and they have used up you / And still, and still, you have not written the poem."[20]

The evocation of those chosen moments or things or people will be repeated throughout Borges' entire poetic work, although never in quite the same way. Specifically it will appear in the poems: "Somebody," "Elegy," and "Another Poem of Gifts." In some cases, the poem enumerates not the things that life gave the poet but those it didn't; poems about gifts not received, like "Limits," expanded into "An Elegy of the Impossible Memory," and tried once again in "Things That Might Have Been." In other poems, there are just inventories of things dear to the poet's memory, like "The Things," reenacted in "Things," and repeated once again in "Inventory." In poems like "The Threatened One" and "To the Sad One," personal things and interests are listed together. There are also poems whose enumerations are intended to give not a portrayal of the poet but of somebody else, or of animals, places, countries, cultures, books, or questions, such as "Descartes," "The Righteous Ones," "The Orient," "Israel," "Buenos Aires," "Iceland," "The Islam," "England," "A Thousand and One Nights," and "Insomnia." Finally, in a poem like

"John, I, 4" the enumeration foregoes the particulars and concentrates on the abstract side of gifts from life.

But the more interesting and the more relevant to this study are those instances of enumeration addressed to a survey of the poet's life. In addition to the already mentioned, the following should be added: "I," "I Am," "Talismans," "The Thing I Am," "A Saturday," "The Causes," "The Maker," "Yesterdays," and "Fame." What pertains to the first three poems applies to these also; each has its own focus, its own inflection and tone. Yet all share the condition of enumeration as a means of evoking the poet's past and reflecting upon his present. The theme is recast, again and again, each time to strike a different chord, or a different poem. The method was essentially set forth in that early poem of 1925; time completed it, skill refined it. The early hesitant and elementary lyrics evolved into the perfection and complexity of Borges' recent poetry in which we hear the same intrinsic melody, but the music now has the balance, the harmony and serenity that befit a master.

A final and concluding remark. Borges' penchant for summaries is proverbial. He has insisted that "to write vast books is a laborious nonsense" and suggested that "a better course is to pretend that those books already exist and then offer a summary, a commentary."[21] Such a tendency applies to his poetry as well. The poems mentioned as examples of enumerations are summaries of the poet's major themes and motifs, indexes of his poetic production, or metonymies of his main subjects. His ancestors' battles and deaths, splendidly sung in numerous poems, are now resolved in a single and slim line: "I am the memory of a sword." His entire poetic endeavour is compressed into a single verse: "I have woven a certain hendecasyllable," and the plots and counter-plots of his fiction are encapsulated in a terse line from the poem "Fame": "I have only retold ancient stories." There is no need for more. Borges, the master of metonymy, understands that having constructed a literary world of his own, an artful intimation suffices.

I also believe that this type of enumeration expresses his long held notion that "memory is best fulfilled through oblivion." Everything must be forgotten so that a few words remain. But those few words, in turn, condense and contain everything—personal Alephs, indeed—. Oblivion thus becomes the ultimate realization of memory: "Viviré de olvidarme": "I shall live out of forgetting about myself," he says. What is left is an echo, a trace, a single line, the wake of a long journey that the poem proceeds to compile.

NOTES

1. Leo Spitzer, *Lingüística e historia literaria* (Madrid: Gredos, 1961): 245–291. Second edition.
2. Spitzer, *Lingüística*, 258.
3. Leo Spitzer, "Explication de Text." Applied to Walt Whitman's poem "Out of the Cradle Endlessly Rocking." Included in *Essays on English and American Literature* (Princeton University Press, 1962): 23.
4. Spitzer, *Lingüística*, 261.
5. Jorge Luis Borges, "El otro Whitman." Included in *Discusión* (Buenos Aires: Emecé, 1957): 52. My own translation.
6. Borges, "El otro Whitman," 52.
7. Borges, "El otro Whitman," 52.
8. Jorge Luis Borges. *La cifra* (Buenos Aires: Emecé, 1981): 105.
9. Spitzer, *Lingüística*, 258.
10. Jorge Luis Borges, *Selected Poems 1923–1967*. Edited by Norman Thomas di Giovanni. (New York: Delacorte Press, 1972): 43.
11. Spitzer, "Explication de Text," 22.
12. Jorge Luis Borges, "Note On Walt Whitman." Included in *Other Inquisitions*. Translated by Ruth L. C. Simms. (New York: Washington Square Press, 1966): 73–4.
13. Walt Whitman, "A Backward Glance o'er Travel'd Roads." Included in *Leaves of Grass, Authoritative Texts, Prefaces, Whitman On His Art, Criticism* (New York: A Norton Critical Edition, 1973): 573–4.
14. Whitman, "Backward Glance," 574.
15. Jorge Luis Borges, *Elogio de la sombra* (Buenos Aires: Emecé, 1969): 11.
16. Borges, *Elogio de la sombra*, 128.
17. Jorge Luis Borges, *El otro, el mismo* (Buenos Aires: Emecé, 1969): 11.
18. Borges, *Selected Poems*, 93.
19. Borges, *El otro, el mismo*, 18.
20. Borges, *Selected Poems*, 93.
21. Jorge Luis Borges, *Ficciones* (Buenos Aires: Emecé, 1956): 11.

BIBLIOGRAPHY

Borges, Jorge Luis. *Elogio de la sombra*. Buenos Aires: Emecé, 1969.
Borges, *El otro, el mismo*. Buenos Aires: Emecé, 1969.
Borges, "El otro Whitman." In *Discusión*. Buenos Aires: Emecé, 1957.
Borges, *Ficciones*. Buenos Aires: Emecé, 1956.
Borges, *La cifra*. Buenos Aires: Emecé, 1981.
Borges, "Note on Walt Whitman." In *Other Inquisitions*. Translated by Ruth L. C. Simms. New York: Washington Square Press, 1966.
Borges. *Selected Poems 1923–1967*. Edited by Norman Thomas Di Giovanni. New York: Delacorte Press, 1972.
Spitzer, Leo. "Explication de Text." In *Essays on English and American Literature*. Princeton: Princeton University Press, 1962.

Spitzer. *Lingüística e historia literaria*. Madrid: Editorial Gredos, 1961.
Whitman, Walt. "A Backward Glance o'er Travel'd Roads." In *Leaves of Grass, Authoritative Texts, Prefaces, Whitman On His Art, Criticism*. New York: A Norton Critical Edition, 1973.

II. *Borges and Poetic Traditions*

GRACIELA PALAU DE NEMES

Modernismo and Borges

"One of the cardinal functions of poetry"—wrote Octavio Paz—"is to show the other side, the wonders of everyday life: not poetic irreality, but the prodigious reality of the world."[1] Borges' poetry performs this function. It may seem paradoxical to say this of a writer who has won worldwide acclaim by the imaginative character of his prose work, but the works of Borges the poet seem well anchored in the world of reality, from where he probes the other side of things.

Borges and his poetry resist classification. He broke away from Spanish Ultraism whose message he propagated. He had become an Ultraist in reaction to the previous movement, Spanish Modernism, to eliminate ornamentation, confessionalism, circumstantial evidence, preaching and deliberate vagueness.[2] And yet, when his first three collections of poems appeared, he was, in essence, closer to the Modernists than to any other group. These first books, *Fervor de Buenos Aires*, (1923), *Luna de enfrente*, (1925), and *Cuaderno San Martín*, (1929), were reviewed by leading Hispanic critics who found them classic in versification (Enrique Díaz Canedo); adhering to norms (Ramón Gómez de la Serna); and more nostalgic for the perennial structures than desirous of new modulations (Guillermo de Torre).[3] At the same time, they mentioned elements which were present in the poetry of the Modernists, such as its sensorial character, its mysticism and its contradictions, but they did not relate them to Modernism.

Rafael Cansino Assens, an outstanding Spanish critic of the period who exerted a direct influence in the Ultraist adventure noticed, in a penetrating article about Borges' first books, that to perceive and to know were his two primary desires shown in *Fervor de Buenos Aires* and *Inquisiciones* (a book of essays published by Borges in 1925). That his muse was mystic and religious, was a fact he was able to confirm after reading Borges' second book of poetry, *Luna de enfrente*, and that in his "criollismo" or nativeness, he established a mystic relation between his native Buenos Aires and the true ideal reality of things. Cansino Assens had noted previously that in spite of the vivid, distinctive highlights of Buenos Aires in Borges' poetry, it had a mystic and ideal value. When Guillermo de Torre wrote about *Luna de enfrente*, he noticed that in Borges' identification with the familiar landscape there was a longing for a unifying spiritual reintegration as if repudiating the plurality of the world's suggestions. Finally, Cansino Assens saw a contradictory aspect in Borges' verse and prose, which he attributed to an aristocratic preoccupation with language which made the poet use words for their etymological value, as if to demand the purest of the lexical material, while at the same time, by the same elitist tendency, he forced the expression of the concept, incurring a pleasant and archaic baroque style. There are other contradictions in these first books of Borges.

Borges' poetic vision is like the Modernists in the elements we have mentioned: for his avowed willingness to perceive and to know; for the mystic quality of his vision of reality and his adherence to a unifying concept of the universe; and for his cognizance of its contradictions, embodied in his poetic expression.

Spanish Modernism was a metaphysical quest which used beauty as its most eloquent symbol, as in the poetry of the Spanish-American master Rubén Darío, or the Spanish Modernist master, Juan Ramón Jiménez. It was also an exaltation of the real world, which offered the Modernist poet, consciously or unconsciously, proof of the unifying elements between the material and spiritual worlds. More than any contemporary writers, Modernists were forced, by the empirical beliefs and attitudes prevalent at the end of the 19th century, to take cognizance of perceptual space. In *An Essay on Man: An Introduction to a Philosophy of Human Culture*, Ernst Cassirer explains that perceptual space "is not a simple sense datum; it is of a very complex nature, containing elements of all the different kinds of sense experience—optical, tactual, acoustic, and kinesthetic. The manner in which all these elements cooperate in the construction of perceptual space has proved to be one of the most difficult questions of the modern psychology of sensation."[4] The data from perceptual space, reinterpreted, gave the Modernists their symbolic vision of the universe. Cassirer tells us, that instead of defining man as an *animal rationale*, we should define him as an *animal symbolicum* and that without symbolism, "man's life would be confined within the limits of his biological needs and his practical interests; it could find no access to the 'ideal world' which is opened to him from different sides by religion, art, philosophy, [and] science." The modernists turned to symbolism to gain access to the ideal world in an epoch when the practical interests of their society superceded their concern with the realms of the ideal. If we accept this fact, we can speak in a similar vein of such different modernist authors as the Cuban, José Martí, the initiator of the movement in 1882, and Darío, its propagator from 1888 on. Borges more closely resembles Martí, in spite of the fact that the philosophical concepts of Martí are based on intuition rather than erudition. Martí believed that the only philosophical source was observable nature and that man, the observer, was the only philosophical agent. To Martí, *nature* meant everything, that is in every form except man's soul and heaven. He believed that to know, it was necessary to examine nature and that the most reliable source of truth derived from this observation.[5] In Borges' first books of poetry, the speaker is first of all an observer, who takes his time as he walks, but hurries up to meet the sunset; who notices the serenity of the tombs at the cemetery and the juncture of the marble and the flower; the sameness of some houses; and the trees, the moon, the butcher shop. Furthermore, Martí barely diversified the meter or experimented with rhyme, nor did the Post-Modernists, whose simple discourse and native themes marked a return to the roots of the movement, as in Martí's poetry. On the other hand, Darío's ultra-refined vocabulary and at times excessive ornamentation gave poetic discourse an appearance of frivolity, affectation and insincerity. But as noted by Blanco Fombona, an early and important critic of Modernism, had Darío limited himself to the witty, frivolous, rhetoric novelties, he would not have been the great poet he was.[6]

In the prologue to the first edition of *Fervor de Buenos Aires*, Borges claims that this book is a reaction against the decorative visual and lustrous lyricism inherited from Góngora through Darío, his executor; that he (Borges) meant to oppose it with a pensive lyricism made of spiritual adventures. But Darío's lyricism, as that of the other modernists, is also a spiritual adventure.

In his work, *Poesía y conocimiento*, Ramón Xirau, a contemporary critic, notes that even before romanticism reached its peak it was thought that poetry and philosophy were akin.[7] He thinks that philosophy and poetry serve in an effort to grasp this world we encounter and in which we find ourselves.

Cassirer, a philosopher of the physical and cultural sciences had already addressed this topic: "Poetry is one of the forms in which a man may give the verdict on himself and his life. It is self-knowledge and self-criticism. Such criticism is not to be understood in a moral sense. It does not mean appraisal or blame, justification or condemnation, but a new and deeper understanding, a reinterpretation of the poet's personal life. The process is not restricted to poetry; it is possible in every other medium of artistic expression."[8] To elucidate this phenomena of human culture, Cassirer refers to Goethe, who entitled his autobiography *Poetry and Truth*, not because he used imaginary or fictional elements in the narrative of his life, but because the truth about his life "could only be found by giving to the isolated and dispersed facts of his life a poetical, that is a symbolic, shape." This is what Borges does in his first three books of poetry. He gives the scattered facts of his life symbolic shape.

In his excellent study *Borges, el poeta*, Guillermo Sucre says that he finds in Borges' first books a climate of fervent intimacy, of confessionalism, a marked animism which makes the vision of things warmer and deeper.[9] Even those critics who look for the Ultraist elements in these first books, call attention to their confessionalistic tone.[10] The speaker tells the listener most intimately, that he is one with everything. In the first poem, "Las calles," he confesses that the streets of Buenos Aires are already the innermost recesses of his soul; in "La Recoleta," his soul runs over the streets; in "Sala vacía," old things run after his soul; in "Los llanos" the plain is a barren copy of his soul.

There is a progression in the poetic vision of Borges. In *Fervor de Buenos Aires*, he is forever walking the streets, feeling, perceiving; in *Luna de enfrente*, away from Buenos Aires, he recreates it; in *Cuaderno San Martín* acutely aware of the passing of time, he turns Buenos Aires into a myth. Guillermo Sucre says that Borges recreates the Buenos Aires of his infancy, which he lost during his long residence in Europe. Borges confesses the same thing in *Fervor de Buenos Aires*, in his poem, "Arrabal": "this city which I thought to be my past / is my future and my present; / the years that I have lived in Europe are an illusion / I have always been (I shall always be) in Buenos Aires." [11] Like the Modernists, Borges recreates a mythical space which he thought was lost. The poetic vision is essentially the same; the Modernists tried to recreate the mythical space of religion, of God, which they thought lost, but they lacked the spatial data which Borges possessed. Octavio Paz has dealt with this topic in *Children of the Mire*. He implies that Modernism became a metaphysical search because the Modernists felt the necessity of giving a contradictory answer to the spiritual void created by the Positivists in their criticism of religion and metaphysics. In the Post-Modernistic period, coming to terms with their new circumstances, most poets abandoned or postponed the metaphysical search and took cognizance of the more immediate voids in their spaces. This would account for Modernism being first exotic and then regional or nativistic. In Borges' poetry, the native space provided the elements for the mystic search. The streets of Buenos Aires are sublimated because in their great extension into the plains they communicate with the sky, making heaven attainable. The sky is everywhere, it spills over the houses and the patios, which are, in turn, exalted because they hold it, limit it, and then copy it. Patios are grounded in the two primal things of existence, heaven and earth. The sunset also has symbolic meaning. It sets limits; breaks the infinite distance; it is a hallucination imposed by space upon those who fear the shadows; it is a dark ornamental jewel, set in time, to redeem the streets from the humble presence, since the poverty of the houses show under the clear sky.

There are few mornings in this early poetry of Borges. The afternoon, leading to a sunset, is the favorite time of day. But the sunset is also a tyrant, it drives the street crazy with its flashy crowding, it is like an unhealed wound hurting the street, and it is the visualization of time. Night also has a dual, contradictory function; it cancels space, it does away with things, invalidates the immensity and makes it sterile but it increases time, since dreaming is the time for the expansion of the soul.

In *Luna de enfrente*, the space-consciousness of the poems increases; the pampa assumes the symbolic meaning first attributed to the streets.

As the speaker says in the poem "Al horizonte de un suburbio": "Pampa: / You are clear as the moon, you are even as the water / your truth is in the symbol." The plain is a passage between heaven and earth. The ocean provided this passage for the Modernists and the sea journey abounds as a motif in their poetry, but Borges does not need the sea as a mediator, since the plain is a sea of grass. In the text of *Luna de enfrente*, one reads: "the sea is an old language that I can't quite / decipher" ("Singladura"). The afternoon, the sunset and the sky are still favorite elements but the vision is more universal. On the high seas, the speaker feels proximity to his native land through the sight of the stars. They seem to have dropped from the molding of a wall, or to come from the patio's well, or from an afternoon in the province, or from the same sky shining on the dusky extension of the fields. They are like a clear country and Buenos Aires is within its bounds ("La promisión en alta mar"). The last poem in *Luna de enfrente* is a song to the poet's city, praising the intermixture of space and day: "street corners crowned by the sunset / and blue slums made of sky," as he says in "Versos de catorce."

In *Cuaderno San Martín*, Buenos Aires is seen in relation to time, not space, and becomes a myth. Memory is then symbolic matter. The speaker remembers the founding of the city but denies that it had a beginning. He judges it eternal, like water and air ("Fundación mítica de Buenos Aires").

The main theme of the book is death. There are poems about the death of the caudillo Facundo Quiroga; of Borges' ancestor, Colonel Francisco Borges; of the old neighborhood; of the vice district which should not have existed; and the cemetery appears again, as in *Fervor de Buenos Aires*. In the last stanza of a poem entitled "Isidoro Acevedo," the speaker confesses: "I was then a child who knew nothing about death, I / was then immortal," and the listener realizes at last that by affirming his existence within the space of his childhood, Borges was also trying to attain immortality. In the poem, "Remordimiento por cualquier defunción," a dead man, "everywhere no one" is "but the loss and absence of the world." (Trans. W. S. Merwin.)

Fervor de Buenos Aires is a passage, by sense experience, to the space of immortality, the space of his childhood. And yet, Borges the prose writer proposes in "La penúltima versión de la realidad," an essay of the same period (1928), that humanity would forget that space existed.[12] He is commenting on *The Manhood of Humanity*, by Alfred Korzybski. He had not read this book, but based his arguments on what he knew from a review, according to which Korzybski states the view that animal is defined by a hunger for space, but man, a superior being and as such, more original, accumulates time (he means depth, intensity of living). He laments materialism which told man to become space rich, then man forgot his noble task and began to acquire visible things, persons and territories, and the fallacy of progress was born. But human life should be more intense—he says—instead of more extended. Borges opposes this philosophical concept of horizontal and vertical life. He considers space an incident in time and not a universal form of intuition; spatial relation is not a continuity, he says, adding that if mankind were only to be able to hear and smell and not to see or taste, it would continue plotting its history just the same.

There is one further argument in the comparison of Borges and the Modernists. Count Korzybski's phrase, "hunger for space" is reminiscent of the famous verses of Darío: "I hungered for space / and thirsted for heaven."[13] Borges himself wrote, in the prologue to *Luna de enfrente* ("Al tal vez lector"): "Our daily existence is a dialogue between life and death, made of memories (which are forms of having been and having ceased to be) or else of projects that are a mere hunger to be."

Perceptible space was an obsession in the poetry of the Modernists, who seemed more preoccupied with space than with time, perhaps because time was not an empirical object. It was at this point that Borges differed from the ontological concerns of the Modernists. What may account for this difference is the fact that Borges was not trying to affirm the unifying character of the universe, which the Modernists were beginning to doubt. Borges only wished to decipher the universe, but the Modernists wanted to recreate its harmonious vision. It is for this reason that Pythagoras is forever present in their poetry, from Rubén Darío on, but there is hardly a mention of Heraclitus. (Martí would be the exception, since he still believed in a harmonious universe.) In Borges' poetry, Pythagoras and Heraclitus coexist but there is not the Pythagorean music of the spheres. In the prologue of *Luna de enfrente*, Borges says that he is not interested in the auditive aspects of poetry. But according to Octavio Paz, poetic rhythm is the manifestation of universal rhythm and he chastizes those who fail to see the spiritual rootlessness in the musical style of the Modernists.[14] There is also philosophical justification for the Modernists' search for Pythagorean rhythm. Cassirer says that symbolic thought translates into the language of numbers all of our knowledge of space and spatial relation, which in turn makes man arrive at a concept of a unique, systematic, cosmic order.[15] Only towards the end of the Modernist period, in the work of Juan Ramón Jiménez, the poet who resolved the mystic search of Modernism by creating a mystical space for contemporary man, do we find the presence of Heraclitus, and it appears as an epigraph for a work entitled "Tiempo," as yet unpublished, and parallel to his famous work entitled "Espacio," both written in the forties. Borges anticipated him by many years.

Thus the relation between Borges and the Modernists is established. In Borges' collection of poems, *El otro, el mismo*, published in Buenos Aires in 1969, there is a poem entitled "Líneas que pude haber perdido o escrito hacia 1922," in which he summarizes his poetic vision of the twenties. He speaks of silent battles at sunset in far away slums; of the ever old defeat in a war in the sky; of the debris of many dawns which came to him from space-deserted depth and from the depth of time. He mentions some of the space data that appears in his first poetry: the moon upon the marble, the everlasting trees, the night, the expected afternoon, and he concludes: "Am I those and the other things / or are they secret keys and arduous algebra / for that which we shall never know?" Darío, whose vision of existence was less clear than that of Borges, also questioned himself in his poem "Fatality" ("Lo fatal"): "To be, and to know nothing and to lack a way / and the dread of having been, ... / and not to know where we go / nor whence we came! . . . ."[16]

NOTES

1. Octavio Paz, *Children of the Mire*. Translated by Rachel Phillips. (Cambridge: Harvard University Press, 1974): 51.
2. Jorge Luis Borges, "Ultraísmo." *Nosotros* (Buenos Aires, Ano XXIX, Num. 151. Dec., 1921): 468.
3. The opinions about Borges' early works cited here are from the collection of critical articles by Jaime Alazraki, *Jorge Luis Borges* (Madrid: Taurus, 1976), as follows: "Enrique Díaz Canedo, '*Fervor de Buenos Aires*'.": 22; "Ramón Gómez de la Serna, '*Fervor de Buenos Aires*'.": 26; "Guillermo de Torre, '*Luna de enfrente. Poemas*'.": 32; "Rafael Cansino Assens,

'Jorge Luis Borges (1919–1923)'." The pages refer to Alazraki's collection, which gives the original date and provenance of the reviews.

4. Ernst Cassirer, *An Essay on Man* (New Haven: Yale University Press, 1944): 43.

5. For Martí's philosophical thought see "Estudios sobre las ideas de Jose Martí" in *Antología crítica de Jose Martí*. Edited by Manuel Pedro González. (México: Publicaciones de la Editorial Cultura, 1960).

6. Rufino Blanco Fombona, *El modernismo y los poetas modernistas* (Madrid: Editorial Mundo Latino, 1929): 36.

7. Ramon Xirau, *Poesía y conocimiento* (México: Joaquín Mortiz, 1978): 11.

8. Cassirer, *An Essay on Man*, 52.

9. Guillermo Sucre, *Borges, el poeta* (Venezuela: Monte Avila Editores, 1968): 39.

10. Thorpe Running, *Borges' Ultraist Movement and its Poets* (Michigan: International Book Publishers, 1981): 48–9.

11. I have translated into English Borges' verses quoted in the text.

12. Jorge Luis Borges, *Prosa completa*, I (Barcelona: Bruguera, 1980): 39. The concepts attributed to Korzybski are as found in Borges' essay.

13. "Yo soy aquél . . . ," in Rubén Darío, *Cantos de la vida y esperanza* (Madrid: Tipografía de la Revista de Archivos, Bibliotecas y Museos, 1903). My translation.

14. In "Translation and Metaphor." Octavio Paz. *Children of the Mire.*

15. Cassirer, *An Essay on Man*, 49.

16. Lysander Kemp, trans., *Selected Poems of Ruben Darío* (Austin: University of Texas Press, 1965): 90.

BIBLIOGRAPHY

Alazraki, Jaime. *Jorge Luis Borges*. Madrid: Taurus, 1976.
Borges, Jorge Luis. *Prosa completa, I*. Barcelona: Bruguera, 1980.
Borges. "Ultraísmo." *Nosotros*, 151 (Dec. 1921), 468.
Cassirer, Ernst. *An Essay on Man*. New Haven: Yale University Press, 1944.
Darío, Rubén. *Cantos de vida y esperanza*. Madrid: Tipografía de la Revista de Archivos, Bibliotecas y Museos, 1903.
Fombona, Rufino Blanco. *El modernismo y los poetas modernistas*. Madrid: Editorial Mundo Latino, 1929.
Kemp, Lysander, trans. *Selected Poems of Ruben Darío*. Austin: University of Texas Press, 1965.
Paz, Octavio. *Children of the Mire*. Translated by Rachel Phillips. Cambridge: Harvard University Press, 1974.
Running, Thorpe. *Borges Ultraist Movement and its Poets*. Michigan: International Book Publishers, 1981.
Sucre, Guillermo. *Borges, el poeta*. Venezuela: Monte Avila Press, 1968.
Xirau, Ramón. *Poesía y conocimiento*. México: Joaquín Mortiz, 1978.

MARÍA KODAMA

Oriental Influences in Borges' Poetry: The Nature of the Haiku and Western Literature

In the foreword to his *Collected Writings* (1969), and in other works, Borges has expressed many judgments on poetry and style which indicate the way he gradually assumed the essential poetic forms of the Japanese *tanka* and *haiku*. He attempted those two forms for the first time in *El Oro de los Tigres* (1972) and in *La Cifra* (1981). Borges began his prologue to the Collected Writings by claiming: "I have not rewritten the book. I have toned down its Baroque excesses, I have trimmed rough edges, I have blotted out sentimental verses and vagueness and, in the course of this labor sometimes pleasing and sometimes annoying, I have felt that the young man who in 1923 wrote those pages was essentially— what does essentially mean?—the elderly gentleman who now resigns himself to what he penned or emends it. We are both the same; we both disbelieve in success and in failure, in literary schools and in their dogmas; we both are true to Schopenhauer, to Stevenson and to Whitman. In my opinion, *Fervor de Buenos Aires* foreshadows all that came afterwards." He ends by saying: "In those days, I sought sunsets, outlying slums and unhappiness; now, mornings, downtown, and serenity."

These words express not only the writer's feelings on his work, and on himself, but reflect also an essential search, foreshadowed as he tells us, from the beginning. This search, or attempt, is the oldest in the world. It began with Homer, and will continue as long as men write. Its aim is to discover with the utmost formal rigor the center, eternity. This search has often been attempted in the East, particularly in Japan and in the West, and particularly in Borges.

In the West, literature begins with the epic, with poems which throughout Europe tell the tales of heroes in hundreds and hundreds of lines. A perfect expression is found in the famous beginning of Virgil's *Aeneid*: "Arma virumque cano." *"Arms and the man I sing,"* as Dryden translated. The mind accepts the word "arms" immediately; it refers, of course, to the deeds of man. In the West those poems throughout the centuries grow briefer and briefer until they reach the avant-garde schools, among them Ultraism. In the case of Spanish literature this generated some of the most important changes since the introduction of the Italian sonnet by Garcilaso, not so much by itself, but by the changes wrought by its impulse.

Borges' career began with a flirtation with Ultraism, and then followed in his own personal way, a way that led him, in a wide circle, to Japan. He, the maker, even as God Himself, sought what is essential to all poetry and especially to Japanese poetry. Japanese poetry tries to carve into a few precious lines of seventeen syllables the meeting of time and space in a single point. The maker, even as God Himself tries to abolish succession in space.

In his own way Borges has tried to express the same wish in the foreword to his *Historia de la Eternidad* (1936):

I don't know how on earth I compared to 'stiff museum pieces' the archetypes of Plato and how I failed to understand, reading Schopenhauer and Scotus Erigena, that they are living, powerful and organic. Movement, the occupation of different *places* in different moments is inconceivable without time; so is immobility, the occupation of the same place in different points of time. How could I not perceive that eternity, sought and beloved by so many poets, is a splendid artifice, that sets us free, though for a moment, of the unbearable burden of successive things.

In *The Aleph* (1949) he also says:

The Aleph's diameter must have been two or three inches, but Cosmic Space was therein, without diminution of size. Each object (the mirror's glass, for instance) was infinite objects, for I clearly saw it from all points in the universe . . . I saw the Aleph from all points; I saw the earth in the Aleph . . . I saw my face and entrails . . . and felt dizziness and wept because my eyes had seen that conjectural and secret object whose name men take in vain but which no man has

looked on: the inconceivable universe. I felt infinite veneration, infinite pity . . .
For the Kaballah, this letter the En-Sof, the limitless and pure God Head . . .

These ideological elements form converging aspects sympathetic to
the intent of Japanese poetry, which must be examined in some detail in
order to understand both its poetic patterns and their purpose.

As in the case of Western literature, Japanese literature begins by
groping its way. The task of finding a precise date for the birth of regular
forms in prose and verse is not an easy one. The earliest example is the
Kojiki, a record of ancient matters, compiled *circa* A.D. 712. Afterwards
came the *Nihon Shoki*, a chronicle of Japan, A.D. 720. In the year A.D. 751
there appeared a compilation of Chinese verses written in Japan, the *Kai-
fūsō: Fond Recollection of Poetry*. Therein are found texts dating from the
last part of the seventh century. The Nara Period offers the first great anthology of poetry, the Manyōshū Collection of *A Myriad Leaves*. This
compilation was undertaken towards the end of the eighth century. In
the *Kojiki* and in the *Nihon Shoki* the length of the lines in the poems and
in the songs varies from three to nine syllables though even in this early
period we find the habit of repeating five and seven syllables. In the
Manyōshū the poems have already a fixed number of lines and the forms
are regular. The lines are invariably compounded of five and seven syllables passing from one to the other. An example is the poem in which
Prince Arima is getting ready for a journey:

> Iwashiro no
> Hamamatsu ga e wo
> Hikimusubi
> Masakiku araba
> Mata kaerimimu.

*On the beach of Iwashiro. I put the knot together. The branches of the pine. If my
fate turns out well, I shall return to see them again.* This particular form of
thirty-one syllable poems in five lines of 5, 7, 5, 7, 7 each is the most
frequent and the most lasting of the three forms evolved in the Manyōshū Period. In Japanese poetry it is called *tanka* or *waka*. The other two
are the *sedoka* and the *choka*. The *choka* is a long poem with no limit to the
number of lines. The longest of these poems attains one hundred and
fifty lines. It passes, like the *tanka*, from 5 to 7 syllables ending in a line
of 7 syllables. It could also be completed by one or two or more *hankas* or
envoys written after the manner of *tanka* and summing up the subject of

the whole poem. However, of all stanzas to be found in Japanese poetry, the most congenial to the Japanese mind seems to be the *tanka*, since it still survives, along with the *haiku* that is engendered by an evolution of the *tanka* towards a greater brevity and a greater conclusion.

During the Manyū Period, poetry tended toward a private lyricism. The *tanka*, however, underwent a considerable evolution, which ended in a new form, the *haiku*. A crucial point was the transition of the caesura or pause in the syntax. In the *Manyū* Period most *tankas* had their caesura after the second or the fourth line. The poem is thus divided into three units of 5, 7 (12) and 5, 7 (12) and 7 syllables. This pattern hinders the attempt to pass from a short line to a long one and is weakened by the last short unit.

A verse from Hitomaro Kashū provides an example:

> Hayabito no
> Na ni ou yogoe
> Ichishiroku
> Waga na wa noritsu
> Tsuma to tanomase.

Clear and loud as the night call of a man of Haya, I told my name. Trust me as your wife. [The Haya, a southern Kyūshū tribe, famous for the clarity of their voices, were employed at the Imperial Palace as watchmen. A woman tells her name to signify her assent to a proposal of marriage.]

Towards the end of the Heian Period (794–1185) and in the Kamakura Period (1185–1603), the caesura comes after the first and the third line. The poem is thus divided into three longer units of 5, 12 and 14 syllables. As an example the poem of Narihira is given, from the novel *Ise Monogatari*:

> Tsuki ya aranu//
> Haru ya mukashi no
> Haru naranu//
> Waga mi hitotsu wa
> Moto no mi nishite.

Can it be the moon has changed, can it be that the spring is not the spring of old times? Is it my body alone that is just the same? This division gave the poet a greater freedom. It favoured the evolution of the imayō style, where the 12-syllable line had a caesura after the seventh. Far more important is the fact that the second caesura is stronger than the first.

This latter style of *tanka* was divided into the two principal parts, the first three lines and the last two lines (17 syllables and 14 syllables). From this division came the form of linked verse, the *renga*, whose initial stanza comprises three lines, the second two lines, the third three lines, and so on. In due time, the initial stanza of the *renga* became independent and took the name of *haiku*. The curious fact that the season of the year was always recorded or hinted at in those first three verses may have favored the process. A mild surprise clung to it, a sudden enlightenment akin to the *satori* of Zen Buddhism. This is the origin of *haiku*, which was essentially in its beginning the old linked poem of the fourteenth century, ruled by the ideas and conventions peculiar to the *tanka*.

Bashō (1644–1694) fixed forever the road of the *haiku*. Bashō stated that the *haiku* should use the common speech of men avoiding, let it be understood, vulgarity. He abounded in images and words forbidden to the *tanka*. Sparrows instead of nightingales; snails instead of flowers. The poet should be "one with the crowd but his mind should always be pure." He should use "common language and somehow make it into a thing of beauty." He should feel pity for the frailness of all things created and feel keenly *Sabi*, a word that stands for solitude, for lonely sadness, and for the melancholy of nature. Above all, he should so express the nature of the particular as to define, through it, the essence of all creation. His seventeen syllables should capture a vision of the nature of the world.

The best example of this teaching is his famous *haiku*:

> Furu ike ya
> Kawazu tobikomu
> Mizu no oto.

An old pond. A frog jumps in, sound of water. First, we have something changeless, the pond, then something quick and moving, the frog, and lastly the splashing water, which is the point where both meet.

In an examination of Borges' poem "Un Patio" from *Fervor de Buenos Aires* (1923), we find many elements in common, metrics apart.

> With evening
> the two or three colors of the patio grew weary.
> The huge candor of the full moon
> no longer enchants its usual firmament.
> Patio: heaven's watercourse.

> The patio is the slope
> down which the sky flows into the house.
> Serenely
> eternity waits at the crossway of the stars.
> It is lovely to live in the dark friendliness
> of covered entrance way, arbor, and wellhead.
> [*trans. Robert Fitzgerald*]

Unknowingly, this poem follows the indications of Bashō.

How could a South American poet, after so many centuries, attain the very essence of the *haiku*? A possible explanation may be found in the fact that the essence of poetry is timeless and universal and when a writer attains it, as in the case of the Greek tragic poets, the achievement has no ending. An altogether different clue may be given us by Borges' childhood. His paternal grandmother was English, knew her Bible by heart and was continually quoting from it. I have been told that she could recite chapter and verse for any sentence in the Holy Writ. After Grimm, Borges read and reread the *Arabian Nights* in an English version and then went on to a now forgotten book, *Fairy Tales from Old Japan* by Mitford, an American scholar. During the first World War, the works of Schopenhauer sent him to the study of Buddhism. Borges explored with eagerness the books of Hermann Oldenberg on the Buddha and his teaching. These many interests gave him an open mind, a hospitable mind, sensitive to the most different cultures. Thus unaware of his path, he followed the century-old road of Japanese poetry towards the discovery of the *haiku*. Things done unconsciously are done well, and writers should not watch too closely what they are writing. If they do, the dream betrays them.

In the early 1970s, Borges deliberately undertook the composition of *tankas* and crowned that attempt in the 1980s with the composition of *haikus*. The stanza has seventeen syllables; Borges wrote seventeen *haikus*. Some may be chosen and examined more closely. The form will not be taken into account, since seventeen Spanish or English syllables may not be heard as seventeen syllables by an Oriental ear and vice versa. Japanese verse is meant not only to be heard but to be seen; the *kanjis* make a pattern that should be pleasant and moving to the eye. This kind of picture is unfortunately lost in a Western translation.

The *haiku* may be defined as an ascetic art. The ascesis is by far the most important element and the most difficult to attain. Therein we find a fundamental difference between East and West. Ascesis, in the West, is a mean towards an end. We instinctively think of passing from pleasure to suffering; from happiness to sanctity. In the East, ascesis is an end in itself and therefore stands in no need of explanation or justification. Strangely enough, the rigor of ascesis is linked in the East to art. In the West, art passes from life to artifice, from the simple to the complex. The *haiku* is as near to life and nature as it can be and as far as it can be from literature and a high flown style. This ascesis is the reverse of vulgarity.

The chief contribution of Japan to world literature is a pure poetry of sensations, found only partially in Western letters. The great difference between the *haiku* and western poetry is this material, physical, immediate character. It is an exaltation of the flesh, not of the sexual. In the *haiku* we find blended in equal proportions, poetry and physical sensation, matter and mind, the creator and creation. The choice of subjects is significant; war, sex, poisonous plants, wild animals, sickness, earthquakes, that is to say all things dangerous or threatening to life, are left out. Man should forget those evils if he aspires to live a life of mental health. The art of *haiku* rejects ugliness, hatred, lying, sentimentality and vulgarity. Zen, on the other hand, accepts those evils, since they are part of the universe. The heat of a summer day, the smoothness of a stone, the whiteness of a crane are beyond all thought, emotion or beauty which the *haiku* tries to capture. Japanese literature, with particular regard to the *haiku*, is not a mystic one. The *haiku* is, of all artistic forms, perhaps the most ambitious. In seventeen syllables it grasps, or tries to grasp, reality. Intellectual and moral elements are ruled out.

The *haiku* has nothing in common with Good, Evil or Beauty. It is a kind of thinking through our senses; the *haiku* is not a symbol. It is not a picture with a meaning pinned on its back. When Bashō says that we should look for the pine in the pine and for the bamboo in the bamboo, he means that we should transcend ourselves and learn. To learn is to sink into the object until its inner nature is revealed to us and awakens our poetic impulse. Thus a falling leaf is not a token or symbol of autumn, or a part of autumn; it is autumn itself.

Here is a *haiku* by Borges and another by Kitō, Buson's disciple:

> Hoy no me alegran
> los almendros del huerto.
> Son tu recuerdo.

The almond blossoms hold no cheer for me today; they are but your memory. Kitō wrote:

> Yū-gasumi
> Omoeba hedatsu
> Mukashi kana.

The mists of evening when I think of them, far off are days of long ago. In the last poem the mist of evening reminds him of days past. The dim twilight is akin to the dim past. For Borges the almond blossoms bring back a happy, and perhaps recent past. The starting point of both pieces is nature. In another *haiku* Borges says:

> Desde aquel día
> no he movido las piezas
> en el tablero.

Since that day I've not moved the pieces on the chessboard. And Shiki's *haiku* expressed a similar thought:

> Kimi matsu ya
> Mata kogarashi no
> Ame ni naru.

Are you still waiting? Once more penetrating blasts turn into cold rain. Shiki looks back on a woman who may still be expecting him. Her (or his) loneliness may be hinted at by the penetrating blasts of wind and rain. Solitude is also the theme of the Borges *haiku*. The lonely chessboard stands for the lonely man. In this *haiku*, solitude is the solitude of the poet; in Shiki's *haiku* solitude is the solitude of the other.

In another *haiku*, Borges suggests:

> Algo me han dicho
> la tarde y la montaña.
> Ya lo he perdido.

The evening and the mountain have told me something; I have already lost it.
Teishitsu (1610–1673) also composed a similar idea:

> Kore wa kore wa
> To bakari, hana no
> Yoshino-yama.

My, oh my! No more could I say; viewing flowers on Mount Yoshino. Teishitsu is overwhelmed by a powerful beauty that he cannot describe; in Borges' case a revelation has been given him by a fleeting moment, a revelation that he is unable to express.

Further, Borges writes:

> El hombre ha muerto.
> La barba no lo sabe.
> Crecen las uñas.

The man is dead. The beard is unaware of it. His nails keep growing. Which is similar to the composition by Bashō (1644–1649), who wrote:

> Ie wa mina
> Tsue ni shiraga no
> Haka mairi.

All the family equipped with staves and greyhaired, visiting the graves. Death, in Borges' *haiku*, is not represented as pathetic or memorable, sorrowful or fatal, but rather as disgusting and strange, as a curious physical happening. In this particular *haiku* Borges fulfills a requisite we have already noted; that the stanza is a meeting point of something everlasting, death, and something going on for a while, such as the grim circumstance of the growing beard and nails. Death in Bashō's *haiku* is presented in a casually indirect way: the poet sees the family visiting graves and feels that those old men and women will soon be dead. The theme of death was forbidden to the writers of *haiku*; Bashō, a follower of Zen Buddhism, dared to use it.

The moon presents another image to Borges:

> Bajo el alero
> el espejo no copia
> más que la luna.

Under the eaves the mirror holds a single image. The moon.

This is complemented by an earlier *haiku* by Kikaku (1661–1707) who composed:

> Meigetsu ya!
> Tatami no ue ni
> Matsu no kage.

A brilliant full moon! On the matting of my floor shadows of pines fall. Kikaku sets a picture before us. The shadows of the pines can be seen because the moon is in the sky. In both poems solitude is signified by the full moon, absence is the real subject of both, and a fleeting point of time is held by the words. An image of eternity in the Japanese poem is in the full moon; eternity in Borges' *haiku* is reflected in a quiet mirror.

The sense of loneliness may also be found in two other *haikus* by Borges:

> Bajo la luna
> la sombra que se alarga
> es una sola.

Under the moon the growing shadow is but a single one.

> La luna nueva.
> Ella también la mira
> desde otra puerta.

The new moon. She too is gazing on her from another door.

Let us now compare a Western *haiku* and an Oriental one. First here is one by Borges:

> ¿Es un imperio
> esa luz que se apaga
> o una luciérnaga?

This dying flash is it an empire or a firefly? Compare it to a *haiku* by Bashō:

> Natsu-kusa ya!
> Tsuwamono-domo ga
> Yume no ato.

You summer grasses! Glorious dreams of great warriors now only ruins. The subject of both poems is commonplace: the mortality of all things. We should recall, by the way, Seneca's memorable sentence: *Una nox fuit inter urbem maximam et nullam*, in which the last word speaks of the destruction of the entire city. The two *haikus* quoted express the futility of all human endeavours.

Next we might look at this *haiku* by Borges:

> La vieja mano
> sigue trazando versos
> para el olvido.

This old hand goes on writing verses for oblivion. A *haiku* by Jōsō is complementary:

> No mo yama mo
> Yuki ni torarete
> Nani mo nashi.

Both plains and mountains have been captured by the snow. There is nothing left. Jōsō (1662–1704) was one of the ten special disciples of Bashō and a follower of Zen Buddhism. He tells us that nothing lasts. Even the mountains and their strength are blotted out by the most immaterial things such as snow. In Borges' *haiku*, the *haiku* itself is written for final and relentless oblivion.

Two other *haikus* are presented for comparison. Borges writes:

> La vasta noche
> no es ahora otra cosa
> que una fragancia.

The endless night is now but a fragrance. And the poet Mokudō (1665–1723) wrote:

> Haru-kaze ya!
> Mugi no naka yuku
> Mizu no oto.

A gentle spring breeze! Through green barley plants rushes the sound of water. Perhaps this last *haiku* by Borges is one of his best. The poem refers to a single instant where the unseen night reveals herself to the poet. The last line of Mokudō's *haiku* had been used already by his teacher Bashō in his most famous poem. Nobody thought of repetition as plagiarism; nobody thought in terms of personal vanity. The *haiku* is a splendid habit of a whole country, not of an individual. It is considered that poetry in Japan is a living thing, and every person from a laborer to the Emperor is a poet.

In examining these poems it is necessary to ask if there is a certain virtue common to all poetry in all ages and lands. The answer may be sought in Borges' foreword to *El Oro de los Tigres*, that: "to a true poet every single moment of his life, every deed or dream should be felt by him as poetic, since essentially it *is* poetic" . . . "Beauty is common in this world." In the foreword to *El Otro, El Mismo* Borges tells us that "the fate of a writer is very strange. At the beginning he is Baroque, insolently Baroque; aftger long years he may attain, if the stars are auspicious, not simplicity, which is meaningless, but a shy and secret complexity." This is the way of the *haiku*. The brief *haiku* is the apex of a vast pyramid.

III. *Borges and Other Poets*

CHRISTOPHER MAURER

The Poet's Poets: Borges and Quevedo

Caminas por el campo de Castilla
Y casi no lo ves. Un intrincado
Versículo de Juan es tu cuidado
Y apenas reparaste en la amarilla

Puesta del sol. La vaga luz delira
Y en el confín del Este se dilata
Esa luna de escarnio y de escarlata
Que es acaso el espejo de la Ira.

Alzas los ojos y la miras. Una
Memoria de algo que fue tuyo empieza
Y se apaga. La pálida cabeza

Bajas y sigues caminando triste,
Sin recordar el verso que escribiste:
Y su epitafio la sangrienta luna.[1]

I would like to declare the meaning of Borges' sonnet on Quevedo, the meaning of Quevedo to Borges, and the meaning of both of them to me.

The sonnet "A un viejo poeta" ("To an Old Poet") belongs to the oldest genre in Castilian literature—the poetic gloss. Borrowing an image from one of Dámaso Alonso's essays on the *jarchas*,[2] we can think of line 14 (borrowed from one of Quevedo's sonnets to the Duke of Osuna[3]) as a precious stone which "because of its brevity and extreme concentration" allowed itself to be set in precious metal.

The precedents of Borges' sonnet are remote and illustrious. The Italian critic Giovanni Caravaggi reminds us that some of the earliest Castilian sonnets were in fact glosses: Boscán began his experimentation with Italian meter by glossing verses of Petrarch, and occasionally placed the line or lines being glossed at the poem's "point of maximum tension," just as Borges does here.[4] Petrarch himself ended each stanza of his *canzone* 70 with a line from one of his favorite poets, and that encouraged Garcilaso to end his sonnet 22 with a line of Petrarch: "non esservi passato oltra la gonna."

But Borges' use of the gloss is far more interesting than that of Boscán or Garcilaso or Petrarch, for Borges believes that "it is not so much the text, as the way the text is read, that makes one literature differ from another. . . ."[5] Before pursuing this, let us listen to what he has said about the line "Y su epitafio la sangrienta luna."[6]

Borges does not seem to think very highly of the sonnet to which it belongs, "the one about the geographical burial of the Duke of Osuna, who is mourned by rivers and has volcanos at his wake."[7] But he discusses lines 7 and 8 of Quevedo's sonnet apropos of certain verses by the Nordic poet Egil Skalagrímson, "The falcon of the dew of the sword," and "Serpents of the pirates' moon." Borges believes that such lines as these

give one an almost organic satisfaction. It does not matter what they strive to transmit; what they suggest is nil. They do not invite one to dream, nor do they provoke images or passions. They are not points of departure, rather ends in themselves. Their pleasure—a sufficient, minimal pleasure—lies in the heterogeneous contact of their words. I look for the classical equivalent of such pleasure, and I come upon Quevedo's famous sonnet to the Duke of Osuna. . . . It is easy to prove that the splendid efficacy of these two lines,

> Su tumba son de Flandes las campañas
> Y su epitafio la sangrienta luna

is previous to, and independent of, any interpretation. I say the same of the expression which follows, *llanto militar* [military wailing], whose meaning is as trivial as it is clear: the wailing of the soldiers. As for the *sangrienta luna* [the blood-red moon], it is better not to know that it is a symbol of the Turks, eclipsed by I know not what piracies of don Pedro Téllez Girón.[8]

Spanish poets seem to have been finding their way towards that line ever since the Battle of Lepanto in 1571, about fifty years before Quevedo wrote his sonnet and had long taken pleasure in confusing the Turkish crescent and the real moon.[9] "Who can pity you now," asks Herrera, "you who follow the moon, adulterous Asia, sunken in vice?"[10] Like so many of his most memorable lines, Quevedo's *"sangrienta luna"* is the sublimination of a literary commonplace.

But in the context of Borges' poem, that venerable commonplace comes alive. It is as though Borges were emulating Pierre Menard, author of the Quijote. It is a revelation to compare Borges' line with that of Quevedo: "La sangrienta luna: ¡la idea es asombrosa!"[11] It is hardly true that the phrase suggests nothing, transmits nothing. What was once a tired symbol is now a genuine metaphor that reminds the reader of some secret relation between the moon and human blood.[12] In 1921 Borges wrote that this very metaphor, and others like it, contort objective reality and help to create a new one.[13]

Let us return now to Borges' use of the gloss. I am using the term "poetic gloss" to mean any poem which deliberately provides a new context for words taken from another text. Not all glosses are explicative, but all of them remind us to what extent meaning depends upon context. For example, the meaning of the same *estribillo* changes from one *letrilla* to another, and it might even be argued that the *estribillo* acquires a different meaning each time it returns within any given poem. Borges' sonnet places a well-known expression in new surroundings: obviously, the words *"Y su epitafio la sangrienta luna"* mean one thing in Quevedo's sonnet and another in Borges'. The lack of "identity" of those words, their lack of semantic *sameness* seems to me to reinforce the message of Borges' sonnet and of the book to which it belongs.

The pathos of that sonnet lies in Quevedo's inability to remember a line of his own verse. This is doubly ironic, for not only does the old poet look at the real moon, he is meditating upon a verse from Revelation, Chapter 6: "And I beheld when he had opened the sixth seal, and, lo, there was a great earthquake; and the sun became black as sackcloth of hair, and the moon became as blood."[14] John's words describe the day of wrath, *dies irae*, which justifies the reference in line 8 to the moon as a mirror of wrath. It is, after all, a mirror.[15] Here the moon is the mirror of the Lamb, of a wrathful God. The afterglow of sunset, any sunset, reminds us of Judgment Day:[16] the old poet himself stands in judgment. In the dying light (light of the sun, light of consciousness) he is no longer himself; he is no longer a writer, only a reader (in the background is Quevedo's lovely sonnet on reading, one of Borges' favorites, "Retirado a la paz de estos desiertos").

It is not difficult to discover the meaning of Quevedo's inability to remember what he once wrote. *El otro, el mismo* is a book of elegies. The elegy compares, either implicitly or explicitly, what is present and what is absent—in this case what is remembered and what is forgotten. What Borges compares most frequently in *El otro, el mismo* is Divine Providence, on the one hand, "the infinite web of cause and effect" and, on the other hand, the course of human events. The writer's ignorance of his own work, or of the significance of his work, reminds us of man's ignorance of Divine Providence. The sonnet to Cervantes entitled "Un soldado de Urbina" alludes to precisely the same ignorance of divine purpose. Line 14 thus deepens the irony, if not the pathos, of the sonnet. Even had Quevedo remembered his line, he could not have foreseen what it would mean to us. In a luminous page entitled "Mutaciones," Borges observes that "there is not a single thing on earth that oblivion does not erase, or that memory does not alter; and no one knows into what images the future will translate him." [17]

Perhaps this is the right moment to speculate upon Borges' image of Quevedo.

We will ignore, for the moment, the verbal habits that Borges admired and studied in Quevedo, among them the use of certain types of metaphor. *La hora de todos* seemed to him to be "a seedbed of tropes"; [18] the use of the epithet that contains an entire metaphor (Borges says of Quevedo, "Abrevió en sus epítetos la entereza de una metáfora," and provides numerous examples); [19] the verb or epithet that gives material properties to abstract nouns, the love of paradox and of the little paradox called oxymoron; [20] the coining of verbs from adjectives and nouns, and the use of the second person singular to engage the reader and to anticipate his objections. [21] Quevedo's discovery of words within words and Borges' use of words according to their etymological meaning hardly spring from the same impulse, but both make the commonplace seem very strange.

We shall pass over all this, because much has been said of the stylistic affinities between Borges and Quevedo, but all too little about their spiritual affinity. [22] Borges once called Torres Villarroel "our brother in Quevedo,"[23] but he was not thinking of a fraternity of style. In 1927 he wrote, "I cannot remember when I first began to read Quevedo; he is now the author I visit most."[24] "His work is before us," he wrote in 1925, "with its apparent diversity of purpose. How can one reduce it to unity and coin a symbol for it? The only thing that ought to interest us is Quevedo's myth: the banner and the meaning that we make of it."[25]

The Quevedo who accompanied Borges in the mid-1920s offered apparently an image of freedom and an example of self-truth. Quevedo meant rebellion against the "stilted provincialism" of the Real Academia Española, with its ideal of timeless propriety. In his introduction to an anthology of Latin American poetry in 1926, Borges wrote defiantly that in the "new American poetry"

language frees itself. Intransitive verbs become active ones, and the adjective does duty as a noun. Barbarisms flourish, as do neologisms and archaisms. In the face of the affected provincialism exercised by the Academy, our language is enriching itself.[26]

Not since those tireless nights in which . . . Quevedo took his pleasure with the Spanish language have there been such . . . images, such floodtides, such Indian raids of metaphors as the ones you will find in this book.[27]

The "rebellious Quevedo who took words from Latin and Greek and even from *germanía*, the cant of ruffians" served as justification for Borges' own raid on *el lenguaje criollo*.[28]

To certain Spanish and Latin American writers in the 1920s Góngora was no less a symbol of artistic freedom than Quevedo, but as Borges admired the *conceptismo* of Quevedo, he rejected the *culteranismo* of don Luis[29] and his modern disciples. Borges unjustly thought of Rubén Darío as Góngora's *albacea*, his literary executor.[30] Many of Quevedo's attacks on don Luis allude to color and light; so do Borges' attacks on so-called *rubenianismo*, with its *matices borrosos* and *apuntaciones de colores*.[31] Quevedo mocked Góngora for his *crepusculallas* and Borges reproached *Rubén y sus secuaces* for their *palabras crepusculares*. Quevedo laughed at the *platería de los cultos* and Borges ridiculed the *crisolampos, amatistas*, and *carbunclos* of the early work of Herrera y Reissig.[32] The battle between *culteranismo* and *conceptismo* was being relived in Buenos Aires in the early 1920s.

Borges was following Quevedo's example when he penned the "Ejecución de tres palabras," in which he burns at the stake the three words *inefable, misterio*, and *azul*. The precedents were the "Sueño del infierno," the "Cuento de cuentos," and perhaps also the *premáticas*. Borges detested the *jerigonza* (the word Quevedo applied to the language of don Luis) of the Modernists and those of their disciples who "vocean nubes y gesticulan balbuceos,"[33] a phrase which either Borges or Quevedo might have written. The joyous idea of burning them at the stake is Quevedo's, as is the ridicule of poets whose thoughts are dictated by rhyme. Quevedo had called a woman *absoluta*; the law of rhyme had made her a *puta*. The *modernistas*, Borges noticed, were condemned to rhyme *azul* with *tul, gandul, abedul*, and even *baúl*.[34]

Borges' line-by-line commentary of a sonnet by Góngora, his analysis of certain lines by Cervantes and by Herrera y Reissig owe their form, or at least their cruel irreverence, to Quevedo's *Comento contra 73 estancias de don Juan Ruíz de Alarcón*. "Las alarmas del doctor Américo Castro", in which don Américo is dismissed as an "incoherent writer of orthopedic devices that gather sheep, literary genres that play football, and torpedoed grammar books," recalls Quevedo's *Perinola*,[35] the book in which Borges read the strange words, "Historia infinita temporis atque aeternitatis."

As for the Quevedo who turned Apollo into a fat red silversmith of mountain peaks ("Bermejazo platero de las cumbres") and Daphne into a bat ("pues vais del sol y de la luz huyendo"), Borges shared his hatred of empty mythology and poetic untruth, protesting against "the coiners of false art who force upon us their rusty mythological figures."[36]

For a time, Borges *was* Quevedo. It seems that Quevedo did more than provide him with literary poses, verbal techniques or polemical tricks. He helped Borges fight his battles, and those battles were far from trivial. The polemic between *culteranismo* and *conceptismo* revolves, after all, around a timeless problem: the relative importance of what one says and how one says it; substance and form, the idea and its verbal expression. Jaime Alazraki observes that for Borges style is not silverwork but ironwork, not ornament but function, utility, and efficacy.[37] In recent years Borges has spoken apologetically of his early enthusiasm for Quevedo and for other seventeenth-century writers; he declares that he once thought literature was nothing more than technique.[38] It is as though he had forgotten that Quevedo was once his dearest symbol of the stylistic "utility" mentioned by Alazraki. In the 1920s Borges believed that *conceptismo* was an attempt to follow "con más veracidad las corvaduras de un pensamiento complejo."[39]

In recent years Borges has spoken of a public Quevedo more or less incapable of writing intimate poetry.

> My destiny is the Castilian tongue,
> The bronze of don Francisco de Quevedo.[40]

This is the "bronze" of the *Marco Bruto*, the bronze from which Quevedo cast epitaphs like the one to Osuna.

In *Other Inquisitions* and elsewhere, Borges declares that Quevedo's greatness is fundamentally verbal greatness. "To judge him a philosopher or a theologian or . . . a statesman is an error allowed by the titles of his works, but not their contents."[41] No doubt Borges is correct. But what of Quevedo as a man, Quevedo as an attitude towards life, as a *sentidor del mundo?*[42] What of the Quevedo who wrote the so-called "metaphysical poems" that ponder, as Borges himself has pondered, the nature of time and death?[43]

There is a certain stoic calm in Borges' later verse which I cannot help but associate with Quevedo. Quevedo forbade himself from taking delight in the creation:

They will tell me to turn my eyes to the beauty of the earth, to the light of the sun, to relatives, to parents, to my estate, to delights and tastes. They tell me that I should weep when someone is swept away from these things halfway through his life. But it consoles me to see someone free of these things, for the beauty of the earth reminds us only of its end.[44]

Borges could never have written those melancholy words. He writes in "Evigkeit," "I shall not deny, like a coward, what my clay has blessed," and he has ridiculed the Spanish commonplace that the hour of death is more real than the hour of life.[45]

And yet, Borges and Quevedo write of detachment from human passions and calmness in the face of death. Quevedo's stoic persona closely resembles that of Borges: in the poems, the poets' awareness of the inevitability of death give both a sense of invulnerability. The source of Quevedo's calm lies in the contemplation of death in everyday life. "You are invulnerable," Borges tells his reader. "Have not the spirits who govern your destiny / given you the certainty of dust?" And he adds, "Reflect that in a way you are already dead." [46]

What of the sonnet we have just examined? There is comfort in one's ignorance of divine purpose and in the conviction that oblivion conquers all, erasing personal identity. This is the dark lesson taught by both Borges and Quevedo. Quevedo, remembering Vergil, calls upon death thus:

> Come now, oh fear of sages and of the strong.
> The indignant, moaning body will go down
> Beneath the shades, and my dry lips will drink
> Their fill of oblivion. [47]

Borges seems to be remembering Quevedo in a sonnet about death:

> Quiero beber su cristalino Olvido,
> Ser para siempre; pero no haber sido.
>
> (I want to drink her clear Oblivion,
> and be forever, never having been.) [48]

Terror of dissolution, or yearning for dissolution govern Quevedo's best poems. As a young man, Borges saw that one of Quevedo's sonnets, "Cerrar podrá mis ojos la postrera / sombra que me llevare el blanco día," (to which Borges devoted a fine essay,) seems to promise immortality: "Intensity promises [Quevedo] immortality; not the intensity of *any* feeling, but rather the intensity of amorous craving, or, better said, of the act of love." [49] The early poem entitled "Inscripción en cualquier sepulcro" departs from that idea. [50] But in more recent years Borges seems to have written and spoken more often about the longing to be rid of himself: "*Defiéndeme de mí*. The words were spoken / By Montaigne and Browne and a Spaniard I forget." [51] That Spaniard was probably Quevedo: "*Desnúdame de mí*." [52] Certainly the idea is his: "Soy en mi defensa un peligro sumo," [53] "Descanso ya de andar de mí cargado." [54] Quevedo's admirer Francisco López de Zárate wrote these words, which are worthy of Borges: "Hacedme, con no ser tan yo, dichoso." "Make me less myself, and therefore blessed." [55]

Is Quevedo's greatness verbal greatness, as Borges insists? Gómez de la Serna once wrote these memorable words: Quevedo's work is "una sustancia activa que da bravura al corazón y a la conciencia, aprendiendo cómo, desde el que lo ve todo, nos llega la enseñanza de menospreciarlo todo." [56] Perhaps Quevedo's greatness, like that of Borges, lies in having given enduring verbal form to a certain attitude towards life. Among the poet's poets is this seventeenth-century Spaniard who, like Borges himself, provides consolation in the face of death; this stoic who, like Borges, wonders at Time ("el es, y el será, y el fue"), who makes us feel that life is a dream, that we cannot know God's plans for us, that death is a law, not a punishment; and that God will somehow defend us and deliver us . . . from ourselves.

NOTES

1. Jorge Luis Borges, *El otro, el mismo* (Buenos Aires: Emecé, 1969): 79.
2. Dámaso Alonso, *Primavera temprana de la literatura europea: lírica, épica, novela* (Madrid: Ediciones Guadarrama, 1961): 61–2.
3. "Memoria inmortal de don Pedro Girón, Duque de Osuna, muerto en la prisión" Edited by J. M. Blecua. Francisco de Quevedo, *Poesía original completa* (Barcelona: Planeta, 1981): 268–9.
4. One technique of Boscán was to "orientare la costruzione del sonetto verso una citazione autorevole, che viene collocata nel punto di massima tensione." G. Caravaggi, "Alle origini del petrarchismo in Spagna," *Miscellanea di studi ispanici*, 24 (1971–1973): 92.
5. Jorge Luis Borges, *Otras inquisiciones*, 3rd edition (Buenos Aires: Emecé, 1966): 218. "una literatura difiere de otra, ulterior o anterior, menos por el texto que por la manera de ser leída." As an example Borges quotes the words "amica silentia lunae," which "significan ahora la luna íntima, silenciosa y luciente, y en la *Eneida* significaron el interlunio, la oscuridad que permitió a los griegos entrar en la ciudadela de Troya." (217–18).
6. Borges' poem on the moon landing of 1971 ends with a reminiscence of the very line of Quevedo: ". . . La luna, / Que el amor secular busca en el cielo / Con triste rostro y no saciado anhelo, / Será su monumento, eterna y una." Jorge Luis Borges, *El oro de los tigres* (Buenos Aires: Emecé, 1972): 53.
7. "Un soneto de don Francisco de Quevedo" in Jorge Luis Borges, *El idioma de los argentinos* (Buenos Aires: Colección Indice, 1928): 75. Edited by M. Gleizer.
8. "Las kennigar" in Jorge Luis Borges, *Historia de la eternidad*, 6th edition (Buenos Aires: Emecé, 1969): 45–6. Borges returns to this sonnet in 1982 in the prologue to an anthology of Quevedo's verse: "La línea *Y su epitafio la sangrienta luna* permite dos interpretaciones: la luna, debidamente roja, sobre los campos de batalla de Flandes, y la blanca medialuna, sobre fondo rojo, de la bandera turca. Quevedo habrá imaginado las dos; lo significativo es el hecho de que nuestra emoción precede a las interpretaciones y no depende de ellas." Francisco de Quevedo, *Antología poética* (Madrid: Alianza Editorial, 1982): 10. I am grateful to Robert Katz for calling this book to my attention.
9. José López De Toro, *Los poetas de Lepanto* (Madrid: Instituto Histórica de Marina, 1950): 121. For similar verses by Quevedo himself see *Poesía original*, 262, 265.
10. Fernando De Herrera, *Obra poética*. Edited by J. M. Blecua, vol. I (Madrid: Anejos del BRAE, 1975): 253.
11. "Pierre Menard, autor del *Quijote*" in Jorge Luis Borges, *Ficciones* 8th edition (Buenos Aires: Emecé, 1956): 55.

206 / *Borges the Poet*

12. Ovid's witch Dipsas alludes to the same relation: "songuine, si qua fides, stillantia sidera vidi; / purpureus Lunae sanguine vultus erat" (*Amorum Liber I*, VIII, 11–12). Cf. Lope de Vega, *El caballero de Olmedo*, Act III, verse 860.

13. Jorge Luis Borges, "Apuntaciones críticas: la metáfora," *Cosmópolis*, (Nov. 1921): 401. I have not been able to see this essay and am following Zunilda Gertel's paraphrase in "La metáfora en la estética de Borges," in *Jorge Luis Borges*, edited by J. Alazraki, (Madrid: Taurus, 1976): 92.

14. Revelation 6:12.

15. Borges, "1924" and "La luna," *El otro, el mismo*, 75, 175.

16. ". . . el Juicio Final de cada tarde," writes Borges in *Fervor de Buenos Aires*. Cf. "Ultimo sol en Villa Luro" in *Luna de enfrente*.

17. "Mutaciones," Jorge Luis Borges, *El hacedor* (Buenos Aires: Emecé, 1971): 37.

18. "La adjetivación," Jorge Luis Borges, *El tamaño de mi esperanza* (Buenos Aires: Editorial Proa, 1926): 53.

19. Quevedo's expression *boca saqueada*, given as an example, reappears in Borges' sonnet to Walt Whitman (*El otro, el mismo*, 161). Another direct imitation of Quevedo occurs in the poem "Juan I, 14" (*Elogio de la sombra*), where Borges' line "Yo que soy el Es, el Fue y el Será" recalls Quevedo's "Soy un fue, y un será, y un es cansado." (*Poesía original*, 4).

20. On the use of the oxymoron in Borges' prose see Alazraki, *La prosa narrativa de Borges*, 2nd. ed., (Madrid: Gredos, 1974): 223 ff.

21. See, for example, "Ejercicio de análisis" (*Tamaño*, 107–114) and the "Prólogo" and "La nadería de la personalidad" (*Inquisiciones*). The use of *vos* is mentioned by Ana María Barrenechea in "Borges y el lenguage" (Alazraki, 221). Giuseppi Bellini observes that the prologue of *Fervor* "per lo stile stringato e vivace, per il ricorso improviso al 'tuteo' del lettore, non certo per il contenuto nichilista, rinconduce ai prologhi quevedeschi dei *Sueños*." *Quevedo nella poesia ispano-americana '900* (Milano: Editrice Viscontea, 1967): 83.

22. An exception is Bellini's admirable essay, just cited: he writes of the "clima di spiritualita affine" of Borges and Quevedo, and their common interest in "i temi del tempo e dell'eternita della vita e della morte."

23. Borges, *Inquisiciones*, 7.

24. Borges, "La fruición literaria," *El idioma de los argentinos*, 102.

25. Borges, "Menoscabo y grandeza de Quevedo," *Inquisiciones*, 39.

26. *Indice de la nueva poesía americana*. Prólogo de Alberto Hidalgo, Vicente Huidobro y Jorge Luis Borges (Buenos Aires: Sociedad de Publicaciones *El Inca*, Ediciones Especiales, 1926): 17.

27. Hidalgo, *Indice*, 17.

28. In defense of *lunfardo* Borges writes: "La germanía fue el lunfardo hispánicao del Renacimiento, y la ejercieron escritores ilustres: Quevedo, Cervantes, Mateo Alemán. El primero, con ésa su sensualidad verbal ardentísima, con ése su famoso apasionamiento por las palabras, la prodigó en sus bailes y jácaras, y hasta en su grandiosa fantasmagoría 'La hora de todos.'" See "Invectiva contra el arrabalero," *Tamaño*, 139–40.

29. Verbal reminiscences of Góngora's moral poetry are easily found in Borges; for example, his many variations on the last line of Góngora's sonnet 149, "en tierra, en humo, en polvo, en sombra, en nada," and on the last line of sonnet 163, "los días que royendo estan los años."

30. In *Fervor* ("A quien leyere") Borges writes: "A la lírica decorativamente visual y lustrosa que nos legó don Luis de Góngora por intermedio de su albecea Rubén, quise oponer otra. . . ."

31. Speaking of his days as an *ultaísta*, Borges writes: "Abominamos los matices borrosos del rubenismo, y nos enardeció la metáfora por la precisión que hay en ella, por su algébrica forma de correlacionar lejanías."

32. Borges, *Inquisiciones*, 141.

33. Borges, *Inquisiciones*, 153.
34. Borges, *Tamaño*, 103–4 and 120; *Inquisiciones*, 157; and *Indice*, 15.
35. I am thinking especially of this sentence from the *Perinola*: "De manera—dijo la bermejuela—que Montserrate cuanto al monte es capote, cigüeña, río atollado, cuatro lentiscos, cuatro huevos, lagarto de damasco, lobo con tajón y trinchante, toros con estoques de marfil, tigre con montante, rogativa de rosales, monje enfermo, ermitaño inquieto, lenteja y vieja." Quevedo, *Obras completas*. Edited by F. Buendía, Vol. I (Madrid: Aguilar, 1969): 455.
36. Borges, "Ultraísmo," *Nosotros* (Dec. 1921): 466.
37. Alazraki, *La prosa narrativa*, 161.
38. Alazraki, *La prosa narrativa*, 153.
39. Borges, *Inquisiciones*, 107, a propos of Unamuno.
40. Borges, *El oro de los tigres*, 81.
41. Borges, *Otras inquisiciones*, 56. In *Leopoldo Lugones* Borges writes, "Como el de Quevedo, como el de Joyce, como el de Claudel, el genio de Leopoldo Lugones es fundamentalmente verbal." 2nd ed. (Buenos Aires: Editorial Pleamar, 1965): 11.
42. A phrase Borges himself applies to Quevedo in *Inquisiciones*, 45.
43. See Bellini, 84 ff.
44. From a letter of 1631 to don Antonio de Mendoza, in *Obras completas*, 921.
45. "No sé por qué razón la hora de la muerte ha de ser más verdadera que las de vivir y el viernes que el lunes." *El idioma de los argentinos*, ed. cit. Cf. *Inquisiciones*, 101–3.
46. From "A quien está leyéndome," in *El otro, el mismo*, 181.
49. "Un soneto de don Francisco de Quevedo," *Fervor de Buenos Aires*, 79.
50. The poem "Inscripción sepulcral" from the same book, *Fervor de Buenos Aires*, is perhaps the early work where one hears Quevedo's voice most distinctly.
51. Borges, "Religio Medici, 1643," *El oro de los tigres*, 49.
52. Quevedo, *Poesía original completa*, 20.
53. Quevedo, *Poesía original*, 13.
54. Quevedo, *Poesía original*, 5.
55. Francisco López de Zárate, *Obras varias*. Edited by José Simón Díaz, Vol. II (Madrid: CSIC, 1947): 204.
56. Gómez de la Serna, *Quevedo* (Buenos Aires: Austral, 1953): 227.

BIBLIOGRAPHY

Alazraki, Jaime. *La prosa narrativa de Borges*. Madrid: Gredos, 1974.
Alazraki, ed. "La metáfora en la estética de Borges." In *Jorge Luis Borges*. Madrid: Taurus, 1976.
Alonso, Dámaso. *Primavera temprana de la literatura europea: lírica, épica, novela*. Madrid: Ediciones Guadarrama, 1961.
Bellini, Giuseppi. *Quevedo nella poesia ispano-americana del '900*. Milan: Editrice Viscontea, 1967.
Borges, Jorge Luis. "Apuntaciones críticas: la metáfora." *Cosmópolis*, (Nov. 1921), 401.
Borges, *El oro de los tigres*. Buenos Aires: Emecé, 1956.
Borges, *El otro, el mismo*. Buenos Aires: Emecé, 1969.
Borges, *Fervor de Buenos Aires*. N.p.,n.d.
Borges, "La adjetivación." In *El tamaño de mi esperanza*. Buenos Aires: Editorial Proa, 1926.
Borges, "Las kennigar." In *Historia de la eternidad*. Buenos Aires: Emecé, 1969.
Borges, *Leopoldo Lugones*. Buenos Aires: Editorial Pleamar, 1965.
Borges, "Mutaciones." In *El hacedor*. Buenos Aires: Emecé, 1971.
Borges, *Otras inquisiciones*. Buenos Aires: Emecé, 1966.

Borges, "Pierre Menard, autor del Quijote." In *Ficciones*. Buenos Aires: Emecé, 1956.
Borges, "Ultraísmo." *Nosotros*, (Dec. 1921), 466.
Borges, "Un soneto de don Francisco de Quevedo." In *El idioma de los argentinos*. Buenos Aires: Colección Indice, 1928.
Gómez de la Serna, Ramón. *Quevedo*. Buenos Aires: Austral, 1953.
Hidalgo, Alberto, Vincente Huidobro y Jorge Luis Borges. *Indice de la nueva poesía americana*. Buenos Aires: Sociedad de Publicaciones, 1926.
Herrera, Fernando de. *Obra poética*. Edited by J. M. Blecua. Madrid: Anejos del BRAE, 1975.
Quevedo, Francisco de. *Antología poética*. Madrid: Alianza Editorial, 1982.
Quevedo. *Poesía original completa*. Edited by F. Buendía. Madrid: Aguilar, 1969.
Toro, José López de. *Los poesas de Lepanto*. Madrid: Instituto Histórico de Marina, 1950.
Zárate, Francisco López de. *Obras varias*. Edited by José Simón Díaz. Madrid: CSIC, 1947.
Zárate, Francisco López de. *Obras varias*. Edited by José Simón Díaz. Madrid: CSIC, 1947.

W. KENNETH HOLDITCH

Borges and Emerson: The Poet as Intellectual

Perhaps the most remarkable aspect of Borges' deep love for the literature of the United States is the high position in which he has repeatedly, in writing and in interviews, placed Ralph Waldo Emerson as poet. One is certainly not surprised at his appraisal of Walt Whitman as an epic poet, or Emily Dickinson as "perhaps the greatest poet that America . . . has as yet produced," or when he speaks with admiration of the ideas expressed in Emerson's essays; but the praise for Emerson as a poet is another thing altogether. Traditionally Emerson has been admired by American readers and critics, rightly or wrongly, as a philosopher, thinker, and creator of pithy and memorable aphorisms that generously pepper the prose of his famous essays. His poetry, however, interesting insofar as it conveys some of the same philosophical concepts belonging to American romanticism, has generally been relegated to a distant second place. Yes, we remember the farmers who gathered by "the rude bridge that arched the flood" and "fired the shot heard round the world" and may even recall isolated lines such as "Things are in the saddle / And ride mankind," but when we quote Emerson, it is usually from unforgettable lines in his prose; and such essays as "Nature," "Self-Reliance," and "The American Scholar," for example. Borges' praise for the poems, then, places them in a new and intriguing light in which we can identify those aspects of Emerson's poetry Borges finds of particular interest and merit; examine specific poems which he singles out for comment or commendation; and distinguish any Emersonian elements which are present as allusions or influences in Borges' own works.

The one aspect of Emerson's poetry most often commented upon by Borges is its intellectual quality. His most recent published remarks on the subject appear in *Borges at Eighty* in which he states that Emerson, like Walt Whitman, is "one of those men who cannot be thought away," that "literature would not be what it is today" without Poe, Melville, Whitman, Thoreau and Emerson, then singles out Emerson for particular commendation: "I love Emerson and I am very fond of his poetry. He is to me the one intellectual poet—in any case the one intellectual poet who has ideas. The others are merely intellectual with no ideas at all. In the case of Emerson, he had ideas and was thoroughly a poet." [1] The "intellectual poet who has ideas"—this is the characterization that surfaces again and again whenever Borges has written or spoken of the great Transcendentalist.

What exactly does Borges mean by the phrase "intellectual poet"? Is his definition of the word *intellectual* a restrictive one, or are we to accept it as meaning merely rational as opposed to emotional, merely possessed of ideas as opposed to being devoid of same? Part of the answer may be found in his assertion that the "breadth of his mind was astonishing," [2] and his comparison of Emerson to three other writers may illuminate this evaluation. In 1949, in the prologue to *Representative Men*, which he had translated into Spanish, Borges identifies Emerson as a classical writer in opposition to Thomas Carlyle the romantic—whom Borges had earlier loved but later declared unreadable—and asserts that Emerson is far superior to those "compatriots who have obscured his glory: Whitman and Poe." [3] In *An Introduction to American Literature* he states that Friederich Nietzsche had remarked "that he felt himself so close to Emerson, that he did not dare to praise him because it would have been like praising himself." [4] Borges counters that identification between the two philosophers, however, by observing that Emerson is "a finer writer and a finer thinker than Nietzsche, though most people wouldn't say that today." [5] Granted that Borges reserves much of his praise and respect related to philosophers for that other German master, Schopenhauer, his comparison of Nietzsche to Emerson attests surely to his admiration for the philosophy of the American and suggests that it is in the philosophical realm, not only in his prose but also in his poetry, that Emerson excels intellectually. This is true especially in poetry, one might argue, since Borges has elsewhere asserted that Emerson's prose has a "disconnected character" and suffers from the fact that he does not construct valid, sequential arguments in the essays but merely strings together "memorable sayings, sometimes full of wisdom, which do not proceed from what [has] come before nor prepare for what [is] to come."[6]

When he mentions Emerson in connection with Poe, Borges observes rather ambiguously that "the most curious" volume of the twelve that contains Emerson's collected works is the one devoted to his poetry, then reiterates his belief that Emerson was "a great intellectual poet" and that Poe, "whom he called, not without disdain, the 'jingle man,' did not interest him."[7] In the short fiction entitled "The Other Death," the persona argues that Emerson is "a poet far more complex, far more skilled, and truly more extraordinary than the unfortunate Poe."[8]

In the preface to *Doctor Brodie's Report*, Borges states that "the art of writing is mysterious" and "the opinions we hold are ephemeral." He prefers, he continues, "the Platonic idea of the Muse to that of Poe, who reasoned, or feigned to reason, that the writing of a poem is an act of the intelligence. It never fails to amaze me that the classics advance a romantic theory of poetry, and romantic poets a classical theory."[9] Here he is referring, of course, to Poe's famous "explanation" in "The Philosophy of Composition" of the allegedly rational procedure through which he wrote that seemingly irrational poem "The Raven."

Later Borges was to reaffirm this belief when in a 1980 conversation he stated that "opinions come and go, politics come and go, my personal opinions are changing all the time. But when I write I try to be faithful to the dream, to be true to the dream."[10] This rejection of Poe's belief that writing a poem is "an act of the intelligence" and the assertion that our opinions are "ephemeral" might seem markedly contrary to his praise for Emerson as an intellectual poet: a paradox, and how should it be solved? Probably Borges would not want it solved, since much of his work attests to love of the paradoxical, but critics never tire of trying.

The answer to the seeming dilemma lies perhaps in "A Vindication of the Cabala" where writers are categorized as journalists, verse writers, and intellectuals. The journalist, Borges states, in his "ephemeral utterances . . . allows for a noticeable amount of chance," while the verse writer subjects "meaning to euphonic necessities (or superstitions)," but the intellectual is another matter. Although he has not eliminated chance, either in prose or verse, "he has denied it as much as possible, and limited its incalculable concurrence. He remotely resembles the Lord, for Whom the vague concept of chance holds no meaning, the God, the perfected God of the theologians, Who sees all at once (*uno intelligendu actu*), not only all the events of this replete world, but also those that would take place if even the most evanescent of them should change, the impossible ones also." [11] This presumably is the kind of poet that Borges believes Emerson to be, and the introduction of the notion that the intellectual poet sees all—not only that which exists, but that which might have been—relates to a favorite theme of Borges' own poetry. His admiration for the intellectual process as exemplified in Emerson's versifying surely relates to the idea of the nineteenth-century writer that all poetry derives from "meter-making arguments" rather than from meter.

Emerson is admired by Borges not only for his intellectuality, but, as Ronald Christ points out, for being a "man of letters" of the caliber of G. K. Chesterton, H. G. Wells, Thomas DeQuincey, George Bernard Shaw, and Robert Louis Stevenson—all, the critics note, "lovers of words, poets, or storytellers, weavers of theories, manifestations of the writer as *grammaticus*." In addition, Borges has commented on the writer as *vate* or *místico*, the writer, as Christ defines him, "who looks through the solidness of our reality and reveals another world and perhaps a secret scheme or logic which controls our world." Emerson's transcendentalism, the critic concludes, "is explicitly vatic in the Borgesian sense. . . ." [12] In his discussion of Transcendentalism in *An Introduction to American Literature*, Borges points out that the New England version of Romanticism has its origin in, among other sources, Hindu pantheism and "the visionary theology of Swedenborg"—a favorite of Borges', of course—who proposed a belief that "the external light is a mirror of the spiritual." [13]

Emerson's theory of art obviously holds an appeal for Borges, since he refers often to its principles. In *Borges at Eighty*, he is quoted as observing, "I remember what Emerson said: language is fossil poetry. He said every word is a metaphor. You can verify that by looking a word up in the dictionary. All words are metaphors—a fossil poetry, a fine metaphor itself." In the same work, he remarks that "a book, when it lies in the bookshelf — I think Emerson has said so (I like to be indebted to

Emerson, one of my heroes) — a book is a thing among things . . . A book is unaware of itself until the reader comes."[14] Often he has reiterated his agreement with Emerson that creative reading is as important as creative writing, the reader as essential in the scheme of things as he who writes the poetry. Another aspect of Emerson's esthetic, as Christ points out, is the belief that "a work of art is an abstract of the epitome of the world" and Borges has created in "The Aleph" "one of the points of the universe which contains all the points" so that it becomes "a symbol of all Borges' writing."[15]

The works of Emerson to which Borges most often refers in his own writing include three remarkable poems, "Days," "The Past," and "Brahma." The first two are concerned with the passage of time and its relationship to man, the third embodies the doctrine of the unity of all that exists.

In "Days," the persona describes the subjects as "Daughters of Time," hypocritical, dumb, like dervishes, who offer to each man "gifts after his will." Forgetting his own "morning wishes," the persona accepts from one of them "a few herbs and apples" and the day departs, a look of scorn upon her face. The poem is decidedly ambiguous, open to at least two interpretations. Certainly the persona may be complaining that he has not taken full advantage of the opportunities offered to him by the days (and months and years) of his life, but has settled rather for something less than the rewards accorded kings and martyrs. On the other hand, the two items he employs to symbolize his choice—herbs and apples—are objects of nature, not worldly baubles, and given Emerson's devotion to the natural world, to the simple; given his belief that man even in his most trivial activities may be involved in the serious labor of eternity, it is surely at least as likely that he is arguing that his decision is correct and the scorn of the "hypocritic" Daughter of Time is not to be accorded credence.

Borges has opted for the former interpretation. In a 1967 interview with Cesar Fernández Moreno, cited by Carlos Cortínez in his study of Borges' poem "Emerson," Borges interprets "Days" as meaning that when Emerson, offered anything he wants on earth, takes only "a few herbs and apples," the days make fun of the poet's absurd moderation ("*la absurda moderación del poeta*"). This leads Borges to speculate that there was in Emerson a secret discontent ("*una secreta insatisfacción*"), and that he regretted having chosen the life of the mind over the life of action.[16]

The powerful sonnet to Emerson portrays the "tall New Englander" closing a volume of Montaigne and going out into the fields one evening. The walk, as much a pleasure for him as reading, takes him toward the sunset, as well as through the memory of Borges who writes of him. Emerson thinks of the important books he has read, the imperishable books he has been granted the privilege to write, and of his national fame and concludes, surprisingly, that "I have not lived. I want to be someone else." In his note to the poem, Emir Rodríguez Monegal observes that the sonnet was written in 1962 after Borges had visited New England and that in the work the North American poet becomes a "mask" for the Argentine poet. Cortínez has argued that Borges creates a contrast in the poem between Emerson, the contemplative man, and Don Quixote, the man of action. Although as I have suggested, the opposite interpretation may be given to "Days," Emerson's belief in the necessity for action certainly was often expressed; consider, for example, his criticism of Thoreau, even as he eulogized him, for being content to be "the captain of a huckleberry-party" when he could have been "engineering for all America."[17]

The opening line of "The Other Death," Borges' story of the soldier who behaved in a cowardly manner in battle and may—or may not—be allowed to relive the event and die bravely, refers to a proposed first translation of Emerson's "The Past" into Spanish. In that poem, Emerson's intellectual idea is that what is past is finished; there is no altering any event: "All is now secure and fast; / Not the gods can shake the Past. . . ." "The Other Death" would seem to posit as one of the interpretations of the strange events it contains, a contradiction of Emerson's argument; to offer the possibility, at least, that the past can be relived.

The nostalgic and rather tragic recognition of the immutability of things and events that have been, however, is on other occasions, in other works, embraced by Borges. In "Things That Might Have Been," for example, the poet envisions literary masterpieces that were never written, empires that never existed and "History without the afternoon of the Cross and the afternoon of hemlock. / History without the face of Helen." Or, after "the three labored days of Gettysburg, the victory of the South." In the conclusion of the poem, the persona envisions the "son I did not have."[18] In "Things That Might Have Been," Borges obviously concurs with Emerson's past that "is now secure and past," even though he may elsewhere assert, as in a 1980 conversation, that "as to the past, we are changing it all the time. Every time we remember something, we slightly alter our memory."[19] On the other hand, remember that one of the attributes of the "intellectual poet," as noted above, is the ability to see "all at once," not only what was, but what might have been; and it is to this category, of course, that he assigns Emerson.

The poem "Brahma" is based on the pantheistic unity which Emerson had derived from his reading of Hindu scriptures. Borges quotes the entire poem in *An Introduction to American Literature* and in *Other Inquisitions* identifies as "perhaps the most memorable line" that in which the persona, Brahma, states paradoxically "When me they fly, I am the wings."[20] The concept of the contradictory unity of all things as Emerson conveys it in the poem manifests itself often in Borges' works. Consider the passage in *DreamTigers* called "A Problem" in which he speaks of the possibility of Don Quixote's having been reincarnated as a Hindustani king who stands over the body of the enemy he has slain and understands "that to kill and beget are divine or magical acts which manifestly transcend humanity. He knows that the dead man is an illusion, as is the bloody sword that weighs down his hand, as is he himself, and all his past life, and the vast gods, and the universe."[21] Not only is the idea of the passage parallel to the argument of "Brahma," but the phrase "the vast gods" is surely an echo of Emerson's line "The strong gods pine for my abode."

In addition to Emerson's concepts reflected in the poems considered above, other themes of his that have been influential in the works of Borges include the doctrines of the Over-Soul and the Universal Poet and man; of Compensation and Undulation; the concepts of Illusions and Miracles, and the ethical considerations of the Concord genius. Of these, Emerson's most important influence on the thought and work of Borges would seem to be the basic Transcendental concept of the Over-Soul, particularly as embodied in the Universal Man, or, more to the point here, the Universal Poet.

In "The Flower of Coleridge," Borges quotes Paul Valéry as saying that literary history should not be constituted by the lives of poets and their careers but rather "the history of the Spirit as the producer or consumer of literature." Borges adds that "It was not the first time that the Spirit had made such an observation," for in 1844, "one of its amanuenses in Concord" wrote,

I am very much struck in literature by the appearance that one person wrote all the books; . . . there is such equality and identity both of judgement and point of view in the narrative that it is plainly the work of one, all-seeing, all-hearing gentleman.[22]

This passage from Emerson's essay "Nominalist and Realist" introduces a theme that obviously has a strong appeal for Borges, since he turns to it again and again. In a 1980 conversation, for example, he commented on how little we know of Shakespeare's life, a fact which does not trouble us, he insists, because Shakespeare has converted that life into plays and sonnets. The best thing for any author is to be a part of a tradition, a part of the language, which is in itself a kind of immortality, he argues, since language and tradition go on, while the books may be forgotten: "or perhaps every age rewrites the same books, over and over again. . . . Perhaps the eternal books are all the same books. We are always rewriting what the ancients wrote, and that should prove sufficient."[23] Emerson makes exactly the same point in his essay "The Poet" where he states that "poetry was all written before time was."

A more generalized implication of the Over-Soul concept—the belief that not only are all poets one poet, but all men are one man—has intrigued Borges and provided inspiration in several works. In *An Introduction to American Literature*, he observes that for Emerson, every man is a microcosm and the "soul of the individual is identified with the soul of the world," so that all "each man needs is his own profound and secret identity."[24] The prologue to Borges' translation of *Representative Men* contains the observation that since the tragedy of human life results from individuals being "restricted by time and space," nothing is "more gratifying than a belief that there is no one who is not the universe."[25] This being the case, for Emerson, men are immortal through their universality; and for Borges, as he states elsewhere, "my days and nights are equal in poverty and richness to those of God and those of all men."[26]

Any attempt to make a case for Borges as a Transcendentalist in the Emersonian sense would be foolish and futile, but what is apparent from the evidence offered above, incomplete as it may be, is the fact that

Borges feels for that "tall gentleman" of Concord both an admiration and an affinity. The value of finding and analyzing such a relationship is the evidence it offers for the value of tradition and the relationship of that tradition to poets and poetry, and the insight which such a study can afford readers to the writings of two great "intellectual" poets, one of the nineteenth century, one of the present; of two—as Borges himself might express it—"amanuenses" of the one great Spirit that connects all literature of the past and present and—if human beings continue to read—of the future.

NOTES

1. Willis Barnstone, ed. *Borges at Eighty: Conversations* (Bloomington: Indiana University Press, 1982): 5.
2. Jorge Luis Borges, In collaboration with Esther Zemborain de Torres, *An Introduction to American Literature*. Trans. L. Clark Keating and Robert O. Evans (Lexington: University Press of Kentucky, 1973): 26.
3. Carlos Cortínez, "Otra Lectura de 'Emerson' de Borges," *Revista Chilena de Literatura* 19 (1982): 98.
4. Borges, *An Introduction to American Literature*, 25.
5. Cited by Ronald J. Christ, *The Narrow Act* (New York: New York University Press, 1969): 42.
6. Borges, *An Introduction to American Literature*, 26.
7. Borges, *An Introduction to American Literature*, 26.
8. *Borges: A Reader*. Edited by Emir Rodriguez Monegal and Alastair Reid. (New York: E. P. Dutton, 1981): 215.
9. Borges, *Doctor Brodie's Report*. Trans. Norman Thomas di Giovanni (New York: E. P. Dutton, 1972): 10.
10. Barnstone, *Borges at Eighty*, 12.
11. Monegal and Reid, *Borges: A Reader*, 24.
12. Christ, *The Narrow Act*, 11–12.
13. Borges, *An Introduction to American Literature*, 24.
14. Barnstone, *Borges at Eighty*, 67, 165.
15. Christ, *The Narrow Act*, 11–12.
16. Cortínez, "Otra Lectura de 'Emerson' de Borges," 95.
17. Perry Miller, ed. *Major Writers of America* (New York: Harcourt, Brace and World, Inc., 1966): 307.
18. Monegal and Reid, *Borges: A Reader*, 327.
19. Barnstone, *Borges at Eighty*, 14.
20. Jorge Luis Borges, *Other Inquisitions: 1937–1952* trans. Ruth L. C. Simms (Austin: University of Texas Press, 1964): 69.
21. Jorge Luis Borges, *DreamTigers*. Trans. Mildred Boyer and Harold Morland (Austin: University of Texas Press, 1964).
22. Monegal and Reid, *Borges: A Reader*, 163.
23. Barnstone, *Borges at Eighty*, 9.
24. Borges, *An Introduction to American Literature*, 25.

25. Christ, *The Narrow Act*, 131.
26. Barnstone, *Borges at Eighty*, 42.

BIBLIOGRAPHY

Barnstone, Willis, ed. *Borges at Eighty: Conversations*. Bloomington: Indiana University Press, 1982.
Borges, Jorge Luis. *Doctor Brodie's Report*. Translated by Norman Thomas di Giovanni. New York: E. P. Dutton, 1972.
Borges, *DreamTigers*. Translated by Mildred Boyer and Harold Morland. Austin: University of Texas Press, 1964.
Borges. *Other Inquisitions: 1937–1952*. Translated by Ruth L. C. Simms. Austin: University of Texas Press, 1964.
Borges, Jorges Luis, and Esther Zemborain de Torres. *An Introduction to American Literature*. Translated by L. Clark Keating and Robert O. Owens. Lexington: University of Kentucky Press, 1973.
Cortínez, Carlos. "Otra Lectura de 'Emerson' de Borges." In *Revista Chilena de Literatura*, 19 (1982): 95, 98.
Christ, Ronald J. *The Narrow Act*. New York: New York University Press, 1969.
Miller, Perry, ed. *Major Writers of America*. New York: Harcourt, Brace and World, Inc., 1966.
Rodríguez Monegal, Emir. and Alastair Reid, eds. *Borges: A Reader*. New York: E. P. Dutton, 1981.

JULIE JONES

Borges and Browning: A Dramatic Dialogue

In a rather backhanded tribute to Robert Browning, Jorge Luis Borges comments that "si hubiera sido un buen escritor de prosa, creo que no dudaríamos que Browning sería el precursor de la que llamamos literatura moderna."[1] In a writer who has repeatedly emphasized his preference for plot over character and his suspicions about the nonexistence of personality, this interest in the work of a poet who described himself as "more interested in individuals than abstract problems"[2] is curious, yet despite his claim in *Introducción a la literatura inglesa* of this widely accepted view of Browning, Borges seems drawn to a different reading. For him, Browning is "el gran poeta enigmático,"[3] and, with Dickens, one of "dos grandes artífices góticos."[4] In the introduction to English literature, Borges summarizes a poem he must have especially liked, "How It Strikes a Contemporary": "el protagonista puede ser Cervantes o un misterioso espía de Dios o el arquetipo platónico del poeta,"[5] and among "Los precursores de Kafka," he numbers another of Browning's poems, "Fears and Scruples," in which the speaker defends a stubbornly enigmatic friend who, it is hinted in the last line, may be God. Borges appears particularly interested in *The Ring and the Book*, with its deployment of multiple narratives on the part of the different characters, each of whom presents his own version of the same murder.[6] Browning's development of point of view, along with his ambiguity and what Borges sees as a quality of irreality are probably the basis for his argument that

Browning be considered a precursor to James and Kafka and, through them, to much modern literature. Considering his own bent for the exotic, Borges must have been intrigued by the perspectives Browning opens on distant times and places, although he does not mention it. Although Borges' reading of Browning is quirky enough—he has nothing to say about the enormous energy or about the determined optimism that so offended T. S. Eliot—he is not alone in his evaluation of Browning's influence on modern literature. Ezra Pound, for example, claimed Browning as his literary father and pushed him tirelessly. In an essay on the relation between Browning and the Anglo-American Modernists, G. Robert Stange points out three primary reasons for Browning's prestige: his attempt to render spoken speech in verse; his use of an elliptical method with startling jumps and juxtapositions that put the onus of interpretation on the reader; and his elaboration of the dramatic monologue, a form with obvious importance for the literature of perspective developed by James, Conrad, Proust, Joyce, Woolf and Faulkner.[7] Like so much modern literature, the dramatic monologue insists on the fragmentary, the incomplete; it opens up new areas of experience and conveys them through a single, and therefore limited, perspective.

The use of a conversational tone and an elliptical approach is widespread throughout twentieth-century poetry, but the dramatic monologue, perhaps the dominant form now in Anglo-American poetry, has never really caught on in Hispanic verse. Borges, however, uses the form rather frequently. That he does so may be the result of his intellectual formation in a library composed of English books; still, this fondness for a form that has traditionally been a vehicle for the presentation of character is odd. It is best seen by focusing on Borges' adaptation of the dramatic monologue, as it was developed by Browning, to suit his own ends.

In 1947, Ina Beth Sessions listed the characteristics of the "perfect dramatic monologue": "that literary form which has the definite characteristics of speaker, audience, occasion, revelation of character, interplay between speaker and audience, dramatic action, and action which takes place in the present."[8] The problem with this schema is that it excludes many of Browning's best monologues and is totally inadequate for dealing with such modern examples as "The Love Song of J. Alfred Prufrock" or Pound's "The Tomb at Akr Çaar," in which a soul addresses its mummified body. Although development of character is central to the majority of Browning's monologues, there are notable exceptions—"Saul," "Rabbi Ben Ezra," "Fears and Scruples," "How It Strikes a Contemporary." Sessions' description is useful as an index of features that often are presented in the form, but it should not be taken as prescriptive. In his seminal study, *The Poetry of Experience*, Robert Langbaum argues that it is more important to consider effect rather than mechanics. For him, the essential effect is to give "facts from within,"[9] but he offsets this contention by observing that "there is at work in [the monologue] a consciousness . . . beyond what the speaker can lay claim to. This consciousness is the mark of the poet's projection into the poem."[10] Ultimately, Park Honan's definition may offer the most useful rule of thumb: "a single discourse by one whose presence in the poem is indicated by the poet but who is not the poet himself."[11]

Before examining the dramatic monologue in Borges, it should be helpful to take a brief look at one of Browning's more representative monologues. In his introduction to English literature, Borges mentions "An Epistle of Karshish," in which "un médico árabe refiere la resurrección de Lázaro y la extraña indiferencia de su vida ulterior, como si se tratara de un caso clínico."[12] The entire poem takes the form of an epistle written from Karshish to his mentor, Abib. Karshish writes at some length about his journey into Judea, including details about the political situation and his medical discoveries. Finally, he gets around to the real reason for his writing—his encounter with Lazarus. Even though he dismisses Lazarus as a "case of mania—subinduced / By epilepsy,"[13] it is evident that he is rationalizing an experience that haunts him, and at the end of the letter, having apologized repeatedly for "this long and tedious case" and actually written his good-byes, he suddenly bursts out:

> The very God! think, Abib; dost thou think?
> So, the All-Great, were the All-Loving too—
> The madman saith He said so: it is strange.

"An Epistle of Karshish" is representative of the Browning monologue as it takes up a character at a specific point in time, at a moment of personal as well as historical crisis. It is thick with detail which establishes time and place and, more importantly, delineates character (a reference to the herb borage, for example, not only demonstrates Karshish's attempt to circumvent his discovery, it also reveals the scientist's practiced eye). The protagonist addresses a particular person, but the communication is really a pretext for a "dialogue between self and soul" in which, while attempting to come to grips with a disturbing incident, he sums up his entire life. The letter is an expression of self *and* an exploration: what if Lazarus is right? The poem is open-ended; the outcome of the struggle, unresolved. An ironic tension is established between the speaker, who has an incomplete understanding of a firsthand experience, and the reader, whose knowledge is much greater, but who is separated from the event by two millenia.

It is not difficult to see why the poem appeals to Borges. In its oblique approach to a great historical moment, it brings to mind his speculations about why the thief asked to be saved in "Lucas XXIII" and why Judas betrayed Christ in "Tres versiones de Judas." Browning's ironic manipulation of point of view in the monologue looks ahead to "La busca de Averroes," Borges' narrative about the Arab translator of Aristotle, a man of high intelligence, who is prevented by his belief in Islam, on which his strength is founded, from accomplishing the task he has set himself, defining comedy and tragedy. Although repeatedly exposed to clues about the nature of the theater, he is doomed to ignore them. The story is told from the third person (except for an intrusion by Borges at the end to remind us that he is as ignorant of Averroes as Averroes is of drama), but the perspective is so carefully limited and so free of analysis that it is almost internal,[14] and its effect is close to that of the dramatic monologue: it gives the facts "from within."

However, rather than discussing possible analogues in his fiction, it is preferable to examine what Borges does with the dramatic monologue in his poetry. Among the speakers are his ancestor Francisco Laprida; Alexander Selkirk; Hengist, the Jutish king of Kent; God; Heraclytus; a Chinese library guard; Tamerlan, an English madman; Browning himself; Ulysses; an unknown Saxon warrior; an unknown inquisitor; an unknown conquistador; the Altamira painter; the Caliph Omar; Alonso Quijano; and Descartes. For the most part, these are short poems; a number are sonnets. There is neither room to develop nor an intention of developing the kind of psychological complexity that is Browning's peculiar characteristic. Instead, Borges tends to offer just a glimpse of the other.

"Hengist Cyning"[15] is a fine example of the use of the dramatic monologue to open a perspective on the distant past by showing, instead of explaining, a way of thinking that is distinctly not modern. The poem opens with an epitaph that substantiates the claims made by the voice of the dead ruler, Hengist the first Jutish king of Kent, whose monologue makes up the body of the poem. Hengist is concerned with clearing up a misunderstanding about his life. The British accuse him of betrayal because he killed his king but what Hengist wants clarified is that the real betrayal lay in the selling of his strength and courage. By turning on the British Vortigen, he reaffirms his personal worth: "yo *fui* Hengist el mercenario" (v. 7, italics mine); and *now* he speaks as king. His speech is laconic, as austere as the epitaph engraved on stone, and appropriate for a Northern warrior king. His reference to the murder is understated and curiously touching: "Le quité la luz y la vida" (v. 16). In an economy based on limited good, the only way to attain "luz y vida" is to deprive someone else of these things (the following verse is, "Me place el reino que gané"). In any event, the murder needs no more justification than the comment that "la fuerza y el coraje no sufren / que las vendan los hombres" (vv. 12–13). That he should lay waste the British cities and enslave the subjugated populace is simply taken for granted. Like many dramatic monologues ("My Last Duchess" is a good, if far more complex, example), the poem is a gratuitous assertion of self. The real brunt of the message is: This is what I am, "Yo he sido fiel a mi valentía" (v. 27). To whom is Hengist speaking? A chance passerby at the grave? Future generations? The sole possible audience is Borges, sensitive to these cries from the past, and through him, the reader on whom he now confers a privileged insight into the workings of an archaic sensibility.

Borges has always been interested in what Browning calls that "moment, one and infinite,"[16] when a man recognizes his destiny. Hengist turned on Vortigen because he realized that he was meant to rule rather than be ruled. The body of the poem deals with the upshot of that discovery. "El advenimiento"[17] focuses on the moment itself, when the anonymous painter of the Altamira cave saw the herd of buffalo he later painted (like "Hengist Cyning," the narration here takes place centuries after the event and is addressed to the void—or the ears of the poet):

> Son los bisontes, dije. La palabra
> No había pasado nunca por mis labios,
> Pero sentí que tal era su nombre.

Era como si nunca hubiera visto,
Como si hubiera estado ciego y muerto
Antes de los bisontes de la aurora.
Surgían de la aurora. Eran la aurora.
No quise que los otros profanaran
Aquel pesado río de bruteza
Divina, de ignorancia, de soberbia.
Pisotearon un perro del camino;
Lo mismo hubieran hecho con un hombre.
Después los trazaría en la caverna
Con ocre y bermellón. (vv. 23–37)

Like many of Borges' poems, "El advenimiento" arises from an intellectual question: how did the Altamira caves come to be painted? Borges answers the question with an impression that is vivid because it is rendered from within. The speaker is neither described nor analyzed. He simply tells us what, not why, he thought, and we instinctively feel— yes, it must have been like that. Through his use of the monologue, Borges allows a very distant, hazy event to become real. For the speaker, the critical moment comes when he sees the herd; the painting, which has had such a great impact on twentieth-century art, is an afterthought. The real genius, Borges suggests—and this notion obviously has wider application—lies in seeing.

In the last verses of the poem, Borges dissolves the image he has created:

. . . Nunca
Dijo mi boca el nombre de Altamira.
Fueron muchas mis formas y mis muertes. (vv. 38–40)

Rodríguez-Monegal writes that for Borges, "All men who perform the same basic and ritual act are the same man."[18] As an artist, the speaker has more in common with other artists than he does with his other, non-artist self, the primitive man who must traffic with his tribe, hunt for food, sleep, make love. Since Borges conveys to the reader *only* what is relevant to the epiphanic moment, it is possible for this individual to be subsumed into the species. This type of transformation does not much interest Browning. For the most part, he builds up portraits of the whole man, full of troublesome details that cannot be wished away, even when he concentrates, say, on a man's art, as in "Fra Lippo Lippi" and "Andrea del Sarto."

Borges uses the monologue to explore situation rather than character: how did the cave paintings come about? what is the reason for an apparent act of treason? Silvia Molloy comments that in Borges' fiction, character and situation usually coincide.[19] In general, this is true of the poetry as well. As a form, the dramatic monologue is suited to this kind of overlapping since it involves the presentation of character *in situ*. Eliot, too, uses the monologue in a way similar to Borges—if "Prufrock" is a rounded portrait of a shattered man, "The Journey of the Magi" and "The Wasteland" (a series of monologues uttered by Tiresias in different times and places) are more concerned with situation.

Like "El advenimiento," "Poema conjectural"[20] is an example of a monologue concerned with what Mary Kinzie calls "hidden history," the point when the individual merges with the archetype.[21] The poem takes place at a specific historical moment. The prefatory note explains: "El doctor Francisco Laprida, asesinado el día 22 de setiembre de 1829 por los montoneros de Aldao, piensa antes de morir." The action is dramatic, but the narrative is secondary to Laprida's discourse. He is even now being hunted down. Although he accepts his approaching death "sin esperanza ni temor," (v. 11), he is confused and bitter about the *kind* of death being doled out to him since it represents a denial of the grounds of his existence, his "Yo, que estudié las leyes y los cánones, / yo, Francisco Narciso de Laprida" (vv. 6–7). He is lost, not because he is about to die, but because his ending makes no sense in terms of his life. The representative of civilization is being done in by the forces of barbarism.

In the second stanza, Laprida reaches for an analogy that may help him understand his peculiar fate. "Aquel capitán del Purgatorio," to whom he refers, Buonconte da Montefeltro, falls into the group of the Late Repentant. In 1289, he commanded the Aretines in an unsuccessful attempt against the Florentines at Campaldino. Following the defeat, he was hunted down; his throat was cut, and his body carried away by the Arno. According to Dante, at the moment of his death, he repented his life of violence and called out the name of Mary, thus saving his soul. The manner of Buonconte's death coincides with Laprida's, but more important is Laprida's identification with a figure who reaches understanding just before he dies, and the fact that Laprida looks to the universal, embodied in literature, to come to terms with his individual situation; that is, the particular has meaning only in relation to the general. In the remainder of the stanza, Laprida returns to the narrative of his flight. His killers are drawing closer. Earlier he heard shots; now he hears hooves. The outer hunt parallels the inner search; time is running out for both. The situation is similar to that in "El milagro secreto."

At the beginning of the third stanza, Laprida thinks back to his life, much in the terms he used earlier, but the fourth verse signals a change:

> pero me endiosa el pecho inexplicable
> un júbilo secreto. Al fin me encuentro
> con mi destino sudamericano. (vv. 25–27)

The analogy in the previous stanza opens the way for a revelation, a recognition not of Christian divinity, but of the collective unconscious of his race. Seen in this fresh light, Laprida's death is a confirmation, not a denial of self.[22] At this critical juncture, Laprida discovers his "insospechado rostro eterno" (v. 37); he becomes one with the archetype—not only of the gaucho, but of warriors over the centuries, including Dante's Aretine captain, whose death he reenacts.

In the last stanza, it only remains to consummate his fate. Laprida, like Buonconte, narrates his own death. This point of view produces a disturbing close-up effect: "Pisan mis pies la sombra de las lanzas" (v. 39):

> Ya el primer golpe,
> ya el duro hierro que me raja el pecho,
> el íntimo cuchillo en la garganta. (vv. 42–44)

In the poem, we find a number of elements typical of the dramatic monologue. The protagonist is forced to formulate his thoughts at a moment of dramatic intensity. Through his discourse, he arrives at a revelation and subsequent understanding. Although the language is pure Borges, it is not beyond the reach of an educated forebear who is, in any event, not speaking out loud.

Through the prefatory note and the title, as well as the language, Borges reminds the reader of his shaping presence in the poem. The "conjectural" establishes the same relationship between creator and creation as does the last paragraph in "La busca de Averroes." The tension thus set up between past and present, between reality and literature, is associated with the odd notion that only through recourse to letters does Laprida recognize that he is destined to be a man of action. The world of literature provides access to the universal. Yet even though he is, so to speak, disseminated through history, Laprida remains simultaneously fixed for the reader in the memorable gesture of his death, just as the Altamira painter is fixed in the moment he sees the herd.

In her study of his oscillations between the impersonal and the personal, Molloy points to Borges' use of gesture which, she argues, is much like Stevenson's: it gives shape to character, idea or emotion by means of an act or an attitude that captures our attention.[23] Even though he sweeps a character away, Borges often leaves us with something akin to the Cheshire cat's furious grin, a gesture that stays with us. The monologue provides Borges with a ready source of irony—the character who announces his "yo" most tenaciously finds that the only appropriate term is "nosotros," but it also offers a means of making the experience vivid—the character's own perspective. Because in "El advenimiento" we see the herd through the protagonist's eyes, join him imaginatively at the crack through which he peers, both he and the herd, in short, the entire situation, are sharply etched in our minds. Similarly, for an instant, we also find ourselves with Laprida at his death just because our angle of vision is exactly his. It is for this reason that Langbaum describes the dramatic monologue as a "poetry of sympathy."[24] Actually, the disparity between Langbaum's insistence that the monologue give the "facts from within" and his contention that there is a greater consciousness at work in the poem is only apparent, as these poems demonstrate. Borges manipulates point of view here to provide additional tension between the particular and the universal, the individual and the archetype. There is a great pathos to these creations that seem to be so bright and are suddenly sent up in smoke.

It is precisely because Borges does not take advantage of the speaker's perspective that "Browning resuelve ser poeta,"[25] a poem inevitably in this discussion, is less successful than many of his other dramatic monologues. The title suggests that the poem will focus on a specific occasion—the point when Browning decided to become a poet—but the great moment eludes the poem. The speaker's remark, "descubro que he elegido / la más curiosa de las profesiones humanas" (vv. 2–3) is under-cut by the next comment—"salvo que todas, a su modo, lo son" (v. 4), which reveals a diffidence characteristic of Borges, but quite alien to Browning. The poem turns on a playful series of allusions that con-tinually remind the reader of the author's presence in the poem. For ex-ample, the reference to Browning's use of colloquial language:

> haré que las comunes palabras—
> naipes marcados del tahur, moneda de la plebe—
> rindan la magia que fue suya
> cuando Thor era el numen e el estrépito (vv. 5–12)

does double duty since the two metaphors for common words point to-ward Borges' own work. "Los naipes del tahur" is the composition for which the Borges persona does not win an award in "El Aleph"; the coin is probably the "zahir." The poem is graceful and clever, but it lacks the tension that gives a number of other monologues strength. Here the speaker, Browning, is simply swallowed up by the central theme, which is the intertextuality of all literature. Other poems discussed involve identifiable circumstances even though their speakers may now be dis-embodied voices monologizing centuries after an event; nevertheless, there is an experience and an attitude to remember. The real location of "Browning resuelve ser poeta" is in the pages of universal literature, rather than the "rojos laberintos de Londres" (v. 1) that are dismissed in one verse, and it takes place not at some point in the 1820's, but over the centuries. What is missing here is the memorable gesture that would, as Stevenson suggests, capture our attention.

The true power of the dramatic monologue as Borges uses it lies in its ability to create tension between the temporal and the eternal, between the individual speaker and the archetype, and to offer us a privileged perspective on a situation or mode of thought that would otherwise be inaccessible. If his tribute to Browning falls short of this potential and is—to this reader's mind—less successful, the vivid images that so many of the other dramatic monologues leave testify to Borges' brilliant use of a traditional form.

NOTES

1. Richard Burgin, *Conversaciones con Jorge Luis Borges* (New York: Holt, Rinehart and Winston, 1968): 48.

2. Jorge Luis Borges, *Introducción a la literatura inglesa* (Buenos Aires: Editorial Columba, 1965): 46. My translation.

3. María Esther Vásquez, "Entrevista a Borges," *Jorge Luis Borges*. Edited by Jaime Alazraki. (Madrid: Taurus, 1976): 71.

4. Jorge Luis Borges, *Obras completas III. Otras inquisiciones* (Buenos Aires: Emecé, 1957): 121.

5. Borges, *Introducción a la literatura inglesa*, 47.

6. Burgin, *Conversaciones*, 48–9.

7. G. Robert Stange, "Browning and Modern Poetry," in *Browning's Mind and Art*. Edited by Clarence Tracy. (New York: Barnes and Noble, 1968): 153.

8. Ina Beth Sessions, "The Dramatic Monologue," in *PMLA*, 62 (1947): 508.

9. Robert Langbaum, *The Poetry of Experience* (New York: W. W. Norton, 1963): 85.

10. Langbaum, *Poetry of Experience*, 94.

11. Park Honan, *Browning's Characters* (New Haven: Yale University Press, 1961): 122.

12. Borges, *Introducción a la literatura inglesa*, 47.

13. Robert Browning, *Poetical Works: 1833–1864*, edited by Ian Jack. (London: Oxford University Press, 1970): 594, vv. 79–80. The poem appears on pp. 594–602.

14. Mary Kinzie, "Recursive Prose," *Prose for Borges* (Evanston, Ill.: Northwestern University Press, 1974): 28.

15. Jorge Luis Borges, *Obra poética* (Madrid: Alianza Editorial, 1975): 213.

16. Browning, "By the Fireside," *Poetical Works*, 586, v. 181.

17. Borges, *Obra poética*, 409–10.

18. Emir Rodríguez-Monegal, "Borges: The Reader as Writer," *Prose for Borges*, 120.

19. Silvia Molloy, *Las letras de Borges* (Buenos Aires: Editorial Sudamericana, 1979): 76.

20. Borges, *Obra poética*, 129–30.

21. Kinzie, "Recursive Prose," 34.

22. The poem is, of course, an attempt to find consolation for a needless death—like W. B. Yeats' "An Irish Airman Foresees His Death" and "In Memory of Major Robert Gregory." Interesting in this connection is Jaime Alazraki's discussion of "El Sur," the story in which a librarian who lies dying of septicemia in a hospital in Buenos Aires dreams that he is killed defending his honor in a knife fight somewhere in the South. He sees the "death" as both a wasteful reminder of the country's barbarism and an effort to return to an epic past: "es un exceso y una privación, una destrucción y una forma de realización, una negación y un acto de afirmación." [Jaime Alazraki, *Versiones, Inversiones, Reversiones* (Madrid: Editorial Gredos, 1977): 40.]

23. Robert L. Stevenson cited in Molloy, 124. (I am paraphrasing in English.)

24. Langbaum, *Poetry of Experience*, 79.

25. Jorge Luis Borges, *The Gold of the Tigers: Selected Later Poems*, a bilingual edition, ed. and trans. Alastair Reid. (New York: E. P. Dutton, 1976): 52, 54.

BIBLIOGRAPHY

Alazraki, Jaime. *Versiones, Inversiones, Reversiones*. Madrid: Editorial Gredos, 1977.

Borges, Jorge Luis. *The Gold of the Tigers: Selected Later Poems*. Edited and translated by Alastair Reid. New York; E. P. Dutton, 1976.

Borges, *Introducción a la literatura inglesa*. Buenos Aires: Editorial Columba, 1965.

Borges, *Obras completas*. Buenos Aires: Emecé, 1957.

Borges. *Obra poética*. Madrid: Alianza Editorial, 1975.

Browning, Robert. *Poetical Works: 1833–1864*. Edited by Ian Jack. London: Oxford University Press, 1970.

Burgin, Richard. *Conversaciones con Jorge Luis Borges*. New York: Holt, Rinehart and Winston, 1968.

Honan, Park. *Browning's Characters*. New Haven: Yale University Press, 1964.

Kinzie, Mary. *Prose for Borges*. Evanston: Northwestern University Press, 1974.
Langbaum, Robert. *The Poetry of Experience*. New York: W. W. Norton, 1963.
Molloy, Silvia. *Las letras de Borges*. Buenos Aires: Editorial Sudamericana, 1979.
Rodríguez-Monegal, Emir. "Borges: The Reader as Writer." In *Prose for Borges*. Evanston: Northwestern University Press, 1974.
Sessions, Ina Beth. "The Dramatic Monologue." In *PMLA*. n.p, 1947.
Stange, G. Robert. "Browning and Modern Poetry." In *Browning's Mind and Art*. Edited by Clarence Tracy. New York: Barnes and Noble, 1968.
Vásquez, María Esther. "Entrevista a Borges." In *Jorge Luis Borges*. Edited by Jaime Alazraki. Madrid: Taurus, 1976.

MARÍA LUISA BASTOS

Translated with Daniel Balderston
Whitman as Inscribed in Borges

For many years I believed that literature, which is almost infinite, was in one man.
BORGES

You shall listen to all sides and filter them from your self. WHITMAN

For the last sixty years, the literature of Borges, an unending text, has been unfolding the variants, the arrangements, the enthusiasms configured in his first books. Tautologically, as Guillermo Sucre observed when commenting on *Elogio de la sombra* (*In Praise of Darkness*), Borges' latest books return to the first Borges, bringing him into a new focus, illuminating and revealing him to us.[1]

At the beginning of that text, the identity of which is characterized by movement, and which predicts from the start its future versions, those who will become familiar presences for Borges' readers are already there. They are in the two books he has refused to republish—*Inquisiciones* and *El tamaño de mi esperanza*—in his first three volumes of poetry, and in *Discusión*. Familiar presences: raw material which is predictable because it is constant, but which is also endowed with potentially infinite generative power. The most adequate synecdoches of those presences are the names: Torres Villarroel, Joyce, Berkeley, Cansinos-Assens, Milton, Groussac, Flaubert, Góngora, Quevedo, and Macedonio Fernández. Presences which Borges' texts will not only transform into habit but also into surprise: recognizable signs but also secret traces. On the one hand, we want to recognize those traces even when strictly speaking they are not there; or, on the other hand, they may be so intensely interwoven into Borges' writing that we pass over them without noticing. For this reason, much as would occur with any of the names inscribed in Borges' texts, a record of the times Whitman's name occurs in his work would be deceptive, would inevitably prove incomplete even if compiled with an extreme thoroughness. Besides, that record could be much better replaced with the texts that Borges has devoted to the Whitman theme, thus, the following essay does not attempt a more or less systematic inventory of Whitman's name in Borges: rather, it provides arbitrary notes to scattered reading, guided above all by memories of prior readings. Also, these notes are doubly arbitrary, since they deal in part with an already expurgated Whitman, selected and translated by Borges, of a Whitman who became part of Borges' text.

1. *The Wish to Express the Totality of Life*

In 1925, referring to the extreme subjectivity typical of nineteenth century esthetics, Borges pointed out: ". . . any frame of mind, however extraneous, can become the focus of our attention; in its brief totality, it may be our essence. If translated into the language of literature, this means that trying to express oneself and having the wish to express the totality of life are but one and the same thing." Whitman was the first Atlas attempting to bring such a challenge into action, and he lifted the world upon his shoulders.[2]

Years before, the young Borges, astounded by Whitman's ambitious task,[3] wrote verses that, according to the sarcastic reflection of the mature Borges, instead of echoing Whitman echoed the Peruvian Post-*Modernista* poet, Chocano.[4] Here is a sample of those verses, from "Himno del mar," written in 1919:

> I have longed for a hymn of the sea with rhythms
>   as ample as the screaming waves;
> Of the sea when on its waters the sun flutters as
>   a scarlet flag;
> Of the sea when it kisses the golden breasts of
>   virgin, thirstily waiting, beaches;
> Of the sea when its forces howl, when winds shout
>   their blasphemes;

When the polished, bloody moon shines on the steel
     waters. . . .

Oh, protean, I have sprung from you.
Both of us shackled and nomadic;
Both of us intensely thirsty of stars;
Both of us hopeful and deceived;
Both of us air, light, strength, darkness;
Both of us with our great desire,
     and both of us with our great misery![5]

However, in spite of the deliberate grandiloquence with which Borges tried to render the Whitmanesque rhythm, the statements in "Himno del mar," like blurred copies, lessen the optimism of the original. It is useful to compare Borges' verses to Whitman's:

You sea! I resign myself to you also—
     I guess what you mean,
I behold from the beach your crooked inviting fingers,
I believe you refuse to go back without feeling
     of me,
We must have a turn together, I undress, hurry me
     out of sight of the land,
Cushion me soft, rock me in billowy drowse,
Dash me with amorous wet, I can repay you.

Sea of stretch'd ground-swells,
Sea breathing broad and convulsive breaths,
Sea of the brine of life and of unshovell'd yet
     always-ready graves,
Howler and scooper of storms, capricious and dainty
     sea,
I am integral with you, I too am of one phase and
     of all phases.[6]

"Himno del mar" is interesting as a part of the prehistory of Borges' poetry, but the fact remains that many of his lasting early poems are firmly guided by the enticing invitation at the beginning of "Song of Myself": "Stop this day and night with me and you shall possess the origin of all poems" (25).

Also, both *Fervor de Buenos Aires* and *Luna de enfrente* have many echoes of Whitman's decision: "Creeds and schools in abeyance/ Retiring back a while sufficed at what they are, but never forgotten" (24). For the

Borges who wrote *Fervor de Buenos Aires*, to turn away from the schools meant, among other things, having too many different objectives, which he himself mockingly summarized in 1969: ". . . to copy some of Unamuno's awkardnesses (which I liked), to be a Seventeenth Century Spanish writer, to be Macedonio Fernández, to find out metaphors already found out by Lugones, to sing of a Buenos Aires with one story houses and, towards the West or the South, villas surrounded by iron fences."[7] Underlying those contradictory objectives it is possible, however, to detect one guiding principle, an adaptation of Whitman's ambitious plan: "With the twirl of my tongue I encompass worlds and volumes of worlds" (45).

From the very beginning, it is also clear that Borges' project has been designed on a scale totally different from Whitman's. In Borges' first two books of poems and even in *Cuaderno San Martín*, the totality of life has been, paradoxically, envisioned in minute dimensions: the universe is viewed with a very limited focus. Moreover, it is looked for, pointed out and expressed within boundaries. Borges already knew that the poet is not identical to his universe—that he can, and must, keep his distance, accepting the limited dimensions of the poem in relation to the limitless world, to the limitless sectors of the world:

> Africa's destiny lies in eternity, where there are
> deeds, idols, kingdoms, arduous forests and swords.
> I have attained a sunset and a village. (66; transl. MLB)

Even before these lines in "*Dakar*," from *Luna de enfrente*, in "*Las calles*," the opening poem of *Fervor de Buenos Aires*, one can see some sort of a reduction of the Whitmanesque world. In fact, Whitman's "worlds and volumes of worlds" have been replaced by the humble streets which will be Borges' only topography:

> Towards the West, the North, and the South
> streets, which are also the native land, have unfurled:
> may those flags be in the verses I design. (16; transl. MLB)

As echoes of Whitman's project and of Whitman's voice, even the more grandiloquent poems—particularly those collected in *Luna de enfrente*: "Una despedida," "Jactancia de quietud," "Dakar," "La promisión en alta mar"—render the tone of the model at a lower pitch. One could point out the poem, "Casi Juicio Final" ("Almost Last Judgment") as the epitome of that change:

> In my heart of hearts, I justify and praise myself:
> I have witnessed the world; I have confessed the
>   strangeness of the world.
> I have sung the eternal: the clear returning moon and
>   the cheeks longed for by love. (69; transl. MLB)

In *Elogio de la sombra*, Borges acknowledges that he "once coveted the ample breath of the psalms or of Walt Whitman" (975; transl. MLB). The lines quoted above do, in my opinion, recall the almighty Adamic Whitmanesque breath. But it is as if Borges' reproduction had undergone a filtering process. Borges has pointed out very often that language is succession: it can only render a simplified, reduced universe, it cannot reproduce the universe's concurrences. A comparison between Whitman's and Borges' declarations will show the modesty of Borges' project. Whitman says in *Leaves of Grass*:

> My voice goes after what my eyes cannot reach,
> With the twirl of my tongue I encompass worlds and
>   volumes of worlds.
> Speech is the twin of my vision, it is unequal to
>   measure itself. (45)

In "Casi Juicio Final," the poetic voice sums up its accomplishments, its originality:

> I have commemorated with verses the city that embraces
>   me and the shredding outskirts.
> I have expressed wonder where others have merely
>   expressed custom.
> I have held up in firm words my feeling which could
>   have been easily scattered in tenderness.
>   (69; transl. MLB)

It is also worth remembering that "Casi Juicio Final" is like a disturbing anticipation, a matrix of other Last Judgments in Borges' poetry in addition to that in "Mateo, XXV, 30." For instance, in "Otro poema de los dones," from *El otro, el mismo* (*The Self and The Other*), Whitman is a double symbol; his name is equivalent to gratitude and it is also an equivalent of the power of Grace:

> I want to thank the divine
> Labyrinth of effects and causes . . .
> For Whitman and Francis of Assisi
> Who already wrote the poem. (936; transl. MLB)

All of the above can be summarized very briefly: if one had to choose only one poem from Borges' early poetry as an emblem of the powerful, yet silent presence of Whitman—presence explicitly reinforced in other texts—"Casi Juicio Final" could be that poem. In it, Whitman's ambition to witness the world is clearly inscribed. This vision, however, expressed through the modest confines of the topography of Buenos Aires has become typically Borgesian.

2. *Self-Definition through Opposition*

One of Borges' practices has been to define his own literary objectives when characterizing the literature of other writers. This, he has done while dealing with Whitman's poetry; in two notes included in *Discusión*—"El otro Whitman"; and "Nota sobre Walt Whitman"—in his lectures on the poet;[8] in the preface to his selection and translations from *Leaves of Grass* (1969);[9] and in his essay," Valéry como símbolo."

In his essay, "El otro Whitman," written in 1929, Borges wrote that Whitman's themes render "the peculiar poetry of arbitrariness and loss," (208; transl. DB) a phrase which would describe his own poetry with accuracy and concision. He also pointed out the failure of Whitman's critics to see the basic merit of his enumerations, "a merit lying not in their length but in their delicate verbal balance," (206; transl. D.B.) a description which is perhaps ultimately more appropriate for Borges' enumerations than for Whitman's. The essay on Valéry—written on the poet's death in 1945, and collected in *Otras Inquisiciones* in 1952—is an excellent sample of Borges' technique. He defines by closeness or by opposition—*simpatías y diferencias*. He develops an opposition Whitman/Valéry which might serve as a base to define Borges' literature; "Valéry personifies in an illustrious way the labyrinths of the spirit; Whitman, the interjections of the body" (686; transl. DB). Borges says of Whitman: ". . . he wrote his rhapsodies by means of an imaginary self, formed partly from himself, partly from each of his readers." Borges continues that in the face of that quest, of that fiction of a "possible man . . . of unlimited and careless happiness Valéry glorifies the virtues of the mind." Finally, in Valéry's predilections (the antithesis of Whitman's), are without a doubt Borges' pleasures: "The lucid pleasures of thought and the secret adventures of order."

3. *The Memory of an Unending Poem*

In the early poetry of Borges one can notice the presence of Whitman's diction; but these versions even in the young Borges' display of *Ultraísta* baroque, already announce the future Borges. It is well-known that in the work of both Whitman and Borges free verse, marked by the use of long lines, has Biblical resonances. It is also known that such a resonance largely derives from the anaphoric repetitions and the enumerations. (I think it is appropriate to recall here that Michel Foucault, in *The Order of Things*,[10] has aptly described Borges' enumerations as heteroclite, a term more adequate, in my view, than the stylistic "chaotic enumeration" popularized by Leo Spitzer, who, by the way, never mentioned Borges in his essay written in 1944, when Borges had already published twelve books.[11]) Like Whitman's, Borges' diction interweaves somewhat unexpected colloquial language with rather audacious images, linked together by a syntax of a paradoxically grandiloquent ease. That syntax, nonetheless, shows a degree of control which is the privilege of brevity: "he was a poet of a tremulous and sufficient laconism" (207; transl. DB), Borges said of Whitman, a singularly apt characterization of his own poetry. With tremulous and sufficient pithiness, Whitman had announced: "Tenderly will I use you, curling grass" (28), which Borges translated: "Te usaré con ternura, hierba curva."[12] Raised from its elementary condition to a pantheist motif, and ultimately to the level of symbol, the "curling grass" sums up the whole of *Leaves of Grass*, and perhaps provides the main clue to it:

> These are really the thoughts of all men in all ages
> and lands, they are not original with me,
> If they are not the riddle and the untying of the
> riddle they are nothing,
> If they are not as close as they are distant they
> are nothing.
> This is the grass that grows wherever the land is
> and the water is,
> This the common air that bathes the globe. (38)

It is striking to note that Whitman's verses are particularly close to the reflections on "La nadería de la personalidad" ("The Nothingness of Personality") in *Inquisiciones*,[13] and, above all, to Borges' concept of the author of the poem. That concept, repeated so many times, was set forth in the early inscription to the reader in *Fervor de Buenos Aires*: "Our nothings differ little: it is a trivial and chance circumstance that you are the reader of these exercises, and I the writer of them" (16; transl. DB).

Nonetheless, it must be recognized that the point of contact is at once more subtle and more solid than the comparison of the texts might suggest at first sight. The two concepts of poetry depend essentially on a similar intention: on a way of looking at humble and insignificant elements and raising them to poetic stature, to make them poetically prestigious. It is possible to go still further, and one will note that the deeper connection between Whitman's voice and that of the early Borges will be revealed moreover in the echoes of the first Borges in his later work. Such a connection can be established, I think, once the links are found between the early poems by Borges and later reworkings of them. To be sure, here it is necessary to attempt a reading which would reach for one of those secret traces I referred to previously. Like Whitman's grass, some humble and insignificant elements belong for Borges in the category of symbols. The streets of the out-of-the-way neighborhood, the outskirts—the *arrabal*—are one of those symbols. And just as there is a recognizable echo of "tenderly will I use you, curling grass" in the first line of "Para una calle del Oeste" ("For a street in the West"): "You will give me an alien immortality, lonely street" (72; transl. DB). That echo, that exaltation of something insignificant, similar to Whitman's, is repeated when the neighborhood street—freed of its literal meaning—is endowed with symbolic value.[14]

The preceding remarks are based on the following hypothesis: in "La noche cíclica" ("The Cyclical Night"), one of Borges' most characteristic and striking poems dated in 1940, Whitman is subtly inscribed in the affinity of the poetic quest, and in the will to specify a totalizing vision. There is no doubt, to begin with, that formally the regular quatrains of "La noche cíclica" could not be farther from Whitman's free verse. Besides, it is obvious that there are poems in *El otro, el mismo*—"Insomnio," for instance, with which the book begins—in which the influence of Whitman, a "presence" that Borges acknowledges in the preface, is undeniable. But I think that the affinity should also be traced on a more profound level. Perhaps the affinity lies above all in the way of looking at, or in the way of looking for, the substance of poetry. In that respect, Borges transfigures the insignificant neighborhood into a meaningful, relevant poetic symbol:

> They knew it, the fervent pupils of Pythagoras . . . .
>
> But I know that a vague Pythagorean rotation
> Night after night sets me down in the world
>
> On the outskirts of the city. A remote street
> Which might be either north or west or south,
> But always with a blue-washed wall, the shade
> Of a fig tree, and a sidewalk of broken concrete.
>
> This, here, is Buenos Aires. Time, which brings
> Either love or money to men, hands on to me
> Only this withered rose, this empty tracery
> Of streets with names recurring from the past
>
> In my blood. . . .[15]

These stanzas show that, under the umbrella of other much more explicit shades—Pythagoras, Hume, Anaxagoras—Whitman springs forth to give deeper meaning to the non-prestigious sign (the grass / the neighborhood street). But, also, there is another trace of Whitman in the poem: Whitman is also present in the design of Borges' text. The design by which the last stanza (cyclically) returns to the first line of the poem is a version of Whitman's faith in poetic writing:

> It returns, the hollow dark of Anaxagoras;
> In my human flesh, eternity keeps recurring
> And the memory, or plan, of an endless poem
>   beginning:
> "They knew it, the fervent pupils of Pythagoras. . ."[16]

Borges had commented many times on Whitman's intention that his entire work be a single book or poem, and also on the unattainable nature of such an intention: "La noche cíclica" appears to me as a metaphor, a Borgesian transposition of that ambition.

An earlier reference was made to Borges' desire to transcend Whitman's ambition by a process of moderation or restraint, and to conceive of poetry not as the complex expression of a luxuriant world but limiting himself to recording and simplifying an already essential universe; in ordering an "enigmatic abundance."[17] In his works on Whitman, Borges insists on the failures of an ultimately unattainable conception of a poem which would embrace the whole universe. In the preface to the selection from *Leaves of Grass*, he states: "To speak of literary experiments is to speak of exercises which have failed in some more or less brilliant way . . . Whitman's experiment worked out so well that we tend to forget that it was an experiment."[18]

In the work of Borges, there is at least one significant example of failure to which we might say that Whitman is secretly, almost cunningly, inscribed. This is the wild project of the second rate, amateurish character in "El Aleph," Carlos Argentino Daneri, bitten with the idea of composing a poem about "La Tierra" ("The Earth"). It is not by chance that this grotesque imitation, this caricature of a Whitman who has failed completely—or, better perhaps, of a barely embryonic Whitman—provides Borges, the character-narrator, with the experience of the Aleph; that Borges should perceive the qualities of that Aleph from Carlos Argentino's place; and, that he should transmit them in a paradigmatic enumeration. That enumeration not only proves the impossibility of rendering the universe's concurrences, but is at once a culmination and a negation of Carlos Argentino's (and Whitman's) unattainable project.[19]

4. *Exorcism and Generative Power*

To a certain extent, to write, or to speak about the familiar presences in this work was a fertile exorcism, which led Borges to find his own literary voice. The exorcism of the name of Whitman, like that of the other names which are signs in Borges, began early, perhaps becoming intensified during the hiatus in his poetic production after *Cuaderno San Martín* (*San Martín Copybook*)—as is proven by the two notes included in *Discusión*, mentioned above—and culminating when Whitman appears as an explicit sign in poems and prefaces. A final confrontation between a poem by Whitman and a poem by Borges will be useful to show to what extent the exorcism was successful: it will provide an example of how Whitman's name, an explicit sign starting from *El otro, el mismo* keeps on inspiring the poet, as a secret cipher, as in the texts of Borges' prehistory. In his *Nota sobre Walt Whitman*, included in *Discusión*, Borges included a Spanish version of "Full of Life, Now":

Full of life now, compact, visible,
I, forty years old the eighty-third year of the States,
To one a century hence or any number of centuries hence,
To you yet unborn these, seeking you.

When you read these I that was visible am become
    invisible,
Now it is you, compact, visible, realizing my poems,
    seeking me,
Fancying how happy you were if I could be with you
    and become your comrade;
Be it as if I were you. (Be not too certain but I
    am now with you.) (109)

So Borges addresses himself, in *El otro, el mismo*, "To My Reader":

You are invulnerable. Have they not shown you,
The powers that preordain your destiny,
The certainty of dust? Is not your time
As irreversible as that same river
Where Heraclitus, mirrored, saw the symbol
Of fleeting life? A marble slab awaits you
Which you will not read—on it, already written,
The date, the city, and the epitaph.
Other men too are only dreams of time,
Not everlasting bronze nor shining gold;
The universe is, like you, a Proteus.
Dark, you will enter the darkness that expects you,
Doomed to the limits of your traveled time.
Know that in some sense you by now are dead.[20]

Certainly the dialogue of these two texts can be interpreted as a summary of the generative power of poetry, and as a synthesis of a continuity—ultimately beyond all analysis—of a poetic text combined with an idealist belief and with a clear baroque certainty: the continuity which prevents us from separating this poem from the whole of Borges' poetry, a poetry in which Whitman's name is a permanent force, and perhaps more so when it is not spelled out.

NOTES

1. Guillermo Sucre, "Borges: el elogio de la sombra," *Revista Iberoamericana*, 72 (1970): 372.

2. Jorge Luis Borges, *Inquisiciones* (Buenos Aires: Proa, 1925):91. Translated by MLB.
3. James E. Irby, *Encuentro con Borges* (Buenos Aires: Galerna, 1968): 12–13.
4. César Fernández Moreno, "Harto de laberintos," *Mundo Nuevo*, 18 (1967):10.
5. In Carlos Meneses, *Poesía juvenil de Jorge Luis Borges* (Barcelona: Otañeta Editor, 1978): 57–8. Translated by MLB.
6. Walt Whitman, "Song of Myself," 3. In *Leaves of Grass* and *Selected Prose* (New York: the Modern Library, 1950):25. Further references to Whitman belong to this edition, and the page number is given in parenthesis in the text. As I have said, in this paper I refer only to poems by Whitman which Borges chose to translate into Spanish for his selection of *Leaves of Grass*.
7. Jorge Luis Borges, *Obras completas* (Buenos Aires: Emecé, 1969): 13. Translated by MLB. Further references to this edition are given in parenthesis in the text.
8. Apparently, the first public lecture that Borges gave on Whitman took place in Buenos Aires in 1958. Cf. *La Prensa*, Buenos Aires, August 2, 1958, p. 3. To my knowledge, there is a transcription of another lecture on Whitman he gave in Chicago in 1968. Cf. Jorge Luis Borges, "Walt Whitman: Man and Myth," *Critical Inquiry*, 1 (1975): 708–711. James East Irby has mentioned Borges' project to give a lecture on Whitman in Texas in 1961. Cf. Irby, *Encuentro con Borges*, 12. Irby has told me that Borges lectured on Whitman at Princeton University in 1968 or 1969.
9. Walt Whitman, *Hojas de hierba*. Selección, traducción y pró-logo de Jorge Luis Borges (Buenos Aires: Juárez Editor, 1969).
10. Michel Foucault, Preface. *The Order of Things* (New York: Vintage Books, 1973): XVII.
11. Leo Spitzer, *La enumeración caótica en la poesía moderna* (Buenos Aires: Facultad de Filosofía y Letras, 1945).
12. Whitman, *Hojas de hierba*, 45.
13. Borges, *Inquisiciones*, 84–95.
14. I have developed this idea in "La topografía de la ambigüedad: Buenos Aires en Borges, Bianco, Bioy Casares," *Hispamérica*, 27 (1980): 33–46. The opposition: Literal meaning/ symbolic value is based in A. J. Greimas' theory, in *Du Sens* (Paris: Seuil, 1970): 7–17.
15. Jorge Luis Borges, *Selected Poems, 1923–1967* (New York: Dell, 1972): 79. Translation by Alastair Reid.
16. Borges, *Selected Poems*, 81.
17. Borges wrote in "Examen de metáforas," *Inquisiciones*, 65: "Language is an efficient ordering of the world's enigmatic abundance." Translation by MLB.
18. Jorge Luis Borges, "Prólogo," Walt Whitman, *Hojas de hierba*, 29. Translation DB.
19. There is, I think, another echo of that unattainable project in the drama in verse, *The Enemies*, by the second-rate writer Jaromir Hladíc, victim of the Nazis, protagonist of "El milagro secreto" ("The Secret Miracle") in *Ficciones*.
20. Borges, *Selected Poems*, 183. Translated by Alastair Reid.

BIBLIOGRAPHY

Borges, Jorge Luis. *Inquisiciones*. Buenos Aires: Proa, 1925.
Borges, *Obras Completas*. Buenos Aires: Emecé, 1969.
Borges. *Selected Poems, 1923–1967*. New York: Dell Publishing Co., 1972.
Foucault, Michel. *The Order of Things*. New York: Vintage Books, 1973.
Irby, James E. *Encuentro con Borges*. Buenos Aires: Galerna, 1968.
Meneses, Carlos. *Poesía juvenil de Jorge Luis Borges*. Barcelona: Otañeta Editor, 1978.
Moreno, César Fernández. "Harto de laberintos." In *Mundo Nuevo*, 18 (1967), 10.
Spitzer, Leo. *La enumeración caótica en la poesía moderna*. Buenos Aires: Facultad de Filosofía y Letras, 1945.

Sucre, Guillermo. "Borges: el elogio de la sombra." In *Revista Iberoamericana*, 72 (1970), 372.

Whitman, Walt. *Hojas de Hierba*. Translated by Jorge Luis Borges. Buenos Aires: Juárez Editor, 1969.

Whitman. "Song of Myself." In *Leaves of Grass and Selected Prose*. New York: The Modern Library, 1950.

JAMES M. HUGHES AND CARLOS CORTÍNEZ

Where Do You Stand with God, Ms. Dickinson, Señor Borges?

God in the Poetry of Emily Dickinson

Where does Emily Dickinson stand with God? She stood stubbornly outside the congregation of those officially designated "godly" in her community and her family. This courageous or foolish or perverse personal attitude is central to the posture of the poet as it is expressed in her poems. But remember, she has been called both the witch and the nun of Amherst!

Dickinson's views anticipate moderns like Borges. In her case, as possibly in Borges', such convictions seem on the edge, at the border, of the possibly provincial frontier of a creative re-evaluation of acquired wisdom. For the language of these early rebels must also be the very language of conventional communities against which, but also in which, their stands are made.

In Dickinson, and possibly in spite of himself, in Borges, there are suggestions or elements of orthodoxy. In Dickinson's case there is a significant amount of what might be called orthodox anxiety, as if a fear that such and such a stance with or against God were indeed warning proof of damnation. In response to this anxiety, some Dickinson poems appear conventionally pious. Nevertheless, one's overall impression of Dickinson's *oeuvre* suggests that even these "safe" poems are part of a restlessly continuing experimentation with words and the possible relationships with God words can reveal or assure. Dickinson's religious poems can be called wagers (in Pascal's sense of that word), or possibly pragmatic prayers.

Dickinson's uneasy but persistent experimentation with the language and postures of life is her most instructive legacy to those, like Borges, who come after her. If any doubts seemed willfully perverse in her place and time, they appear now as refreshingly honest evidence of an unfortunately troubled integrity. What Borges said at Dickinson College about his hearing Dickinson's voice, testifies to the lasting impact of her example.

I can only suggest the range of Dickinson's attitude towards God. Four poems and one letter may reveal for her poetic heirs the questioning complexity of these pioneering examples. The first poem is considered conventional enough to become a favorite of school anthologies.

> I never saw a Moor—
> I never saw the Sea—
> Yet know I how the Heather looks
> And what a Billow be.
>
> I never spoke with God
> Nor visited in Heaven—
> Yet certain am I of the spot
> As if the Checks were given—[1]

Even in the absence of experience, the believer can ascertain the existence of heaven. But might it not be significant that God appears reduced to "the Spot," a designation more appropriate to the geographically located Heaven and obviously departing from the parallel expectations of the first stanza? Furthermore, this popular poem begs the question of proof that lies behind belief, the very question at the heart of Dickinson's persistent experimentation.

Before returning to the critically interesting question of Dickinson's choice of the word "Checks," let me quote a second poem, one that raises a fundamental question about the nature of the kind of knowing that faith exemplifies.

> The Brain—is wider than the Sky—
> For—put them side by side—
> The one the other will contain
> With ease—and You—beside—

> The Brain is deeper than the sea—
> For—hold them—Blue to Blue—
> The one the other will absorb—
> As Sponges—Buckets—do—
> The Brain is just the weight of God—
> For—Heft them—Pound for Pound—
> And they will differ—if they do—
> As Syllable from Sound—[2]

Here the believing, certain Brain is "just" as heavy as God. Where does Dickinson stand with God? Here she stands side by side, weighing all in the balance by the audacity of a creative verbal act. The Brain that creates syllables out of sounds, poems out of experience, creates belief and even, perhaps, the object or subject of that belief.

Many other Dickinson poems, of course, posit a personal view on behalf of God's objective existence. But even in these poems, as in some of Borges' "religious" poems, the attributes given God are not orthodox. That last line of "I never saw a Moor," for example, introduces one of these daring notions: "As if the Checks were given—." Dickinson's official editor, Thomas H. Higginson, notes the "use of the word 'Checks' perplexed the early editors, who altered it. She seems to be using it in the accepted colloquial sense of railroad tickets: 'My assurance of the existence of Heaven is as great as though, having surrendered my checks to the conductor, I knew I had arrived there.'"[3] Johnson's explanation of "Checks" fails to account for the implications of that explanation: the certainty of Heaven, if not God, depends upon the surrendering of proofs not of existence but of purchase. Surrendering tickets purchased in the promise of a destination suggests arrival, as well as a schedule and a price scale. This may be analogous to the Puritans' designated stages in spiritual development from an initially embarking Election and Life of Sin to a finally disembarking Glorification. What Bunyan called *Pilgrim's Progress* and Hawthorne a "Celestrial Railroad," Dickinson, like Hawthorne, sometimes uses terminology of this spiritual journey in less than orthodox ways.

But another look at "Checks" in Dickinson's own Noah Webster's *Dictionary of the American Language,* suggests even more.[4] The primary meanings of the noun "Check" all refer to stops (as on a train?!), hindrances, rebuffs, continued restraints, curbs, controls, governments, rebukes, fears: all these are Dickinson attributes of the God who created both death and sin to check the conceivably endlessly uninterrupted Eden of living.[5] Consider too the financial meaning of the word "Check": "The correspondent cipher of a bank note; a corresponding indenture; any counter-register." Cipher? Indentured servant of God? Checks that counter and register symbolic proofs of and against some ultimately real accounting? Noah Webster continues: "An order for money, drawn on a banker or on the cashier of a bank, payable to the bearer." Where does Dickinson stand with God? Sometimes as bearer not only of tickets purchased and surrendered, but as bearer of an IOU, a creative collector of God's indebtedness for His arbitrary or at least unreasonable checks and restraints, those imbalancing riddles of deaths and sins and loves.

Another poem may summarize, over-simply, Dickinson's stand with God in terms of her delightful but dangerous play with terms of belief and accountability.

> I never lost as much but twice,
> And that was in the sod.
> Twice have I stood a beggar
> Before the door of God!
>
> Angels—twice descending
> Reimbursed my store—
> Burglar! Banker—Father!
> I am poor once more![6]

Dickinson's version of the Trinity here is central to her lifelong conflict with that believed, but ambivalent certainty, which checks again and again our immortal longings and lovings. Thus Dickinson may not be able to share Borges' trust in death. Coupling "Burglar" and "Banker" may anticipate, quite unwittingly of course, the Marxist sense of an economic system, capitalism, that specializes in waylayings of the potentially free spirit. "Burglar! Banker—Father!" It is a trinity one might or might not expect from the rebellious daughter and sister of lawyers in a frontier orthodox capitalist community whose Puritan deity specializes in keeping seemingly unfair accounts, exchanging checks of one kind for checks of another, with power only in obscure reserve, with at least as much alien theft as fatherly love.

Where does Dickinson stand with God the Father, the Burglar and the Banker?

> "Heavenly Father"—take to thee
> The supreme iniquity
> Fashioned by thy candid Hand
> In a moment contraband—
> Though to trust us—seem to us
> More respectful—"We are Dust—"
> We apologize to thee
> For thine own Duplicity—[7]

Dickinson might mean: forgive us for making us the way you did. Forgive us for your trespasses. Forgive us for your indebtedness to us.

In 1845, Dickinson explained her sentiments against a highly pressured group effort to convert her:

I was almost persuaded to be a Christian. . . . I can say that I never enjoyed such perfect peace and happiness as the short time in which I felt I had found my savior. But I soon forgot my morning prayer or else it was irksome to me. One by one my old habits returned and I cared less for religion than ever. . . . I hope at sometime the heavenly gates will be opened to receive me and the angels will consent to call me sister. I am continually putting off becoming a Christian. Evil voices lisp in my ear—[8]

For better or worse, those "evil voices" may well be the poet's own restlessness, her own inquiring mind, her own pragmatic faith in facts and the marvellously manifold words and meanings that express and define them.

Dickinson describes the ubiquity of whatever God

> Perennial beholds us—
> Myself would run away
> From Him—and Holy Ghost—and All—
> But there's the "Judgment Day"![9]

Perhaps that possibly blaming, checking, cost-accounting homiletics was arguing God too narrowly for Dickinson's romantic imagination and modern skepticism.[10] Borges once offered us Anglos, us Yankee heirs of Dickinson's litigatious liturgical legacy, "the loyalty of a man who has never been loyal."[11] Borges stands nearer Dickinson than one might expect; the two of them may really offer us seemingly endless poetic proof that when all has been said and done, there may be no last stands where God is concerned. God the Father? Dickinson's father was a not very nurturing, enigmatic, devout lawyer. Borges' father was an anarchistic free thinker. A fundamentally modern designation of deity is, as Dickinson and Borges show, ambiguous at best.

J. H.

God in Borges' Poetry

Speaking of his countrymen Borges says that they believe in a supernatural world but that they are not interested in it. On the contrary, he himself is interested in it but does not believe.[1] He gives this answer every time that he is asked about his religious convictions. For the record, Borges is neither a Catholic nor a Christian.

When asked to name the most important book ever written he immediately answers *The Divine Comedy,* but is quick to add that, of course, he shares neither the Christian vision of Dante nor his faith. Borges appreciates the poem exclusively for its literary qualities.[2]

The person who limits his knowledge of Borges to the interviews that are incessantly printed all over the world by magazines and newspapers knows very well—because those interviews all are so similar—that the author is not only an agnostic but perhaps—since he himself says so—an outright atheist.

Everyone is aware that Argentina, like all the countries of Latin America, is a Catholic nation. The Church there enjoys certain privileges regardless of which dictatorship is in control at any given moment. It is virtually a spiritual monopoly, and woe to anyone who dares to defy it. During the first administration of Perón, attacks on the Catholic Church were encouraged by the "justicialismo," and finally brought down the dictator. On the other hand, Catholic support for Rosas during the previous century kept that tyrant in his palace for an intolerably long period of time.

Borges' parents offered their son a contradictory example: his father was an anarchist, a free thinker; his mother, a devout Catholic. The son followed the paternal path from an early age but lived most of his life close to his mother. After his father died in 1938, Borges spent almost forty years in close dialogue with his mother, Doña Leonor. His mother's influence became more intense during the fifties, when Borges' almost total blindness forced her to become also his secretary, reader, amanuensis, travel companion and of course, confidant. Only to satisfy her insistent request did Borges receive communion before her death.

Thus it was not surprising to a casual observer of Argentine life to learn of a more or less noisy polemic, in 1976, between the ecclesiastical hierarchy and the "atheist" writer.

But moving away from what journalists tell us about Borges' thoughts (a rather superficial source of information), and turning toward his works, a much less simplistic situation is evident.

The first thing that stands out is a preponderance of theological motifs. It is true that philosophical subjects, in particular the question of time, abound in Borges' works. Neither is there a lack of labyrinths, knives, and hoodlums. But, quantitatively, it appears that the theme of God and related concerns, such as theological discussion, biblical gloss, mystical characters, and heretics, clearly predominates in his extensive literary corpus.

In his short stories, nevertheless, in spite of the intensity with which some of them (for instance, "The Zahir," "God's script," "The Secret Miracle") deal with a religious subject, we cannot transfer to the author the concerns or the mystical experiences of their characters. At the same time, of course, the writer cannot totally distance himself from the subjects that his literature treats. One really has to wonder if it isn't a bit suspicious that God strolls around so ubiquitously through the fictional works of an author who is a professed atheist.

Concentrating upon Borges' poetry, a genre that allows us to identify the lyric voice with that of its author, the findings are of another nature. There are still an overwhelming number of references to the Deity. Some of them are direct invocations of that Almighty Being, and are identified in the traditional terminology as God. In other poems references are made to a Supreme Being but with a more non-committal name: "Something" or "Somebody," or even "the divine labyrinth of causes and effects."[3] In many poems there are allusions to Christ, and the Bible is mentioned frequently as a Holy Book and is the inspiration for several poems written about certain favorite passages.[4]

Granted that from the quantity of poems, more than a hundred with religious themes or significant allusions, we cannot identify an orthodox religious belief. Many poems presuppose a God and the lyric voice in the poem invokes Him. Many others, however, question His existence or attribute to Him very different characteristics from those which the Judeo-Christian tradition assign Him. God appears, then, as a created Being (not eternal) or is indifferent to human destiny, or antagonistic towards human beings. At times God's will is depicted as ironic (giving the poet, for instance, books and blindness simultaneously) or generous (because blindness proves to be advantageous to thought) or selfish (because He has created human diversity only in order to expand His own possible experiences and perceptions).[5]

With respect to life after death, Borges fluctuates between poems that assure Truth (that is to say, the Archetypes, the Rose, our own enigma) will be revealed to us after our death, and others in which, following the paternal example, he pleads to die "entirely," both in body and soul.[6]

Although Borges' atheism is not, by any means militant or belligerent,[7] it is voiced occasionally in disrespectful or provocative terms, as when he mocks dogmas such as that of the Holy Trinity (and speaks of "teratology"!) or when he makes corrections of passages in the Gospels or replaces the Lord's Prayer with a revised version.[8]

Adding to this his total lack of interest in the notion of sin, one can readily judge why it is not easy to consider Borges an orthodox Roman Catholic, in spite of the fact that there are also statements from him—rare, to be sure—insisting that he is a Catholic because he has been raised in a Catholic environment.[9]

In this very brief outline of an immense subject within the work and thought of Borges, it may only be suggested that the so-called "agnosticism" of the Argentine writer is an oversimplified, hastily-arrived-at conclusion.[10]

Perhaps Borges is really skeptical of theological constructions that are formulated by human beings in order to sustain their intuitions with dogmatic force. Reason does not allow us to "know" with certainty. As the title of one of his poems expresses it: "De que nada se sabe": "That Nothing is Known." It is mentioned in this poem that perhaps human destiny does not belong to men, and may belong to someone else, but calling that someone else "God" does not help us at all. Therefore, it makes no sense to fear, to doubt, to pray.[11]

Unwilling to accept as evidence that which is not self-evident, Borges, of necessity, distances himself from any dogma or faith. He proves himself nevertheless interested, curious to explore every religion (Christianity, Judaism, Islam, Buddhism, and Shintoism) but reluctant to join any of them.[12] The closest that he has been to a formal declaration of a concrete faith is his "Autobiographical Essay," in which he declares himself an "amateur Protestant."[13]

But if the poetical works of Borges are read carefully, the reader can perceive something more than a mere insistence upon religious subjects and an incessant speculation, almost obsessive in nature, about the intentions of the Creator (or the "Dreamer" as he would say). I think the poems reveal that, despite what reason tells the author, there is an intuition, perhaps a certainty, that there is a Divine Being—one that gives us its truth in small brief glimpses, perhaps keeping the total revelation for after our death.[14]

Unlike Hölderlin or Rilke, who justify God's silence by reminding us of the terrible consequences that a revelation could cause to man, Borges does not have a satisfactory answer for the mystery. Declaring himself an agnostic, Borges misleads the superficial inquirer and remains free to continue his incessant probing from all possible points of view and without the constraints of religious bias, of the subject that obsesses him. Emily Dickinson has advised, "Tell all the Truth, but tell it slant." Borges seems to agree with her when he says that Homer was not unaware that things should be said in an indirect way.[15]

In contrast to flat journalistic statements, the poetical works of Borges —which fortunately are non-confessional—tell his readers, in a subtle but forceful way that the poet indeed possesses a religious faith, not a blind one but an expectant one, an intuition regarding a "divine" labyrinth of causes and effects, a "Something" or "Somebody" who will in fact face us with the Archetypes and Splendors, who will reveal to us, finally, who we have been, who we are. That's why he sees death as a "hidden treasure," a "dark marvel that lies in wait for us" ("un oculto tesoro," "una oscura maravilla que nos acecha").[16]

C. C.

NOTES

God in the Poetry of Emily Dickinson

1. Thomas H. Johnson, ed. *The Poems of Emily Dickinson* (Cambridge: Harvard University Press, 1958), Vol. II: 72. Poem #1052.
2. Johnson, *The Poems of Dickinson*, 486. Poem #632.
3. Johnson, *The Poems of Dickinson*, II, 742.
4. *An American Dictionary of the English Language*, 1828. Two volumes.
5. Johnson, *The Poems of Dickinson*, III, 838. Poem #1205:
    Of heaven above the firmest proof
    We fundamental know
    Except for its marauding Hand
    It had been Heaven below.
6. Johnson, *The Poems of Dickinson*, I, 38. Poem #49.
7. Johnson, *The Poems of Dickinson*, III, 1009–10. Poem #1461.
8. Thomas H. Johnson, ed. *The Letters of Emily Dickinson* (Cambridge: Harvard University Press, 1958), I, 27. Letter #10.
9. Johnson, *The Poems of Dickinson*, I, 322. Poem #413.
10. Johnson, *The Poems of Dickinson*, III, 839. Poem #1207.
11. Jorge Luis Borges, "Two English Poems, II." *Selected Poems 1923–1967*. Edited by Norman Thomas di Giovanni. (New York: Delacorte Press, 1972): 77.

God in Borges' Poetry

1. Jorge Luis Borges, *Obras completas* (Buenos Aires: Emecé, 1974): 282.
2. ". . . the best book Literature has yet produced . . ." J. L. Borges, *Nueve Ensayos Dantescos* (Madrid: Espasa-Calpe, 1982).
3. "Something" or "Somebody" ("Algo" or "Alguien") in reference to God, in the following poems: "Alguien", "Islandia", "Una brújula", "La clepsidra". In the poem "El fin", it is called "Perhaps" or "Nobody" ("Tal vez" or "Nadie"), quite significantly because it is a poem about the writer's mother. In two other poems the reference to God is done with the formula "labyrinth of causes and effects": "Otro poema de los dones" and "Al iniciar el estudio de la gramática anglosajona."
4. Christ in: "La noche que en el sur lo velaron," "Poema del cuarto elemento," "Baltasar Gracián," "Al vino," "Milonga de Manuel Flores," "Buenos Aires," "No eres los otros," "Things that might have been," "Acevedo." Biblical passages in: "Juan I, 14," "Lucas XXIII," "Mateo XXV, 30."
5. a) a created God: "Ajedrez II," "Cosmogonía," "Baruch Spinoza."
    b) an indifferent God: "No eres los otros," "La moneda de hierro."
    c) a terrible God: "El golem."
    d) an ironic God: "Poema de los dones."
    e) a generous God: "Versos de catorce," "La mañana."
    f) a selfish God: "Él," "Juan I, 14."
    g) a not almighty God: "Amanecer."
    h) a subtle God: "Los espejos," "Una brújula."
    i) a capricious God: "In memoriam A.R."
    j) a fair God: "El otro."
    k) a lyric voice sure of its immortality: "Composición escrita en un ejemplar del *Beowulf*."
    l) a lyric voice open to the possibility of God: "Los enigmas."
6. In reference to his father: "A mi padre." In reference to himself: "The thing I am."

7. "I am neither a missionary of Christianity nor of agnosticism . . . Everything is possible, even God . . . We are not even sure that God does not exist . . ." in Oswaldo Romero, "Dios en la obra de J. L. Borges: su Teología y su Teodicea," *Revista Iberoamericana*, n. 100: 465–501.

8. About the Holy Trinity: J. L. Borges, *Obras completas*, 283–4; and "El budismo" in J. L. Borges, *Siete Noches* (N.p.,n.d.)

9. ". . . being a Catholic, I feel attracted to Protestantism . . ." Interview with Rita Guibert, *Life en Español*, XXXI, n. 5 (March 11, 1968): 58. "I have been raised in a Catholic environment; my grandmother knew the Bible by heart, my mother was a Catholic, my father was an atheist, but not in a belligerent or political way . . ." (Polemic with the president of the University of Jujuy, December 1976) in Manuel Caldeiro, "Yo acuso a Borges," (*Gente* XII, n. 597, Jan. 6, 1977): 74.

10. The most complete study on the subject, even if it focuses mainly on Borges' answers to journalists and only deals with a few of his poems, is the already mentioned article by Oswaldo Romero.

11. "De que nada se sabe," Jorge Luis Borges, *La rosa profunda* (Buenos Aires: Emecé, 1975).

12. When in his lecture on Buddhism, for example, he states that he is not sure of being a Christian, although he is sure of not being a Buddhist.

13. "Autobiographical Essay" in *The Aleph and Other Stories* (New York: Dutton, 1970); and Selden Rodman, *Tongues of Fallen Angels* (New York: New Directions, 1972): 24.

14. In this way, among others, in the following poems: "Everness," "Elogio de la sombra," "The unending rose," "A mi padre," "La clepsidra."

15. Emily Dickinson in Poem #1129, in T. Johnson, ed., *The Complete Poems of Emily Dickinson* (Boston: Little, Brown & Co., 1958): 506.

16. Lines in the poems "Blind Pew" and "1964, II," respectively.

BIBLIOGRAPHY

God in the Poetry of Emily Dickinson

An American Dictionary of the English Language. 1828.
Jorge Luis Borges, "Two English Poems, II." In *Selected Poems 1923–1967*. Edited by Norman Thomas Di Giovanni. New York: Delacorte Press, 1972.
Thomas H. Johnson, *The Letters of Emily Dickinson*. Cambridge: Harvard University Press, 1958.
Johnson. *The Poems of Emily Dickinson*. Cambridge: Harvard University Press, 1958.

God in Borges' Poetry

Borges, Jorge Luis, "Autobiographical Essay." In *The Aleph and Other Stories*. New York: Dutton, 1970.
Borges, "De que nada se sabe." In *La rosa profunda*. Buenos Aires: Emecé, 1975.
Borges, "El budismo." *Siete Noches*. N.p., n.d.
Borges, *Nueve Ensayos Dantescos*. Madrid: Espasa-Calpe, 1982.
Borges, *Obras completas*. Buenos Aires: Emecé, 1974.
Borges, "Un escolio." *Historia de la Noche*. Buenos Aires: Emecé, 1977.
Caldeiro, Manuel. "Yo acuso a Borges." *Gente*, XIIn.597 (Jan. 6, 1977), 74.
Guibert, Rita. *Life en Español*, XXXI n.5 (March 11, 1968), 58.
Johnson, T. *The Complete Poems of Emily Dickinson*. Boston: Little, Brown & Co., 1958.
Rodman, Selden. *Tongues of Fallen Angels*. New York: New Directions, 1972.
Romero, Oswaldo. "Dios en la obra de Jorge Luis Borges: su Teología y su Teodicea." *Revista Iberoamerica*, 100, 465–501.

D. L. SHAW

Some Unamunesque Preoccupations
in Borges' Poetry

So far as I am aware only three short studies have been published on Unamuno and Borges. One is Anthony Kerrigan's essay "Borges/Unamuno" in the *Tri-Quarterly* homage volume to Borges.[1] The second is an interesting article by Stelio Cro, "Jorge Luis Borges e Miguel de Unamuno."[2] The last is an essay of my own, published in an obscure magazine.[3] Hence there may be room to return to the subject, with special reference to Borges' poetry. For one cannot wholly agree with Kerrigan that "the truest testaments from these two meditative Spanish bookmen are necessarily in their fictions." Certainly in the case of Borges, we cannot overlook his remark to Keith Botsford in 1964,[4] that "en última instancia soy poeta" or to Madelaine Chapsal "Creo que no soy más que eso. Un poeta . . ."[5] The aim here is to suggest with respect to Borges the poet, that as Hispanists we can perhaps understand some of his preoccupations in a clearer and more familiar perspective by looking at them beside Unamuno's rather than by comparing them to those of non-Hispanic writers such as Chesterton, Emerson, Bloy, Hawthorne or Nabokov.

One of the intriguing aspects of Borges' work is that after "Acerca de Unamuno, poeta"[6] and the necrological article "Inmortalidad de Unamuno,"[7] Borges rarely mentions Unamuno.[8] Roberto Paoli[9] quite rightly speaks of "Unamuno, un autore la cui influenza su Borges, cosi manifesta, non è stata adeguatamente riconosciuta da chi l'ha subita." For although to Burgin[10] Borges asserted that Unamuno was "a very great writer" whom he greatly admired, he went on to say that Unamuno was interested in things that he, Borges, was not.

This is not always the case. Hardly less intriguing is that while Barrenechea, Enguídanos and Irby among others, also refer to Unamuno in connection with Borges, Sucre never mentions him once and Gertel is content with a reference to the 1923 essay; this despite affinities which seem to cry out for comment. Nor are these affinities casual. In his autobiographical statements, Borges has regularly emphasized his infatuation with Macedonio Fernández, the roots of whose work are very clearly in Unamuno's, so much so that Fernández once referred to himself jokingly as "Ningunamuno." In fact, Cro shows convincingly that throughout most of the 1920s Borges remained deeply interested in Unamuno. He makes the dangerous suggestion that the latter's influence may have been "decisive" in bringing on Borges' break with *Ultraísmo* between 1922 and 1923; and he notes the interesting parallel between Borges' hope for a kind of "criollismo universal" and Unamuno's similar postulate that a writer may reach the universal via the national tradition. In the end, however, Cro tends to restrict himself to remarks connected with Unamuno's *Rosario de sonetos líricos* and in practice suggests that the only major poem of Borges in which parallels with Unamuno can be detected is "La Recoleta," which he compares with "La oración del ateo." Perhaps this is too limited a view.

Above all what unites the work of Borges and Unamuno and makes any comparison possible is of course the philosophical, or rather metaphysical, basis on which it rests. Both men are essentially concerned with exploring, and inducing their readers to explore with them the problematic natures of being and reality. For this reason both deliberately blur the difference between analytic thought and creative imagination. Both seek, in differing degrees, to transcend the contingency of life through art, knowing the attempt to be vain. Sucre's description of the poetry of Borges as "una angustiosa meditación" is equally descriptive of Unamuno's. Unamuno, a man of his time, expresses his anguish in rather more religious terms; Borges, a man of our time, in rather more secular ones. But many of the roots are the same, for both belong to a historical pattern of collapsing confidence in what Sherman Eoff called "a fatherly world according to design."

At the center of the collapse is the sense of our individual identity, which we think of as real. We recall Victor Goti's remark in chapter thirty of Unamuno's *Niebla* that "el lector de la nivola llega a dudar de su propia realidad." We note in Unamuno that this is the end of a process which began with the acquisition of metaphysical awareness via rational, analytical thought. In Borges, on the other hand, it is a starting point, that of his intuition of "nuestra esencial nadería." [11] It is preceded by that most Unamunesque of all the lines in Borges' youthful verse, the second line of "La Recoleta," which reminds me that we are "irrealizados por tanta certidumbre de anulación." [12] All the threat to our ultimate substantiality, which Unamuno perceived in the inevitability of death, rings in that line. It condemns the ". . . deseable / dignidad de estar muerto" promised by the tombstones, to exist as mere *vanilocuencia*.

Life, "La Recoleta" tells us, is the absolute. Time and space are projections of the conscious mind only. Things, objects in what seems to be external reality, may be "ajenas de substancia" [13] and a street in the very suburbs which Borges celebrates with such warmth and tenderness may have only the reality of a legend or a line of poetry. [14] Borges toys with the idea which he and Unamuno shared sporadically with Berkeley and Schopenhauer that perception creates reality. This is certainly a major point of convergence between the two poets, as Cro recognizes:

È impossible trasferire a un piano metafisico delle dimensioni fisiche. Questo è l'asse della problematica della poesia di Borges: l'impossibilità di penetrare il mistero con la ragione, ma la necessità di esprimere l'esperienza emotiva suscitata dal mistero. È chiaro a questo punto la profonda analogia con la poesia di Unamuno. [15]

But what is perception? "Amanecer" contains the telling juxtaposition ". . . una actividad de la mente, / un sueño de las almas" [16] and suddenly we are back in the heartland of Unamuno territory.

For Unamuno, dreaming was both a comfort and a threat. Blanco Aguinaga in his well-known *El Unamuno contemplativo* [17] long ago distinguished four categories of dreaming in Unamuno's work: the conventional Calderonian concept of earthly life as unreal compared to life after death; the concept of man as a dream of God and vice versa; the *ensueño* or daydream of those who attempt to demonstrate God's existence or non-existence; and finally the *buen sueño* of unquestioning faith and ontological security. But to these we must add a fifth category which is clearly present in Unamuno's *La novela de don Sandalio, jugador de ajedrez* and in his play *Soledad*. It is this category which reveals the affinity with Borges. It rests on Unamuno's hope that "El sueño de dos es ya la verdad, la realidad,"[18] the proof of existence is to exist in the minds of others.

There are three possible consequences. On the one hand it may be possible, as Unamuno suggests in his late play *El hermano Juan*, to provoke others, through love, to dream their dreams of us and thus strengthen our substantiality. The notion is present in another early poem of Borges' "El jardín botánico" in which love differentiates us from the trees "que balbucean apenas el ser,"[19] but which nonetheless seek to join the quest for the unknown. This existential or ontological dimension of the love relationship is deeply Unamunesque. Secondly, as Frances Weyers has pointed out, "'La vida es sueño' may mean that someone else is dreaming us; the dream becomes a symbol of self-estrangement."[20] Lastly, there is the possibility that both we ourselves and others who dream us are all no more than dreams, but dreams in God's mind.

These last two possibilities surface in the second phase of Borges' poetic work in his well-known "El golem." Its theme combines two fundamentally Unamunesque ideas. First, the aspiration to add something to existing reality, to ". . . agregar a la infinita / serie un símbolo más."[21] This is very similar to Fulgencio Entrambasmares' doctrine of the *morcilla*. Don Fulgencio, a character in Unamuno's *Amor y pedagogía* in whom we recognize a kind of self-caricature by Unamuno, explains in chapter four: "morcilla se llama . . . a lo que meten los actores por su cuenta en sus recitados, a lo que añaden a la obra del autor dramático." Only by intercalating one's own *morcilla* into pre-existing reality, by adding one's own creation to God's creation, can one achieve a "momento metadramático" and guarantee one's own immortality. Borges' rabbi had attempted to bring about a "momento metadramático" of his own, like the wizard in the earlier tale "Las ruinas circulares." But the end of the poem forces us to recognize, like don Fulgencio, that the *morcilla* was merely one which "también nos sopla al oído el gran Apuntador." As the rabbi contemplates his creation (in all its inadequacy), so God ironically contemplates the rabbi. Borges himself underlined the totally Unamunesque quality of the poem when he declared to Burgin ". . . in the end it is suggested that as the golem is to the magician, to the cabbalist, so is man to God."[22] It is hardly by chance therefore that when Don Quixote in "Ni siquiera soy polvo" (*Historia de la noche*) asserts "Mi Dios, mi soñador, sigue soñandome," he is unconsciously—or consciously—echoing the situation that is at the base of the ending of *Niebla*. If we are the stuff that dreams are made of in this sense, we are, to use another of Borges' (and Unamuno's) favorite images, mere reflections in a mirror. But to speak of ourselves as dreams or reflections at least implies the existence of a dreamer to dream us or a mirror to reflect us. In moods of deepest scepticism both Unamuno and Borges were prepared to deny man even this vestige of substantiality. Unamuno both in his plays and in *San Manuel Bueno, martir* introduces the idea that life is not merely a dream, whoever dreams it, but a dream within a dream. So in "Arte poética" Borges can refer to the notion that ". . . la vigilia es otro sueño / que sueña no soñar."[23] There is, of course, a fundamental difference between Borges' treatment of the theme and Unamuno's, to which we shall return presently.

First we may glance at Borges' double sonnet "Ajedrez," whose theme is profoundly familiar to all students of Unamuno. The bulk of the second, and far better, of the two sonnets rehearses in four lines to essences of Unamuno's *La novela de don Sandalio*, which in turn expresses preoccupations which go far back in his work. In *La esfinge*, the hero, Angel, in the course of a chess game, asks: "¿No estamos los hombres con nuestras luchas matando la eternidad a un Ser Supremo que con nosotros juega?" Later, in *Del sentimiento trágico de la vida*, Unamuno asserts explicitly: "Y si las piezas de ajedrez tuviesen consciencia, es fácil que se atribuyeran albedrío en sus movimientos."[24] Echoing the idea, Borges writes of the chessmen in "Ajedrez":

> No saben que la mano señalada
> Del jugador gobierna su destino,
> No saben que un rigor adamantino
> Sujeta su albedrío y su jornada.[25]

The source of Borges' poem was not Unamuno, however, but Fitzgerald's translation of Omar Khayyam, stanza 49:

> Impotent pieces of the game he plays
> Upon his chequered board of Nights and Days
> Hither and thither moves, and checks and stays;
> And one by one back in the closet lays.

What is interesting is that in the first edition of Fitzgerald's translation the subject of the verb in the first line of the above quotation was not God but Destiny. Hence the progression in the sestet of Borges' sonnet:

> También el jugador es prisionero
> (La sentencia es de Omar) do otro tablero
> De negras noches y de blancas días.
> Dios mueve el jugador, y éste, la pieza.

But this follows:

> ¿Qué dios detrás de Dios la trama empieza
> De polvo y tiempo y sueño y agonías?

We think at once of Tzinacán's vision in "La escritura del Dios" in which among other things Tzinacán tells us "Vi el dios sin cara que hay detrás de los dioses." The idea of a faceless God (Destiny) behind the personal God of the Christian religion is one which as D. G. Turner has shown,[26] obsessed Unamuno no less than Borges (and Fitzgerald). For, if Unamuno is understood correctly, the chessboard in *Niebla*, *La novela de don Sandalio* and *La esfinge*, as well as elsewhere, is a patent symbol of determinism. What is not plain is the form of the determining force. Is it chance, Providence or destiny?

Borges and Unamuno share a consuming interest in the roles of design and chance in the workings of the universe. Some critics have insisted that Borges' central symbol, the labyrinth, is essentially a man-made object, and have related it to what they see as Borges' exposure of man's obstinate tendency to impose a pattern or structure on the chaos and flux of reality. Even this is a prominent Unamunesque idea. We see it in Augusto Pérez's reflection in Chapter Seven of *Niebla* that "esa idea de la necesidad no es sino la forma suprema que el azar toma en nuestra mente." Compare Borges' reference in "Las metáforas de las 1001 noches" in *Historia de la noche* to "el arbitrio del Destino / o del Azar, que son la misma cosa." But more important is the fact that a labyrinth is a chaos with the appearance of regularity or design. This is what fascinates both Unamuno and Borges: the idea enunciated by don Fermín in *Niebla*, Chapter Six: "Rigen a los hombres y a sus cosas enigmáticas leyes, que el hombre, sin embargo, puede vislumbrar." We are immediately reminded of Borges' lines in "In memoriam Alfonso Reyes": "El vago azar o las precisas leyes / que rigen nuestro sueño, el universo";[27] and the cognate but more explicit "El claro azar o las secretas leyes / que rigen este sueño, mi destino"[28] of "Oda compuesta en 1960." Just as a labyrinth appears to have a meaningful design, with a discoverable way to its center, so at intervals, as with Unamuno, Borges seems to have thought he could intuit a mysterious but significant design in his experience. Hence he could write in "Poema de los dones": "Algo que ciertamente no se nombra / con la palabra azar, rige estas cosas"; and much later in "Poema de la cantidad" from *El oro de los tigres*:

> Acaso cada hormiga que pisamos
> Es única ante Dios, que la precisa
> Para la ejecución de las puntuales
> Leyes que rigen su curioso mundo.
> Si así no fuera, el universo entero
> Sería un error y un oneroso caos.[29]

The labyrinth in Borges' work has only a deceitful appearance of order and regularity. In fact it is a meaningless and circular trap, a maze without an outlet or a center. This being so, there is no escape from the conclusion that God, Providence, Fate and determinism mean one and the same thing. The "despiadado dios que no se nombra" of "El otro,"[30] the "minuciosa Providencia / que administra lo pródigo y lo parco" of "In memoriam Alfonso Reyes,"[31] and the "hado o el azar" of "La luna"[32] are merely interchangable concepts. The temptation at this point is to qualify this last affirmation in the light of occasional glimpses of doubt and longing for immortality.[33] Thus, for example, in the second of two very moving poems concerned with Borges' parents in *La moneda de hierro*, "El fin" and "A mi padre," we read the strikingly Unamunesque line ". . . Nadie sabe / De qué mañana el marmol es la llave" with its suggestion of *ultratumberías*. In the first of the two poems Borges writes: "Dios o Tal Vez o Nadie, yo te pido / Su inagotable imagen, no el olvido." Is this a hint of *agonismo*? Even though the image in question is that of Borges' father, not his own, the yearning for its survival rather than resigned acceptance of its annihilation is noteworthy in a man who has almost always insisted that for him death is the end.

I incline to the view that a more detailed study of Borges' later poems might cast doubt on Cro's affirmation that Borges never carries his *problemática* beyond the interplay of mere ideas, rational exercises and theoretical speculation. While for Unamuno the essence of human tragedy was the recognition that life may be ephemeral, that existence may be definable as "ser sueño de una sombra," for Borges the opposite is normally true. In "El otro Whitman" (*Discusión*) he wrote of life that "su misma contingencia es una riqueza." It is life with all its precariousness and brevity which allows us to confer value on things. And yet quite recently Borges wrote in "Elegía del recuerdo imposible" (*La moneda de hierro*):

> Qué no daría yo por la memoria
> De haber sido auditor de aquel Sócrates
> Que, en la tarde de la cicuta,
> Examino serenamente el problema
> De la inmortalidad. . . .

The poem contains eight rhetorical questions in each of which the poet expresses his regret that certain experiences, and therefore the memory of them, have been denied him. Seven of the experiences are directly related to reality, whether historical or psychological, while the last belongs to a quite different order of aspiration. The first seven longed-for experiences thus form a separate group, arranged climactically. The climax-image is that of Socrates discussing immortality as he lies slowly dying. We have to ask why Borges placed this *recuerdo imposible* in this important position. The last pages of Plato's *Apology* indicate that Socrates believed strongly in the soul's immortality. It is hard to avoid the conclusion that, in expressing at this point in the poem the wish to have heard Socrates' conclusions, Borges is implicitly admitting that what for Unamuno was the question of questions was even for him, despite his often-expressed scepticism, a recurrent preoccupation underlying the repeated affirmation of his desire merely for oblivion.

However, the difference of emphasis between Unamuno and Borges subsists. At various times and with various degrees of conviction, Unamuno was prepared ultimately to affirm the existence of a true reality, of a Divine Mind, behind the illusion which we call the real. For Borges there is in the end no First Cause and only the most sporadic aspiration towards belief in one. There is only an infinite regression into which everything meaningful ultimately dissolves. Although he could speak in "Lectores" of "algo inmortal y esencial,"[34] which possibly survives corporeal death, it is not Unamuno's "alma de bulto." Borges very often writes in much the same key as Unamuno, but the latter's yearning to discover a true self, to recover ontological confidence—not just in *ser* but in *serse*—is more intimately anguishing. When he reaches the most fearful possibilities, the total illusoriness or the final annihilation of our personalities, for example, Unamuno draws back and takes refuge in mystiques. Borges seems to possess the tragic vision no less than Unamuno. "Nuestro destino es trágico" he wrote in a prologue to a translation of Emerson's *Representative Men*, "porque somos irreparablemente individuos, coartados por el tiempo y el espacio." But he seems able to face this tragic destiny for the most part with serenity and even with humor, though, as I have implied, the poetry contains occasional hints that this serenity is less than complete.

What a comparison of the work of Unamuno and Borges underlines is that both belong to that current of literature which has flowed out of the "European Crisis of Confidence" which Morse Peckham, among others, has analyzed so brilliantly in his *Beyond the Tragic Vision*.[35] But they represent two distinct and in large measure separate moments in the development of our modern *Weltanschauung*. Unamuno was much closer to the moment of full realization that the absolute had been lost. Borges, in the next generation, accepts that loss more readily. In his work we perceive one of the noblest ways of accommodating our minds and spirits to that loss.

NOTES

1. Anthony Kerrigan, "Borges/Unamuno." *Tri-Quarterly* 25 (Fall 1972). Later published in *Prose for Borges*. Edited by Charles Newman and Mary Kinzie. (Evanston: Northwestern University Press, 1974).

2. Stelio Cro, "Jorge Luis Borges e Miguel de Unamuno." *Annali di Ca' Foseari* 6 (1967): 81–90.

3. D. L. Shaw, *Spanish Studies* 3 (London, 1981): 3–10.

4. Keith Botsford, "Sobre y al margen de Jorge Luis Borges." *Revista Mexicana de Literatura* Mayo/junio (1964). Cit. M. Ferrer. *Borges y nada* (London: ———, 1971): 45.

5. G. Sucre, *Borges, el poeta* (Venezuela: Monte Avila, 1968): 32.

6. Jorge Luis Borges, "Acerca de Unamuno, poeta." *Nosotros* 175 (1923). Later included in *Inquisiciones* (Buenos Aires: Proa, 1925).

7. Borges. "Inmortalidad de Unamuno." *Sur* 28 (1937): 92–3.

8. But Cro lists references in *El tamaño de mi esperanza* (Buenos Aires: Proa, 1926), *El idioma de los argentinos* (Buenos Aires: Coleción índice, 1928) and *Historia de la eternidad* (Buenos Aires: Emecé, 1969). As late as 1937 in the *Sur* necrological article Borges wrote,

"El primer escritor de nuestro idioma acaba de morir; no sé de un homenaje mejor que proseguir las ricas discusiones iniciadas por él y que desentrañar las secretas leyes de su alma."

9. R. Paoli, *Borges, percorsi di significato* (Mesiana/Firenze, 1977): 49.

10. Richard Burgin, *Conversations with Jorge Luis Borges* (New York: Holt, Rinehart and Winston, 1968).

11. Jorge Luis Borges, "Calle desconocida." *Obra poética* (Buenos Aires: Emecé, 1964): 21.

12. Borges. *Obra poética*, 19.

13. Borges. "Amanecer." *Obra poética*, 48.

14. Borges. "Calle desconocida." *Obra poética*, 22.

15. Stelio Cro, "Borges e Unamuno." 86.

16. Borges. *Obra poética*, 47.

17. Blanco Aguinaga, *El Unamuno contemplativo* (Mexico: ———, 1959).

18. Miguel de Unamuno, *Niebla* (Madrid: Espasa-Calpe, 1966).

19. Borges. *Obra poética*, 23.

20. Frances Weyers Weber, *Miguel de Unamuno. The Contrary Self*. (London: ———, 1976): 62.

21. Borges. *Obra Poética*, 72.

22. Burgin. "Conversations." 75.

23. Borges. *Obra poética*, 223.

24. Miguel de Unamuno. *Obras completas* XVI (Madrid: A. Aguado, 1958): 257.

25. Borges. *Obra poética*, 182.

26. D. G. Turner, *Unamuno's Webs of Fatality* (London: ———, 1974): 162–7.

27. Borges. *Obra poética*, 203.

28. Borges. *Obra poética*, 209.

29. Borges. *Obra poética*, 177.

30. Borges. *Obra poética*, 225.

31. Borges. *Obra poética*, 204.

32. Borges. *Obra poética*, 193.

33. Cited from the very well-documented study by Oswaldo Romero, 'Dios en la obra de Jorge Luis Borges." *Revista Iberoamericana* 100/101(1977): 465–501.

34. Borges. *Obra poética*, 227.

35. Morse Peckham, *Beyond the Tragic Vision* (New York: G. Braziller, 1962).

BIBLIOGRAPHY

Aguinaga, Blanco. *El Unamuno contemplativo*. México, 1959.

Botsford, Keith. "Sobre y al margen de Jorge Luis Borges." *Revista Mexicana de Literatura*, mayo/junio (1964), 45.

Borges, Jorge Luis. "Acerca de Unamuno, poeta." *Nosotros*, 175 (1923).

Borges, "Calle desconocida." In *Obra poética*. Buenos Aires, 1964.

Borges. "Inmortalidad de Unamuno." *Sur*, 28 (1937), 92–3.

Burgin, Richard. *Conversations with Jorge Luis Borges*. New York, 1968.

Cro, Stelio. "Jorge Luis Borges e Miguel de Unamuno." *Annali di Ca' Foscari*, 6 (1967), 81–90.

Kerrigan, Anthony. "Borges/Unamuno." *Tri-Quarterly*, Fall (1972), 25.

Paoli, R. *Borges, percorsi di significato*. Mesiana/Firenze, 1977.

Peckham, Morse. *Beyond the Tragic Vision*. New York: G. Braziller, 1962.

Romero, Oswaldo. "Dios en la obra de Jorge Luis Borges." *Revista Iberoamericana*, 100/101 (1977), 465–501.

Shaw, D. L. *Spanish Studies*. London, 1981.
Sucre, G. *Borges, el poeta*. Venezuela: Monte Avila, 1968.
Turner, D. G. *Unamuno's Webs of Fatality*. London, 1974.
Unamuno, Miguel de. *Obras completas* XVI. Madrid: A. Aguado, 1958.
Unamuno. *Niebla*. Madrid: Espasa-Calpe, 1966.
Weber, Frances Weyers. *Miguel de Unamuno. The Contrary Self*. London, 1976.

DIONISIO CAÑAS

The Eye of the Mind: Borges and Wallace Stevens

I don't know what mysterious reason Borges had in his 1967 *Introduction to American Literature* by not mentioning the name of Wallace Stevens; to solve the enigma is irrelevant. Nevertheless, it is this omission that impelled me to do a simultaneous reading of the two poets.

In 1944, the literary magazine *Sur* published a translation of the famous Stevens poem "Sunday Morning"; the translators were Bioy Casares and Borges, and some lines from this poem are very close to Borges' own poetry:

> What is divinity if it can come
> Only in silent shadows and in dreams?

At the end of the poem, once more, the obscurity so dear to the author of *In Praise of Darkness* appears in all of its sublimity:

> And, in the isolation of the sky,
> At evening, casual flocks of pigeons make
> Ambiguous undulations as they sink,
> Downward to darkness, on extended wings.

In the twenties, two poetic works were created over the foundations of European verse that would play a preponderent role among American and European writers. Robert Alter, in his article "Borges and Stevens: a Note on Post-Symbolist Writing" (*Prose for Borges*), points out the affinity between Borges and Stevens as part of post-modern literature and its anti-symbolist movement. He writes: "Borges and Stevens are great imaginists whose exercise of imagination—in Borges' case, often fantastication—is directed by a fine skepticism not only about the world of brute matter but also about the imagination itself."

Borges writes about himself, about men and their activities as the splendor and mockery of a god, of gods; Stevens, with irony, writes about the splendor of the world and the presence of the "I" as a mind surrounded by beings created through poetry. Both are solitary poets, but generous in their gifts, and with their poetry they give us abundant fruits of the mind.

In "Poem of the Gifts" Borges writes:

> Let no one debase with pity or reprove
> This declaration of God's mastery
> Who with magnificent irony
> Gave me at once books and the night. . . .
>
> Within my darkness I slowly explore
> The hollow half light with hesitant cane,
> I who always imagined Paradise
> To be a sort of library.

Stevens, in "Of Mere Being," writes that Paradise is

> The palm at the end of the mind,
> Beyond the last thought, rises
> In the bronze decor
>
> A gold-feathered bird
> Sings in the palm, without human meaning
> Without human feeling, a foreign song.

We are facing here a humanistic philosophy, but paradoxically, the human being is absent, and it is his achievements and his imagination that create an Eden for these poets.

As Borges states in his "Ars Poetica," poetry is "humble and immortal," "Art is that Ithaca, / of green eternity." But what does Borges mean by eternity? To what place does the finger of his poetry point? Is a library his eternity, his Paradise? And after all, doesn't a library provide the only surviving visions of the minds of writers from the past? In *The Necessary Angel* Wallace Stevens writes: "The mind of the poet describes itself as constantly in his poems."

But in the poems of Stevens that Borges translated, a more drastic dichotomy appears; blood is a symbol of life which opens a possible space for Paradise:

> Shall our blood fail? Or shall it come to be
> The blood of paradise? And shall the earth
> Seem all of paradise that we shall know?

The answer to Stevens' question is given by Borges in his article "Valéry as Symbol." This article is most illuminating and if we replace the name of the French poet with that of Stevens: ". . . a man who, in an age that worships the chaotic idols of blood, earth and passion, preferred always the lucid pleasures of thought and the secret adventures of order."

Indeed, both poets are the last consequence of a certain faith in the human mind, not as a reasoning form, but rather as an imagining reason. They are the last members of the aristocracy of an imagining wisdom.

Borges and Stevens represent the other side and the ultimate expression of Romantic poetic thought. For both poets the domesticated imagination occupies a principal place in their poetry. In this way, they have overcome the long debate between imagination and reason, and have created the imagining reason.

The two poets have the tendency to claim for their poetry the same essential outlook: one that appears to the eyes as it is—the ordinary, everyday scene. At the same time, this commonplace is projected into an imaginative level, fabulous and mythical. Borges, for example, refers to "the celestial moon of every day," but nevertheless believes that "better than real nighttime moons, I can / recall the moons of poetry" ("The Moon"). Stevens, in "An Ordinary Evening in New Haven" writes: "The moon rose in the mind . . ."

What moon is this that looks like the ordinary moon but is not? What eye that looks like the ordinary eye but is not, describes these moons? It is the moon of the mind, the eye of the mind and it is the sun "half sun, half thinking of the sun; half sky, / Half desire for indifference about sky" ("Extracts From Addresses to the Academy of Fine Ideas"). As a result of this, Stevens writes: "the mind / is the eye, and . . . this landscape of the mind / is a landscape only of the eye" ("Crude Foyer").

For both poets, the poem is a kind of iceberg in which the world seen or thought has been frozen, making it always available to the reader's eyes. For Borges and Stevens poetry is also a sort of window in which the frame creates specific limits. Things are perceived by means of their changing aspects, with their lights and shadows, but circumscribed by a frame, by the boundaries of a precise form. This window can be a book, a word, a painting, a song, a legend or a myth: in any case, always with very clearly defined outlines.

Borges, as a poet, describes himself as someone sitting in a dark room from which he observes the outside world or the world of the mind. And from the darkness he can see without being seen. Stevens, in "Of Modern Poetry," refers to poetry as "metaphysician in the dark." The poet as well as the poem, for both writers, represents poetic form, art and the world, its limitations, its *trompe l'oeil*. In truth, the ultimate raison d'être for writers is a longing to find themselves or a description of the mind that does this.

Borges in his "Ars Poetica" writes:

> Sometimes at evening there's a face
> that sees us from the deeps of a mirror.
> Art must be that sort of mirror,
> disclosing to each of us his face.

Stevens in "An Ordinary Evening in New Haven" views "reality as a thing seen by the mind" and continues:

> Not that which is but that which is apprehended,
> A mirror, a lake of reflections in a room,
> A glassy ocean lying at the door, . . .

And it is because the eye of the mind is what we see reflected in the poem, that every object described in it is sustained by the self of the poet. Simultaneously the separation of the otherness and the self has vanished into the new space of poetic fiction.

> Suppose these houses are composed of ourselves,
> So that they become an impalpable town, full of
> Impalpable bells, transparencies of sound.

The attitude of the two poets originated in an *a priori*: that of a "confidence in language as self sufficient" (as Guillermo Sucre has pointed out in *Borges el poeta*). But it is not a faith in the tautological values of language. Harold Bloom writes in *Figures of Capable Imagination*: "what Wittgenstein means when he speaks of a *deep* tautology, which leads to a true realism, Stevens too knows, as Emerson knew, that what he *says* is wrong, but that his meaning is right."

When Borges wants to talk about the tiger "El otro tigre" ("The Other Tiger") he establishes that his tiger is "a system and arrangement of human language." Conscious about the fallacy of poetic fiction he says:

> . . . I keep on looking
> throughout the afternoon for the other tiger,
> the other tiger which is not in this poem.

Stevens also describes a tiger as "lamed by nothingness and frost." Therefore a faith in language indicates at the same time a distrust of the world that conceived it. This tragic consciousness of an excision between language and world, and the consequent retreat of the poet into an imagining reason, is resolved by Borges and Stevens through irony and sarcasm.

The works of the two poets is modulated by the eye of the mind that sees the world in its totality. This may be sensorial and intellectual in the way of Wallace Stevens, or profoundly intellectual in the manner of Jorge Luis Borges. To quote Borges, though he was talking about Valéry, both poets are: ". . . the symbol of [men] infinitely sensitive to every phenomenon and for whom every phenomenon is a stimulus capable of provoking an infinite series of thoughts."

The concept of the eye of the mind is the ultimate result of the creative impulse formulated by the emotional eye of the Romantic movement. It is possible that the poetry of Borges and Stevens derives from the "Majestic Intellect" mentioned by William Wordsworth in the poem of the same title:

> When into air had partially dissolved
> That vision, given to spirits of the night
> And three chance human wanderers, in calm thought
>
> Reflected, it appeared to me the type
> Of a majestic intellect, its acts
> And its possessions, what it has and craves,
> What in itself it is, and would become . . .

If, as Borges said in his poem "Cambridge,"

> We are our memory,
> we are this chimerical museum of shifting forms,
> this heap of broken mirrors,

I am convinced that in some remote region of his memory Wallace Stevens is looking at Borges with consciousness from the eye of the mind.

BIBLIOGRAPHY

Bloom, Harold. *Figures of Capable Imagination*. New York: Seabury Press, 1976.
Borges, Jorge Luis. "El otro tigre," in *Obra Poética*. Buenos Aires: Emecé, 1977.
Borges. *In Praise of Darkness*. New York: E. P. Dutton, 1974.
Borges, *Introduction to American Literature*. Translated by L. Clark Keating and Robert O. Owens, Lexington: University of Kentucky Press, 1973.
Kinzie, Mary. *Prose for Borges*. Evanston: Northwestern University Press, 1974.
Stevens, Wallace. *The Necessary Angel*. New York: Knopf, 1951.
Sucre, Guillermo. *Borges: el poeta*. México: Unam, 1967.

NICOLAS SHUMWAY

Eliot, Borges, and Tradition

Except for an Eliot poem Borges translated and a footnote in "Kafka y sus precursores," one finds little reason to link Eliot and Borges. Eliot is frequently defined and dismissed by his oft-quoted statement that he was an Anglo-Catholic in religion, a royalist in politics and a classicist in literature. Borges, on the other hand, flees such neat, all-encompassing categorizations, and prefers to cultivate the charming image of a genial skeptic and self-effacing writer who questions everything, including the value of his own work. Despite these obvious differences, in style as well as in substance, on at least two central points, Eliot and Borges are not so far apart as one might think. The first point concerns the role of individual talent and effort in the creative process. The second has to do with the creative process itself—or how a poem gets written. I will offer first a brief overview of the positions Eliot and Borges take on these issues, and then, using two of Borges' poems as examples, it may be shown that Eliot describes how Borges writes poems better than Borges does.

Like Borges, Eliot proclaimed the underpinnings of his criticism early in his career. In his seminal and best-known essay, "Tradition and the Individual Talent," written in 1919, Eliot defended two ideas fundamental to virtually all his thought. The first concerns the importance of tradition as the most significant source of literary creation. Eliot writes:

[Tradition] cannot be inherited, and if you want it you must obtain it by great labour. It involves, in the first place, the historical sense . . . [which is] not only [a sense] of the pastness of the past, but of its presence; the historical sense compels a man to write not merely with his own generation in his bones, but with a feeling that the whole of the literature of Europe from Homer and within it the whole of the literature of his own country has a simultaneous existence and composes a simultaneous order.[1]

Eliot contends that the poet's first responsibility is to read as widely as possible, for only by that method may he or she bring to writing a sense of tradition, a sense of literature as an inherited activity to which one may add, but from which one cannot escape. In Eliot's view of literary history, innovation and individual talent count for little; the best poets can do is take from tradition, add a little to it, and perhaps modify the manner in which their contemporaries read and understand writers of other generations. It was this last idea that purportedly led Borges to maintain in "Kafka y sus precursores" that literature is rewritten each time it is read. Says Borges, "The fact is that every writer *creates* his precursors. His work modifies our concept of the past, just as it must modify the future."[2]

Within Eliot's concept of tradition one discovers two seemingly contrary positions. The first indicates that tradition is inevitable, that we carry it with us in our language, our behavior, and our culture whether it suits us or not. It is this sense of tradition that most resembles Borges' argument in "The Argentine Writer and Tradition," where he contends that the ascendency of Argentine literature incorporates all of Western culture—inevitably.[3] Eliot's second position reflects a conscious awareness that tradition is a vital component of the creative process; it is here that he and Borges differ most. Says Eliot:

The mind of the poet is a [catalyst]. It may partly or exclusively operate upon the experience of the man himself; but, the more perfect the artist, the more completely separate in him will be the man who suffers and the mind which creates; the more perfectly will the mind digest and transmute the passions which are its material.[4]

Eliot goes on to describe the creation of a poem as a process of fusion, of concentration. Elements of that fusion may be the poet's private emotions, or themes such as love, death, absence, or praise, which generate their own inertia in a tradition the poet cannot escape. To the process of that fusion, the poet brings "numberless feelings, phrases, [and] images" which are stored in the poet's mind until "all the particles can unite

to form a new compound."[5] Although Eliot concedes that conscious de-
liberation forms a vital element in the poetic process, ultimately the creation of a poem is beyond the will of the poet; the creative moment occurs
only when the mix of elements is right. In other words, conscious effort
and the rhetorical skills of the poet are indispensable in poetic creation;
but beyond his will is the exact moment when tradition, private emotion
and the poet's skills must combine to make a new poem possible. Despite
Eliot's reputation as a dogmatist, his description of poetic creation is re-
markably inclusive. It gives credence to individual effort, but not at the
expense of tradition; it allows for subconscious elements in creation, but
not if they preclude the effort of reading widely and honing one's rhetorical skills.

As has been amply documented in this symposium, Borges, like
Eliot, plays down the role of individual talent—particularly his own. We
have, for example, those wonderfully audacious essays "The Nothingness
of Personality," and "Berkeley at the Crossroads," where Borges argues
not only against individual talent but also against the very notion of au-
tonomous existence itself.[6] Moreover, Borges frequently maintains that
art is possible only because of the commonality of humankind, and not
because of the genius of any particular individual. As he writes in "Inscripción en cualquier sepulcro":

> Ciegamente reclama duración el alma arbitraria
> cuando la tiene asegurada en vidas ajenas,
> cuando tú mismo eres la continuación realizada
> de quienes no alcanzaron tu tiempo
> y otros serán (y son) tu immortalidad en la tierra.[7]

> Blindly the willful soul asks for length of days
> when its survival is assured by the lives of others,
> when you yourself are the embodied continuance
> of those who did not live into your time
> and others will be (and are) your immortality on earth.

The intention of these lines is clear enough. We are all mirrors of the
past; individuality is an arbitrary illusion thwarted by our common human essence. The dead live in us, just as we shall live in those who follow us. Similarly, writers often reflect other writers who in their collec-
tivity add to that organic unity called literature.

We see then with regards to tradition, that Borges and Eliot are in substantial agreement. In describing the creative process, however, Eliot considers the poet's efforts to be a necessary, though not sufficient, ingredient of the poetic process. Borges, on the other hand, allows an individual even less a role. Typical of his descriptions concerning how he writes a poem is the following statement taken from a lecture given at Columbia University in 1971:

This is a kind of central mystery—how my poems get written. I may be walking down the street, or up and down the staircase of the National Library . . . and suddenly I know that something is about to happen. Then I sit back. I have to be attentive to what is about to happen. It may be a story, or it may be a poem, either in free verse or in some form. The important thing at this point is not to tamper. We must, lest we be ambitious, let the Holy Ghost, or the Muse, or the subconscious—if you prefer modern mythology—have its way with us. . . . All this boils down to a simple statement: poetry is given to the poet. I don't think a poet can sit down at will and write.[8]

As a religious man, Eliot would no doubt disapprove of Borges' suggestion that the Muse, Fate, the Holy Ghost and the subconscious all refer to the same thing. In substance, however, both agree that poetry in some sense lies beyond the will of the poet, that it cannot be forced. Eliot, however, allows the poet a more active role than Borges in maintaining that the poet is at least a catalyst who must bring to the creative moment a conscious sense of tradition that will be actively deployed in writing poetry. Borges, with typical modesty, casts attention away from his erudition and its role in his poetry; on this point, however, it may be said that Eliot describes Borges better than Borges does himself.

Perhaps the best place to study Borges' relationship to tradition, or at least his conscious use of tradition (the kind of thing Eliot advocates), is in those moments when he deliberately appeals to a non-Hispanic literature. A good example of such an appeal is the poem "Fragmento." Borges' thematic intention in "Fragmento" parallels that of his famous "La forma de la espada" where he inverts the order of invention and suggests that the human hand was created to grasp the sword and not vice versa.[9] In "Fragmento" this idea is linked specifically to the hand of Beowulf and thus to Anglo-Saxon poetry. The linguistic reflection of that link lies in Borges' deliberate inclusion in the poem of several kennings, or at least kenning-like images which were previously identified in his article "Las kenningar."[10] For example, "Igualarán al hielo y al fuego" is clearly derived from "hielo de la pelea"; similarly "la selva de lanzas" resembles the "bosque de picas" which again appears on Borges' list of kennings.[11] Professor Karen Lynn identifies no fewer than eight images in "Fragmento" taken from Borges' list of kennings.[12] However, the specific identification of the kennings is less interesting than the question of why Borges includes them at all. His attitude towards the kennings is at best ambivalent. On the one hand, he belittles them, calling them "cold aberrations, . . . belabored and useless, . . . rancid rhetorical flowers" which "transmit indifference and suggest nothing."[13] On the other hand, he cannot stay away from them and even dignifies the deplorable kennings by incorporating them into his poetry. Lurking behind this inclusion is precisely the sense of tradition and its influence on literary creation that Eliot so clearly outlines. In Borges there is combined information on kennings, poetic talent, rhetorical skill, intuitive knowledge of humankind's bellicose nature, and a deep appreciation of the Beowulf story; from that fusion the poem was written. Moreover, the inclusion of kennings in the poem is clearly an indication of Eliot's conscious use of tradition. Indeed, few poems could better illustrate his notion of the contemporaneous nature of literature regardless of its age.

But the most ineluctable demonstration of tradition as a real presence in poetry is in language itself, and it is in this connection that Borges shows even greater coincidence with Eliot's dicta on tradition. At this juncture, no statement serves our purposes better than one of Borges' own. In his 1969 foreword to *El otro, el mismo*, Borges writes:

> The languages of Man are traditions which embody something predestined. Individual experiments are, in point of fact, minimal, except when the innovator resigns himself to sculpt a museum piece, a game directed to historians of literature, or a mere scandal.[14]

In other words, poets are inevitably controlled by their language; as Eliot often repeats and Borges seems to agree, language carries with it an inescapable past. Unlike Eliot, however, Borges allows little room for the poet's conscious participation in that linguistic tradition, preferring to speak of the Muse and the Holy Ghost. By examining one of Borges' English poems, perhaps it can be shown that in actual practice, Borges is much closer to Eliot than may be expected.[15]

Thematically, the poem is a love poem and, like most of Borges' love poetry, it is not particularly convincing. Beyond the thematic intention, however, is the linguistic intention: to write a poem in English using what, in Borges' mind at least, is most "English" about the English language. On this level, he not only adheres to linguistic convention and peculiarity; he revels in it, trying to exploit to their fullest the peculiarities of the English linguistic system which have no equivalent in Spanish. For example, in the lines

> Nights are proud waves: dark blue topheavy
> waves laden with all hues of deep spoil,
> laden with things unlikely and desirable . . .

several interesting points stand out. The first line, for example, except for the last syllable, consists entirely of adjacent stresses. In Spanish, one rarely finds more than two adjacent stresses since the language offers only a very limited number of stressed monosyllabic words. With great difficulty one can create four-stress combinations like "algún buen ron blanco," but it is most unlikely such a phrase would occur in natural speech, much less in poetry. English, on the other hand, is rich in stressed monosyllabic words and can, theoretically at least, string together any number of adjacent stresses; in this sense, Borges' first line indicates a playful indulgence in prosodic capabilities unavailable in his native Spanish. The problem is that, although English permits any number of adjacent stresses, English speakers tend to avoid them. This is one of the reasons the phrase "Big, black bug's blood" is a tongue twister. It is also the reason that Borges' line of poetry is so hard to read without weighty, uncomfortable pauses. One might say that the line is too English to be English. But more importantly, it reveals a conscious manipulation of tradition in exactly the fashion described by Eliot. In no way did this line spring from the Muse or the Holy Ghost; it resulted from a sophisticated awareness of English that unfortunately got out of hand.

In the same poem, one finds a similar problem in Borges' choice of words. In ordinary English discourse, fully one third of the words would be expected to be of Romance origin. In this particular poem, however, the percentage of Latinate words is less than ten percent. Moreover, the words Borges chooses from the native Germanic word stock are either monosyllables or very common disyllables. The remarkable line

> I turn them over in the dawn, I lose them, I find
> them; I tell them to the few stray dogs and
> to the few stray stars of the dawn . . .

consists entirely of Germanic monosyllables, as do many of the short, powerful lines like "The big wave brought you," or "What can I hold you with?" When he does introduce a Latinate word, it is conspicuous by its contrast; witness the last stanza, for example,

> I must get at you somehow: I put away those
> illustrious toys you have left me, I want
> your hidden look, your real smile—that
> lonely, mocking smile your cool mirror knows.

The lonely word "illustrious" springs out at us precisely because of its Latinate difference. Again, in Borges' near exclusion of Romance derivatives, we find a deliberate appeal to tradition in exactly the fashion Eliot has argued to be the conscious province of all good poets. Unfortunately, as in the case of the adjacent stresses noted earlier, Borges ends up being more English than the English: the result is an almost unreadable poem.

In conclusion, it seems that there is a real affinity between Eliot's and Borges' theoretical positions concerning the volitional role poetry plays in its own creation. Similarly, it appears that both Borges and Eliot agree that no poet escapes the weight of tradition, and that it is futile to try. Finally, regarding the one area where they disagree, it can be safely concluded that Borges' attempts to diminish the role his conscious knowledge of the past plays in his own poetry is largely belied by evidence in the poems themselves—particularly in the English poems where his erudition becomes too heavy for the verses to carry.

NOTES

1. T. S. Eliot, "Tradition and the Individual Talent," *Selected Prose of T. S. Eliot*, ed. Frank Kermode (New York: Harcourt Brace Jovanovich, 1975): 38.
2. Jorge Luis Borges, "Kafka y sus precursores," *Obras completas* (Buenos Aires: Emecé: 1974): 712.
3. Borges, "El escritor argentino y la tradición," *Obras completas*, 273–4.
4. Eliot, *Selected Prose*, 41.
5. Eliot, *Selected Prose*, 41.
6. Jorge Luis Borges, *Inquisiciones* (Buenos Aires: Proa, 1925): 84–95, 109–119.

7. Jorge Luis Borges, *Selected Poems 1923–1967*, ed. Norman Thomas di Giovanni (New York: Dell Publishing Co., 1968): 16–17.

8. *Borges on Writing*. Ed. Norman Thomas di Giovanni (New York: E. P. Dutton, 1973): 72–3.

9. Borges, *Selected Poems*, 158–9.

10. Borges, *Obras completas*, 368–381.

11. Borges, *Obras completas*, 372–375.

12. Karen Lynn and Nicolas Shumway, "Borges y las kenningar," unpublished article.

13. All these assertions are found in Borges' article "Las kenningar." (Buenos Aires: Emecé, 1969).

14. Borges, *Obras completas*, 857.

15. Borges, *Obras completas*, 861.

BIBLIOGRAPHY

Borges, Jorge Luis. "El escritor argentino y la tradición." In *Obras completas*. Buenos Aires: Emecé, 1974.

Borges, *Inquisiciones*. Buenos Aires: Proa, 1925.

Borges, "Kafka y sus precursores." In *Obras completas*. Buenos Aires: Emecé, 1974.

Borges. *Selected Poems 1923–1967*. Edited by Norman Thomas di Giovanni. New York: Dell Publishing Co., 1968.

Di Giovanni, Norman Thomas, ed. *Borges on Writing*. New York: Delacorte Press, 1973.

Eliot, T. S. "Tradition and the Individual Talent." In *Selected Prose of T. S. Eliot*. Edited by Frank Kermode. New York: Harcourt Brace Jovanovich, 1975.

Lynn, Karen and Nicolas Shumway, "Borges y las kenningar." Unpublished article.

IV. *On Borges' Poetry Collections*

JOAN WHITE

Allegory in *Dreamtigers*, and the Theory of Reality

In his 1960 Epilogue to *Dreamtigers*, Jorge Luis Borges called this collection his most personal because it "abounds in reflections and interpolations."[1] The poet has used a vocabulary expressive of his life's concentration on profoundly personal reactions. Memories of sensations deeply rooted in childhood, and material from many levels of reading, are transformed and blended into a rare poetic fabric.

A selection of certain poems from *Dreamtigers*, may provide a discussion of two inherent tendencies common to Borges' poetry: to construct paradisiac images and themes, and to explore problems in knowledge and reality, even though Borges does not trust philosophical systems. He is an architect of intellectual territories, of imaginary and reconstructed historical beings as well as gods. Also, a third connecting theme cannot be disregarded, such as the nature of art, which, in Borges' interpretation, relates to the metaphysical leanings shown in his poetry.

"Adrogué" (87–88) is a poetic memory of a place revisited in darkness, first a park where the poet is walking among trees and black flowers. He assures the reader or himself: "Let no fear be that in indecipherable night / I shall lose myself. . . ." He knows by heart the shapes, sounds, and odors; the smell of eucalyptus trees, the lion's head biting a ring (like a mythic beast who guards entrances), the dripping faucet in a patio where his footsteps have brought him. At the threshold of a building, the stained glass windows "reveal to a child wonders / Of a crimson world and another greener world," and he thinks of the dead sleeping behind the door in an eternal dream. The flood of memory is so intense that the barrier between past and present has slipped away; dawn and evening are the same, life and death the same. The patios and the gardens of the past are preserved in "that forbidden round," a world which one can never physically enter again, where the dripping faucet marks time without advancing the hours. This time-stopped atmosphere is characteristic of several poems involving reminiscences of Borges' earlier days and in general evoking his response to Buenos Aires as the first and continuing environment of his life. In "Adrogué" he asks:

> How could I lose that precise
> Order of humble and beloved things,
> As out of reach today as the roses
> That Paradise gave to the first Adam?

In a sonnet entitled "The Rain" (67) Borges again meditates on fragments of the past, once again organized into poetic wholeness by the rain, which is "falling, or it fell"; because the persistent force of memory pulls the past into the present, the present into the past, the rain is falling in both times at once. A patio, and in the last stanza, his father's voice, come to life again through the power of that continuity of memory which is imagination. The nostalgic feeling of the poem links with the paradisal content of "Adrogué," adding the symbol of the father, who can be extended into the parental archetype of God, now lost.

Dreamtigers contains another Paradisal symbol: a library filled with infinite books: infinite knowledge and the attractions of pursuing the unknown. The subject of "Poem about Gifts" (55–56) is expulsion from the library's world-in-itself, from the richness of access to written words, by fate, by God whose "excelling irony/ Gives me at once both books and night," a recognition that great human happiness and freedom may bear the seeds of destruction. For one who considers himself first a reader and secondly a writer,[2] blindness can be irremediable. Because Borges has said that his mind contains more memories of books than of places —"In fact, I hardly remember my own life"[3]—the library may thus be more nostalgic than the patio, representing the sensory less and the intellect more. The library, infinite and unseeing, takes its place as one of the many labyrinths in Borges' poetry, a maze in which the poet searches tirelessly for the experience of knowledge, moving slowly among encyclopaedias and atlases without being able to read them.

Slow in my darkness, I explore
The hollow gloom with my hesitant stick,
I, that used to figure Paradise
In such a library's guise.

Not mere chance but some kind of purpose is indicated, and the poet, connecting himself with others suffering from the same deprivation questions his identity: is he this self, or another?

Which of us two is writing now these lines
About a plural I and a single gloom?
What does it matter which word is my name
If the curse is indivisibly the same?

Following Hebrew-Christian tradition, the punishment of Adam is now assumed by the poet, whose role becomes allegorical. In "Adrogué" and "The Rain" there appears a garden of youthful happiness, representing a security that is later forbidden. Perhaps the library may be interpreted as a tree of knowledge actualized into life, the hubris-motivated choice of learning for its own sake, a passion for reading. The word *curse* has been used in "Poem about Gifts." In the context of the poet's allegorical projection, the ironic giving and taking away suggests that the expiation due is suffering through deprivation, the blindness which makes reading a lost joy.

The poems in *Dreamtigers*, although sometimes incompletely and sometimes antagonistically, relate to each other by means of themes and symbols. Hovering around these mythic connections in varying moods, Borges touches on only a part, not forcing a systematic parallel. Whatever picture of salvation is offered is not theological but personal, and expresses itself in the poems' existence: they are here, composed of a life's subject matter which includes not only events but endurance, reflection, creation, and the self-knowledge that intensifies imagination. Much has been gained in this strong and individual salvation. Looking back, Borges has said in a Preface to *El otro, el mismo*, "More than by any school, I have been educated by a library—my father's—and despite the vicissitudes of time and space, I believe I have not read those beloved volumes in vain."[4]

Not only the poems of religious meaning but those of philosophical bearing are enriched by sensory images and fictive actions, for although

Borges deals with abstractions he cloaks ideas in physical guise. In "The Game of Chess," reflective of the *Rubaiyat* and of Heraclitus, the players sit in their "grave corner" moving the pieces. The shapes—king, queen, horse, bishop, pawn—seem alive in the antagonistic plays; in fact, after the players' deaths the game will go on. At the end of the first part we are told that the game is a world game and is infinite. The second part continues to invest the pieces with human motives:

> They do not know it is the artful hand
> Of the player that rules their fate,
> They do not know that an adamant rigor
> Subdues their free will and their span.

But the players are also controlled, by God who keeps them prisoners. The final question is:

> What god behind God originates the scheme
> Of dust and time and dream and agony?

The poem is grounded in an oriental fatalism which denies free will, whether or not this is believed by the poet, or is under consideration, or is an artistic game in itself.

Another large-scale, impersonal look at the universe is found in "The Hourglass" (57–58), in which the forces of nature have nothing to do with our individual lives. The hourglass shows the regular flow of sand piling up "With an urgency wholly human," or so it seems to human observation. But the sand represents "Unwoundable eternity" and marks the time without stopping, its chill inevitability making the brief stance of human life seem especially frail. Cosmic time sees us all destroyed.

> This tireless subtle thread of unnumbered
> Sand degrades all down to loss.
> I cannot save myself, a come-by-chance
> Of time, being matter that is crumbling.

Time is of great fascination to this poet. He has declared in *Borges at Eighty*: "I think that time is the one essential mystery. . . . We can go on making guesswork—we will call that guesswork philosophy, which is really mere guesswork. We will go on weaving theories, and being very much amused by them, and then unweaving and taking other new ones."[5] To Borges all philosophy is like art, personal, created, ready to be compared to other human productions; yet in his own work the involvement of the self in a poem, the depth of emotion, can suggest philosophical affinities and explorations if not absolute purchase-holds.

Two poems about women known to Borges provide examples of lives seen against an indifferent or malignant universe. "Elvira de Alvear" (62) is a study in contrasts between an earlier span of beauty, freedom, and luxury—"That wealth which annuls all distance / Like the magic carpet"—and the downward path to loss of all things but one, the subject's natural courtesy, surviving against an irreversible illness. But this was a poet whose book contained a preface by Borges; he universalizes the tragedy of her fate and the role of art, which "transforms our actual sorrows / Into a music. . . ." It was the stars that, friendly at first, went against her, the inexplicable nature of human destiny.

A companion piece, "Susana Soca" (63), describes a woman less related to the world than Elvira de Alvear, preferring greys to strong red colors, a woman of afternoon or evening. Susana observed life from outside the labyrinth, "Just like that other lady of the mirror." But once more the forces of the universe do not align themselves with human justice: Susana Soca was killed in the terror and violence of an airplane crash, or as Borges interprets it:

> Gods who dwell far-off past prayer
> Abandoned her to that tiger, Fire.

The poem "Mirrors" (60-61) links questions about reality with implications about knowledge. The "horror of mirrors," Borges says, has haunted him because "They prolong this hollow, unstable world / In their dizzying spider's-web" of duplications that never stop, reflecting reflections into infinity. It is another kind of Borgesian labyrinth where one wanders and is lost. The poem is a brilliant statement by a mind that, having contemplated the shifting nature of perception, has come to the admission that we can know nothing. The concluding stanzas consider the creative agent of such a universe:

> God (I keep thinking) has taken pains
> To design that ungraspable architecture

> Reared by every dawn from the gleam
> Of a mirror, by darkness from a dream.
>
> God has created nighttime, which he arms
> With dreams, and mirrors, to make clear
> To man he is a reflection and a mere
> Vanity. Therefore these alarms.

The comings and goings of night and day, of dreams and mirrors, leave us nothing but our illusory existence; even the great globe itself, mirrored in our rooms, is an illusion.

Borges has also had a long, imaginative involvement with the moon. The twenty-three stanzas of his poem called simply "The Moon" (64–66) review mythic treatments of this object which has so attracted his poetic attention; and a warning is announced applying to the moon in particular and to everything in general. A man once "conceived the unconscionable plan" of making a condensed description of the universe in a single volume, but when it was finished he realized that he had forgotten the moon. "The essence is always lost." When fate decided that Borges would be a poet, he reasoned that he too had inherited the obligation to define the moon, that a poet's function is to give things their exact names, "like red Adam in Paradise" naming the animals, but later he came to understand how futile it is to attempt true definitions of anything. The moon is its own essence, the *moon*, and there is no verbal equivalent. Using his familiar alternatives, he ascribes to fate or chance the gift of the moon to us, and at the poem's end a guarded hope is suggested: one day by using the symbol of the moon in its complex relatedness to all things, man may discover and write "his own true name / Uplifted in glory or in agony."

A like problem governs one of the key poems to the collection, which begins:

> I think of a tiger. The gloom here makes
> The vast and busy Library seem lofty
> And pushes the shelves back. . . .

"The Other Tiger" (70–71) is about reality and art. The entrance place to imagination is the library again, perceived through a dimmed vision which, by turning inward, enlarging, makes room for a forest where a young tiger roams. Time and space present no obstacles to the poet's mind; leaping all distances he pursues the tiger in Sumatra or Bengal, to see the stripes and feel the skin with the intensity of experience. The poet's soul begins to understand that the tiger of his poems is only a ghost and not the real tiger, for describing it

> Makes it a figment of art and no creature
> Living among those that walk the earth.

In a final stanza Borges announces a search for the third tiger. This one will be his invention also—and here we have a Berkeleyan concept that one cannot get outside his own impressions, or, to state it in William James' language, one cannot catch anything on an errand of its own. Nevertheless, as he speaks through this poem, Borges is irresistibly drawn to track down the pure reality of the tiger-in-itself, and in so doing to go beyond his own poetry.

> I know well enough
> That something lays on me this quest
> Undefined, senseless and ancient, and I go on
> Seeking through the afternoon time
> The other tiger, that which is not in verse.

There is a tinge of Platonic idealism in the mystical force of this quest for reality, as often in Borges' poems the reader suspects counter-affinities: up to the archetypes, down to the senses. In "The Other Tiger" what is skillfully blended is a double attraction, to the physical animal for its enviable freedom and beauty, and to its symbolic representation of some spiritual energy in the universe—even though the first cathexis appears to be dominant and to occupy most of the poem's content. This work acknowledges the lure of discovery against odds, the hope of finding a hidden essence underlying the appearances of nature and the enigmas of our human drama.

The final work to be discussed, "Ars Poetica," reflects the Heraclitean flux, as is shown in the opening stanza:

> To gaze at the river made of time and water
> And recall that time itself is another river,
> To know we cease to be, just like the river,
> And that our faces pass away, just like the water.

Because this poem, in its rhythms and repetitions of language, concerns theories of change and opposites, things and conditions become each other in an eternal round. Waking is sleep, dreaming it is not asleep. Death is the same as every night's sleep from which we wake. Through this perception of human life, Borges finds it is the function of art:

> To transform the outrage of the years
> Into a music, a rumor and a symbol. . . .

And in almost identical lines from 'Elvira de Alvear," Borges shows the Lady herself possessed that talent in verse

> That transforms our actual sorrows
> Into a music, a hearsay, and a symbol. . . .

But as the river flows and all things change, so do the concepts fluctuate in "Ars Poetica." Art is not one fixed entity any more than the nature of reality is an end-stopped universe. Art, Borges explains, must be a mirror that reveals to us our faces, as in a sudden glance we may experience a flash of comprehension (even though in "Mirrors" he expresses a horror of this stare). Art is not something extraordinary, but something humble. From tales about Ulysses we learn how he wept on reaching home:

> Art is that Ithaca
> Of green eternity, not of wonders.

Finally, absorbing the fluctuations of water into the endlessness of its flow, and appearing to contradict the meaning of the opening stanza, Borges assigns eternity to the river, compares art to the river, and makes art a mirror reflecting the shifting yet eternal Heraclitus:

> It is also like an endless river
> That passes and remains, a mirror for one same
> Inconstant Heraclitus, who is the same
> And another, like an endless river.

Not only is art a reflection of something which is itself a reflection, but as we experience the things of this world we form our own interpretations, and our creations are dependent upon us who in turn are dependent upon the changing, insubstantial universe. These paradoxes are not evasions on Borges' part but recognitions that reality is open: the mind searching for truth about nature is, as Plato said, a changing observer trying to understand a changing object. This is why, to the Greek idealist, the quest for Being must fix itself upon the permanent, transcendent forms—a lure that Borges sometimes seems to dangle in front of his own eyes, though he won't be caught in any absolute dogma of philosophy. To him, the power in the universe is fascinating to search for through his art, but he does not identify it as a traditional personal God. Pantheistically, God and the universe are one; we are at the service of a blind, uncaring destiny, such as that "tiger, Fire" that burned Susana Soca. And yet, behind the pessimistic view often found in the *Dreamtiger* poems, there lurks a vital spiritual need. The long life of this poet, Borges, devotes itself to reflection, memory, and to the "senseless" quest for knowledge, because it brings delight. He gives us poetry of elegance and truth.

NOTES

1. Jorge Luis Borges, "Epilogue" to *Dreamtigers*. Translated from *El Hacedor* by Mildred Boyer and Harold Moreland, with a Preface by Victor Lange and Introduction by Miguel Enguídanos (New York: E. P. Dutton, 1970): 93. All quotations from the poems will refer to this edition.
2. Jorge Luis Borges, "Foreword" to *Selected Poems 1923–1967*. Edited, with an Introduction and Notes by Norman Thomas di Giovanni (New York: Delacorte Press, 1972): xv.
3. Jorge Luis Borges, *Borges at Eighty*. Edited by Willis Barnstone (Bloomington: Indiana University Press, 1982): 7.
4. Borges, "Preface to *El otro, el mismo*," *Selected Poems 1923–1967*, 279.
5. Borges, *Borges at Eighty*, 110.

BIBLIOGRAPHY

Barnstone, Willis, ed. *Borges at Eighty: Conversations*. Bloomington: Indiana University Press, 1982.
Borges, Jorge Luis. *Dreamtigers*. Translated by Mildred Boyer and Harold Morland. Austin: University of Texas Press, 1964.
Borges, *El otro, el mismo*. Buenos Aires: Emecé, 1967.
Borges. *Selected Poems 1923–1967*. Edited by Norman Thomas di Giovanni. New York: Dell Publishing Co., 1968.

ANA CARA-WALKER

Borges' Milongas: The Chords of Argentine Verbal Art [1]

Jorge Luis Borges has claimed that "the milonga is one of the great conversational forms of Buenos Aires," [2] and in his book of milongas, entitled *Para las seis cuerdas*, his poetry turns to such "talk." In the prologue, he invites the reader to participate and to collaborate in the dialogue. He writes: "All reading implies a collaboration and almost a complicity" (EE1). [3] Yet since the publication of *Para las seis cuerdas* (For the Six Guitar Strings) in 1965, almost no academic attention has been paid to this collection of poems. [4] Not only have the milongas remained quietly ignored even by scholars who treat traditional Argentine elements in Borges' work, they are conspicuously absent from the text and indices of books dedicated to the author's comprehensive works. In contrast to the recognition and critical acclaim received otherwise by this noted Argentine writer, the lack of response to his milongas is particularly dramatic and puzzling. It poses the question: Why is it that readers have failed to respond to Borges' milonga compositions?

Perhaps a necessary familiarity with the milonga genres or mode is missing, since it is essential for an understanding of milongas to understand the historical and cultural Argentine context for this expressive form, and to develop an awareness of the social and aesthetic character of traditional milonga performances. Yet, in order to comply with the author and to fully participate in and appreciate *Para las seis cuerdas*, actual historical and ethnographic data by itself proves less important than an understanding of the dialogic relationship which exists between Borges' verses and those of the milonga tradition.[5]

In *Para las seis cuerdas* the author adopts an attitude, a mode, required by the milonga which inform his voice and shape his compositions. He engages in that "great conversational form" styled by *criollos* before him, both in oral and literary creations. In order to respond to and to collaborate in this work, therefore, the reader must be able to hear in Borges' understated verses not only the strings of a guitar (as the author prescribes in his prologue), but the voice of the poet alternating and merging with a polyphony of voices from the folk and erudite verbal art of generations.

Let us examine, then, the roots and character of the milonga, and briefly outline the relationship of Borges' compositions to the art of past milongueros. By thus placing the poems within a milonga tradition, we can begin to uncover a way of reading *Para las seis cuerdas*.

Of African origin, the name "milonga" comes from one of the Bantu languages. It is the plural form of *mulonga*, meaning "word" or "wordiness" and suggesting, by extension, verbal entanglement and intricacy.[6] Such oral manifestations took various forms and tones in the Argentine context. "Milonga" was used, for example, to refer to disputes, confusion, or disorder, but also, for instance, to indicate a mischievous lie or gossip.[7] A "milonguero" utterance might be characterized by a boastful, provocative tone, or by a light and humorous sense of verbal play. In each case, though, verbal display and flaunting highlight the speaker's mastery of words.

The milonga spirit, however, could also take non-verbal dimensions. The term is used in Argentina, for instance, to name a dance, a musical form, and to characterize rowdy, festive, or permissive behavior.[8] A *milonguero*, furthermore, was one who singled himself out through his dancing and singing, and one who at a gathering took command of the social moment through boastful, defiant, and masterful behavior. In fact, mastery and display for the purposes of artistic and social control, and for personal recognition, mixed with playful *desafío* (challenge), lay at the heart of the milonga.

Milonga, therefore, came to signify more than simply "wordiness," as its etymology suggests. Its parameters were in no way bound to a single genre. More important to its essence was the style and tone, the stance and attitude with which not only words but dance, or song, or behavior in general were *performed*. For a better understanding of Borges, however, let us focus here on the *verbal* dimensions of the milonga.

Traditional milonga verses varied in their meter, their themes, and their temper. Although classically octosyllabic, they could range to fit the music, and the interests of the moment. Their tone and themes could be patriotic, political, critical, jocular, provocative, philosophical, amorous, and at times even narrative. These songs "could be either the repetitions of previously memorized couplets, or its strophes were the fruits of sudden inspiration." Given its often improvised lines the milonga "was also used to *payar*" (to engage in an improvised, contrapuntal, poetic contest common among gauchos).⁹ In fact, to say "milonguear" in the Porteño suburb was synonymous to saying *payar* or *cantar*.¹⁰

While the payada was the verbal counterpoint or duel of the gauchos, however, the milonga belonged to the men of the outskirts. Ethnomusicologist Lauro Ayesterán explains: ". . . next to the traditional payador, acquiring greater stature (around the year 1870) appears the 'milonguero' who was to the suburban surrounding what the former had been to the countryside environment . . ."¹¹ This milonguero type emerged around the time when the impact of immigration, urbanization, and industrialization pushed the Buenos Aires city limits outward toward the pampa while simultaneously drawing men from the countryside to its outskirts. In the tension of this transition the milonga flourished. "The payador gradually vanished into the milonguero," Vicente Rossi summarized, adding: "that is why the milonga is the citified payada."¹²

Borges, of course, knew all this well. He had read Vicente Rossi's book *Cosas de negros* as a young man and had written in 1928: "This yet unheard of and solitary Vicente Rossi, will be *discovered* one day with our, his contemporaries', disrepute and with the scandalous confirmation of our blindness."¹³ He had also come in contact, if only as an onlooker, or guest, with the whereabouts of the milonga. Ulises Petit de Murat, for example, tells of such incidents:

We frequented the neighborhood cafes that were the meeting places for cart drivers, *cuarteadors* (horsemen who made their living by pulling vehicles out of the mud—and who, incidentally, still operate on some Argentine byways), workingmen who would stay up all night talking, toasting friends, and listening to the music of a sad guitar. Borges still remembers, and admires, a couplet we learned from one of those men. It ends like this: 'La muerte es vida vivida, la vida es muerte que viene (Death is life that has been lived, life is coming death). Their inventiveness has always fascinated him.[14]

Similarly, José Gobello notes:

In his youth—it is known—he walked the *barrios* and befriended some condescending *compadres* from Palermo, whom he later immortalized in his literature. They were compadres not yet Italianized, introverted and axiomatic; compadres of the guitar and sweet cane, capable of singing things like this: 'la vida no es otra cosa / que muerte que anda luciendo' (life is nothing more / than death sporting about). From one of those compadres, Nicanor Paredes, Borges learned the philosophy of the compadre world.[15]

As early as 1928 what Borges had seen, heard, and what he had learned were integrated into an essay about the milonga, included in *El idioma de los argentinos*. In it, he points out not only the milonga's suburban character, but its gaucho, countryside roots. He writes: ". . . the milonga was of the outskirts. The wooden counter and the compadrito's guitar generated it and it was perhaps a decantation of the *cantar por cifra* . . . ."[16] In the same essay, Borges notes the milonga's defiant, challenging tone, often intended to provoke, in the spirit of a verbal duel. He explains:

That milonga, happy to defy, is the well-known one, it is the one that made itself bold and insolent in bravados about places in Buenos Aires, around the 1880's. It is the one that got along well with couplets like:

Soy del barrio e Monserrá	I'm from the barrio of Montserrat
donde relumbra el acero;	where the steel blade shines
lo que digo con el pico	what I contend with my lip
lo sostengo con el cuero.	I back up with my hide.[17]

As in the payada, which Borges called "a kind of duel, but a duel carried out with guitars," the verbal tension of this "shove" or "thrust" (of this *"empuje,"* as Borges calls it) is also present in the milonga.[18] "Not only of fights; that frontier was also made of guitars,"[19] he noted, and "milongas express directly what poets have tried to say with words: the conviction that fighting can be a celebration."[20]

The physical duel, both in the pampa and in the city, was thus elevated by the guitar to poetic and musical metaphor. Milonga verses captured the spirit of a social *"enredo"* and transformed it into a verbal and literary *enredo* through a weaving of words.[21] In the course of this process and as a result of this artistry, an Argentine way of narrating and versifying was fashioned which made for a native, *criollo* way of speaking. Indeed, it rendered an integrally Porteño "conversational form," as Borges explains in "La canción del barrio":

The milonga is truly representative. Its common version is an infinite greeting, a ceremonious gestation of flattering verbiage, corroborated by the ponderous pulsation of the guitar. It sometimes narrates bloody events without hurry, duels which take their time, deaths of valiant spoken provocations; other times it pretends to simulate the themes of destiny. Its airs and arguments will vary; what does not vary is the singer's entonation, pulled along, with rushes of weariness, never loud, between conversational and sung . . . The milonga is one of Buenos Aires' great conversational forms . . .[22]

It is precisely within this conversational, dialogized mode that Borges writes his own milongas. By so doing he actively engages himself in the Argentine, payadoresque tradition—a tradition which speaks to and from a historic, folkloric, musical, and literary, as well as a personal and biographical past. It is a complex, and in some sense, daring undertaking on his part, for he asserts himself as a milonguero, as a wielder of words, and as a descendant of the payadores and creators of *cifras*.[23]

This marks a change, a leap, in Borges' writing. In *Para las seis cuerdas* he no longer writes *about* the milonga and the payada tradition, as he had done in his earlier days. He actually takes up the challenge here to *engage* in "milonguicity." Through his milonga compositions Borges merges his voice with those of other criollos—both erudite singers and popular neighborhood or countryside poets. He puts himself to the test and contest of the milonga. "In my *milongas*," Borges tells us, "I have done my respectful best to imitate the joyous courage of Hilario Ascasubi and of the old-time street ballads [*coplas*] of the different neighborhoods of Buenos Aires."[24] And earlier he had said: "I would like these verses which, granted, need musical backup, to be of the liking of Hilario Ascasubi."[25] Gobello, moreover, observes: "In those lyrics [of Borges' tangos and milongas] a payador-like tone is displayed. I think that the *compadritos* would have written them just like Borges, had they not been illiterate."[26] The latter is a compliment indeed, for it suggests that Borges, without turning to Lunfardo (the street language of the hipster-like compadrito) or to a nostalgic tone, could render (as he hoped) a native, genuine milonga. "I have wanted to elude the exaggerated sentimentality of the inconsolable *"tango canción"* (tango song) and the systematic use of Lunfardo, which infuses the simple couplets with an artificial air," he writes in his *Para las seis cuerdas* preface (EE1). Earlier, he had commented in "La historia del tango":

> Certain composers of today seek that valiant tone and concoct, sometimes felicitously, *milongas* of the lower Battery or of the Barrio Alto, but their works, music and lyrics studiously antiquated, are exercises in nostalgia for what was, laments for what is lost, essentially sad though happy in tone. They are to the rough and innocent *milongas* that Rossi's book contains what *Don Segundo Sombra* is to *Martín Fierro* or to *Paulino Lucero*.[27]

Borges' milonga writings mark an important part in his search for a native, Argentine idiom.[28] Like Hernández' poem, they weave and superimpose a range of Argentine voices and allusions which together render a polyphonic text. As such, *Para las seis cuerdas* assumes a degree of criollo familiarity, and requires that, like Borges, the reader take a leap and engage in a milonga-like reading/response. This, of course, necessitates that we hear the milonga verses as part of a contrapuntal, dialogic discourse shaped and informed by Argentine folk, literary, social, and historical tradition.

"Dialogic" refers here (and earlier) to the term employed by M. M. Bakhtin, where "dialogism" is defined as "the characteristic epistemological mode of a world dominated by heteroglossia."[29] Such a world, in this case, is the Argentine framework in which the milonga emerges and thrives. Here, "milonga talk" defies the kind of authoritative discourse where, although ambiguity or multiple meaning may be present, the voice is rigid: speaking *at* instead of *with*. Quite the contrary, Borges' milongas and milonga renderings in general are "conversational," dialogic. They involve a multiplicity of social voices which thrive on irony, on a tongue in cheek delivery, on a suggestive, understated, and allusive kind of speech which recalls (or implies at least) a previous utterance, a simultaneous aside, or a dialogue. In this manner, each milonga shares authority with its very tradition, and with its audience. It is composed by countless and often anonymous authors. In this type of discourse, Bakhtin suggests, "everything means, is understood, as part of a greater whole," insuring the primacy of context over text.[30]

The notion of "contextuality" has already been thoughtfully discussed, for example, in articles such as Emir Rodriguez Monegal's

"Borges: The Reader as Writer," where he takes up Genette's suggestion of the completion of the text by way of the reader's participation in Borges' work.[31] But what has not been satisfactorily considered are the different conventions which govern our reading, and the different frames which define our "contexts."[32] Borges tells us in the preface to *Para las seis cuerdas*, for instance, that to read *Fausto* or *Martín Fierro*, two gauchesque texts, the reader must make specific admissions (EE1). "In the modest case of my milongas," he says, "the reader must substitute the missing music with the image of a man who hums, on the threshold of his *zaguán* or *almacén*, accompanying himself with a guitar. The hand lingers on the strings and the words count less than the chords" (EE1).

The milonga author requires, in other words, that the reader respond not only to the words of a written text but that he recall a specific contextual frame—and that he do this, furthermore, in the criollo spirit in which the work was composed. The milonguero challenges the listener/reader to enter into dialogue not only with him but with the ethics and the aesthetic of the milonga world. He asks, in short, that we not be limited by that which appears linear or literal ("the words count less," Borges tells us), and that we expand our notion of "text" to include the extra-textual, the sociocultural fabric which perpetuates the milonga.[33]

Although this is not a close analysis of *Para las seis cuerdas*, certain aspects of these poems may be examined and read in the spirit of the reflections expressed in this discussion.

Reminiscent of Martín Fierro, who calls for divine inspiration and the aid of his muse, Borges turns to the guitar to recall past histories and to bring memory to life. He writes in "Milonga de dos hermanos" (Milonga of Two Brothers):

Traiga cuentos la guitarra	Let the guitar bring us tales
De cuando el fierro brillaba,	Of when the knives used to flash,
Cuentos de truco y de taba,	Tales of gambling and of dice,
De cuadreras y de copas,	Horse races and hard drinking,
Cuentos de la Costa Brava	Tales of the Costa Brava
Y el Camino de las Tropas.	And of the old Drovers' Trail.
Venga una historia de ayer	A story of yesterday
Que apreciarán los más lerdos;	Of appeal to all comers;
El destino no hace acuerdos	No deals can be made with fate,
Y nadie se lo reproche—	So no one should reproach it—

Ya estoy viendo que esta noche	I'm aware now that tonight
Vienen del Sur los recuerdos.	Memories come from the South.[34]

The story which follows in this milonga is one that Borges has already written in prose. It is the story of the eternal duel, always present in Argentine history and folklore. In this instance it occurs between Juan Iberra and his brother, and more generally represents the contest between North and South, the counterpoint between payadores, the rivaling versions of a same story. Implicit, one could even argue, is the poem's allusion to the duel between Fierro and el Negro, and to the consequent dialogic relationship between Hernández and Borges.[35]

But Borges' milongas do not echo only Hernández' poetry or the literary gauchesque tradition. The author of *Para las seis cuerdas* also engages in dialogue with common, though heroic, compadres. He relates:

I was once at a meal, and the payador, a good man, dedicated verses to all those present, and I liked the strophe he addressed to me, because it began 'Y a usted, compañero Borges / lo saludo enteramente.' That idea of . . . a kind of . . . 'social greeting' seemed very nice to me and I asked him to write it down later.[36]

Not only did the payador write it down, but Borges responded to this "social greeting" years later when he composed "Milonga de Nicanor Paredes," which opens:

Venga un rasgueo y ahora,	Give us a strum and now,
Con el permiso de ustedes,	With the permission of those
Le estoy cantando, señores,	present,
A don Nicanor Paredes. (EE20)	Gentlemen, I'm going to sing
	To *Don* Nicanor Paredes.

This kind of greeting—this dedication or celebration—however, is also a "fórmula" which adheres to the traditional milonguero's repertoire, and which in these poems render a milonga-like discourse. Borges himself noted that his milongas were largely composed from verses sung by his predecessors, by other criollos. These depended on formulas and turns of phrases such as "con el permiso de ustedes" or "aquí me pongo a cantar."[37] Similarly, for example, Borges calls on traditional proverbs "En casa del jabonero / el que no cae se refala" (EE22), or on popular sayings "Más bravo que gallo inglés" (EE36). He turns to folk humor "Un balazo lo tumbó/En Thames y Triunvirato; / Se mudó a un barrio vecino, / El de la Quinta del Ñato" (EE32). And he includes the mordant, ironic kind of understatement common among *paisanos* and compadres "Un acero entró en el pecho, / Ni se le movió la cara; / Alejo Albornoz murió / Como si no le importara" (EE46).

Yet the "social greeting" mentioned earlier serves not only to recall "milonga talk" but also to address or to identify an audience, and to establish thereby a familiar and conversational tone. Borges begins, for example:

A un compadrito le canto	I sing to a compadrito
Que era el patrón y el ornato	Who embellished and protected
De las casas menos santas	The least holy houses
Del barrio de Triunvirato. (EE30)	In the barrio of Triunvirato.

and

Alta la voz y animosa	The voice loud and animated
Como si cantara flor,	As if about to say "*flor*,"
Hoy, caballeros, le canto	Today, gentlemen, I sing
A la gente de color. (EE34)	To the people of color.

and

Milonga que este porteño	Milonga which this Porteño
Dedica a los orientales,	Dedicates to the *Orientales*,
Agradeciendo memorias	Grateful for the memories
De tardes y de ceibales. (EE38)	of afternoons and *ceibales*.

Often Borges' "responses" to other milongueros are not as explicitly stated as the one to Nicanor Paredes, yet we hear echoes of past popular milonga verses woven into Borges' poems. Such is the case with the words of the milonguero Arnold. Borges tells us:

I have heard in a suburb of Buenos Aires a milonga, a milonga composed by a jail-bird in Tierra del Fuego, a convict who, curiously had the same name as Matthew Arnold: Arnold's milonga. And in that long milonga, almost metaphysical like the end of *Martín Fierro*, I have found extraordinary verses like the following:

La muerte es vida vivida,	Death is life lived,
la vida es muerte que viene,	life is coming death,
ya la vida no es otra cosa	soon life is nothing more
que muerte que anda luciendo.	than death sporting about.[38]

Borges' reference here is to Enrique Vicente Arnold whose composition "De profundis" includes other such metaphysical concerns, which defy popular expression. Arnold's milonga, for example, says:

En la humana comprensión,	In our human comprehension,
con majestad grave y muda,	with grave and silent majesty,
germina en todo la duda,	doubt germinates in everything
según mi interpretación.	given my interpretation.
Las cosas son y no son,	Things are and they are not,
por ley de su propio ser,	by law of their own being,
nada es eterno a mi ver,	nothing is eternal to my seeing
pero fin tampoco tiene:	nor does it have an end:
del hoy el mañana viene	from today tomorrow comes
y el hoy viene del ayer.	and from yesterday comes today.[39]

We see this philosophy echoed in Borges' "Milonga de Manuel Flores" where a similar understated, deceptively simple, and apparently logical reasoning about life and death occurs:

Manuel Flores va a morir.	Manuel Flores is doomed to die.
Eso es moneda corriente;	That's as sure as your money.
Morir es una costumbre	Dying is a custom
Que sabe tener la gente.	well known to many.
Mañana vendrá la bala	Tomorrow comes the bullet,
Y con la bala el olvido;	oblivion descending.
Lo dijo el sabio Merlín:	Merlin the magus said it:
Morir es haber nacido. (EE48)	being born has an ending.[40]

Again in "Milonga de Calandria," the reader/listener is drawn back to voices and personages from the past. One recognizes in Calandria, for example, that "last Argentine outlaw" carefully sketched for us and immortalized by Paul Groussac. Groussac's narrative, in turn, perpetuates the story told to him by an *estanciero* from Entre Ríos of the courageous, defiant, and playful gaucho/*peón*, Calandria, famous for his duels.[41] Similarly, we are reminded by this milonga of an early tango written by Villoldo, a milonguero and author of those festive tangos which Borges likes and which scholars argue are derived from the milonga.[42] Villoldos' version, also entitled "Calandria," sings the following boasts which, though defiant, are most endearing. It opens:

Aquí tienen a Calandria	Here you have Calandria
que es un mozo de renombre,	a well-known chap,

and continues:

el que cantando milongas	who singing milongas
siempre se hace respetar.	knows how to get respect.
No hay compadre que me asuste,	No compadre frightens me,

por más guapo y cuchillero,	not even the bravest knife fighter,
porque en casos apurados	because I know, when pressed,
sé manejar el acero.	how to handle a steel blade.
El miedo no lo conozco:	I've never known fear
y jamás me sé asustar,	and I never get scared,
y el que pretenda ganarme	and if anyone wants to top me
tiene mucho que sudar.	they've got a lot to sweat.[43]

Borges' version, in turn, sounds like this:

Servando Cardoso el nombre	The name is Servando Cardoso
Y Ño Calandria el apodo;	And the nick-name Ño Calandria;
No lo sabrán olvidar	Not even oblivious time
Los años, que olvidan todo.	Will be able to forget it.
No era un científico de ésos	He wasn't one of those scientists
Que usan arma de gatillo;	Who used weapons with a trigger;
Era su gusto jugarse	He was pleased to stake his life
En el baile del cuchillo.	In a dance with his knife.
Fija la vista en los ojos,	With his eyes and sights fixed,
Era capaz de parar	He was capable of stopping
El hachazo más artero.	The most dexterous "axe" blow.
¡Feliz quien lo vio pelear! (EE52)	Happy those who saw him fighting![44]

A song about Calandria is particularly interesting here, furthermore, since the *apodo* (nickname) of the character is also the name of a native Argentine bird. Not just any bird, the calandria represents a symbol of freedom to the country people, and is known for its ability to sing in any voice. The bird is a perfect mimic, known by the folk as the poet of the countryside. Its name thus inspires popular sayings which celebrate, as does Borges, the gaucho singer's values and his verbal art. "Libre o muerto, como la calandria" or "Calandria y gaucho, dejarlos libre" are examples which underline the gaucho's resistance to authority. And "Tiene pico e calandria" or "Calandria pa el amor" indicate the seduction, cleverness, and sweetness of a "calandria's" song or words.[45]

Another device used in Borges' milongas to create a dialogic tone is a series of questions which are posed to the audience. His readers are challenged to reconsider the past and to redefine the future by looking back on Argentine history and tradition. Such is the case, for example, in "¿Dónde se habrán ido?," where Borges responds to the interrogation at the end of this milonga with an insistent refrain: "No se aflija. En la memoria." (Don't worry. In memory.) Earlier in the poem, perhaps echoing the verses of Fierro and Hernández ("Me tendrán en su memoria/ para siempre mis paisanos"), Borges declares:

—No se aflija. En la memoria	—Don't worry. In the memory
De los tiempos venideros	Of coming days
También nosotros seremos	We also will be
Los tauras y los primeros.	The foremost and the brave.

To similar questions posed previously in the poem "El tango," Borges had responded:

En la música están, en el cordaje	They are in the music, in the strings
De la terca guitarra trabajosa	Of an obstinate and elaborate guitar
Que trama en la milonga venturosa	Which weaves a fiesta and the innocence
La fiesta y la inocencia del corage.	Of courage into a fortuitous milonga.[46]

Both answers, in essence, bring us back to the milonga, and to the six (guitar) strings. There, in the music of the lyrics/poems, memory (history, folklore, popular voices, etc.) is recalled by the milonguero/poet, and celebrated by the collaborative reader willing to draw up "the image of a man who hums . . . accompanied by the guitar" (EE1).

When questioned why he had "condescended to the milongas," Borges replied "I have not condescended. I have elevated myself to them! But it is not I who have written them." He added, "It is all the criollos I carry in my blood."[47] Similarly, we too must read these compositions against a backdrop of their full criollo tradition—a challenge to which this essay has only begun to respond. Indeed, much more unravelling of Borges' milongas remains to be done. The following are defiant, traditional milonga lines:

Caballeros milongueros	Milonguero gentlemen
la milonga está formada.	the milonga is formed and there
El que sea más milonguero	let the one most milonguero
que se atreva y la deshaga.	try to undo it if he dare.

Perhaps they will invite readers to "elevate" themselves (like Borges) to the challenge posed by *Para las seis cuerdas*.

NOTES

1. Some revisions have been made in the text as it was delivered at the Symposium on the Poetry of Jorge Luis Borges, Dickinson College, April 6–8, 1983. I wish to thank Linda Taranik Grimm, Güneli Gün, and Diana Grossman Kahn for their critical comments and editorial suggestions after reading a draft of this paper.

2. Jorge Luis Borges, "La canción del barrio," *Evaristo Carriego*, in *Obras completas de Jorge Luis Borges* (Buenos Aires: Emecé, 1970): 133. All translations of prose or poetry are mine unless otherwise noted.

3. Jorge Luis Borges, *Para las seis cuerdas*, 2nd. ed. (Buenos Aires: Emecé, 1970): 1. Several versions of *Para las seis cuerdas* are available. In its first edition (Emecé, 1965) the collection included "Alguien le dice al tango." For the second edition (Emecé, 1970) J. L. Borges omitted this poem, and added three new milongas written in 1970: "Milonga de Albornoz," "Milonga de Manuel Flores," and "Milonga de Calandria," (see editorial note in the Emecé, 1970 edition). The Emecé 1970 version also includes an opening poem entitled "Buenos Aires," and closes with "Los compadritos muertos," neither of which appear as part of the collection in the *Obras completas*. Henceforth, references to *Para las seis cuerdas* come from the 2nd edition. (Buenos Aires: Emecé, 1970). This edition subsequently appears in the text as EE. Pagination begins with the Preface as page 1.

4. In spite of the limited treatment of *Para las seis cuerdas* by scholars, it is interesting to note that Borges' milongas have been acknowledged and recorded by popular singers. These include tango interpreters as well as singers of more traditional and rural folk music (e.g., Edmundo Rivero, Josefina, Susana Rinaldi, the Cuarteto Zupay).

5. By "dialogic" I refer to the term as it has been employed by M. M. Bakhtin, *The Dialogic Imagination* (Austin: University of Texas Press, 1981).

6. Vicente Rossi, *Cosas de negros*, ed., Jorge Horacio Becco, 2nd ed. (Buenos Aires: Hachette, 1958): 116–117. See especially, footnote number 4 on page 116, where Horacio Jorge Becco offers, among other references, the following: "En el trabajo de Beaurepaire-Rohán, *Diccionario de vocabulos brazileiros*, 94, hallamos sobre *milongas*: 'E vocábulo de origen bunda. Milonga é o plural de mulonga, é significa "palavra"; y que ella ha conservado su origen africano, o sea "emredo"'. . . . P. Andrés Febrés. *Diccionario araucano-español*, apéndice por Juan M. Larsen (Bs. As., 1882) anota: 'la voz *milonga* en Mogialuá, *mulonga* en Abundá y *ulonga* en Congo, significa "palavra".'" Another etymological explanation given is that by Josué Teófilo Wilkes and Ismael Guerrero Cárpena in "Formas musicales rio-platenses," as quoted in Robert Selles, "La milonga," *La historia del tango*, No. 12 (Buenos Aires: Ediciones Corregidor, 1978): 2086. They believe that "milonga" is a contraction of "melos-longa," long melody, attributed to the long duration of the milonga when sung as a counterpoint.

7. Robero Selles, "La milonga," *La historia del tango*, No. 12 (Buenos Aires: Ediciones Corregidor, 1978): 2086. See also footnote 6.

8. Rossi, *Cosas de negros*, 117–126; Horacio Ferrer, "Milonga," *El libro del tango* (Buenos Aires: Editorial Galerna, 1977): 568–570; José Gobello, "Milonga," *Etimologías* (Buenos Aires: Ediciones Corregidor, 1978): 117–180; Félix Coluccio, "Milonga," *Diccionario Folklórico Argentino*, vol. II (Buenos Aires: Luis Lasserre y Cía. S.A., 1964): 311–312.

9. Selles, "La milonga," 2091.

10. Rossi, *Cosas de negros*, 120.

11. Lauro Ayestarán, as quoted in Ernesto Sábato, *Tango, discusión y clave*, 3rd ed. (Buenos Aires: Editorial Losada, 1963): 41.

12. Rossi, *Cosas de negros*, 115.

13. Rossi, *Cosas de negros*, 24.

14. Ulyses Petit de Murat, "Borges as I Know Him," *Américas*, 11 (January 1959): 10.

15. José Gobello, *Conversando tangos* (Buenos Aires: A Peña Lillo Editor, 1976): 14. Note

also that in his essay "History of the Tango," *Obras completas*, 159, Borges himself reports: "I have spoken with (tango composers) José Saborido, author of "Felicia" and "La morocha," with Ernesto Poncio, author of "Don Juan," with the brothers of Vicente Greco, author of "La Tablada," with Nicolás Paredes, a *caudillo* from Palermo, and with some *payador*. I let them talk; I carefully avoided formulating questions which might suggest determined answers."

16. Jorge Luis Borges, *El idioma de los argentinos* (Buenos Aires: M. Gleizer, 1928): 135. The *cifra*, briefly, was a contrapuntal way of verbal dueling used to payar, in which the singer improvised verses. For a definition, see Félix Coluccio, *Diccionario folklórico argentino*, vol. I (Buenos Aires: Luis Laserre y Cía. S.A., 1964): 78. Roberto Selles, furthermore, writes about the milonga: "It was, and still is common, in this type of music, to apply the same melody for different lyrics. This is called '*cantar por milonga*.' The same had occurred with the *cifra*, the *estilo* and, even, with other genres, like the *vals*,": 2099.

17. Borges, *El idioma de los argentinos*, 136.

18. Jorge Luis Borges, "El gaucho Martín Fierro," A lecture delivered to the Department of Spanish, University of Bristol on Friday, February 22, 1963 (London, 1964): 34.

19. Jorge Luis Borges, "Palermo de Buenos Aires," *Evaristo Carriego*, in Borges, *Obras Completas de Jorge Luis Borges* (Buenos Aires: Emecé, 1974): 111.

20. Jorge Luis Borges, "Historia del tango," *Evaristo Carriego*, in Borges, *Obras Completas*, 161.

21. See footnote 4.

22. Borges, *Obras Completas*, 133.

23. See footnote 16.

24. Jorge Luis Borges, *In Praise of Darkness* (New York: E. P. Dutton, 1974): 11.

25. J. L. Borges as quoted in *Todo Borges y . . .* (Buenos Aires: Editorial Atlantida, 1977): 130.

26. Gobello, *Conversando tangos*, 15.

27. Andrew Hurley, trans. "History of the Tango," in el. E. R. Monegal and Alastair Reid, *Borges, A Reader* (New York: E. P. Dutton, 1981): 262.

28. See Jorge Luis Borges, "The Spanish Language in South America—A Literary Problem," The Tenth Canning House Annual Lecture delivered at Canning House, February 19, 1963 (London, 1964): especially pp. 10–11.

29. M. M. Bakhtin, *The Dialogic Imagination* (Austin: University of Texas Press, 1981): 426–427. Also see "heteroglossia," p. 428, and the fourth essay, "Discourse in the Novel," in particular. The specific pages cited correspond to the glossary offered by editor Michael Holquist and translators Caryl Emerson and Holquist.

30. Bakhtin, *Dialogic Imagination*, 426–427.

31. Emir Rodríguez Monegal, "Borges: the Reader as Writer," *TriQuarterly*, 25, No. 25 (1972): 102–143.

32. I suggested undertaking an "ethnography of literature" as a step toward achieving a more holistic type of reading, in a paper entitled "Creolization in Argentina: Folk Poetry, Tango, and Literary Criticism," *American Folklore Society* (Philadelphia, 1976).

33. This, of course, has been suggested, and excellently discussed by Clifford Geertz in "Deep Play: Notes on the Balinese Cockfight," in *Myth, Symbol, and Culture*, ed. Clifford Geertz (New York: W. W. Norton, 1971): 1–37. See also Karl Reisman, "Contrapuntal Conversations in an Antiguan Village," *Explorations in the Ethnography of Speaking* (London: Cambridge University Press, 1974): 110–124.

34. Jorge Luis Borges, *Selected Poems 1923–1967*, trans. Norman Thomas di Giovanni (New York: Delacorte Press, 1972): 225.

35. At the end of this milonga, in the lines: "Así de manera fiel / Conté la historia hasta el fin," we are reminded of Borges' need to give us "the end" of Martín Fierro's and el Negro's duel in the story "El fin." By so doing, Borges enters into contest / dialogue with José Hernández.

36. Borges, "El gaucho Martín Fierro," 34.
37. Personal interview with Jorge Luis Borges, Oberlin, May 7, 1983.
38. Borges, "El Gaucho Martín Fierro," 35.
39. Selles, "La milonga," 2109.
40. Alastair Reid, trans. *Borges, A Reader*, by Jorge Luis Borges, ed. E. R. Monegal and Alastair Reid (New York: E. P. Dutton, 1981): 294. Note that the version in Spanish varies from that in Borges' *Obras completas*.
41. When asked for the source of inspiration for his milonga "Calandria," J. L. Borges cited Paul Groussac's narrative. (Personal interview with J.L.B., Oberlin, May 7, 1983.) See "Calandria" in *Jorge Luis Borges selecciona lo mejor de Paul Groussac* (Buenos Aires: Editorial Fraterna, 1981): 137–144.
42. See Rossi, *Cosas de negros*, 147, for example, or José Gobello, "Tango, vocablo controvertido," *La historia del tango*, No. 1 (Buenos Aires: Ediciones Corregidor, 1976): 143. Examples of sheet music also attest to this, where compositions are labeled "milonga-tango" or "tango milongueado."
43. Enrique Horacio Puccia, *El Buenos Aires de Angel G. Villoldo 1860 . . . 1919* (Buenos Aires: n.p., 1976): 316–317.
44. The last word in this stanza could be "it" or "him" since the last line can refer both to the person or to his name. See also the translation by Norman Thomas di Giovanni in Borges, *In Praise of Darkness*, 8.
45. E. F. Sánchez Zinny, *Integración del folklore argentino* (Buenos Aires: Editorial Stilcograf, 1968): 97–98.
46. Anthony Kerrigan, trans. *A Personal Anthology*, by Jorge Luis Borges, ed. Anthony Kerrigan (New York: Grave Press, 1967): 158–160.
47. Carlos Cortínez, "Con Borges," *Anales de la Universidad de Chile*, (enero-diciembre 1967): 142–143. It is also worth noting here that the poem Borges considers to be among his most accomplished in this interview is, "y por qué no, algunas de las milongas . . ."

BIBLIOGRAPHY

Bakhtin, M. M. *The Dialogic Imagination*. Austin: University of Texas Press, 1981.
Borges, Jorge Luis. "El gaucho Martín Fierro." Lecture delivered to the Department of Spanish, London University of Bristol. February 22, 1963.
Borges, *El idioma de los argentinos*. Buenos Aires: M. Gleizer, 1928.
Borges, *In Praise of Darkness*. New York: E. P. Dutton, 1974.
Borges, *Obras completas*. Buenos Aires: Emecé, 1974.
Borges, *Para las seis cuerdas*, 2nd. ed. Buenos Aires: Emecé, 1970.
Borges, *Selected Poems 1923–1967*. Translated by Norman Thomas di Giovanni. New York: Delacorte, 1972.
Borges, "The Spanish Language in South America—A Literary Problem." Lecture delivered at Canning House. London, February 19, 1963.
Borges. *Todo Borges y . . .* Buenos Aires: Editorial Atlantida, 1977.
Coluccio, Félix. *Diccionario folklórico argentino*, Vol. I. Buenos Aires: Luis Laserre y Cía, 1964.
Cortínez, Carlos. "Con Borges." *Anales de la Universidad de Chile*. Enero-diciembre, 1967.
Geertz, Clifford, ed. *Myth, Symbol, and Culture*. New York: W. W. Norton, 1971.
Gobello, José. *Conversando tangos*. Buenos Aires: A. Peña Lillo, Editor, 1976.
Kerrigan, Anthony, trans. *A Personal Anthology*. New York: Grove Press, 1967.
Monegal, E. R. and Alastair Reid. *Borges: A Reader*. New York: E. P. Dutton, 1981.
Petit de Murat, Ulyses. "Borges as I know Him." *Américas* 11 (January 1959).
Puccia, Enrique Horacio. *El Buenos Aires de Angel G. Villoldo 1860 . . . 1919*. Buenos Aires: n.p., 1976.

Reisman, Karl. *Explorations in the Ethnography of Speaking.* London: Cambridge University Press, 1974.

Rodriguez Monegal, Emir. "Borges: the Reader as Writer." *TriQuarterly* 25, No. 25(1972).

Rossi, Vicente. *Cosas de negros,* 2nd ed. Ed. Jorge Horacio Becco. Buenos Aires: Hachette, 1958.

Zinny, E. F. Sánchez. *Integración del folklore argentino.* Buenos Aires: Editorial Stilcograf, 1968.

THOMAS E. LYON

Intimations on a Possible Immortality:
Ambiguity in *Elogio de la sombra*

Just a few months after the publication of *In Praise of Darkness* (*Elogio de la sombra*),[1] 1969, Borges spoke at the University of Wisconsin. His short prose piece from this book, "A Prayer," was read and then the author commented on it. The next day, the very reputable *Wisconsin State Journal* carried an article, supposedly quoting the English translation, stating that in the story Borges had said: "My wish is to die *holy*." The Spanish original says, "Quiero morir del todo," which translates, "I want to die *wholly*," completely, forever. The reporter had simply missed a small phoneme and then had to justify the word *holy* with a paragraph of unnecessary and inaccurate explanation.

In this instance, the error is obviously the reporter's, yet it demonstrates the ambiguity that Borges himself has often loosed in his poetry and prose. Scores of critics have noted ambiguities in Borges' works, unresolved dichotomies relating to both the physical world and metaphysical concepts of the universe, man's mind, and existence in general. A recent article even points to ambiguity with respect to Buenos Aires, and Borges' constant wavering between urban amenities and the dangers of the unsettled pampa.[2] Borges would probably settle right on the edge of town, the suburbs, to be able to enjoy the best of two contrasting worlds. Ambiguity relating to death and the possibility of an afterlife is a dominant motif in Borges' work and forms the basis of the present study, an examination of this motif with special emphasis on the poetry and prose of *In Praise of Darkness*.

The initiated reader has already been exposed to preoccupations with death and immortality in the writer's earlier fiction and essays. "The Circular Ruins" and "The Immortals" depict helpless, almost pitiful souls, anguishing over the discovery of their immortality, and the inability to control their own destinies, to die *wholly*. "The Secret Miracle" is quite the opposite: Hladik mentally projects himself into timeless immortality but is suddenly brought to a realization of impending death inflicted by German bullets. These are only three of scores of stories whose characters fight and play with immortality. Some characters attempt, and at times succeed, to multiply their own image endlessly, into an eternity of timelessness or mirrored repetition. Borges' stories, essays and early poetry often depict an endless universe which represents "the endlessness of endlessness of endlessness ad infinitum."[3]

This early expressed motif of immortality recurs with dramatic emphasis in the little-studied *In Praise of Darkness*. It was published on Borges' seventieth birthday and many thought that it would be the author's last major work, his final gift to an anxious world. It was quickly followed, however, by a new book of stories, four more books of poetry and by many other original prose selections. *In Praise of Darkness* was eclipsed by the success and rapidity of publication of these later books; and criticism has not caught up with the author and his recent poetry. A few isolated poems in *In Praise of Darkness* have been analyzed, usually with structural criticism,[4] and Guillermo Sucre has devoted a brief chapter to the book.[5] Much still remains for the energetic critic: ordering, analyzing and interpreting.

In Praise of Darkness consists of thirty-four poetic pieces, twenty-nine of which are obviously poems, and indeed "look" like poems, and five other mini-short stories, narrative outbursts of poetic prose. Fourteen of these thirty-four creations deal directly with death, finality, mortality, or immortality, the single most dominant idea in the book. It would be erroneous to interpret all these poems and narrations in an autobiographical sense—Borges is *not* Pedro Salvadores nor Fred Murdock. Yet Borges' personal experiences and feelings loom closely behind most of the poems. Alazraki has already pointed out that the author's recent books of poetry have turned inward, with little concern for sunlit patios, plazas and the South, and deal with the intimate, subjective life, usually that of the author.[6] Gone are most of the obtuse metaphors and verbal plays of Ultraism, replaced by enumerations of nouns, usually relating to the author's familiar world and experiences. Borges the poet expresses many personal reflections and concerns in *In Praise of Darkness*; if they are not always consistant and clear, neither is life, nor death. A fallacy of much Borgesian criticism is the desire to see only the author behind each poem and analyze the work in terms of his personal experience, or his own personal anguish. This approach unduly limits the poetic significance and requires a knowledge of the author's life and innermost feelings for understanding, thus limiting the possible scope of the poetry. This study examines seven of the pieces in *In Praise of Darkness* as creations with universal expressiveness and meaning.

Several of the fourteen poems dealing with death and immortality project a despair, a desire to "end it all at the end." The prose piece "A Prayer" typifies this desire for oblivion. The few critics who have discussed the work have overlooked the fact that despite the title, the piece is not really a prayer; rather, a few mental wanderings about prayer. The poet reminds himself that he cannot really ask for miracles (that darkness not wholly descend on his eyes), nor can he ask for mercy, for to do so would be to change a major link in the chain of eternity. Finally, toward the end of the long paragraph comes the first supplication: "I want to be remembered less as a poet than as a friend." A simple request, curiously affirming that the poet desires some salvation from oblivion; he wants to live on in the memory of others, as a friend. The last sentence is a final entreaty to divinity, perhaps the only real prayer in the entire piece: "I want to die wholly; I want to die with this companion, my body." Within the work the poet presents a somewhat ambiguous request—a desire for complete oblivion but at the same time prolonged life in the memory of others. Nevertheless, the desire to disappear completely is the predominant idea. In the first sentence, the poet indicates that his mouth regularly recited the Lord's Prayer. He is removed personally; it is his *mouth*, not his mind, or heart, which pronounces this rote prayer, and after struggling for a whole paragraph for the right thing to say, the poet only expresses one wish—complete oblivion and no immortality. Even the title of the piece is ambiguously ironic, since the poet offers a prayer to some type of divine being, assumed to be immortal, and begs nothing more than complete oblivion. This petitioner is similar to so many Borgesian characters, a heresiarch who depends on God for his being or lack of being.[7]

A similar attitude toward a future is expressed in the excellent sonnet, "Things." In a type of ordered enumeration, as Richard Ford has shown,[8] the poetic voice laments that things last longer than man. The poet moves from the personal to the universal, reminding the reader that "things will last beyond *our* memory / they will never even know that *we* have departed." A delightful but despairing line recalls a violet, "monument to an unforgettable evening, now forgotten." Even memory fades as man disappears. In short, there is no expectation of a future existence, of a life beyond the present.

A third poem, "Heraclitus," reflects on the river of life as a mystery that vanishes into nothingness, and postulates that

> Perhaps the source is in me.
> Perhaps from my shadow
> Days spring forth, deadly, imaginary.

Night and nothingness are the winners; existence began with the poet and will obviously end with him. There is to be no continuance.

Several other poems from the book postulate a similar end for man and for human endeavor—nothingness. This is not new; any careful reader recognizes this familiar direction in the author's works. But the same reader must be careful to weigh the three poems here quoted against an equal number of poems from the same collection, for these contradict and counter the above described ideas on death as finality, resulting in excellent literary ambiguity. "The Unending Gift" (the title in English, perhaps because Borges already had too many "poemas de los dones") relates the event of an unfulfilled promise of a painting and the poet's gratitude that it was not completed, because "Men may also make promises; there is something immortal in a promise." *Man* is not part of any immortality yet, but at least it exists, for unfulfilled promises. This profound poem is filled with hope—there seems to be sufficient time for a promise to be completed. Fulfilling the promise would have locked the painting into a fixed time; unfulfilled, it exists in the vastness of an eternity.

"John 1:14" proffers a direct view of immortality. The biblical passage that inspired Borges' poem claims that the Word was with God in the beginning and was made flesh and dwelt on earth. This indicates an ante-mortal life, some pre-mortality, which, of course, would be part of the broader immortality (immortality cannot only refer to life after death, but to life before this present existence). Borges' poem follows the tragic thoughts of the "Word in the Flesh," who, like the poet himself, does not know his destiny but does know that he will be something or someone in another tomorrow, after this life. Christ will live on, and states that "From My Eternity fall these signs," that is, signs as words; so the poem comes to the reader from some eternal fount where deity is now dwelling, and the words have perpetuity of their own.

In the poem "Israel," one Jew may be all Jews—Sampson, Shylock, Spinoza, Moses are all mentioned. Further, a Jew is

> A man who insists on being immortal,
> One who has again taken up the battle,
> In the violent light of victory,
> As beautiful as a lion at midday.

Here man's will projects him beyond this life; by his actions he can have some effect on his future existence. Borges marvels at the Hebrew race and religion which have outlasted and will continue to outlive their enemies, their borders, their time. The familiar Borgesian "one man / all men" motif is obviously present in the poem; an immortality is achieved as one man fights the same battles as his distant predecessors.

"His End and His Beginning" (again, the title is in English; how curious that the only two compositions with English titles project man and memory into immortality!) also postulates a very plausible cycle of existence. In this short prose selection the narrator relates the story of a man who slips effortlessly into a seeming dream world, only to realize that he has entered heaven. "He deserved grace; since his death he had always been in heaven" and did not realize it. Echavarría Ferrari wisely argues that Borges here refers to a literary reality, to the author's works continuing and transforming themselves in the minds of unknown, innumerable and hence immortal readers.[9] This is certainly one plausible explanation but it is not the only interpretation. The use of the word "grace" argues for some type of spiritual or religious being who grants eternal favors, and the word projects a being, an entity, in an eternal sphere, not just a poem or a book. Death occurs and is referred to as the end—heaven is the beginning; there is no line between the two. A more normal title might have been "His Beginning and His End"; beginnings usually precede endings. Borges has purposefully placed the end as the first noun, since death usually concludes existence. But here the end (death) is merely an imperceptible beginning in a continuous life. Man does not cease *being* even in death.

Some of Borges' writings postulate a continuation of existence beyond the present state. About half of them appear in *In Praise of Darkness*; the other half assume *no* immortality. But even if death is the end, "this darkness is slow and painless," says Borges in the title poem, the most autobiographical of all, "In Praise of Darkness." After a recitation of all the things that had always been too numerous in his life, he writes,

> Now I can forget them.
> I arrive at my center,
> At my algebra and my key,
> At my mirror.
> Soon I will know who I am.

What calmness and serenity! In death comes self-knowledge and satisfaction. Ceasing *to be* may be the most fulfilling of all possibilities, but if there is more to life, that too could be pleasant. The entire poetry of this book exudes an optimistic mood regarding old age, death and a possible future.

Oswald Romero has counted, catalogued and classified references to God, gods, and the divine in Borges' works. He found more than three-hundred, and these before *La Cifra* and other recent works. God certainly exists in the twentieth century, if in no other place than Borges' writing. Romero notes that in the twenty-two interviews he surveyed, Borges talked of God, Christianity, and the afterlife in nineteen of them.[10] The *Saturday Review* records a conversation with Borges: "I'm a happy agnostic, a rollicking agnostic. I suppose every day we're in heaven, we're in hell."[11]

If one wants to know what Borges thinks about immortality, then one must consult his frequent talks and interviews. He has talked freely on the subject:

—I hope that my death will be total; I hope to die in both body and spirit.[12]
—To conclude, I will say that I believe in immortality, not in a personal immortality, rather a cosmic type. We will continue being immortal.[13]
—When I think of mortality, of death, I think . . . in a hopeful way, in an expectant way. I should say I am greedy for death, that I want to stop waking up every morning. . . .[14]

Unfortunately, for the reader who would make Borges his prophet, even the author's personal expressions are ambiguous. The first and the third quotations above seem to deny a continuation; the second affirms it. These statements repudiate Monseñor Mallagaray of the University of Jujuy, who rejected Borges for being an atheist, vain and anti-Christian. Borges, the man, however, tells us that he is an agnostic, not an atheist, and has given us contradictory signals regarding an afterlife. Nor is Borges vain or anti-Christian, either in his life or writings.

From this perspective it should be obvious that the time is now past to decide what Borges the man believes or does not believe about God or immortality. What he believes personally will make little difference; in an age of secular humanism, why try to have Borges foretell his future, as if he were a modern prophet? It is time to return to his works and look at them as literature, not as explanations of the author's life. Borges himself appears to argue for this postulate when he says that concerns regarding "immortality occupy a small place in philosophy [and the historical world] and belong more appropriately to poetry."[15] Thus, critics must turn to his poetry rather than the man himself.

The single most important literary motif apparent in *In Praise of Darkness* is ambiguity; dichotomies relating to life and death, faith and reason, Cain and Abel, heroism and cowardice. Death and immortality are present in nearly every selection. The poet does not "decide" the issues; each poem is a separate reality and contradictions between one and another abound. A type of wondrous mischief leads the reader in one direction, only to be countered in the next poem. The yearning for a final death *and* for a degree of immortality are both positive; the poetry regarding death proposes a calm and peaceful exit from this life and a possible penetration into another—this, a beautiful ambiguity in itself.

Some have suggested that "the Literature of Exhaustion almost totally accounts for Borges' work."[16] They infer that literature is almost all "used up" and hence can only fall back on itself for new energy and inspiration; this type of literature closes the world to new possibilities. To the contrary, the poetry in *In Praise of Darkness* opens up new possibilities, through ambiguity. This time-proven literary device here functions to leave man uncertain of his own future as well as the poet's belief. And why should Borges the poet "solve" this mystery? Life, and literature too, are much more exciting when there is still mystery. Ambiguity and uncertainty reign supreme, even eternal.

NOTES

1. I will use titles in translations. Translations are my own.
2. María Luisa Bastos, "La topografía de la ambigüedad: Buenos Aires en Borges, Bianco y Bioy Casares," *Hispamérica* 9 (December 1980): 33–46.
3. Carlos Navarro, "The Endlessness in Borges' Fiction," *Modern Fiction Studies*, 19:3, 395.
4. See Zunilda Gertel's excellent "Heráclito: Conjunción de opuestos," *Kentucky Romance Quarterly*, 19:237–250.
5. Guillermo Sucre, *Borges, el poeta* (Venezuela: Monte Avila, 1968): 127–147. Also Guillermo Sucre, "Borges: el elogio de la sombra," *Revista Iberoamericana*, 36:371–388.
6. Alazraki, Jaime. "Borges o el difícil oficio de la intimidad: Reflexiones sobre su poesía más reciente," *Revista Iberoamericana*, 43 (1977);449–463.
7. See my study "Heresy as Motif in the Short Stories of Jorge Luis Borges," *Latin American Literary Review*, III, no. 5:23–35.
8. Richard Ford, "La inmortalidad en un soneto de Borges," *Revista de Occidente*, 9 (1976):59.
9. Unpublished paper in possession of the author; Arturo Echavarría Ferrari, "Muerte y transfiguración del escritor: Borges y (en) sus lectores."
10. Romero, Oswaldo. "Dios en la obra de Jorge Luis Borges: Su teología y su teodicea," *Revista Iberoamericana*, 43 (1977): 465–501.
11. Mark Childress and Charles E. McNair, Jr. "The Dark Riddle of Jorge Luis Borges," *Saturday Review*, (March 1983):34.
12. Jorge Luis Borges, *Borges, oral* (Buenos Aires: Emecé, 1979):28.
13. Borges, *Borges, oral*, 41.
14. Cited in Willis Barnstone, *Borges at Eighty: Conversations* (Bloomington: Indiana University Press, 1982):17.
15. Borges, *Borges, oral*, 28.
16. John O. Stark, *The Literature of Exhaustion* (Durham: Duke University Press, 1974):2.

BIBLIOGRAPHY

Alazraki, Jaime. "Borges o el difícil oficio de la intimidad: Reflexiones sobre su poesía más reciente." *Revista Iberoamericana* (36):371–388.
Bastos, María Luisa. "La topografía de la ambigüedad: Buenos Aires en Borges, Blanco y Bioy Casares." *Hispamérica* 9 (December 1980).

Borges, Jorge Luis. *Borges at Eighty: Conversations.* Edited by Willis Barnstone. Bloomington: Indiana University Press, 1982.

Borges. Personal interview.

Childress, Mark and Charles E. McNair, Jr. "The Dark Riddle of Jorge Luis Borges." *Saturday Review* March 1983.

Ferrari, Arturo Echavarría. "Muerte y transfiguración del escritor: Borges y (en) sus lectores. Unpublished paper.

Ford, Richard. "La inmortalidad en un soneto de Borges." *Revista de Occidente* 9 (1976):59.

Gertel, Zunilda. "Heráclito: Conjunción de opuestos." *Kentucky Romance Quarterly* 19.

Lyon, Thomas. "Heresy as Motif in the Short Stories of Jorge Luis Borges." *Latin American Literary Review* III: 23–35.

Navarro, Carlos. "The Endlessness in Borges' Fiction." *Modern Fiction Studies* 19: 3, 395.

Romero, Oswaldo. "Dios en la obra de Jorge Luis Borges: su teología y su teodicea." *Revista Iberoamericana* 43 (1977):465–501.

Stark, John O. *The Literature of Exhaustion.* Durham: Duke University Press, 1974.

Sucre, Guillermo. *Borges, el poeta.* Venezuela: Monte Avila, 1968.

Sucre, "Borges: el elogio de la sombra." *Revista Iberoamericana* 36: 371–388.

ALICE POUST

Knowledge in Borges' *La moneda de hierro*

The idea of poetry as a valid medium for the pursuit and expression of knowledge has become generally accepted in the twentieth century. It has, in fact, become commonplace to speak of contemporary poetry in terms of the knowledge that it offers. What, then, is the nature of the knowledge that Jorge Luis Borges pursues in his poetry? In spite of the fact that the term "scepticism" has been employed by some critics and by Borges himself, [1] regarding his attitude toward the powers of human knowledge, we can observe in the introduction to his recent collection of poetry, *La moneda de hierro*, an affirmation of a special, if limited, kind of knowledge:

Bien cumplidos los setenta años que aconseja el Espíritu, un escritor, por torpe que sea, ya sabe ciertas cosas. La primera, sus límites. Sabe con razonable esperanza lo que puede intentar y—lo cual sin duda es más importante—lo que le está vedado. Esta comprobación, tal vez melancólica, se aplica a las generaciones y al hombre. . . . [2]

En cuanto a mí . . . Sé que este libro misceláneo que el azar fue dejándome a lo largo de 1978, en el yermo universitario de East Lansing y en mi recobrado país, no valdrá mucho más ni mucho menos que los anteriores volúmenes. Este módico vaticinio, que nada nos cuesta admitir, me depara una suerte de impunidad. Puedo consentirme algunos caprichos, ya que no me juzgarán por el texto sino por la imagen indefinida pero suficientemente precisa que se tiene de mí. [3]

In these two passages Borges speaks of a knowledge that pertains to oneself, and by analogy, to people defined by their times, generations, and to man as idea. This knowledge, which begins with a recognition of one's own limits in order to define the space within which human activity and creation will be undertaken, coincides, on this point, with the thinking of the Italian philosopher-historian Giambattista Vico who sought to direct the pursuit of knowledge away from topics that lay outside the limits of human understanding (metaphysics) to the study of man himself.[4] For Vico the only appropriate object of human knowledge was that which man created: history.[5] He envisioned a kind of self-knowledge for mankind, which was based partly on empirical data; the study of language, laws, literature, religious beliefs, and social customs; and partly on one's intuition and self-awareness.[6] Borges' foreword, as well as the poems in *La moneda de hierro* demonstrate that he chose to focus his efforts on knowledge that one may obtain, knowledge of oneself, even though this knowledge may relate to other individuals, and, indeed, cultures. The ideology of Borges and Vico is similar as it extends beyond the parameters that each sets up for the concentration of his own efforts, to include the close ties that exist for both writers between knowledge and creation, as well as a mutual willingness to employ memory as a method for obtaining knowledge.[7] Although it cannot be affirmed that there is a direct link between Vico and Borges, it may be suggested that Vico's thought is an important component of the ideological context within which Borges' *La moneda de hierro* should be considered.

This study is divided into two parts reflecting two types of "knowing" expressed in Spanish as *saber* and as *conocer*. A discussion of knowing as *saber*, which involves one's realizing or understanding, will be followed by a discussion of knowing as *conocer* which means, of course, "to be acquainted with," but often suggests "to experience." Both senses of the verb "to know" refer primarily to self-knowledge in this text.

Fundamental knowledge in the sense of *saber*, is perhaps best expressed in "No eres los otros."[8] The poem is born of the poet's knowledge that he is going to die, an awareness that leads him to feel the solitude of his human condition. The poetic voice addresses a "tú," expressing to the other an intimate knowledge of his ephemeral existence:

> No te habrá de salvar lo que dejaron
> Escrito aquellos que tu miedo implora;
> No eres los otros y te ves ahora

Centro del laberinto que tramaron
Tus pasos. No te salva la agonía
de Jesús o de Sócrates ni el fuerte
Siddhartha de oro que aceptó la muerte
En un jardín, al declinar el día.
Polvo también es la palabra escrita
Por tu mano o el verbo pronunciado
Por tu boca. No hay lástima en el Hado
Y la noche de Dios es infinita.
Tu materia es el tiempo, el incesante
Tiempo. Eres cada solitario instante.[9]

The fact that the "tú" in the poem is a writer and the presence of images and motifs that frequent Borges' literary creation, such as the labyrinth, the garden, time, and death, lead us to believe that the poetic voice is addressing Borges. The direct discourse of the poetic voice creates a moment of realization of the terrible solitude of one sentenced to an irrevocable and lasting death. The poet is clearly not interested merely in portraying cognition, but in evoking a profound emotional impact of this particular knowledge within the individual consciousness. An awareness of death is the most fundamental recognition of one's limits. This is the knowledge that defines the nature of Borges' poetry in *La moneda de hierro.*

Borges recreates the moment of one's realization of mortality in a somewhat more complicated manner in "Heráclito."[10] In this poem Heraclitus appears alongside a river whose name and course he does not know. In a slight alteration of what we might consider normal causality, the philosopher sees his reflection in the water and utters the aphorism "Nadie baja dos veces a las aguas / Del mismo río,"[11] without fully comprehending its meaning for him. The poem provides a new interpretation of Heraclitus' discovery. According to this text, his knowledge has not come as a result of reasoning, or close observation of the water's flow, but is elicited as he sees himself in "the water's fleeting mirror." Heraclitus encounters his image in two complementary senses and in two moments: the water has offered him his reflection, but through analogy, has brought him face to face with his own temporal nature:

Siente con el asombro de un horror sagrado
Que él también es un río y una fuga.[12]

Heraclitus' discovery about time and space achieves its maximum level of significance as it reveals to him a truth about himself.

Borges follows up Heraclitus' feeling of the illusory quality of his existence with the revelation that the philosopher is actually an illusion created by Borges, himself. Instead of dwelling upon faraway Buenos Aires and loved ones, the reader must consider the verses about Heraclitus, not merely in terms of their own poetic content, but as poetic data that refer to Borges. The figure of Heraclitus has served as a substitute for Borges as a knowing subject, a role the poet reclaims at the end of the poem as he confesses his motive to the reader. It is up to the latter, who initially may have been taken aback by the seemingly disjunctive effect of the poet's revelation, to reconstruct the poem's unity on the basis of its emotional quality and knowledge that Heraclitus and Borges possess.

In *La moneda de hierro* both knowledge and ignorance about oneself perform a creative function, as a reading of "Una llave en East Lansing" [13] demonstrates. They not only divide one's consciousness into two spheres, but also serve as a structuring device for the poem, which pits the detailed, if partial, knowledge of the poetic subject (a key) against the reader's lack of knowledge. The key knows its identity: "Soy una pieza de limado acero," [14] recognizes that it was designed for a purpose: "Mi borde irregular no es arbitrario," knows its destiny: "Hay una cerradura que me espera." [15] This knowledge tends to disconcert the reader, for the information offered by the poetic subject raises some fundamental questions about the causal force behind the creation and handling of the key, as well as what will come after the key has fulfilled its role.

The poem leaves little doubt that on the other side of the locked door one will find death. Yet, who is that "one" to be? Perhaps the most meaningful way in which a reader may experience the poem's mystery is by responding to the poet's invitation to wonder if he or she might be the subject for whom the door will be unlocked. In "Una llave en East Lansing," the poet both offers and withholds information which challenges the reader to contribute a personal answer to the questions posed by the poem. In this way the reader assumes a creative role in much the same manner that Borges himself has often done, according to Carter Wheelock's *The Mythmaker*, which is to create effectively from one's lack of knowledge. Thus Borges finds that personal limitation can be turned to esthetic advantage.[16]

Up to this point "knowing" has been discussed in the sense of the verb *saber*, especially with reference to knowing about oneself. Now the discussion will focus upon modes of knowing oneself, and others, as the verb *conocer* implies.

John Sturrock, in his book *The Ideal Fiction of Jorge Luis Borges*[17] comments on the epilogue of *El hacedor*. In this work Borges evokes an image of a man who understakes the task of populating an imaginary space with provinces, kingdoms, mountains, bays, ships, islands, fish, rooms, instruments, stars, horses, and people, only to discover soon before his death that the contours of this labyrinthine creation were those of his own face.[18] Sturrock affirms that this brief story deals less with self-discovery, as some critics believe, than with the process of self-creation through which a man becomes author. Rather than distinguishing knowledge of oneself from a creation of oneself, the two should be viewed as related premises in Borges' work. Returning a moment to Vico's idea that man must have, as object of his knowledge, that which he has created, it may be seen that Borges has in fact carried out this idea by inventing a man who recognizes himself upon contemplating his creation. *La moneda de hierro* thus comprises the subject's knowledge of himself both through creation and through the contemplation of that creation.

Memory performs an important function in *La moneda de hierro*. By dividing consciousness into present and past, to which he has access through memory, the poet may view himself as an object of knowledge. Memory provides a richer knowledge than original experience because it incorporates both an evaluation and an understanding of that experience. Borges himself emphasizes the importance of memory to literary creation in a conversation with Willis Barnstone: "I suppose a poet should live in memory because, after all, what is imagination? Imagination, I should say, is made of memory and of oblivion. It is a kind of blending of the two things."[19]

"Elegía del recuerdo imposible,"[20] the first poem of the collection, defines the nature and function of memory in *La moneda de hierro*. Here the poet finds himself thrice removed from the experience that he desires, first by the passage of time, second by even the lack of a memory of the experience, and third, because in all but perhaps one of the cases, involving the work by Turner, the poet never lived the scenes that he describes. Paradoxically, all of these facts strengthen his poetic creation in which the impossible memory, or its absence, becomes a creative force in evoking an imaginary presence.

> Qué no daría yo por la memoria
> De una calle de tierra con tapias bajas
> Y de un alto jinete llenando el alba
> (Largo y raído el poncho)
> En uno de los días de la llanura,
> En un día sin fecha.
> Qué no daría yo por la memoria
> De mi madre mirando la mañana
> En la estancia de Santa Irene,
> Sin saber que su nombre iba a ser Borges.
> Qué no daría yo por la memoria
> De haber combatido en Cepeda
> Y de haber visto a Estanislao del Campo
> Saludando la primer bala
> Con la alegría del coraje.
> Qué no daría yo por la memoria
> De un portón de quinta secreta
> Que mi padre empujaba cada noche
> Antes de perderse en el sueño
> Y que empujó por última vez
> El catorce de febrero del 38.[21]

"Elegía del recuerdo imposible" was created from both the poet's lack of knowledge, and from his yearning for experiences that he has considered and made a part of his past. At the same time, the poem offers the reader a knowledge of the poetic subject revealing himself in his wishes and in the importance that he assigns to the experiences he seeks and describes.

The poetry of *La moneda de hierro* continues to explore the relationship that Borges has acknowledged in other works, between knowledge of oneself and knowledge of others. These are often figures from the past: Colonel Suarez, Hilario Ascasubi, Herman Melville, Johannes Brahms, Einar Tambarskelver, Baruch Spinoza, or Juan Crisóstomo Lafinur. Knowledge of others is possible in this context since they appear as creations of the poetic consciousness and therefore contain an element of self-knowledge.[22]

Borges begins the poem "Juan Crisóstomo Lafinur" with an awareness of his ancestors as being part of himself; as shadowy figures whom he may conjure up at will. He singles out Lafinur, with whom he feels a special affinity and proceeds to portray him in moments that accentuate the similarities between the poet and his predecessor. Borges' creation supposes his own self-knowledge as well as a familiarity with the presence of Lafinur. The poet's imaginary constructs are founded upon an underlying knowledge of himself and of his ancestor, until the final moment when the poet's fancy actually produces a more radical discovery concerning their relationship.

The poet may invoke the power of memory to recreate, not only his own past, but the past of others. In this poem the poet's self-awareness serves as a point of departure for his knowledge of another. In "Lafinur" the poetic subject, (we suppose that it is Borges) approaches the figure from the past by first reflecting upon himself:

> Cuando en la tarde evoco la azarosa
> Procesión de mis sombras, . . .[23]

The context determines that the word "sombras" refers to the subject's ancestors, yet the image suggests that it may be a projection of Borges himself.

The poet distinguishes Lafinur from his other ancestors, most of whom pursued arms rather than letters. (In this respect Lafinur and Borges have something in common.) The subject then imagines Lafinur arguing with the poet's father about philosophy, evoking an encounter that could not have taken place because the lives of the two did not overlap. (Such a conversation, however, could have taken place between Borges and his father.) Next, the poet envisions Lafinur as he formulates, or perhaps reformulates the theory of eternal forms in the mind, a theory with which Borges himself has toyed in his works. Each of the poet's images of Lafinur reflects, to some extent, on himself, leading up to the final two lines of the poem:

> Del otro lado del ya incierto espejo
> Lo imagino limando este bosquejo.[24]

We have seen that Borges' recognition of his limits as a writer places *La moneda de hierro* within the sphere of the poet's knowledge of himself. The poet is aware of his overall literary creation as a unified body that constitutes an image in which he may discover himself, and by which the public may know him. Borges pursues his self-knowledge within the boundaries established by the temporal nature of man. He does this on a poetic level through the exercise of memory, which, in this text, doubles for imagination. Memory allows the present contemplation of past events or experiences and serves as a vehicle for the knowledge of oneself and of others, much as Vico had envisioned. While the knowing subject in *La moneda de hierro* is first and foremost the poet, Borges, it may also be one of the poet's creations, Heraclitus, a key, or even one who may not realize that he or she is also, in a sense, the poet's creation: the reader.

In *La moneda de hierro* knowledge plays both an existential and an aesthetic role, for the moment of knowing is one of crisis that polarizes consciousness in a "before" and "after" frame of time. The way in which Borges selectively presents knowledge in relation to matters of highest significance for man (identity, death, and the value of life) makes knowing and creating the key functions of the poetic and human consciousness.

NOTES

1. Jorge Luis Borges, "Epílogo." *Otras Inquisiciones. Obras completas 1923–1972* (Buenos Aires: Emecé, 1974): 775.
2. Jorge Luis Borges, *La moneda de hierro* (Buenos Aires: Emecé, 1976): 9.
3. Borges, *La moneda de hierro*, 10.
4. Richard Manson, *The Theory of Knowledge of Giambattista Vico* (Hamden, Conn.: Archon Books, 1969): 11–12.
5. Manson, *Theory of Knowledge*, 11–12.
6. Manson, *Theory of Knowledge*, 29.
7. Donald Phillip Verene, "Memory." *Vico's Science of Imagination* (Ithaca: Cornell University Press, 1981): 96–126.
8. Borges, *La moneda de hierro*, 145–7.
9. Borges, *La moneda de hierro*, 147.
10. Borges, *La moneda de hierro*, 139–140.
11. Borges, *La moneda de hierro*, 139.
12. Borges, *La moneda de hierro*, 139.
13. Borges, *La moneda de hierro*, 27–9.
14. Borges, *La moneda de hierro*, 29.
15. Borges, *La moneda de hierro*, 29.
16. Carter Wheelock, *The Mythmaker* (Austin: University of Texas Press, 1969): 220.

17. John Sturrock, *Paper Tigers: The Ideal Fictions of Jorge Luis Borges* (Oxford: Clarendon Press, 1977): 203.
18. Borges, *El hacedor,* in *Obras completas,* 854.
19. Willis Barnstone, ed. *Borges at Eighty: Conversations.* (Bloomington: Indiana University Press, 1982): 20.
20. Borges, *La moneda de hierro,* 13–14.
21. Borges, *La moneda de hierro,* 13.
22. Borges, *La moneda de hierro,* 133–5.
23. Borges, *La moneda de hierro,* 135.
24. Borges, *La moneda de hierro,* 135.

BIBLIOGRAPHY

Barnstone, Willis, ed. *Borges at Eighty: Conversations.* Bloomington: Indiana University Press, 1982.
Borges, Jorge Luis. "Epílogo." *Otras Inquisiciones. Obras completas 1923–1972.* Buenos Aires: Emecé, 1974.
Borges. *La moneda de hierro.* Buenos Aires: Emecé, 1976.
Manson, Richard. *The Theory of Knowledge of Giambattista Vico.* Connecticut: Archon Books, 1969.
Sturrock, John. *Paper Tigers: The Ideal Fictions of Jorge Luis Borges.* Oxford: Clarendon Press, 1977.
Verene, Donald Phillip. "Memory." In *Vico's Science of Imagination.* Ithaca: Cornell University Press, 1981.
Wheelock, Carter. *The Mythmaker.* Austin: University of Texas Press, 1969.

MIGUEL ENGUÍDANOS

Seventeen notes towards deciphering Borges
(Glosses)

Readers and friends of Borges have always suspected the existence of an underlying secret in his work, and especially in his poetry, which no one has ever been able to unravel. Since 1981, however, there has been available a book of poems entitled—not by mere chance—*La cifra (The Cipher)*. Here, with a deliberately ingenuous aim of *deciphering* Borges, are submitted a few random notes or glosses in miniature.

   1. Yes, there is a woman—and assuredly more than one—in the life of the poet. But in 1981, at the time of publication of *La cifra*, there was just one. The poet announces, and pronounces, her name in the "Inscription": she is María Kodama, the lovely Japanese-Argentinian whom we have known for a number of years. The fact that the poet "pronounces" her name is not fortuitous. Nor does it bow to any kind of amatory exhibitionism. Without a doubt she is an essential piece in the cipher that locks the mystery of Borges' latest work. Her name, her person, her breath, her roots in a distant and mysterious land, all appear and reappear throughout the length of the book. We are told, too, in that initial "Inscription" dedicated to María that transoceanic voyages, mornings and strolls through oriental and western parks have been accompanied by abundant readings of Virgil. Why Virgil?

   2. The final piece of the jigsaw which this collection appears to present, has for its title the selfsame name—"La cifra"—as the book in its entirety. Borges has always relished detective stories, "policiales," as

they say in Argentina, and has himself written several that are outstanding. Why not therefore follow the trail of the poet's final mystery, by calling upon the "science of deduction" as exercised by the greatest character in the genre? Let us be good "mystery" readers, then, and begin with
the ending in order to discover right away the name of the "culprit." For
that is how it would seem. The book finishes where it began: it appears
that Virgil is the poetically inspiring criminal, according to the sworn
and explicit statement of the author in his final page. Virgil? Why Virgil?
The easiest thing for the reader is to pay attention to the poet and not
read any further. But of course, Virgil! "La amistad silenciosa de la luna"
("The friendly silence of the moon"). But what about the woman, what
about María? What is this strange complicity of a woman, the poet—the
poets—and the moon? It is all too simple, is it not?

3. That is the way in which many of us read Conan Doyle and Poe.
By cheating! And why? Was it in order to finish all the sooner? No. What
happened was that in reading the masters of detective fiction, some of us
were more interested in the intrigue itself than the outcome. Therein lay,
and therein continues to lie, the charm of those stories. That trick, then,
won't help us to "decipher" Borges. We must read his book step by step;
and without forgetting the preestablished and ultimate complicity between two poets, a woman, and the moon.

4. There are seventeen *haiku* in *La cifra*; in the seventeenth, Borges
says:

La vieja mano	The old hand
sigue trazando versos	goes on tracing verses
para el olvido.	for oblivion.

Here is the core, the very essence and marrow. What anguish! To be a
poet, to write with the urgent endeavour of transcending the here and
now; and yet, at bottom, to feel that one is writing for oblivion. But is
this, really and truly, what the poet feels? Perhaps . . . , tense agony?
The dark, deep longing for perduration?

5. *La cifra* carries, besides the dedication, a prologue. A strange,
story-laden prologue. In it, Borges tells us of his dilemma in the face of
"el ejercicio de la literatura" ("the exercise of literature"), in other words,
of poetry. These are two paths for the poet: either that of "la cadencia
mágica" ("magic cadence")—Rubén Darío?—or that of intellectual po-

etry, which as Borges says is "casi un oxímoron" ("almost an oxymoron"), Browning, Frost, Unamuno and, he adds with sarcasm, "quizás" ("perhaps") Paul Valéry. No, Borges does not want to travel this latter route. He would prefer to follow the impetuous, impossible flight of the "peregrina paloma imaginaria" ("imaginary pilgrim dove") of Ricardo Jaimes Freyre. The closing words of this prologue, "Estas páginas buscan, no sin incertidumbre, una vía media" ("These pages seek, not without uncertainty, a middle way") are the confession of a trembling fear on the part of the poet. But that fear does not impede recognition of the ultimate truth: the "middle way" is one that can only limp, and with "trembling uncertainty" the poet is aware that poetry is the attempt to capture the impossible flight of the imaginary pilgrim dove.

6. Literature and its core, which is poetry, are among other things, none other than verbal terrorism in moments of emergency. Borges knows that life—and his own is proving to be a long one—is nothing but a hold-up, staged upon the wayfarer-reader: Your money or your life! Speak it now, or perish—perish for ever. It is the knife of Juan Muraña. The dreamed-of deed in a marginal world. Knife that is sword: Mío Cid, Martín Fierro, Don Segundo Sombra, nothingness. Television, perhaps.

7. In "Ronda" the poet encounters the memory of Islam, "que fue espadas que desolaron el poniente" ("which were swords that laid waste the setting sun"—the West) and, still further, "un cóncavo silencio de patios, un ocio del jazmín y un tenue rumor de agua, que conjuraba memorias de desiertos" ("a concave silence of patios, an idleness of jasmine and a faint murmur of water, that conjured memories of deserts"). Borges the poet has the advantage. Others of us were in Ronda performing tedious martial duties. Borges is right; those of us who were there know that he is.

8. The *Quijote* was written in Arabic by Cide Hamete Benengeli and a soldier gave us the Castilian version of the manuscript. Borges inserts a prose poem in *La cifra* to express his admiration for so real a fantasy. An imaginary Arab dreams it; Cervantes held the Arabic manuscript in his hands. "No lo leyó nunca, pero cumplió minuciosamente el destino que había soñado el árabe y seguirá cumpliéndolo siempre, porque su aventura ya es parte de la larga memoria de los pueblos." ("He never read it, but he scrupulously fulfilled the destiny which the Arab had dreamed of

and he will forever continue to fulfil it, because his adventure forms part now of the long memory of all the people.")

9. Borges visits at last one of those remote lands which, as children, seemed to us like a realm of fantasy. He has arrived too late to see it; yet nevertheless blindness does not impede a radical and profound vision of what he himself insists on calling nothing more than surface:

". . . desde una escritura que ejerce la insinuación y que ignora la hipérbole, desde jardines donde el agua y la piedra no importan menos que la hierba, desde tigres pintados por quienes nunca vieron un tigre y nos dan casi el arquetipo . . . desde puentes, mañanas y santuarios, desde una música que es casi el silencio, desde tus muchedumbres en voz baja, he divisado tu superficie, oh Japón. En ese delicado laberinto . . ."

(". . . from a writing that practices insinuation and that ignores hyperbole, from gardens where water and stone matter no less than grass, from tigers painted by people who never saw a tiger and who give us almost the archetype . . . from bridges, mornings and sanctuaries, from a music which is almost silence, from your low-voiced crowds, I have glimpsed your surface, oh Japan. In that delicate labyrinth . . ."). Some "surface," this! Gardens of water and stone, painters who manage almost to trace the archetypal tiger, a music of quasi silence, low-voiced crowds . . . delicate labyrinth! The want of physical vision matters not. That other vision, that of the poet's soul, has seen Japan. And María? We must imagine María Kodama guiding the blind poet through those gardens, bridges and mornings, with the music of her voice, with her sweet patience, through the twists and turns of the labyrinth from whence proceeds half her lineage. (María is to Borges what Virgil is to Dante. Dante? Beatrice? We are beginning to decipher what is coded in the book. Or are we beginning to get dizzy?)

10. María Kodama discovered the lacquer cane with which the poet probes uncertain paths. "Pese a su autoridad y a su firmeza, es curiosamente liviano." ("In spite of its authority and strength, it is curiously light.") The blind poet says that he "mira" ("looks at") his cane. What he "sees," naturally, is the profundity, the meaning, of this simple piece of Chinese craftsmanship: "Siento que es una parte de aquel imperio, infinito en el tiempo, que erigió su muralla para construir un recinto má-

gico." ("I sense that it is a part of that empire, infinite in time, which erected its wall in order to construct a magic precinct.") But he also thinks ". . . en el artesano que trabajó el bambú y lo dobló para que mi mano derecha pudiera calzar bien en el puño" ("of the craftsman who worked the bamboo and bent it so that my right hand could comfortably grasp its handle"), and he feels himself united with it by an undefined but necessary bond. The creative effort of the Chinese craftsman and that of the poet from Buenos Aires coincide at a point in the universe. The certainty of this affirms the poet's raison d'être. Perhaps the seventeenth *haiku* is intentionally fallacious. Perhaps the universe requires that the old hand go on tracing verses, and that is the reason for the fate of the lacquer cane . . .

11. The intrigue is what matters. Be it called life or universe. Everything is linked together in a circle that has neither beginning nor end. Time flows: the dripping of a fountain and the death of Caesar are pieces of the same intrigue. Likewise, Rome and Chaldea. Man is both able and unable to behold the universe altogether. What do the two faces of double-fronted Janus see?

12. Dreams. An old theme in Borges: "La noche nos impone su tarea mágica. Destejer el universo, las ramificaciones infinitas de efectos y de causas, que se pierden en ese vértigo sin fondo, el tiempo." ("Night imposes its magic task. To unravel the universe, the infinite ramifications of cause and effect, which lose themselves in that bottomless whirl which is time.") Three poems are dedicated to dreaming. And also a strange and unexpected dedication to another woman: Viviana Aguilar. Is this the Other Woman? No, that is not the path which will lead us to the discovery of the key. The poet dreams "en el alba dudosa" ("in the doubtful dawn") and of the dream remembers only the fact that "había muchas puertas" ("there were many doors"). All the rest he has forgotten upon awakening. "Sigue la duda y la penumbra crece." ("The doubt continues and the half-light grows.") The trembling of doubt, the mystery of oblivion. Here is the key. Let it not escape us. In the longing to recover what he has dreamed lies the secret of Borges' poetry: "Si supiera qué ha sido de aquél que he soñado, o que sueño haber soñado, sabría todas las cosas." ("If I knew what has become of what I have dreamed, or what I dream I have dreamed, I would know all things.") No less! The poet dreams that he can achieve that supreme wisdom. But let us go back a mo-

ment: towards the beginning of the book is a poem entitled "Descartes" in which systematic doubt is turned upside down. There is no certainty possible. It is not true that I exist because I doubt. All is mere "acasos," mere "perhapses": God, man, earth, moon and time. Even having dreamed, even yesterday, even being born, are doubtfuls. But one night the poet feels a shiver of cold, a quiver of fear. Is existence itself a perhaps? The poet decides to continue to dream "a Descartes y a la fe de sus padres" ("of Descartes and the faith of his forebears").

13. Pierced with the tremor of time is this small book of Borges. A poem entitled "Himno" ("Hymn") begins as follows:

"Esta mañana	This morning
hay en el aire la increíble fragancia	there is in the air the incredible
de las rosas del Paraíso.	fragrance
	of the roses of Paradise.

And in a great, circular, poetic adventure the poet takes us to the first morning of man. "Adán descubre la frescura del agua." ("Adam discovers the coolness of water.") From there to the golden Olympus of Zeus, to Agrigento, to Altamira, to the Rome of Virgil (once again Virgil), who here caresses silk brought from China by caravans and ships to Hungary, where the first nightingale sings: ages, characters and adventures succeed each other in giddy speed in the poem. Pythagoras "revela a sus griegos que la forma del tiempo es la del círculo" ("reveals to his Greeks that the shape of time is that of the circle"). The blind poet arrives, in his hymn, as far as Manhattan and there he hears Walt Whitman sing. But all this traversing of the past is motivated by an erotic force:

Todo el pasado vuelve como una	All the past returns like a wave
ola	and those ancient things recur
y esas antiguas cosas recurren	because a woman has kissed you.
porque una mujer te ha besado.	

14. "Llorado amor, ceniza del deleite" ("Lamented love, ash of delight"): in one poem, "El hacedor" ("The Maker"), which appears to be an appeal to Heraclitus, love is seen dragged along the intangible course of time. All is ashes, all is the image of the irrevocable passage of time— "el tiempo, que ni vuelve ni tropieza" ("time, which neither returns nor stumbles"), said Quevedo. The poet (in this case Borges), nevertheless

proclaims himself, thanks to his work or to his task, victor over time. The "deed" done by the maker will save him:

Otra cosa no soy que esas imágenes	I am no other thing than those images
Que baraja el azar y nombra el tedio.	Which chance shuffles and tedium names.
Con ellas, aunque ciego y quebrantado,	With them, though blind and broken,
He de labrar el verso incorruptible	I have to fashion incorruptible verse
Y (es mi deber) salvarme.	And (it is my duty) save myself.

15. The *haiku* are, in great measure, the key to *La cifra*; or rather, the cipher within the cipher. *Haiku* 15 says:

La luna nueva.	The new moon.
Ella también la mira	She too looks at it
desde otra puerta.	from another door.

Let us remember that the lunar cycle begins with the new moon. Its pallid light announces the hope that one day it will become a full moon. Love too might be able to commence anew and reach its plenitude, however pale it might be. But she . . . , the woman who inspires the *haiku*, and in consequence the book entire, is now in some other place, also looking at the room . . . from another door. Could the new moon reunite the lovers?

16. The poet is alone, without the beloved, in a garden. "Lejos un trino." ("A distant warbling.") The nightingale sings in the night. The poet suffers in his solitude, beneath the moon. He casts a slight shadow: his own, only his own! The poet is alone, but the warble of the nightingale consoles him. The poet will go on "tracing verses." What sorrow to bequeath them only to oblivion! There remains, nevertheless, the hidden hope that some, perhaps just a few, may remember them and, without the poet's knowledge, find in them some comfort for unknown griefs. But the less said of it, the better.

17. Does the number seventeen hold some magic meaning? Borges includes in *La cifra* seventeen *haiku*, as I have already said. Perhaps this is just a matter of chance, or simply tiredness. Yet I do not think so: Borges is one of the most precise and purposeful modern poets. Let us pause here and interrupt for now this small glossary. Let us return for a

moment to Virgil. "Tacitae per amica silentia lunae." Aeneid, ii. 255. ("Through the friendly silence of the mute moon", or "Through the silent friendship of the mute moon".) Virgil's line is transformed in the poem called "La cifra," through a deliberate misquotation by Borges, to become "la amistad silenciosa de la luna" ("the silent friendship of the moon"), which is the companion (woman or ash) of the poet ever since one night, or perhaps one evening, when the almost extinguished light of his eyes "deciphered her for ever." Moon, reflection: light of the blind, light which does not burn, but which is there and which is a sweet companion. Yes, it is a woman. Love of ashes, or ashes of love. Never again will the poet see the "clear moon." No longer will it be of any use to "abrir todas las ventanas del mundo" ("open all the windows of the world"). The poet knows that the final secret of his work lies in that sensation of having arrived always too late. Life has been for him a continual, anguished evening. For ever? "I know," says the poet, "that someone, some day, will truly be able to say to you: Never again will you see the clear moon." Come what may, he knows full well that his poetry is a song, from the very first line to the as yet unwritten last one: a song to the pale light lost in an evanescent past; a song to the love that might have been; to the moment which ought to have been lived as if it were the last. This is the terrible misfortune of the poet; and yet, here before us is his poetry: not the flesh of oblivion, but the supreme attempt of salvation from death, evasion from the void.

Translation by
Mervyn R. Coke-Enguídanos

V. *On Borges' Poems and Characters*

DANIEL BALDERSTON

Evocation and Provocation in Borges: The Figure of Juan Muraña

In Evaristo Carriego's poem "El guapo," dedicated to San Juan Moreira but probably referring to Carriego's contemporary, the *cuchillero* Juan Muraña, Carriego says:

> La esquina o el patio, de alegres reuniones,
> le oye cantar *hechos* que nadie le niega:
> ¡con una guitarra de altivas canciones
> él es Juan Moreira, y él es Santos Vega![1]

No one of course would deny the *guapo*'s deeds to his face because that would be an ostentatious challenge to his manhood, and would inevitably lead to a knife fight. Furthermore, as Borges discovers in his book on Carriego, the provoker of a knife fight is inevitably the loser of it; the successful knife-fighter does not look for fights, but fights to defend himself when necessary.[2]

The *guapo* of Carriego's poem is not the already mythical heroic gaucho (Moreira or Santos Vega), but the electoral thug (*compadre*) or its humbler imitation, the local delinquent (*compadrito*). That is, the *guapo* of the poem is at one or two removes from the heroic world in which he would prefer to live, but through his song he assumes a heroic identity or, better, imposes it on himself and on his listeners:

> El barrio le admira. Cultor del coraje,
> conquistó, a la larga, renombre de osado;
> se impuso en cien riñas entre el compadraje

y de las prisiones salió consagrado.
Conoce sus triunfos y ni aun le inquieta
la gloria de otros, de muchos temida,
pues todo el Palermo de acción le respeta
y acata su fama, jamás desmentida.[3]

The paradox of his fame is that he alone can speak or sing of it: his admirers are condemned to silence. Such is the sensitivity of the *cuchillero* that merely to tell someone that he has renown as a brave man (as in "Hombre de la esquina rosada") is to challenge him to a fight to the death, or at least to the point where one of the fighters "marks" the other, leaving a scar on the face. Thus, the cult of courage is one best practiced in silence, at least during the life (and especially in the presence) of the *cuchillero*.

The exploits of the *cuchillero*, then, can only be sung by himself in the first person, or by someone else in the third person after his death. To sing the hero's deeds in his presence is to invite a *payada*, a song in counterpoint in which the instruments are no longer the voice and the guitar.

Juan Muraña, Carriego's contemporary and *compadre* of Palermo, is for Borges the archetypical *cuchillero*, perhaps because they shared a neighborhood and some mutual friends, although in one poem Borges says he never saw Muraña. Muraña served as thug to the local political boss Nicolás Paredes (whom Borges got to know in the course of writing *Evaristo Carriego*, and to whom he later dedicated a poem). Muraña is mentioned many times in the course of the book on Carriego, most notably at the end of the discussion of "El guapo":

[El guapo] podía no ser un provocador: el guapo Juan Muraña, famoso, era una obediente máquina de pelear, un hombre sin más rasgos diferenciales que la seguridad letal de su brazo y una incapacidad perfecta de miedo. No sabía cuándo proceder, y pedía con los ojos—alma servil—la venia de su patrón de turno. Una vez en pelea, tiraba solamente a matar. No quería *criar cuervos*. Hablaba, sin temor y sin preferencia, de las muertes que cobró—mejor: que el destino obró a través de él, pues existen hechos de una tan infinita responsabilidad (el de procrear un hombre o matarlo) que el remordimiento o la vanagloria por ellos es una insensatez. Murió lleno de días, con su constelación de muertes en el recuerdo, ya borrosa sin duda.[4]

Incidents from Muraña's life were also the inspiration for Borges' first story, "Hombres pelearon" (in *El idioma de los argentinos*, 1928) later expanded slightly under the title "Hombre de la esquina rosada" (*Historia universal de la infamia*, 1935), one of Borges' best-known and most enduring stories. In *El informe de Brodie* (1970), he published a sequel to this story under the same name "Historia de Rosendo Juárez." (Bioy Casares and Borges reworked a version of the same incidents in their filmscript *Los orilleros*.) Furthermore, Muraña appears in numerous Borges poems: he is mentioned in "El tango," "¿Dónde se habrán ido?," and "Milonga de don Nicanor Paredes,"[5] while both "Alusión a una sombra de mil ochocientos noventa y tantos," a poem about Muraña's knife (*El hacedor*, 1960), and the recent "Milonga de Juan Muraña" (*La cifra*, 1981), are devoted wholly to him.[6]

"Alusión a una sombra . . ." reduces Muraña by synecdoche to his knife:

> Por esa brava
> Región anduvo el sórdido cuchillero.
> El cuchillo. La cara se ha borrado.[7]

And in the same poem Borges says that he never met the man, but feels himself in company of this murderer whom he never met. Already in the reduction of Muraña to his knife Borges wipes out his face: he saves the memory of the fighter (symbolized at the end of the poem by the flash of steel) at the expense of the man. Similarly there is a blurring of Muraña's circumstance: the year is 1890-something, the deeds unnamed, the neighborhood itself lower and meaner. Muraña's knife shines out of the past, but the man himself is but a shade to be dismissed rather casually.

The blurring of the face of the dead man and the reference to him as a shade cannot but remind us of the evocation of Muraña at the moment of his death in *Evaristo Carriego*: "Murió lleno de días, con su constelación de muertes en el recuerdo, ya borrosa sin duda." To sing of Muraña, Borges has symbolically marked him, killed off the man to make him into a story. Saving his memory (that is, his memory of his dead) is to appropriate that memory, to remember his victims as if they were Borges' own, and to turn the evocation of the *cuchillero* into yet another deed which none dare challenge.

The same process of evocation and provocation is much more clearly seen in the recent "Milonga de Juan Muraña." The poem reads:

Me habré cruzado con él
En una esquina cualquiera.
Yo era un chico, él era un hombre.
Nadie me dijo quién era.

No sé por qué en la oración
Ese antiguo me acompaña.
Sé que mi suerte es salvar
La memoria de Muraña.

Tuvo una sola virtud.
Hay quien no tiene ninguna.
Fue el hombre más animoso
Que han visto el sol y la luna.

A nadie faltó el respeto.
No le gustaba pelear,
Pero cuando se avenía,
Siempre tiraba a matar.

Fiel como un perro al caudillo
Servía en las elecciones.
Padeció la ingratitud,
La pobreza y las prisiones.

Hombre capaz de pelear
Liado al otro por un lazo,
Hombre que supo afrontar
Con el cuchillo el balazo.

Lo recordaba Carriego
Y yo lo recuerdo ahora.
Más vale pensar en otros
Cuando se acerca la hora.[8]

The poem begins with an affirmation that the young Borges probably crossed paths with Muraña, a contradiction of the declaration in "Alusión," though the future perfect of probability serves to cast this meeting into some doubt. The indeterminacy of the event is confirmed by the indefinite place ("una esquina cualquiera"), though the preterit verb at the end of the stanza ("Nadie me dijo quién era") would seem to confirm that an encounter occurred, even if they did not meet. This mis-meeting is due to a lack of full contemporaneity between the two ("Yo era un chico, él era un viejo"), but given Borges' obsession with circular time this unconsummated encounter suggests that the two will meet fully at some future time (perhaps now in this poem). The following stanza echoes two ideas that appear in "Alusión": that the old *cuchillero* is magically present for Borges and that it is his duty as poet to save Muraña's memory. To save Muraña's memory, that blurred memory of innumerable victims: such is the daring purpose of Borges' *oración* (sentence, oration, prayer).

The choppy, abrupt tone of the octosyllabic verse, broken into a series of short sentences, makes the poem a tense, bold oration for Muraña. That tension and abruptness is especially apt in the third stanza, in which Borges' alleged desire to save Muraña's memory verges on insult. He begins by saying that Muraña had but one virtue (courage), softening the statement by saying that some men have no virtues at all, but none the less reducing Muraña once again to the unthinking fighting machine described in *Evaristo Carriego* or the knife of "Alusión a una sombra . . ." In fact he mentions a second virtue in the following stanza—respect for others—though that respect is qualified by Muraña's professional thoroughness as a killer. (Elsewhere Borges says that Muraña and other *cuchilleros* were more interested in marking their victim than in killing him; here Muraña is reduced to a sort of methodical butcher.) The insulting tone returns in the fifth stanza: Muraña was "faithful as a dog" to the electoral boss, and suffered a dog's life (misery, ingratitude, confinement). The examples of Muraña's bravery in the sixth stanza—a willingness to fight even when tied to his opponent, to face bullets with only a knife for self-defense—suggest a foolhardy, if brave, fool. The heart of the poem, then, gives us an image of a man with far more faults than virtues, though the virtue of courage is supreme in the *cuchilleros'* moral universe, and perhaps in that of Borges.[9]

In the seventh stanza Borges, to maintain the eight syllable line, reduces the two syllable vowel cluster *ea* to the diphthong *ia* in *pelear*, a usage in keeping with gauchesque poetry and with the *milonga* form employed here. The distance between Borges and the world of Muraña is reduced by the popular pronunciation, by what Borges calls the *intonation* of the phrase. The closeness of poet to subject is reflected metaphorically in the same stanza, when Muraña is said to be "capaz de pelear/ Liado al otro por un lazo": though the immediate referent seems to be some exploit of Muraña's, the line can also be read as descriptive of the link between the fighter and the other who provokes him, that other without whom (like the black man in "El fin") he could scarcely exist.

The vagueness of the wording—"liado al otro," linked to the other, any other—suggests the poet's implicit counterpoint, his challenge and the acceptance of that challenge.

The final stanza recalls Carriego's treatment of Muraña in "El guapo" —an equivocal treatment, as we saw initially, since Carriego describes the silence to which the hero condemns his listeners—and then has Borges take Carriego's place (as the shift from past to present confirms). Borges concludes: "Más vale pensar en otros/ Cuando se acerca la hora." The couplet recalls the Muraña of *Evaristo Carriego* who thinks of the blurred images of his victims when his last hour approaches. Borges seems to suggest that he has assumed not only the function of saving Muraña's memory (the memory of Muraña's victims), but also of adding two new victims to the list: Muraña himself, and of course Evaristo Carriego. Many times over the years Borges has been asked why he wrote about such a minor poet as Carriego (the implication being that he should have written about the looming figure of Lugones),[10] but surely part of the point of the exercise of writing a biography of Carriego is to appropriate his text for himself, annihilating the man in the process. Muraña is a less obvious and less willing victim, since he would seem to have had little to fear from the near-sighted boy who lived at 2147 Serrano St. Yet Muraña is a much more total victim of Borges, since his fame must now depend completely on the image created in a series of texts that extend from *Evaristo Carriego* to *La cifra*.

In his great poem on the tango Borges concludes:

> El tango crea un turbio
> Pasado irreal que de algún modo es cierto,
> Un recuerdo imposible de haber muerto
> Peleando, en una esquina del suburbio.[11]

Death at the hands of a *cuchillero* (also sought for by Dahlmann in "El Sur," however we may choose to read that story) is for Borges as impossible as it is vicariously and essentially true. Perhaps he never met Juan Muraña, perhaps he will never have the chance to sing a *payada* or dance that other counterpoint that is a knife fight, yet the essential truth of Borges' role as *payador* flashes like Muraña's knife flashes out of the past. To evoke the world of the *cuchilleros* is to enter it, to provoke the mute violence of the dead, to release their violence in the dance of words and images. As Borges says, again in "El tango,"

> Aunque la daga hostil o esa otra daga,
> El tiempo, los perdieron en el fango,
> Hoy, más allá del tiempo y de la aciaga
> Muerte, esos muertos viven en el tango.[12]

Muraña and his dead live and die, again and again, in Borges' work, not least in his recent *milonga*, again and again evoked and provoked to show their essential manhood, their courage.

NOTES

1. Evaristo Carriego, *Poesías completas* (Buenos Aires: EUDEBA, 1968): 66–7.
2. For simplicity's sake I will refer to the single volume of Borges' so-called *Obras completas* (Buenos Aires: Emecé, 1974): 167–8. See also Borges and Silvina Bullrich, *El compadrito* (Buenos Aires: Fabril, 1968), in which A. Taullard is cited on p. 99: "Peleaban por imposición de las circunstancias, para demostrar que no eran 'flojos' o para mantener su reputación de valientes."
3. Carriego, *Poesías completas*, 66.
4. Borges, *Obras completas*, 129. The first edition of Borges' *Evaristo Carriego* (Buenos Aires: M. Gleizer, 1930), differs slightly from the later versions, in that the verb obró is used twice: "las muertes que obró—mejor: que el destino obró a través de él." I prefer the reading *obró to cobró*.
5. Elsewhere Paredes is consistently named *Nicolás*, not *Nicanor* (see *Obras completas*, 103, 118, 159, 329, 1035).
6. There is also a story, "Juan Muraña," in *El informe de Brodie*, in which Muraña's knife, ten years after its owner's death, continues to protect his family (*Obras completas*, 1044–7).
7. Borges, *Obras completas*, 827.
8. Jorge Luis Borges, *La cifra* (Buenos Aires: Emecé, 1981): 55–6.
9. See the ironic note on courage in Borges' *Evaristo Carriego*: "Si una comunidad resuelve que el valor es la primera virtud, la simulación del valor será tan general como la de la belleza entre las muchachas o la de pensamiento inventor entre los que publican; pero ese mismo aparentado valor será un aprendizaje,"—Borges, *Obras completas*, 128.
10. See, for example, the "Autobiographical Essay" appended to the English version of *El aleph, The Aleph and Other Stories*, Jorge Luis Borges (New York: Dutton, 1970): 233.
11. Borges, *Obras completas*, 889. He says the same thing in the article on the tango appended to the second and later editions of *Evaristo Carriego*: "En un diálogo de Oscar Wilde se lee que la música nos revela un pasado personal que hasta ese momento ignorábamos y nos mueve a lamentar desventuras que no nos occurrieron y culpas que no cometimos; de mí confesaré que no suelo oír *El Marne* o *Don Juan* sin recordar con precisión un pasado apócrifo, a la vez estoico y orgiástico, en el que he desafiado y peleado para caer al fin, silencioso, en un oscuro duelo a cuchillo," in Borges, *Obras completas*, 162.
12. Borges, *Obras completas*, 889.

BIBLIOGRAPHY

Borges, Jorge Luis. *The Aleph and Other Stories*. New York: Dutton, 1970.
Borges, *La cifra*. Buenos Aires: Emecé, 1981.
Borges, *Obras completas*. Buenos Aires: Emecé, 1974.
Borges, Jorge Luis and Silvina Bullrich. *El compadrito*. Buenos Aires: Fabril, 1968.
Carriego, Evaristo. *Poeaías completas*. Buenos Aires, EUDEBA, 1968.

FRANCISCO CEVALLOS

The Poems of the Gifts: The Inverted Image

When studying Borges' literary opus the reader will find a series of symbols and rhetorical devices constantly repeated. The actual bibliography on these technical devices is enormous.[1] Among the many aspects considered by critics, the image of the mirror—reflection—is undoubtedly predominant. It would seem that Borges' work is, in some way, a reflection of itself. This reflecting structure has been studied in detail in Borges' stories. Moreover, many of his poems are also structured like a mirror.[2] It would be easy to expand this idea to his poetic works in general, and it is tempting to consider "The Poem of the Gifts" and the "Other Poem of the Gifts"[3] as images reflected in a mirror: the second poem reflecting the first. However, after an initial confrontation of the texts, the seemingly reflective structure yields to a more contradictory one. In fact, the poems appear to be opposite texts, the second one inverting the structure of the first, and thus, paradoxically, becoming complementary of each other.

First the external structure of the poems must be considered. "The Poem of the Gifts" has ten hendecasyllabic quatrains and, with the exception of the second one, follows a constant rhyme pattern—abba. The poem is written within the conventions of traditional poetry, with a constant verse/stanza model throughout the text. On the other hand, the "Other Poem of the Gifts" is written in free verse. It consists of one stanza, with a total of eighty-one lines. There is no rhyme or metric pattern that can be perceived. So, it seems that the poems are totally different in their external structure. However, it is known that Borges' poetry evolved from an experimental stage towards classical modes.[4] Thus, the fact that he chose to return to the experimental form in the second poem, versus the classical structure of the first is very significant. The fact that both share a title suggests that within the apparent opposite nature of the texts, each poem was perceived as a complementary unit. On the external level, one poem is the inverted image of the other.

A more fruitful analysis is derived from the semantics of the poems. The "Poem of the Gifts" deals with the poetic speaker writing about himself, with the *I* of the poet creating the text.[5] The second poem refers to the poetic *persona* contemplating the world. In a way, it is a list of poetic acknowledgments that the poet pays to authors or books. But Borges has trained his readers to look for the unexpected. Hence, it would be naive to assume that the poems can be reduced to such a simplistic scheme. There are some elements common to both texts that provide a clue for a possible second way of reading them. The first is the presence/absence of God.

Through Borges' works there appears no single concept of God. There is an indifferent deity such as in "The Theologians," or a dreamer who is dreaming a dreamer, as in "The Circular Ruins." Perhaps Borges has been searching for a metaphysical definition of God but has been unsuccessful, and unable to find a single answer. The dual "Poems of the Gifts" present two other possible conceptions of divinity. Both texts start with the idea of God as an active force. The relation of that active being to humanity, however, is quite different. In the "Poem of the Gifts" God is conceived within the Judeo-Christian canon of a paternalistic figure, all-wise and all-powerful, that intervenes in our lives individually. Thus human beings, and Borges, the poet, are His creatures and His inscrutable designs. The poetic persona accepts his destiny. Blindness, for instance, becomes a gift from God in a mysterious way. In the seventh stanza Borges makes clear that *azar*, chance or coincidence, has little to do with the reality of life. The fact that Groussac, the other poet mentioned in the text, was blind, is not a mere coincidence, but part of a carefully conceived plan of the universe.

> Something that certainly is not named
> with the word *azar* rules these things;

> Somebody else already received in other dark
> afternoons the (many) books and the shadows.

The "Other Poem of the Gifts," on the contrary, stems from a rationalistic definition of God:

> I want to thank the divine
> labyrinth of effects and causes
> for the diversity of the creatures
> that form this singular universe.

These lines remind us of the story "The Aleph." There is a place in the universe where all things are contained at once, both in time and space. The "Other Poem of the Gifts" seems to be, to a certain extent, a poetic version of the same idea. There is one point here in the "divine labyrinth of effects and causes," where everything is comprehended at once. This idea, strangely, is closely related to rationalistic thought. Rationalistic philosophy culminated in the ideas of Leibniz. Interestingly enough, he is one of the thinkers that Borges seldom quotes. However, both have many similar ideas. Some of Leibniz's ideas are summarized here.

The German philosopher based his metaphysical system on a concept of the *monad*. According to Leibniz, the monad is *vis*, energy, the capacity to act. But a monad is also unique, there can be no two equal monads in the universe; it is simple, therefore indivisible; the monad has perception, and more important, it has desire, that is a tendency to pass from one perception to another. Thus, the monad corresponds to the metaphysical reality of the *ego*.[6] But monads are also subjected to a hierarchy. Hence, a monad that has perception is only a *soul*, while the monad that has a perception of the act of perceiving is a *spirit*. The third level is the highest level where all monads are perceived, where all the ideas are clear, where the universe is contemplated from all perspectives at once, and the unique and perfect monad is God. God is also the creator of all the monads. In being so, he places in each one the law of internal evolution of its perceptions. With Borges' work in mind, it can clearly be seen how the "Other Poem of the Gifts" follows these ideas. God, the maker of labyrinths, is to be thanked by the existence of the universe. The long list of names and facts that follow are, each one, an individual monad, created by God. The idea of creation is emphasized in the text through the repetition of the deictic *by—por*—which makes of the poem a series of subordinated clauses depending on the verb *to give thanks*. Like in "The Aleph," the whole world is contained in the poem. We can say that the succession of monads is an attempt—limited by form—to capture the whole universe at one glance.

A second concept essential to both poems is the idea of *persona*. Each poem is written from the perspective of the first person singular, *I*. However, the texts reflect a different conception of the poetic *ego*. The "Poem of the Gifts" is based upon an "I" that observes itself, and by doing so, gives reality to its surroundings. But, the poetic speaker is not only one. As it was the case in the famous fragment "Borges and I," the poet wonders "which of the two writes this poem?" The association with Groussac, through blindness and the library, is just a literary device. Borges is changing the reader's focus of attention, but the stanza as a whole makes it clear that the plurality of the "I" is a reflection of a metaphysical view of the universe:

> Which of the two writes this poem
> about a plural I and one shadow?
> What matters the word that names me
> if the anathema is one and indivisible?

Let us consider that plurality from the point of view of one of Borges' favorite philosophers: Berkeley. According to the English bishop, *to be* means to be perceived. Perception is what constitutes the being. Thus, what is unperceived does not exist. In Berkeley's system, this is a very important point. For him, if the material substance is conditioned by perception, the spiritual substance—God—exists in an almost Cartesian way: somebody puts the perceptions in our spirit, therefore, that being is superior, is God. It is clear that the "Poem of the Gifts" is dealing with the plurality—duality—of the persona, and that duality exists between the material and spiritual substances. The poet's spiritual substance perceives the material one, thus giving it existence. In "Borges and I," there is only one name given to both *personae*. In the "Poem of the Gifts" the poet uses a second name, the name of another poet, for if it is the spiritual perception that creates its surroundings, what matters the name of the material substance?

The idea of the "I" in the "Other Poem of the Gifts" is based on a different perspective. Here the persona is reflecting on a series of perceptions about the world. The text is similar to the ideas of Leibniz. The "I" is just one monad, a spirit perceiving the capacity to perceive. In this context, the world has been created by a superior being, who ought to be thanked. The poem lists a series of accomplishments of mankind in the search for knowledge. The poetic "I," thus, does not have to be divided into two different facets, because it belongs to the ultimate monad encompassing all the monads of the world, including books, people, or sunsets.

A third point is the function of the book in both poems. The importance of the written text in Borges' literary creations is well known. It is very difficult to read Borges without thinking of an enormous library included in his works, through quotations, references, paraphrasis, etc. But books go beyond the actual physical texts. "The Library of Babel" is an outstanding example of the multiple values that books have. The story is a quest for the "solution" to a labyrinth, to find a clue that is hidden somewhere in an infinite library. The book becomes a symbol of the universe. In "Poem of the Gifts" Borges mentions the infinite irony of having "books and night" at the same time. He used to think of Paradise, he says, as a library. The poem becomes, then, a text about volumes that cannot be read. The library that surrounds the poetic persona, with all its books, is a magnificent irony that can be deciphered only in dreams. Together with the presence of the unreadable books it is important to mention books that have died, such as the manuscripts in the old library at Alexandria. Hence, there are two kinds of unreadable, or undecipherable texts: the polarity between presence/absence points a real/unreal opposition. However, both possibilities have the same kind of existence in the eyes of the blind poet.

The "Other Poem of the Gifts" is a poem about works that have been read. From Ulysses to Schopenhauer to Whitman, the books have been decoded, assimilated, and thus form part of Borges' poetic conscience. "The world is the manuscript of another, inaccessible to a universal reading and that only experience can decipher," according to Jaspers' phrase.[7] By reading the book of the world, Borges has decoded it, through his experiences with books. However, there is a line in the poem that brings us back to the "Poem of the Gifts." Among the many things that deserve to be praised in the poem, Borges also thanks God for "the name of a book that I have not read: *Gesta Dei per Francos.*" The idea of a book not being read corresponds to the irony of books and night. Nevertheless, the use of the present perfect indicates that the action has not happened yet, but that it may happen.[8] The text may be read, and the universe may still be deciphered.

The presence of books in both poems elicits the concept of an implied reader in the texts. At first place it would seem that the poetic "I" is at the same time its own reader. However, a second reader is implied in both poems. After the world has been decoded by the poet's vision, the poems have to be understood by a receptor who did not participate directly in the act of writing. A message of some kind, perhaps literary, is transmitted by the linguistic signs that structure the texts; a message that is comprehensible to the reader. Both "Poems of the Gifts" present the idea of a reader in a similar and complementary manner.

With regard to "Poem of the Gifts" the text assumes an external reader who is present from the opening words: "Let no one debase . . ." Thus, the poem is indeed a message to be transmitted to a hypothetical decoder, and in being so, the poem acquires a didactical tone. The mood is intensified by the digression in line 13: "Of hunger and thirst (a Greek story has it)." The poet's voice is teaching a lesson that can be summarized in a moral statement of acceptance of one's destiny.

In the "Other Poem of the Gifts" readers are implied through the use of the first person plural pronouns and verbal forms: "things that we do not know," "whose names we ignore," etc. The poetic voice does not assume a didactic tone any more. On the contrary, it joins the *persona* of the text with the voices of the readers of the poems. The reader himself becomes part of the text, and praises the world—or image of the world— that the poet describes. The two poems complement each other in the sense that the reader, implied but absent in the first case, becomes explicit and present in the second.

The two poems have been examined here as antagonistic units. However, the apparent contradiction of the texts yields to a better unity of the same. The Borgesian universe does not have a one and only perspective. In fact, it is multiple, but within an absolute unity: at the end, everything is comprehended in the Aleph. Thus, the two texts, by reason of their polarity, present two perspectives that are complementary: they are part of one contiguous text whose purpose is to decode the universe.

NOTES

1. Jaime Alazraki, *La prosa narrativa de Jorge Luis Borges* (Madrid: Editorial Gredos, 1968); Alazraki, *Versiones, inversiones, reversiones. El espejo como modelo estructural del relato en los cuentos de Jorge Luis Borges* (Madrid: Editorial Gredos, 1977); Ana María Barrenechea, *Borges, the Labyrinth Maker*. Translated by Rober Lima (New York: New York University Press, 1965). Translation of *La expresión de la irrealidad en la obra de Jorge Luis Borges*. (México: El colegio de México, 1957; 2da. edición, Buenos Aires: Editorial Paidós, 1967).

2. Jaime Alazraki, "Outside and Inside the Mirror in Borges' Poetry." *Simply a Man of Letters*. Edited with a foreword by Carlos Cortínez. (Orono: University of Maine Press, 1982): 27–36.

3. Jorge Luis Borges, *Obra poética 1923–1964*. (Buenos Aires: Emecé, 1964): 262–5. Translations mine.

4. Guillermo Sucre, *Borges, El poeta* (Caracas: Monte Avila Editores, 1968); Sucre, *La máscara, la transparencia* (Caracas: Monte Avila Editores, 1975): 161–180.

5. Antonio Carreño, "La negación de la persona en Jorge Luis Borges." *La dialéctica de la identidad en la poesía contemporánea* (Madrid: Editorial Gredos, 1982): 141–169.

6. Gottfried Wilhelm Leibniz, *New Essays on Human Understanding*. Translated and edited by Peter Remmant and Jonathan Benett. (Cambridge: Cambridge University Press, 1981); *The Monadology of Leibniz*, Introduction, Commentary and Supplementary Essays by Herbert W. Carr. (Los Angeles: University of Southern California Press, 1930).

7. Quoted by Jacques Derrida. *De la grammatologia* (Paris: Editions Minuit, 1969): 19.

8. Mauricio Molho, *Sistemática del verbo español*, 2 vols. (Madrid: Editorial Gredos, 1975).

BIBLIOGRAPHY

Alazraki, Jaime. *La prosa narrativa de Jorge Luis Borges*. Madrid: Editorial Gredos, 1968.
Alazraki, *Versiones, inversiones, reversiones*. Madrid: Editorial Gredos, 1977.
Alazraki. "Outside and Inside the Mirror in Borges' Poetry." *Simply a Man of Letters*. Edited by Carlos Cortínez. Orono: University of Maine Press, 1982.
Barrenechea, Ana María. *Borges, the Labyrinth Maker*. Translated by Robert Lima. New York: New York University Press, 1965.
Barrenechea. *La expresión de la irrealidad en la obra de Jorge Luis Borges*. Buenos Aires: Editorial Paidós, 1967.
Borges, Jorge Luis. *Obra poética 1923–1964*. Buenos Aires: Emecé, 1964.
Carreño, Antonio. "La negación de la persona en Jorge Luis Borges." In *La dialética de la identidad en la poesía contemporánea*. Madrid: Editorial Gredos, 1982.
Derrida, Jacques. *De la grammatologie*. Paris: Editions Minuit, 1969.
Leibniz, Gottfried Wilhelm. *New Essays on Human Understanding*. Edited and translated by Peter Remmant and Jonathan Benett. Cambridge: Cambridge University Press, 1981.
Leibniz. *The Monadology of Leibniz*. Los Angeles: USC Press, 1930.
Molho, Mauricio. *Sistemática del verbo español*, 2 vols. Madrid: Editorial Gredos, 1975.
Sucre, Guillermo. *Borges, El poeta*. Caracas: Monte Avila Editores, 1968.
Sucre. *La máscara, la transparencia*. Caracas: Monte Avila Editores, 1975.

"Knight, Death and the Devil"—Dürer Imprint

ROBERT LIMA

"Knight, Death and the Devil"—Dürer's Imprint on Two Poems by Borges

If there are indeed seven types of ambiguity, as the well-known critical study by Empson posits,[1] then Borges has certainly availed himself of every opportunity to manifest them in his tales and poems, sometimes modifying them according to his creative needs.

Not only does he present many of his subjects through the technique of ambiguity, he frequently seeks out that which in itself is ambiguous. A case in point is the famous engraving by Albrecht Dürer popularly known as "Knight, Death and the Devil."

In *Delle Vite de'più eccellenti pittori, scultori ed architettori* (Florence, 1568), Giorgio Vasari refers to Dürer's engraving as one of several by the artist "of such excellence that nothing finer can be achieved."[2] Vasari goes on to laud the technical execution of the engraving's pictorial elements: "In order to depict human fortitude, he engraved an armored knight on horseback with such perfection that even the glitter of his weapons and the skin of his steed can be discerned."[3]

While these external qualities designate the work as technically masterful, they are only means to a higher purpose: to transport the internal meaning of the piece. It is that deeper level of nuance and ambiguity that has made Dürer's engraving both fascinating and controversial. Originally titled "Der Reuter" (The Rider), the 1513 print possesses an esoteric nature founded on issues of identity, placement and symbolism. All of these focus on the Knight, whose very position at the front center of the work leads the eye to his enigmatic face. The Knight looks ahead impassively, his face worn by experience and time, his expression more introspective than fixed.

It has been suggested by Thausing that the Knight is the personification of the sanguine temperament, using the "S" before the date as the clue to that particular humor.[4] But to Sandrart, he was "the Great Christian Knight,"[5] while Weber considers the Knight to have been modeled on a concept formulated by Erasmus in *Enchiridion militis christiani*, an early sixteenth century treatise which promoted the view that every Christian must be a soldier of Christ passing through the dark wood of earthly life armed with the weapons of the Faith.[6]

Whatever his provenance and identity, the Knight is the hub upon which all the other images are arrayed. The circularity of the work is also implicit in the arcs defined by the Knight's lance; were he to rotate the weapon, it would inscribe a circle encompassing everything in the engraving. Since the handle and tip of the lance each culminate well beyond the borders of the engraving plate, the circle would enclose the rectangular area wholly. This circular placement of essentially Medieval images around an impassive Knight in full armor may symbolize the emergence of Man in the Renaissance as the center of his world, no longer perturbed by the anxieties of the earlier age.

Within this encircled rectangle are two juxtaposed triangles. The upper figure has as its base the horizontally dominant horse, while its sides are delineated by the lance on the left and the inclined slope on the right; at the apex of this suggested triangle is the helmeted head of the Knight. This is the *superior* triangle, the one that points to and parallels the distant mountain at whose apex is the turreted city.

The lower triangle is askew, its inverted base formed by an imaginary line between Death and the Devil, while its lower point is the skull, set off at the left. This is the *inferior* triangle, the one that points to the nether regions: the Underworld of Death, the Hell of the Devil.

The superior triangle is composed of "living" elements—the horse Knight (who together signify a cruciform)—while the inferior triangle is composed of "dead" elements—the manifestations of physical death and the eternal death of the soul. The readily-seen superior triangle draws its prominence from its placement in the engraving, a manifestation of Dürer's belief in human fortitude; the less-recognizable inferior triangle owes its obscurity to placement in a secondary position in the engraving, symbolic of the darkness of the nether world and its potential danger, even if no longer the prime concern of civilized man in the Renaissance.

Transmogrified into the beastly he-goat of Medieval European folklore, the Devil lurks behind and to the rear of the rider. His evil eyes display the ire of having been bypassed by the unerring Knight.

Just ahead of the rider and behind his pictorial plane, a satyr-like Death looks askance at the failed Devil. The nag on which Death is mounted looks to earth as if transfixed by the skull placed on a tree stump. The nag is in seeming forward motion; if it reaches the skull, it will form a "toll gate" which the Knight will cross or not at some unknown moment out of time.

Still motion. The progress of Death's decrepit mount, as of the Knight's noble steed,[7] is forever halted in the immutability of the engraving. Never will the nag reach the skull; never will its nagging bell toll a deadly knell. Neither will the Knight's horse encounter Death's divide; it may be almost above the skull, almost at the intersection of the nag's path, but the confrontation will never obtain. And if the dog is indeed symbolic of Veritas, as Panofsky asserts,[8] its lagging behind the horse's pace, if with insistent urgency, underlines the fact that the Knight will never have his ultimate moment of truth—the encounter with Death.

Dürer makes another statement on the fixedness of the scene through the hourglass held by Death. The two chambers are almost equally filled with sand but no more will flow. Time has been stopped. All the elements of the work are fixed in the midst of progressing towards an encounter, accomplishing some task, or fulfilling destiny. There remains only suspended animation.

At this moment of recognition that time has been suspended, another level of meaning emerges. Man, the viewer, is seeing and experiencing Dürer's print within the context of human time. The timelessness of the print is a mockery of the human condition of the viewer, whose linear time elapses as he assesses the suspended time of the Knight.

It is at this juncture of viewer and object viewed that Borges enters the picture. He approaches Dürer's engraving from two perspectives,

each presented in a different poem. In "Ritter, Tod, und Teufel (I),"
Borges first assesses certain figurative elements of the work, proceeds to
an interpretation of the ethical values inherent in the Knight, and makes
a laudatory bow to his valor and worthiness in the face of formidable
enemies.

> Beneath the esoteric helmet lies the stern
> profile, as cruel as the cruel sword that
> lies in wait. Through barren forest
> rides the Knight in his serenity arrayed.
> Torpid, furtive, the obscene throng
> has circled him: the Devil with his abject
> eyes, the labyrinthine snakes,
> the white old man with sandglass in his hand.
> Knight of Iron, whosoever looks at you
> intuits that within there's neither falsehood
> nor the pale of fear. Your lot is hard
> for you command, affront. You're brave as well
> and surely will not prove unworthy,
> German, of the Devil and of Death.[9]

For Borges, the Knight is steadfast in the confrontation with evil and
death, a heroic figure worthy of emulation.

The second poem brings the observer of the first work into the context of the engraving, if not into its cryogenic time. Borges assesses the
metaphysical implications of Dürer's hard statement in "Ritter, Tod, und
Teufel (II)."

> There are two paths. The one the man
> of iron and of pride pursues upon his steed,
> firm in faith, through the uncertain forest
> of the world, between the mocking taunts the Devil mouths
> and the immobile dance of Death. The other,
> mine, the briefer path. Of what forgotten
> night or morning of some ancient day did my own eyes
> discover this fantastic work,
> the everlasting epic scheme that Dürer dreamed—
> the hero and his throng of shades
> which seek, then lie in wait and then encounter me?
> It is I and not the paladin who is exhorted by the white
> old man whose head is crowned by sinuous snakes.
> The clepsydra's successive measure
> counts my time, not his eternal now.

I will become but ash and darkest space;
I, who set out last, will first attain
my mortal end; yet you, who have no life,
you, Knight of the unswerving sword
and of the rigid woods, will hold your path
as long as men endure—
unmoved, imaginary, everlasting.[10]

Borges' concern with Time first becomes evident in terms of his seeking to locate the moment in his own time when he *saw* the work initially. He seems to be trying to locate a time when his eyesight was not impaired, a time when he viewed the engraving and reacted to its visual elements and its deeper structure.

But the poems appeared in print in 1968, when Borges was already unable to distinguish more than "a kind of luminous greyish or bluish or greenish mist," as he himself calls it.[11] If indeed the poems were written around that time, Borges had to have recalled Dürer's engraving rather than actually see it again. His impression of it would, of necessity, have been limited. This would explain why neither poem considers many of the engraving's important visual elements: the dog, the salamander, the skull, the distant city . . . and the mystical geometry in which they are ensconced. Such omissions are consistent with faulty memory, one of the hazards (or, ambiguously, blessings?) of "emotion recollected in tranquility," as Wordsworth so memorably phrased it.

Or is it a matter of selectivity? If the poem is Borges' attempt to recall the moment in which he unlocked the personal meaning of Dürer's engraving rather than the moment when he first saw it, the exclusion of certain elements takes on a different guise. Borges may have chosen for these poems only those elements of the piece which he identified with his personal interpretation of its meaning.

If Dürer's Knight symbolizes the Christian armored by the Faith against the wiles of the Devil and an attendant eternal death, then Borges' exclusion of this theologically oriented motif from his poems is telling evidence that the engraving has another level of interpretation for him. Borges eschews the Christian identification altogether, obviously considering it extraneous to the modern assessment of the engraving. Such elements which were of value to the Christian ethos during Dürer's time are held by an agnostic Borges to be cumbersome, even to detract from the work's modern immediacy.

Immediacy is an important factor to Borges, who has said of his own work: "When I write poetry, I tend to think of something immediate, downright."[12] Thus, he concentrates his attention on the most accessible element in the engraving—the Knight. It is the human condition of the Knight that is of most immediacy to another human being, Borges. Yet in the comparison of the two human existences, the one portrayed and the one being lived, the reality of the poet suffers greatly: the Knight will exist in his "eternal now" while the poet, mortal man, "will become but ash." The great irony, of course, is the comparison of human mortality to the survival of human works. Dürer has passed on, but "Der Reuter" will continue in a state of suspended animation with metaphysical ramifications for human beings, "as long as men endure."

The experience of age behind him, Borges has assessed the main figurative element of the engraving and found in the Knight's serenity, stoicism and relentless pursuit of the goal, despite gruesome hazards, a heroism of magnificent proportions. He does not begrudge the Knight his everness in the ironic context of art's timelessness; Borges has learned to accept the limitations put upon him by his human condition, yet he admires (he cannot emulate) the Knight's existence.

Out of the numerous ambiguities which Dürer's engraving presents, Borges has come to grips admirably with the central enigma, that which has most immediacy. Thus, the imprint of Dürer on Borges is that of one insightful artist upon another, man speaking to man across the centuries about the most ambiguous subject of all, Man.

NOTES

1. William Empson, *Seven Types of Ambiguity* (New York: Harcourt, Brace & Co., 1931).

2. Quoted in Walter L. Strauss, ed., *The Complete Engravings, Etchings & Drypoints of Albrecht Dürer.* (New York: Dover, 1973): 150. Antecedents of "Knight, Death and the Devil" are "Horse and Rider," a large watercolor of 1498 presently in the Albertina in Vienna, and two small pen-and-ink studies titled "Knight on Horseback," done on the recto and verso of the same sheet, now in the Ambrosiana in Milan.

3. Strauss, *Complete Engravings.*

4. Moritz Thausing, *Dürer, Geschichte seines Lebens und seiner Kunst* (Leipzig, 1884). Thausing's theory is faulty on the evidence in the engraving since the warm, passionate, cheerful temperament and ruddy complexion associated with this humor are not present in the Knight's visage. To Campbell Dodgson, [*Albrecht Dürer. Numbered Catalogue of Engravings, Dry-Points and Etchings with Technical Details* (London, 1926)], the "S" stands for *Salus* equivalent to *Anno salutis* (In the Year of Grace), a form of dating employed by Dürer else-

where. My own view is that the "S" may be a stylized snake, a subtle re-statement of the sinuous motifs in Death's headgear and on its shoulders, as well as a third element in association with them and the crawling salamander.

5. Joachim von Sandrart, *Teutsche Academie der Elden Bau- Bild- und Mahlerey Kunste* (Nuremberg, 1675). Other interpretations range from H.S. Husgen's view of the work as "symbolic of the knight's impiety", *Raisonierendes Verzeichnis aller Kupferund Eisenstiche von Albrecht Dürer* (Frankfort-Leipzig, 1778), to Joseph Heller's ideas that the work may either depict Franz von Sickingen, a notorious 16th century knight much feared throughout Germany, or that it may be a variation on a painting "which bears the legend: 'Let all hell break loose and fight, I'll ride down the devil with might.'" However, Dürer's Knight has bypassed the Devil and ignores him.

6. Weber. *Beiträge zu Dürers Weltanschauung* (Strassburg, 1900): 13.

7. Two engravings, "The Great Horse" and "The Little Horse," both dated 1505, show Dürer's interest in heroically executed horses. The Knight's steed in "Der Reuter" is highly modeled, anatomically constructed in idealized proportions, perhaps inspired in Leonardo's Sforza monument, designed for Milan. Also of 1505, is a powerful drawing in charcoal titled "Death on Horseback," which depicts a more traditional skeletal figure with scythe riding a decrepit nag.

8. Erwin Panofsky, *Albrecht Dürer*, I. (Princeton: Princeton University Press, 1943).

9. This poem did not appear first in a periodical but in *Variaciones sobre un tema de Durero* (Buenos Aires: Galerna, 1968). It was published subsequently in Jorge Luis Borges, *Elogio de la sombra* (Buenos Aires: Emecé, 1969). The poem is in my translation.

10. First published in *Atlántida* (Buenos Aires, September 1968). Dürer's Death holds an hourglass or sandglass, not a "clepsidra" as Borges' poem has it. The clepsydra is a device for measuring time through the regulated flow of water or mercury via a small aperture. The translation is mine.

11. Mark Childress and Charles C. McNair Jr. "The Dark Riddle of Jorge Luis Borges," *Saturday Review* (New York, March 1983): 83.

12. Childress and McNair, *Saturday Review*, 34.

BIBLIOGRAPHY

Borges, Jorge Luis. *Variaciones sobre un tema de Durero*. Buenos Aires: Galerna, 1968.

Childress, Mark and Charles C. McNair Jr. "The Dark Riddle of Jorge Luis Borges," *Saturday Review* March 1983: 83.

Dodgson, Campbell. *Albrecht Dürer. Numbered Catalogue of Engravings, Dry-Points and Etchings with Technical Details*. London, 1926.

Empson, William. *Seven Types of Ambiguity*. New York: Harcourt, Brace and Co., 1931.

Panofsky, Erwin. *Albrecht Dürer*, I. Princeton: Princeton University Press, 1943.

Strauss, Walter L., ed. *The Complete Engravings, Etchings and Drypoints of Albrecht Dürer*. New York: Dover, 1973.

Thausing, Mortiz. *Dürer, Geschichte seines Lebens und seiner Kunst*. Leipzig, 1884.

Von Sandrart, Joachin. *Teutsche Academie der Edlen Bau- Bild- und Mahlerey Künste*. Nuremburg, 1675.

Weber. *Beitrage zu Dürers Weltanschauung*. Strassburg, 1900.

Index